CHAMPIONS

WEIRD WAR ONE

Previously: Nova and the Champions responded to a distress
call from deep space, where a group of Chitauri kept
intentionally defenseless by Thanos faced genocide at the
hands of Warbringer's army. They saved the Chitauri, but at a
cost: Thanos destroyed Riri's Ironheart armor, and Sam's Nova
helmet was reclaimed by the Nova Corps. And they're not the
only ones dealing with changes...

COLLECTION EDITOR: JENNIFER GRÜNWALD
ASSISTANT EDITOR: CAITLIN O'CONNELL
ASSOCIATE MANAGING EDITOR: KATERI WOODY   EDITOR IN CHIEF: C.B. CEBULSKI
EDITOR, SPECIAL PROJECTS: MARK D. BEAZLEY   CHIEF CREATIVE OFFICER: JOE QUESADA
VP PRODUCTION & SPECIAL PROJECTS: JEFF YOUNGQUIST   PRESIDENT: DAN BUCKLEY
SVP PRINT, SALES & MARKETING: DAVID GABRIEL   EXECUTIVE PRODUCER: ALAN FINE

CHAMPIONS VOL. 5: WEIRD WAR ONE. Contains material originally published in magazine form as CHAMPIONS #22-27 and ANNUAL #1. First printing 2018. ISBN 978-
1-302-91505-6. Published by MARVEL WORLDWIDE, INC., a subsidiary of MARVEL ENTERTAINMENT, LLC. OFFICE OF PUBLICATION: 135 West 50th Street, New York, NY
10020. Copyright © 2018 MARVEL No similarity between any of the names, characters, persons, and/or institutions in this magazine with those of any living or dead person
or institution is intended, and any such similarity which may exist is purely coincidental. Printed in Canada. DAN BUCKLEY, President, Marvel Entertainment; JOHN NEE,
Publisher; JOE QUESADA, Chief Creative Officer; TOM BREVOORT, SVP of Publishing; DAVID BOGART, SVP of Business Affairs & Operations, Publishing & Partnership; DAVID
GABRIEL, SVP of Sales & Marketing, Publishing; JEFF YOUNGQUIST, VP of Production & Special Projects; DAN CARR, Executive Director of Publishing Technology; ALEX MO-
RALES, Director of Publishing Operations; DAN EDINGTON, Managing Editor; SUSAN CRESPI, Production Manager; STAN LEE, Chairman Emeritus. For information regarding
advertising in Marvel Comics or on Marvel.com, please contact Vit DeBellis, Custom Solutions & Integrated Advertising Manager, at vdebellis@marvel.com. For Marvel
subscription inquiries, please call 888-511-5480. Manufactured between 11/23/2018 and 12/17/2018 by SOLISCO PRINTERS, SCOTT, QC, CANADA.

10 9 8 7 6 5 4 3 2 1

When society became disillusioned with its heroes,
the next generation made a vow to do better.
To make a difference. To change the world. They are the...

CHAMPIONS

WEIRD WAR ONE

CHAMPIONS #22-23
WRITER: **JIM ZUB**
ARTIST: **KEVIN LIBRANDA**
WITH **FRANCESCO MANNA** (#23)
COLOR ARTIST: **MARCIO MENYZ**
COVER ART: **R.B. SILVA** & **NOLAN WOODARD** (#22)
AND **STEFANO CASELLI** & **MARCIO MENYZ** (#23)

CHAMPIONS #24-27
WRITER: **JIM ZUB**
ARTISTS: **SEAN IZAAKSE** (#24-25)
& **MAX DUNBAR** (#25-27)
COLOR ARTISTS: **MARCIO MENYZ** (#24-25), **ERICK
ARCINIEGA** (#24) & **NOLAN WOODARD** (#25-27)
COVER ART: **SEAN IZAAKSE** & **MARCIO MENYZ**

CHAMPIONS ANNUAL #1
WRITERS: **JIM ZUB** & **NYLA INNUKSUK**
ARTIST: **MARCUS TO**
COLOR ARTIST: **JORDAN BOYD**
COVER ART: **R.B. SILVA** & **NOLAN WOODARD**

LETTERER: **VC'S CLAYTON COWLES** CONSULTANT: **NYLA INNUKSUK**
ASSOCIATE EDITOR: **ALANNA SMITH** EDITOR: **TOM BREVOORT**

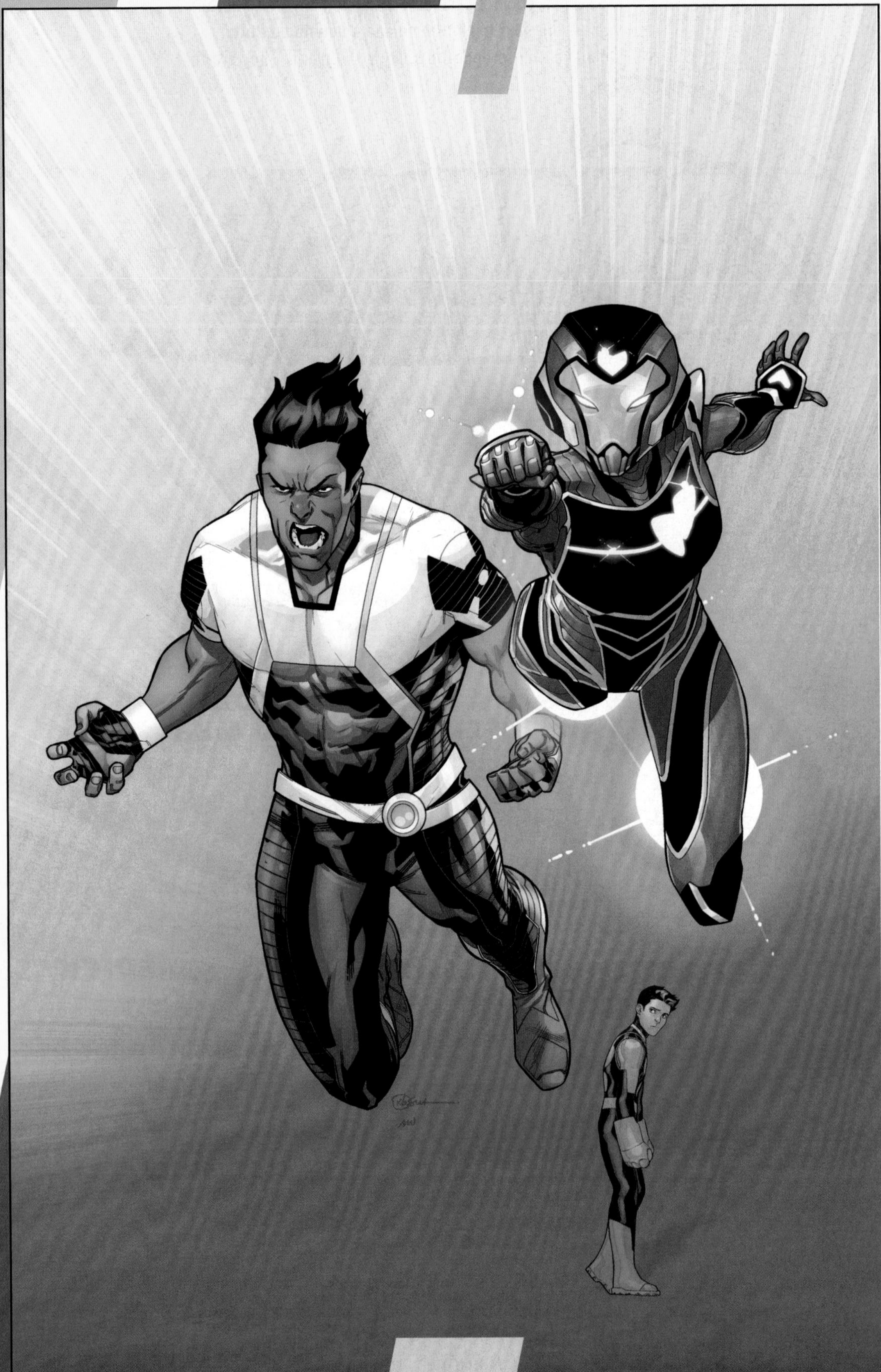

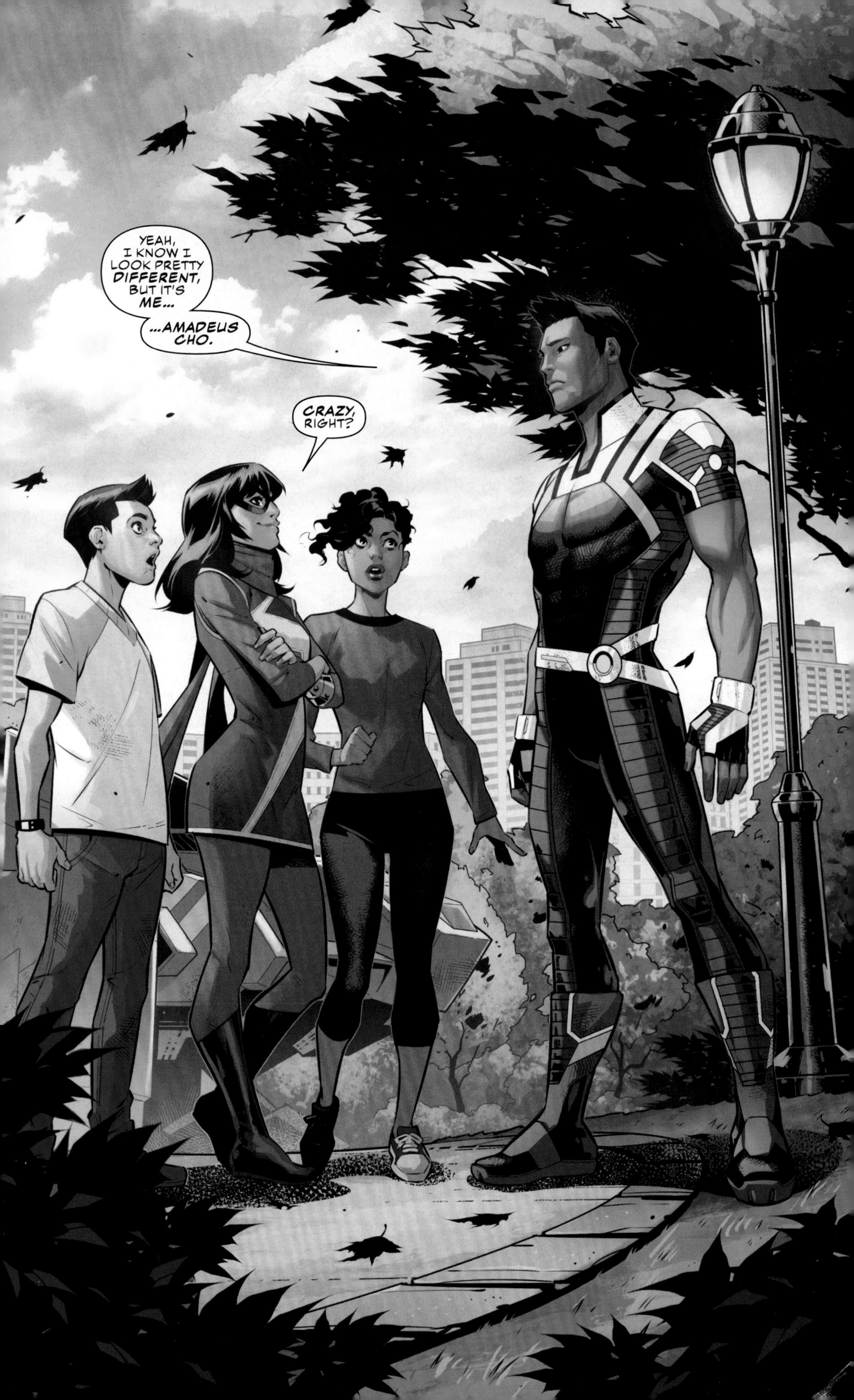
YEAH, I KNOW I LOOK PRETTY DIFFERENT, BUT IT'S ME...
...AMADEUS CHO.
CRAZY, RIGHT?

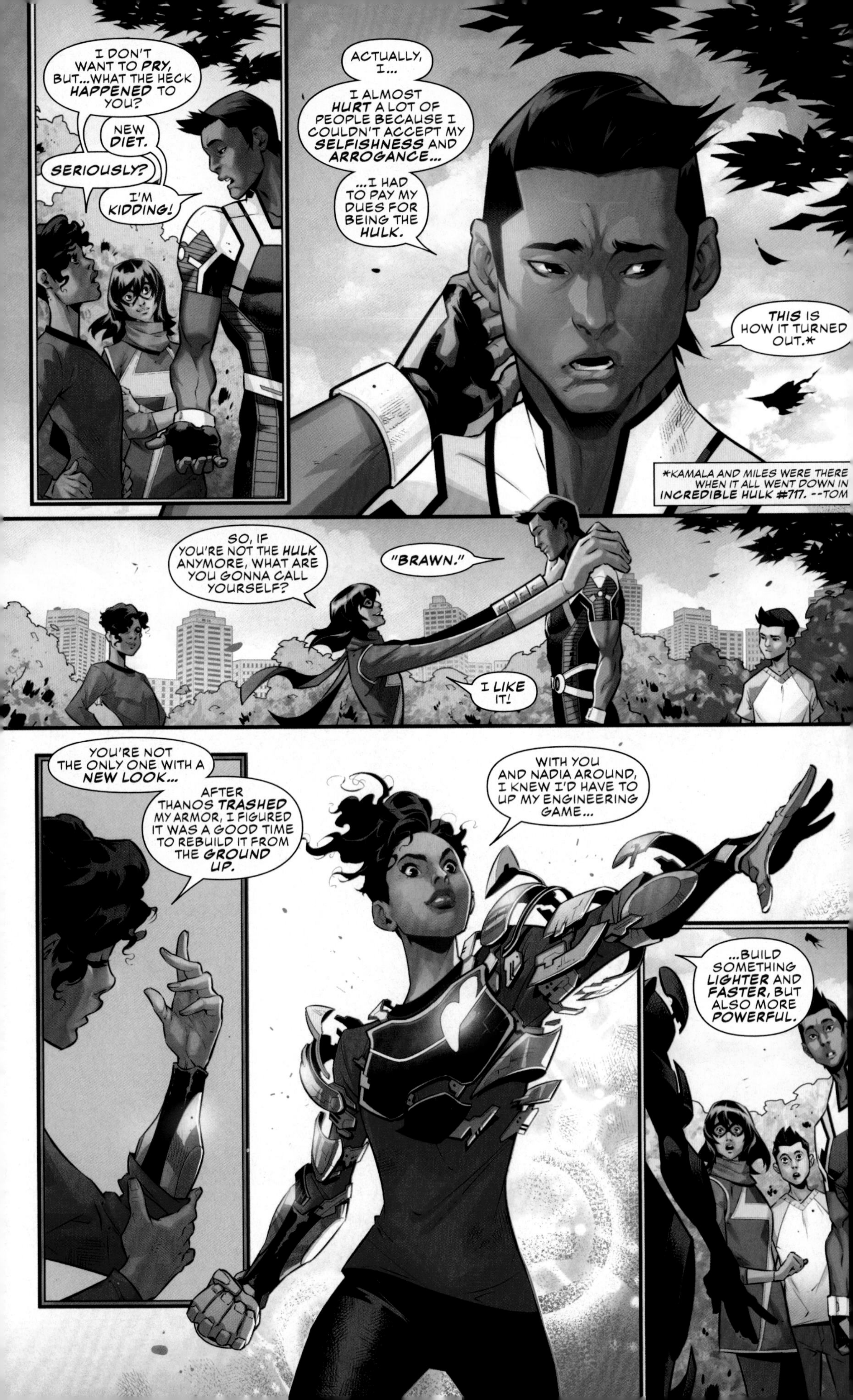

I DON'T WANT TO PRY, BUT...WHAT THE HECK HAPPENED TO YOU?
NEW DIET.
SERIOUSLY?
I'M KIDDING!
ACTUALLY, I...
I ALMOST HURT A LOT OF PEOPLE BECAUSE I COULDN'T ACCEPT MY SELFISHNESS AND ARROGANCE...
...I HAD TO PAY MY DUES FOR BEING THE HULK.
THIS IS HOW IT TURNED OUT.*
*KAMALA AND MILES WERE THERE WHEN IT ALL WENT DOWN IN INCREDIBLE HULK #717. --TOM
SO, IF YOU'RE NOT THE HULK ANYMORE, WHAT ARE YOU GONNA CALL YOURSELF?
"BRAWN."
I LIKE IT!
YOU'RE NOT THE ONLY ONE WITH A NEW LOOK...
AFTER THANOS TRASHED MY ARMOR, I FIGURED IT WAS A GOOD TIME TO REBUILD IT FROM THE GROUND UP.
WITH YOU AND NADIA AROUND, I KNEW I'D HAVE TO UP MY ENGINEERING GAME...
...BUILD SOMETHING LIGHTER AND FASTER, BUT ALSO MORE POWERFUL.

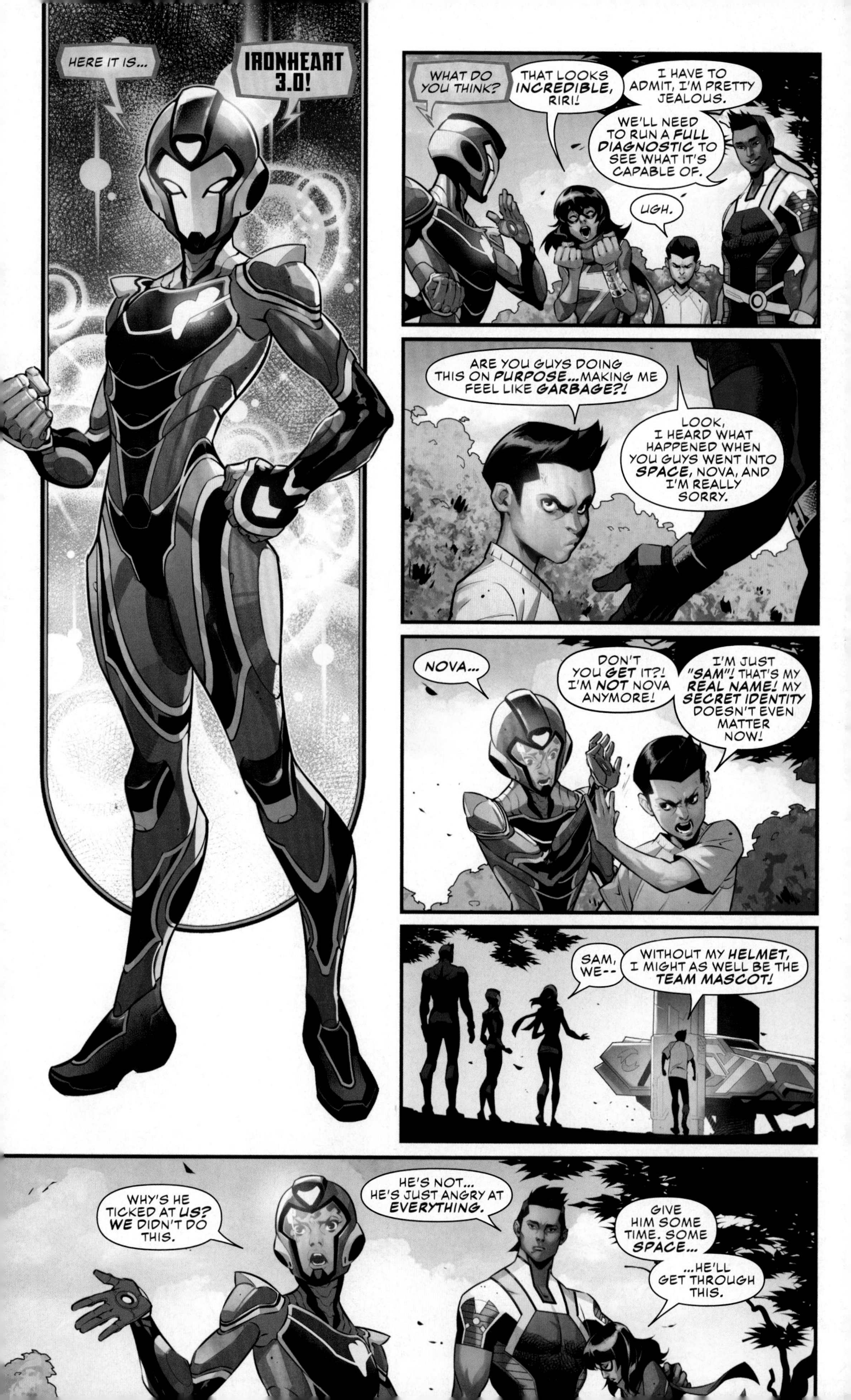
HERE IT IS...
IRONHEART 3.0!
WHAT DO YOU THINK?
THAT LOOKS INCREDIBLE, RIRI!
I HAVE TO ADMIT, I'M PRETTY JEALOUS.
WE'LL NEED TO RUN A FULL DIAGNOSTIC TO SEE WHAT IT'S CAPABLE OF.
UGH.
ARE YOU GUYS DOING THIS ON PURPOSE...MAKING ME FEEL LIKE GARBAGE?!
LOOK, I HEARD WHAT HAPPENED WHEN YOU GUYS WENT INTO SPACE, NOVA, AND I'M REALLY SORRY.
NOVA...
DON'T YOU GET IT?! I'M NOT NOVA ANYMORE!
I'M JUST "SAM"! THAT'S MY REAL NAME! MY SECRET IDENTITY DOESN'T EVEN MATTER NOW!
SAM, WE--
WITHOUT MY HELMET, I MIGHT AS WELL BE THE TEAM MASCOT!
WHY'S HE TICKED AT US? WE DIDN'T DO THIS.
HE'S NOT... HE'S JUST ANGRY AT EVERYTHING.
GIVE HIM SOME TIME. SOME SPACE...
...HE'LL GET THROUGH THIS.

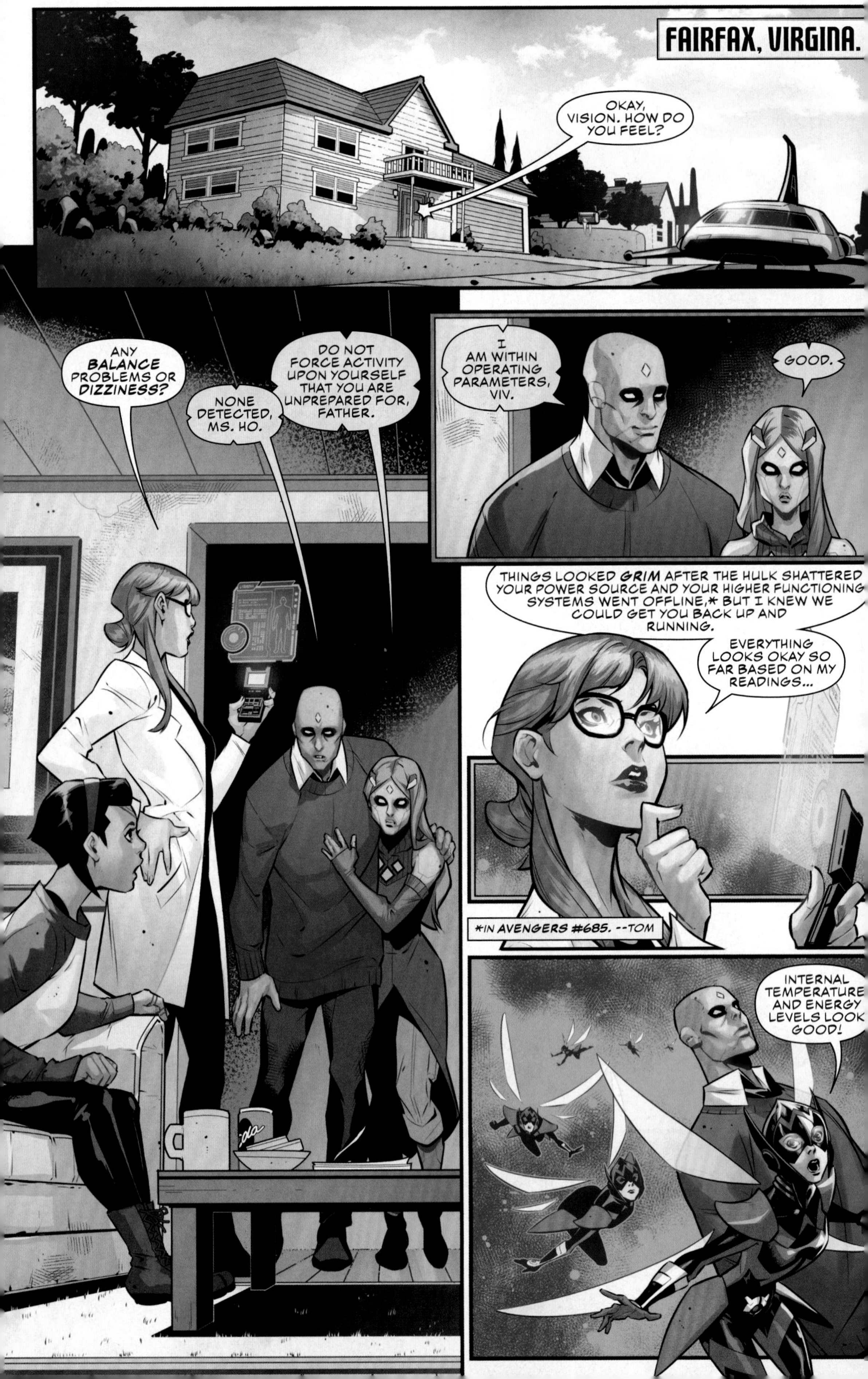
FAIRFAX, VIRGINA.
OKAY, VISION. HOW DO YOU FEEL?
ANY BALANCE PROBLEMS OR DIZZINESS?
NONE DETECTED, MS. HO.
DO NOT FORCE ACTIVITY UPON YOURSELF THAT YOU ARE UNPREPARED FOR, FATHER.
I AM WITHIN OPERATING PARAMETERS, VIV.
GOOD.
THINGS LOOKED GRIM AFTER THE HULK SHATTERED YOUR POWER SOURCE AND YOUR HIGHER FUNCTIONING SYSTEMS WENT OFFLINE,* BUT I KNEW WE COULD GET YOU BACK UP AND RUNNING.
EVERYTHING LOOKS OKAY SO FAR BASED ON MY READINGS...
*IN AVENGERS #685. --TOM
INTERNAL TEMPERATURE AND ENERGY LEVELS LOOK GOOD!

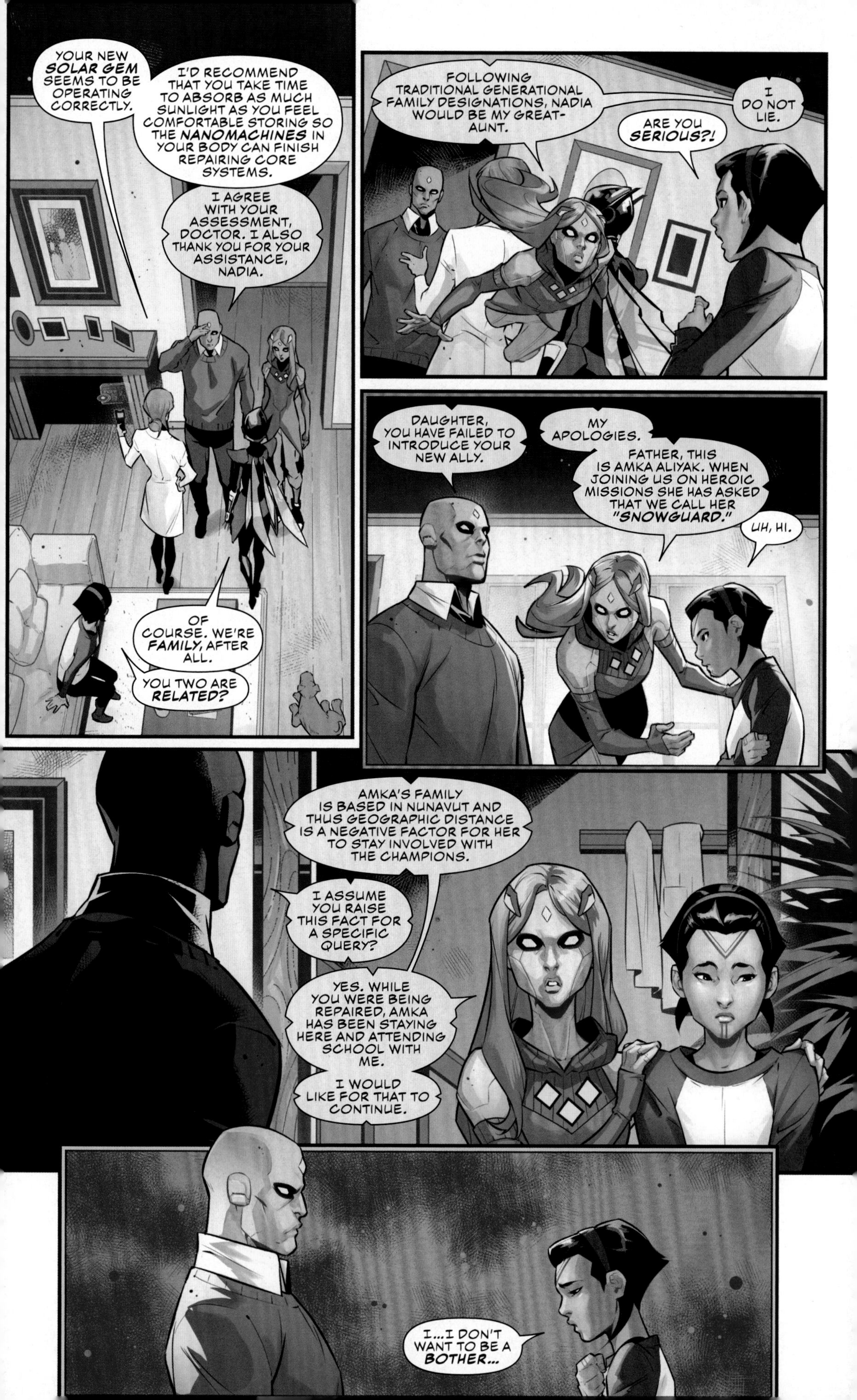
YOUR NEW SOLAR GEM SEEMS TO BE OPERATING CORRECTLY.
I'D RECOMMEND THAT YOU TAKE TIME TO ABSORB AS MUCH SUNLIGHT AS YOU FEEL COMFORTABLE STORING SO THE NANOMACHINES IN YOUR BODY CAN FINISH REPAIRING CORE SYSTEMS.
I AGREE WITH YOUR ASSESSMENT, DOCTOR. I ALSO THANK YOU FOR YOUR ASSISTANCE, NADIA.
OF COURSE. WE'RE FAMILY, AFTER ALL.
YOU TWO ARE RELATED?
FOLLOWING TRADITIONAL GENERATIONAL FAMILY DESIGNATIONS, NADIA WOULD BE MY GREAT-AUNT.
ARE YOU SERIOUS?!
I DO NOT LIE.
DAUGHTER, YOU HAVE FAILED TO INTRODUCE YOUR NEW ALLY.
MY APOLOGIES.
FATHER, THIS IS AMKA ALIYAK. WHEN JOINING US ON HEROIC MISSIONS SHE HAS ASKED THAT WE CALL HER "SNOWGUARD."
UH, HI.
AMKA'S FAMILY IS BASED IN NUNAVUT AND THUS GEOGRAPHIC DISTANCE IS A NEGATIVE FACTOR FOR HER TO STAY INVOLVED WITH THE CHAMPIONS.
I ASSUME YOU RAISE THIS FACT FOR A SPECIFIC QUERY?
YES. WHILE YOU WERE BEING REPAIRED, AMKA HAS BEEN STAYING HERE AND ATTENDING SCHOOL WITH ME.
I WOULD LIKE FOR THAT TO CONTINUE.
I...I DON'T WANT TO BE A BOTHER...

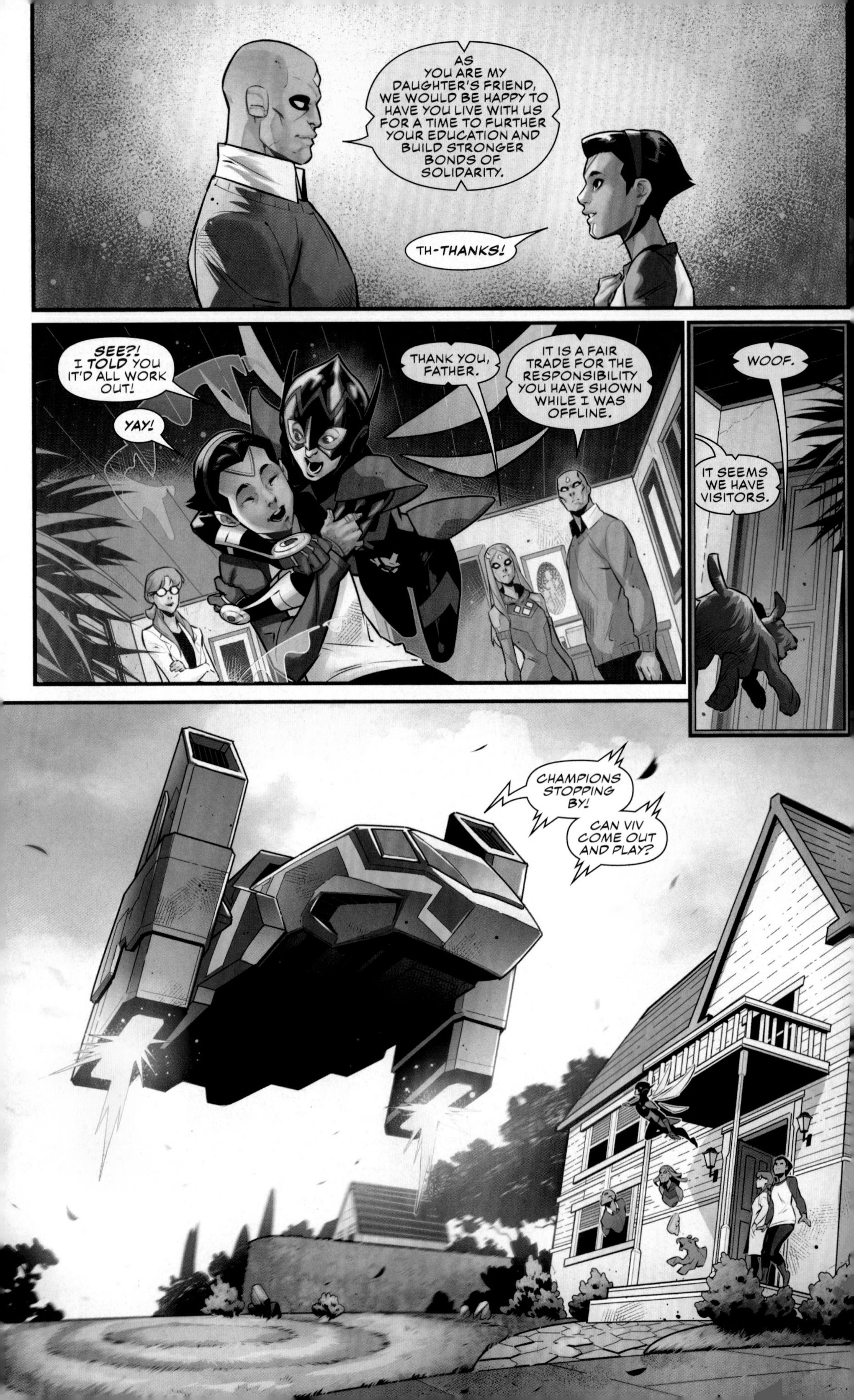
AS YOU ARE MY DAUGHTER'S FRIEND, WE WOULD BE HAPPY TO HAVE YOU LIVE WITH US FOR A TIME TO FURTHER YOUR EDUCATION AND BUILD STRONGER BONDS OF SOLIDARITY.
TH-THANKS!
SEE?! I TOLD YOU IT'D ALL WORK OUT!
YAY!
THANK YOU, FATHER.
IT IS A FAIR TRADE FOR THE RESPONSIBILITY YOU HAVE SHOWN WHILE I WAS OFFLINE.
WOOF.
IT SEEMS WE HAVE VISITORS.
CHAMPIONS STOPPING BY!
CAN VIV COME OUT AND PLAY?

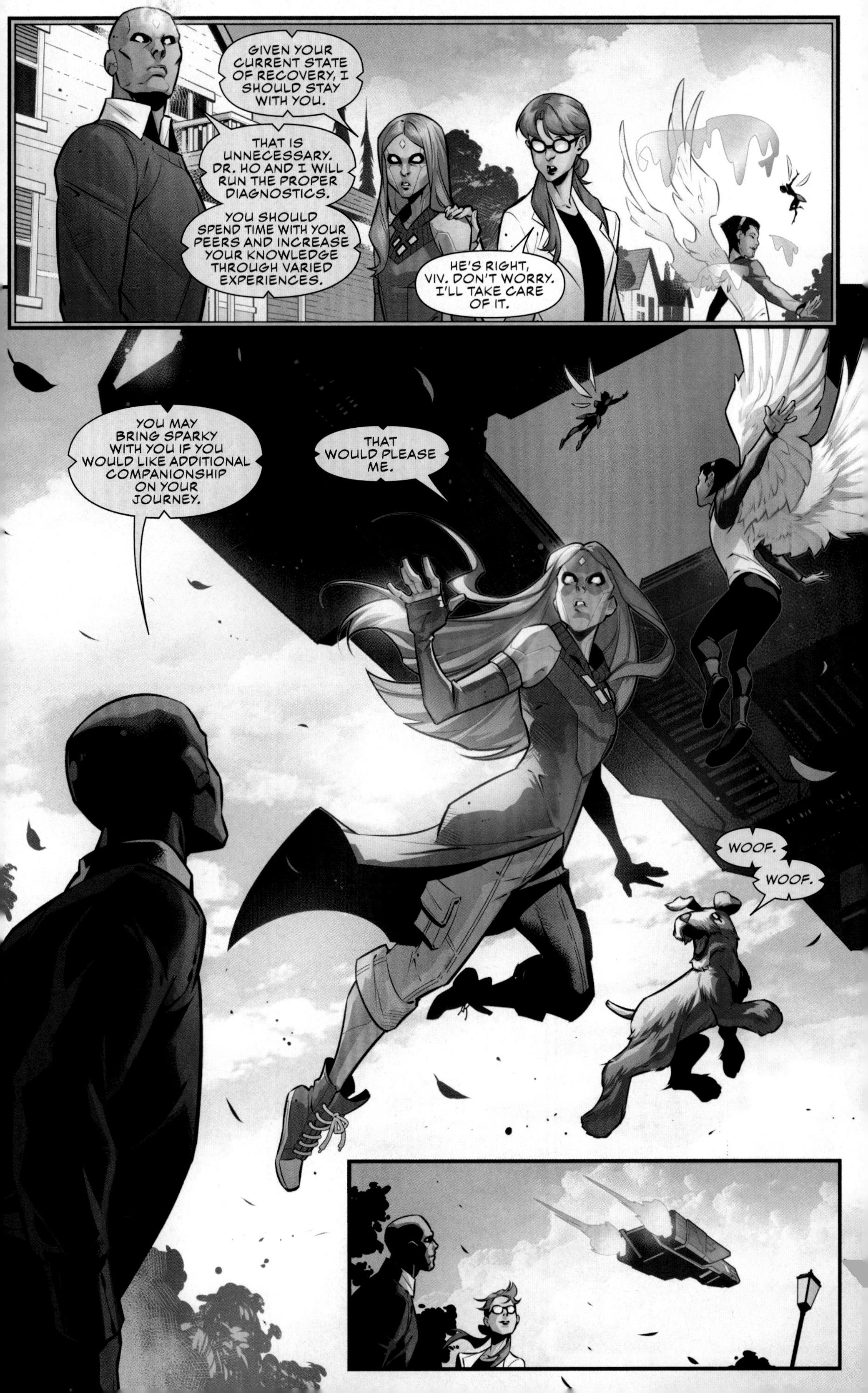
GIVEN YOUR CURRENT STATE OF RECOVERY, I SHOULD STAY WITH YOU.
THAT IS UNNECESSARY. DR. HO AND I WILL RUN THE PROPER DIAGNOSTICS.
YOU SHOULD SPEND TIME WITH YOUR PEERS AND INCREASE YOUR KNOWLEDGE THROUGH VARIED EXPERIENCES.
HE'S RIGHT, VIV. DON'T WORRY. I'LL TAKE CARE OF IT.
YOU MAY BRING SPARKY WITH YOU IF YOU WOULD LIKE ADDITIONAL COMPANIONSHIP ON YOUR JOURNEY.
THAT WOULD PLEASE ME.
WOOF.
WOOF.

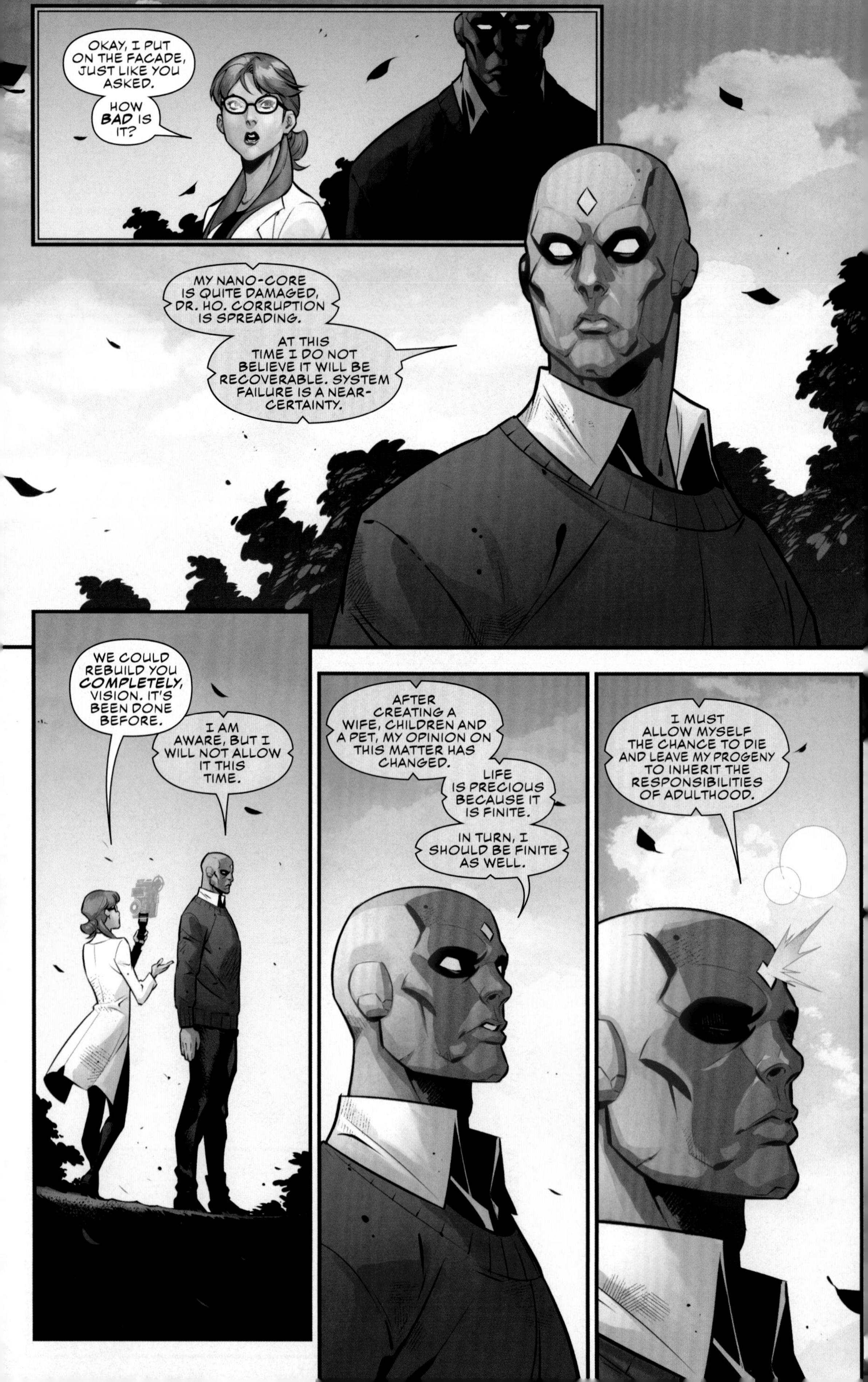
OKAY, I PUT ON THE FACADE, JUST LIKE YOU ASKED.
HOW BAD IS IT?
MY NANO-CORE IS QUITE DAMAGED, DR. HO. CORRUPTION IS SPREADING.
AT THIS TIME I DO NOT BELIEVE IT WILL BE RECOVERABLE. SYSTEM FAILURE IS A NEAR-CERTAINTY.
WE COULD REBUILD YOU COMPLETELY, VISION. IT'S BEEN DONE BEFORE.
I AM AWARE, BUT I WILL NOT ALLOW IT THIS TIME.
AFTER CREATING A WIFE, CHILDREN AND A PET, MY OPINION ON THIS MATTER HAS CHANGED.
LIFE IS PRECIOUS BECAUSE IT IS FINITE.
IN TURN, I SHOULD BE FINITE AS WELL.
I MUST ALLOW MYSELF THE CHANCE TO DIE AND LEAVE MY PROGENY TO INHERIT THE RESPONSIBILITIES OF ADULTHOOD.

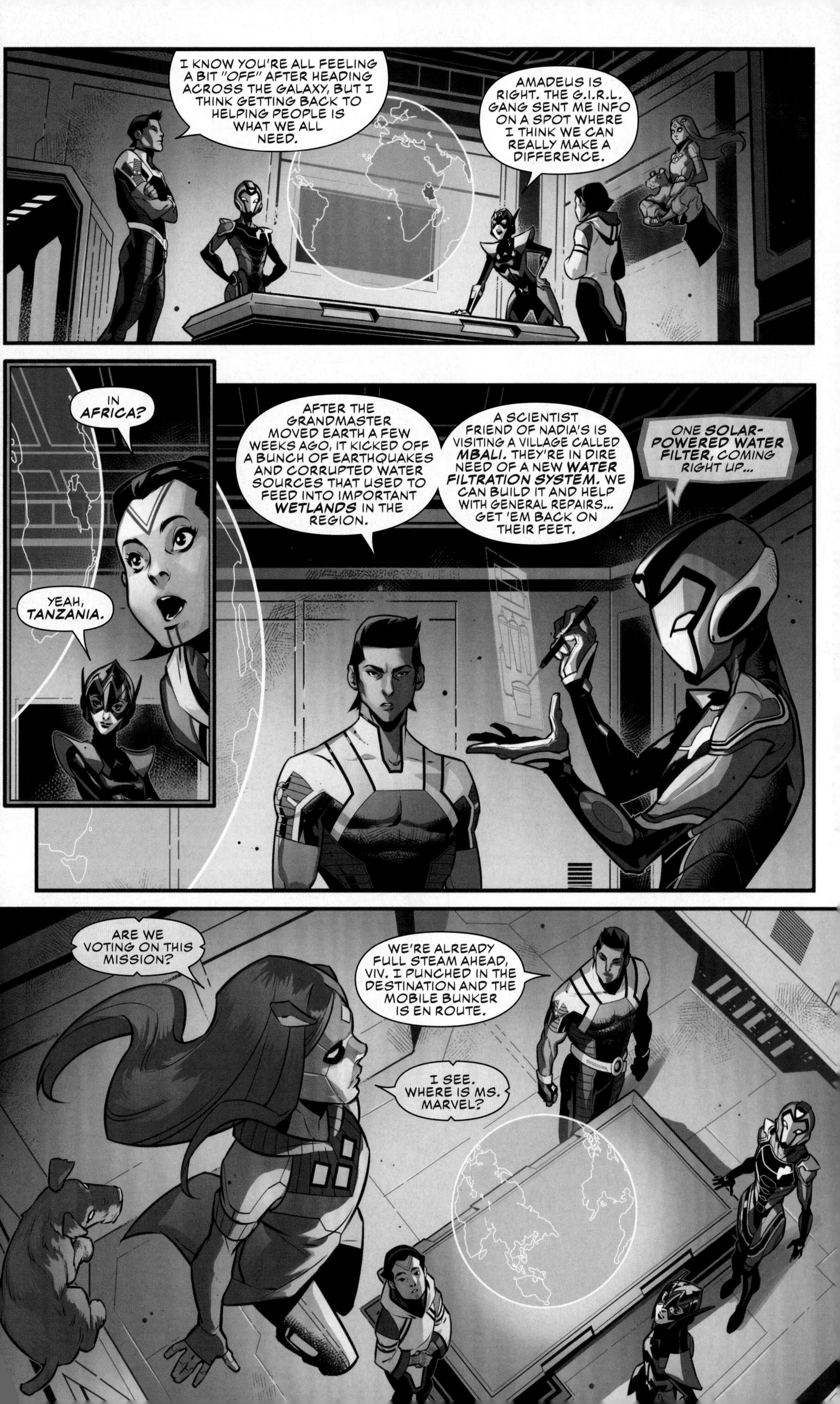
I KNOW YOU'RE ALL FEELING A BIT "OFF" AFTER HEADING ACROSS THE GALAXY, BUT I THINK GETTING BACK TO HELPING PEOPLE IS WHAT WE ALL NEED.
AMADEUS IS RIGHT. THE G.I.R.L. GANG SENT ME INFO ON A SPOT WHERE I THINK WE CAN REALLY MAKE A DIFFERENCE.
IN AFRICA?
YEAH, TANZANIA.
AFTER THE GRANDMASTER MOVED EARTH A FEW WEEKS AGO, IT KICKED OFF A BUNCH OF EARTHQUAKES AND CORRUPTED WATER SOURCES THAT USED TO FEED INTO IMPORTANT WETLANDS IN THE REGION.
A SCIENTIST FRIEND OF NADIA'S IS VISITING A VILLAGE CALLED MBALI. THEY'RE IN DIRE NEED OF A NEW WATER FILTRATION SYSTEM. WE CAN BUILD IT AND HELP WITH GENERAL REPAIRS... GET 'EM BACK ON THEIR FEET.
ONE SOLAR-POWERED WATER FILTER, COMING RIGHT UP...
ARE WE VOTING ON THIS MISSION?
WE'RE ALREADY FULL STEAM AHEAD, VIV. I PUNCHED IN THE DESTINATION AND THE MOBILE BUNKER IS EN ROUTE.
I SEE. WHERE IS MS. MARVEL?

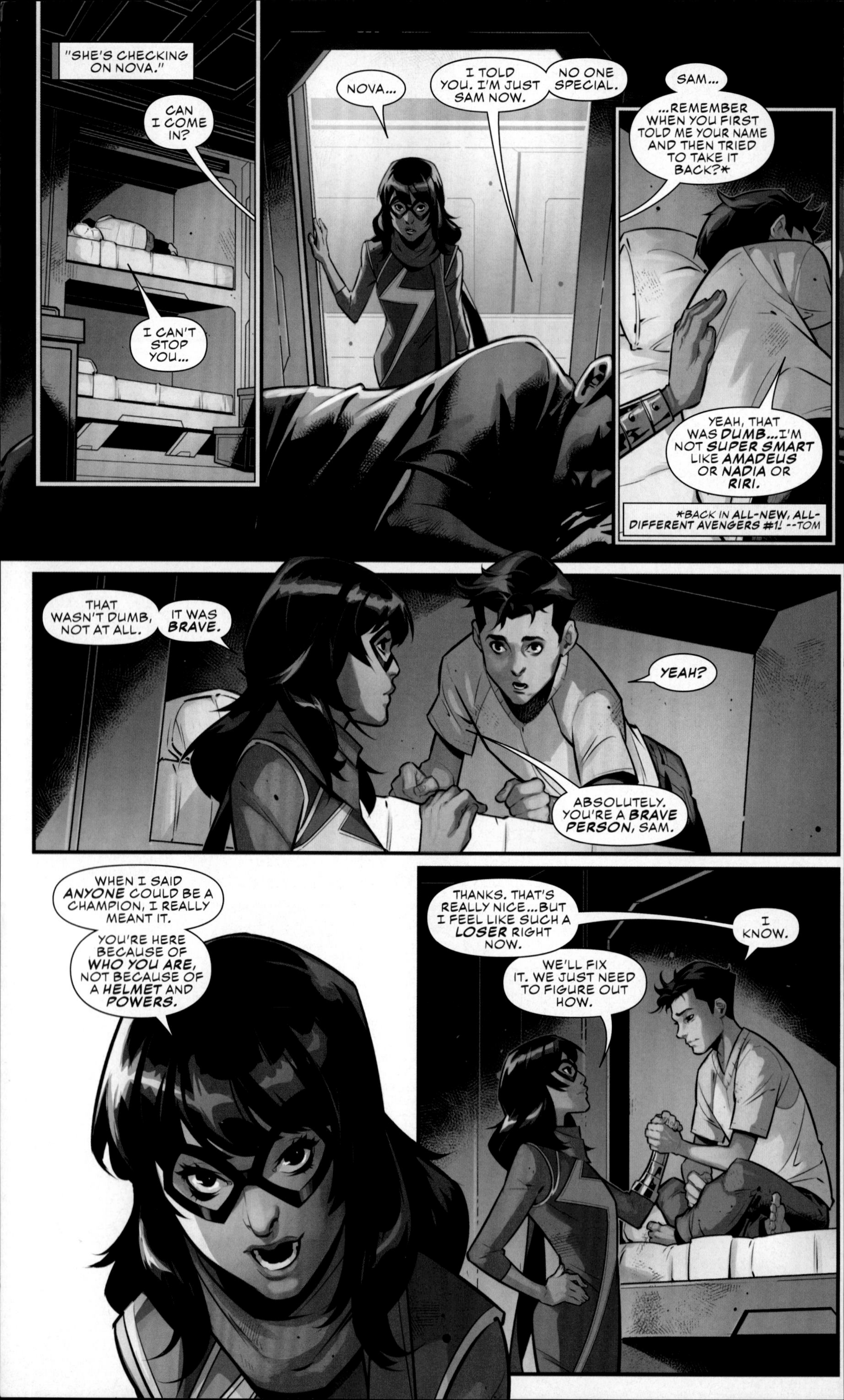
"SHE'S CHECKING ON NOVA."
CAN I COME IN?
I CAN'T STOP YOU...
NOVA...
I TOLD YOU. I'M JUST SAM NOW.
NO ONE SPECIAL.
SAM...
...REMEMBER WHEN YOU FIRST TOLD ME YOUR NAME AND THEN TRIED TO TAKE IT BACK?*
YEAH, THAT WAS DUMB...I'M NOT SUPER SMART LIKE AMADEUS OR NADIA OR RIRI.
*BACK IN ALL-NEW, ALL-DIFFERENT AVENGERS #1! --TOM
THAT WASN'T DUMB, NOT AT ALL.
IT WAS BRAVE.
YEAH?
ABSOLUTELY. YOU'RE A BRAVE PERSON, SAM.
WHEN I SAID ANYONE COULD BE A CHAMPION, I REALLY MEANT IT.
YOU'RE HERE BECAUSE OF WHO YOU ARE, NOT BECAUSE OF A HELMET AND POWERS.
THANKS. THAT'S REALLY NICE...BUT I FEEL LIKE SUCH A LOSER RIGHT NOW.
I KNOW.
WE'LL FIX IT. WE JUST NEED TO FIGURE OUT HOW.

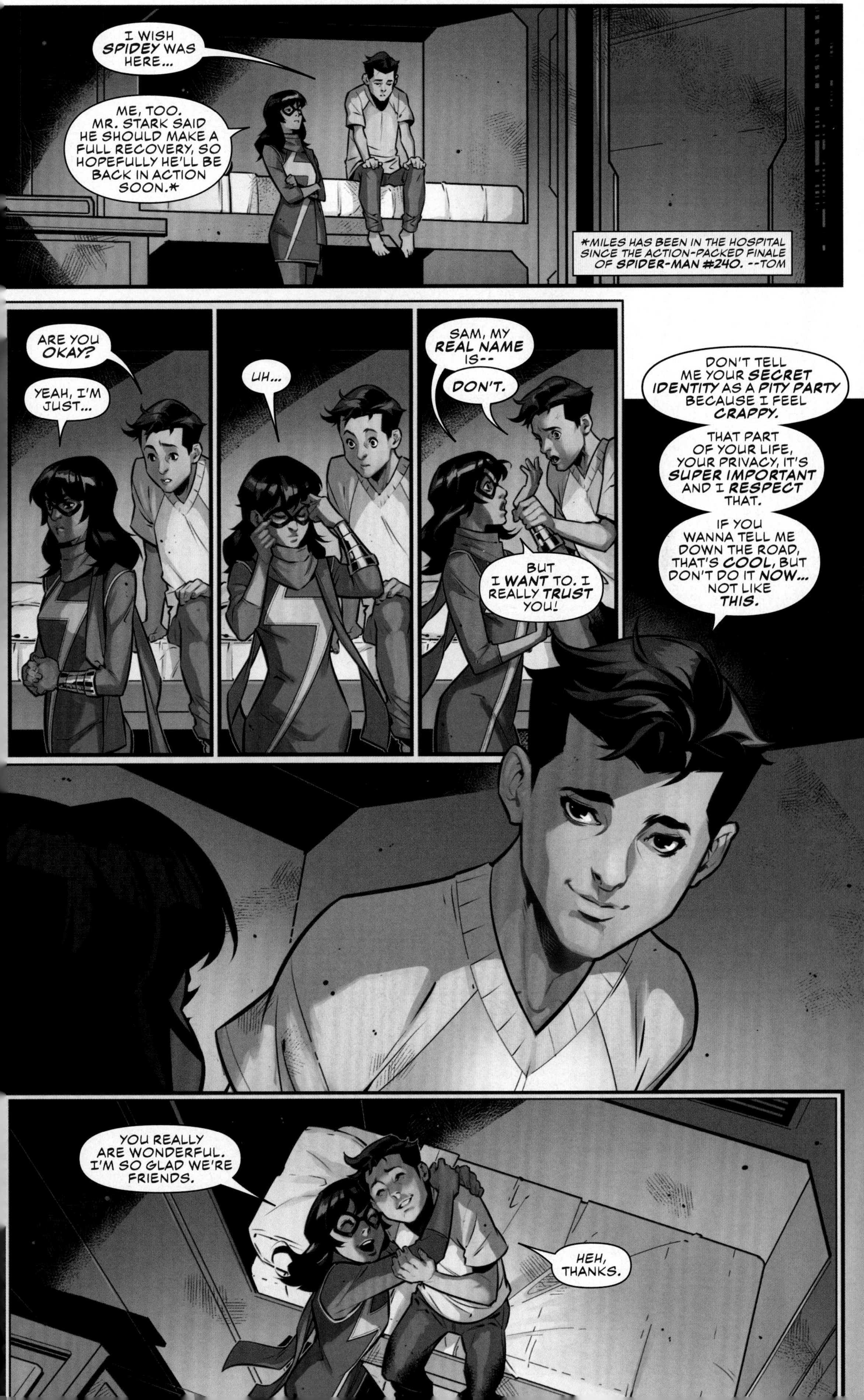
I WISH SPIDEY WAS HERE...
ME, TOO. MR. STARK SAID HE SHOULD MAKE A FULL RECOVERY, SO HOPEFULLY HE'LL BE BACK IN ACTION SOON.*
*MILES HAS BEEN IN THE HOSPITAL SINCE THE ACTION-PACKED FINALE OF SPIDER-MAN #240. --TOM
ARE YOU OKAY?
YEAH, I'M JUST...
UH...
SAM, MY REAL NAME IS--
DON'T.
BUT I WANT TO. I REALLY TRUST YOU!
DON'T TELL ME YOUR SECRET IDENTITY AS A PITY PARTY BECAUSE I FEEL CRAPPY.
THAT PART OF YOUR LIFE, YOUR PRIVACY, IT'S SUPER IMPORTANT AND I RESPECT THAT.
IF YOU WANNA TELL ME DOWN THE ROAD, THAT'S COOL, BUT DON'T DO IT NOW... NOT LIKE THIS.
YOU REALLY ARE WONDERFUL. I'M SO GLAD WE'RE FRIENDS.
HEH, THANKS.

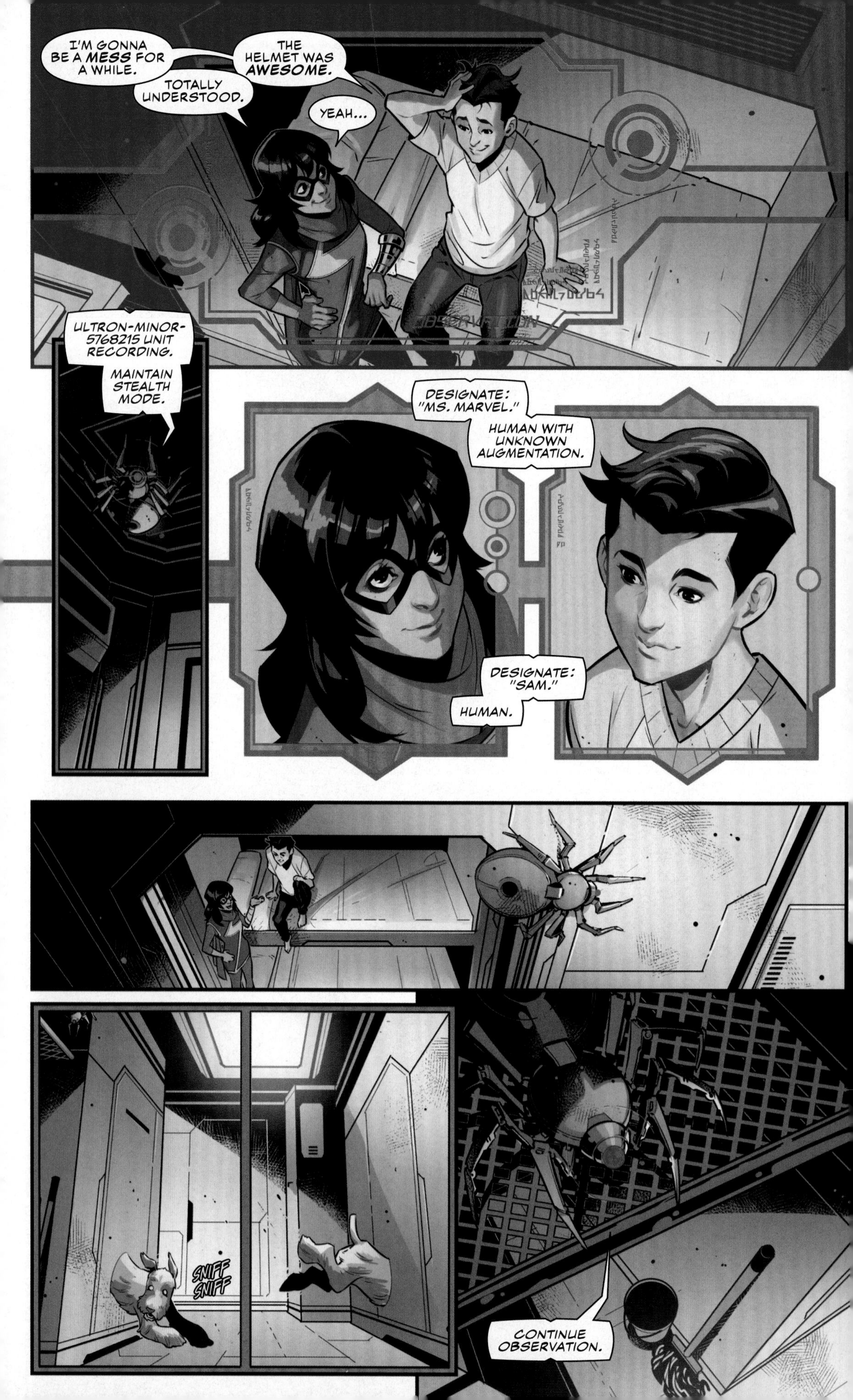
I'M GONNA BE A **MESS** FOR A WHILE.
THE HELMET WAS **AWESOME.**
TOTALLY UNDERSTOOD.
YEAH...
ULTRON-MINOR-5768215 UNIT RECORDING.
MAINTAIN STEALTH MODE.
DESIGNATE: "MS. MARVEL."
HUMAN WITH UNKNOWN AUGMENTATION.
DESIGNATE: "SAM."
HUMAN.
SNIFF SNIFF
CONTINUE OBSERVATION.

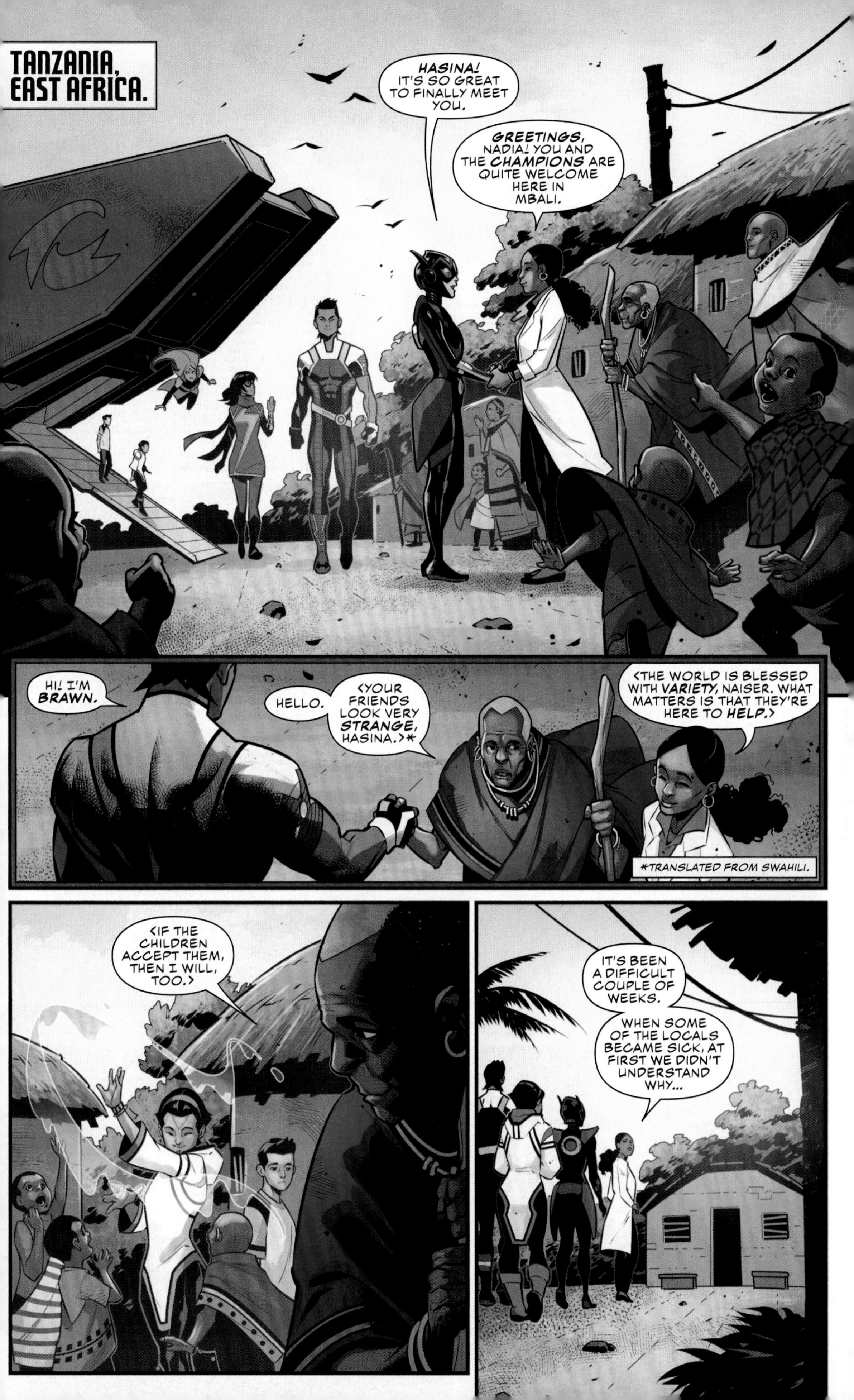
TANZANIA, EAST AFRICA.
HASINA! IT'S SO GREAT TO FINALLY MEET YOU.
GREETINGS, NADIA! YOU AND THE CHAMPIONS ARE QUITE WELCOME HERE IN MBALI.
HI! I'M BRAWN.
HELLO.
<YOUR FRIENDS LOOK VERY STRANGE, HASINA.>*
<THE WORLD IS BLESSED WITH VARIETY, NAISER. WHAT MATTERS IS THAT THEY'RE HERE TO HELP.>
*TRANSLATED FROM SWAHILI.
<IF THE CHILDREN ACCEPT THEM, THEN I WILL, TOO.>
IT'S BEEN A DIFFICULT COUPLE OF WEEKS.
WHEN SOME OF THE LOCALS BECAME SICK, AT FIRST WE DIDN'T UNDERSTAND WHY...

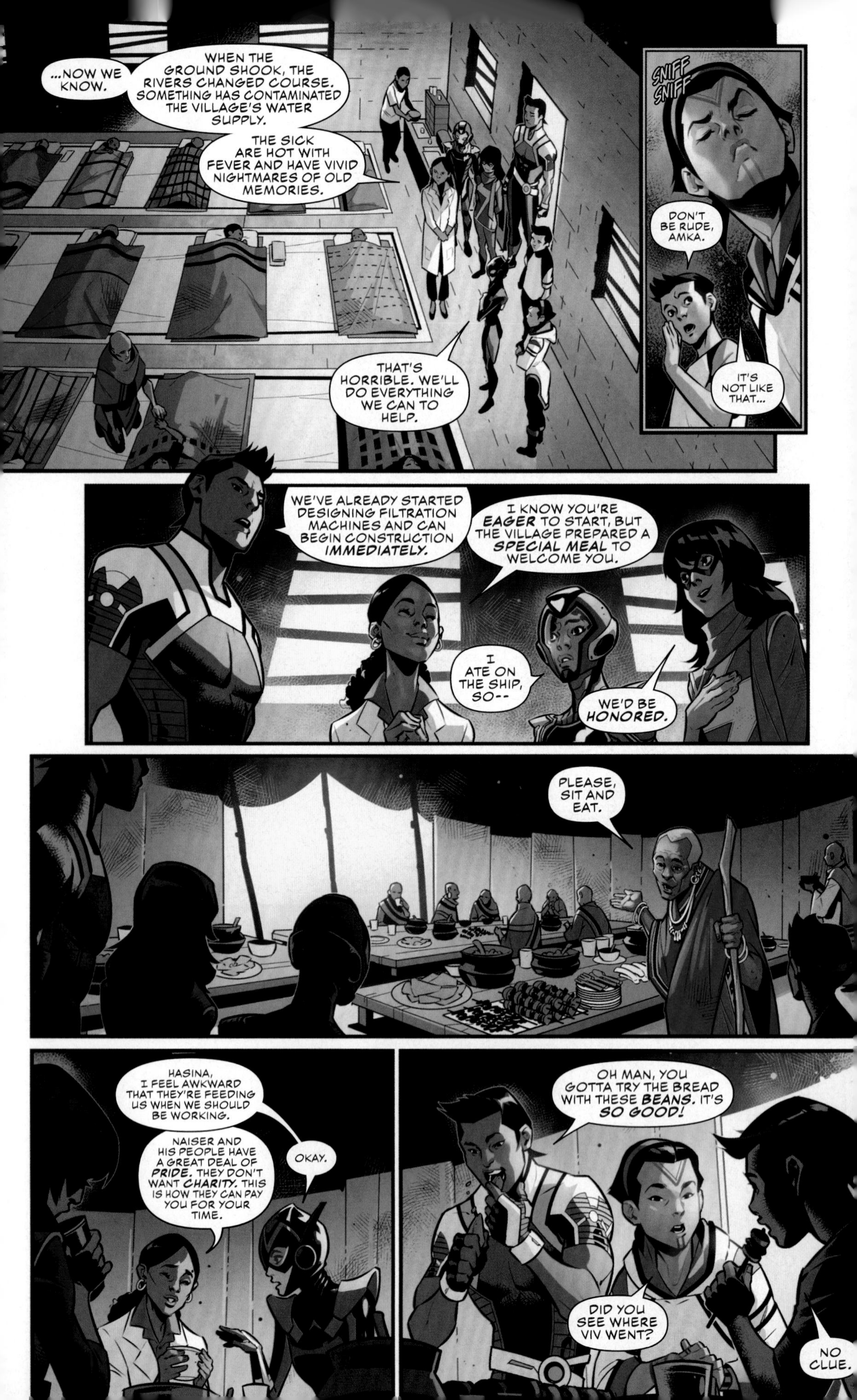
...NOW WE KNOW.
WHEN THE GROUND SHOOK, THE RIVERS CHANGED COURSE. SOMETHING HAS CONTAMINATED THE VILLAGE'S WATER SUPPLY.
THE SICK ARE HOT WITH FEVER AND HAVE VIVID NIGHTMARES OF OLD MEMORIES.
THAT'S HORRIBLE. WE'LL DO EVERYTHING WE CAN TO HELP.
SNIFF SNIFF
DON'T BE RUDE, AMKA.
IT'S NOT LIKE THAT...
WE'VE ALREADY STARTED DESIGNING FILTRATION MACHINES AND CAN BEGIN CONSTRUCTION IMMEDIATELY.
I KNOW YOU'RE EAGER TO START, BUT THE VILLAGE PREPARED A SPECIAL MEAL TO WELCOME YOU.
I ATE ON THE SHIP, SO--
WE'D BE HONORED.
PLEASE, SIT AND EAT.
HASINA, I FEEL AWKWARD THAT THEY'RE FEEDING US WHEN WE SHOULD BE WORKING.
NAISER AND HIS PEOPLE HAVE A GREAT DEAL OF PRIDE. THEY DON'T WANT CHARITY. THIS IS HOW THEY CAN PAY YOU FOR YOUR TIME.
OKAY.
OH MAN, YOU GOTTA TRY THE BREAD WITH THESE BEANS. IT'S SO GOOD!
DID YOU SEE WHERE VIV WENT?
NO CLUE.

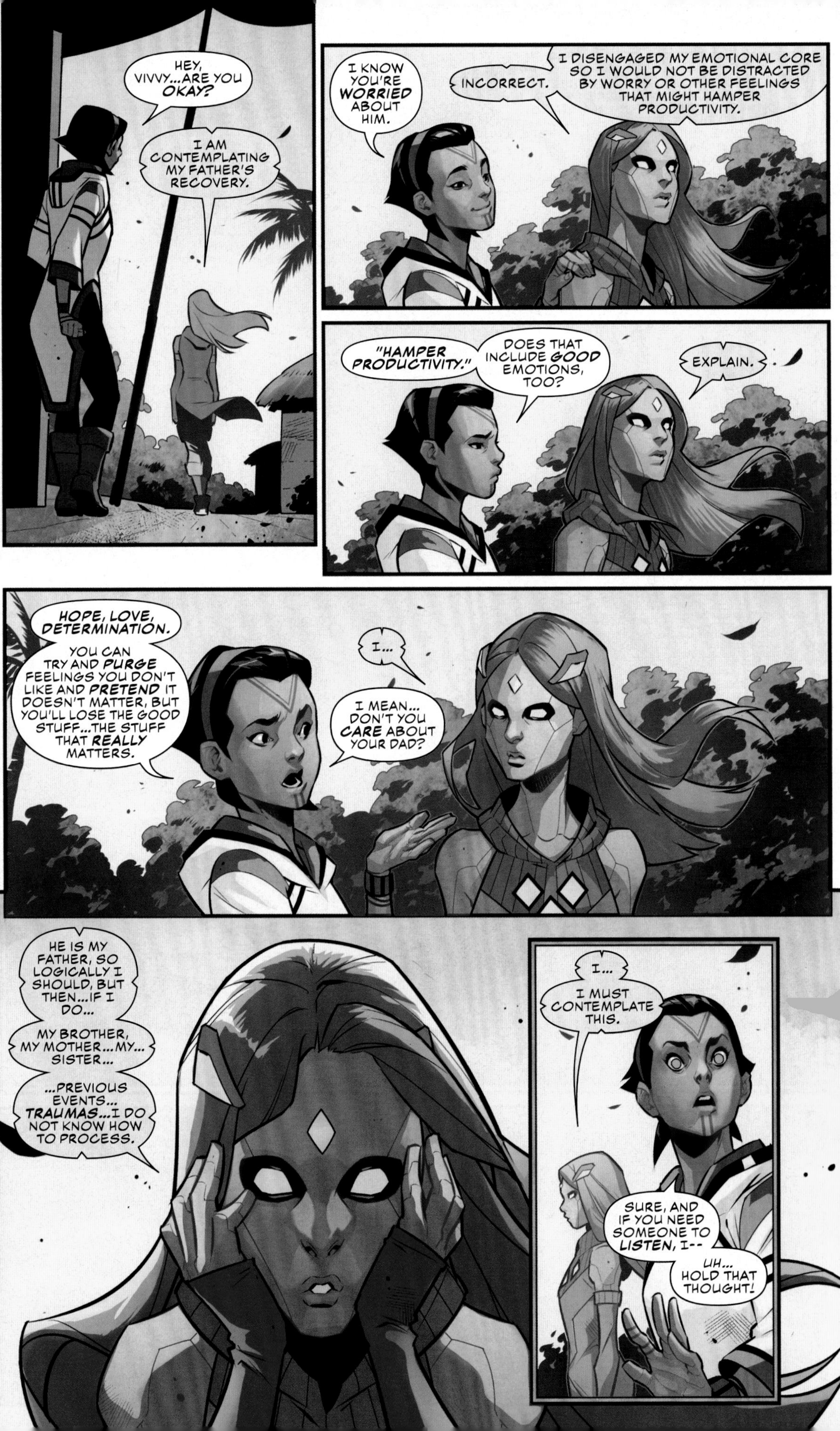
HEY, VIVVY...ARE YOU OKAY?
I AM CONTEMPLATING MY FATHER'S RECOVERY.
I KNOW YOU'RE WORRIED ABOUT HIM.
INCORRECT.
I DISENGAGED MY EMOTIONAL CORE SO I WOULD NOT BE DISTRACTED BY WORRY OR OTHER FEELINGS THAT MIGHT HAMPER PRODUCTIVITY.
"HAMPER PRODUCTIVITY."
DOES THAT INCLUDE GOOD EMOTIONS, TOO?
EXPLAIN.
HOPE, LOVE, DETERMINATION.
YOU CAN TRY AND PURGE FEELINGS YOU DON'T LIKE AND PRETEND IT DOESN'T MATTER, BUT YOU'LL LOSE THE GOOD STUFF...THE STUFF THAT REALLY MATTERS.
I...
I MEAN... DON'T YOU CARE ABOUT YOUR DAD?
HE IS MY FATHER, SO LOGICALLY I SHOULD, BUT THEN...IF I DO...
MY BROTHER, MY MOTHER...MY... SISTER...
...PREVIOUS EVENTS... TRAUMAS...I DO NOT KNOW HOW TO PROCESS.
I...
I MUST CONTEMPLATE THIS.
SURE, AND IF YOU NEED SOMEONE TO LISTEN, I--
UH... HOLD THAT THOUGHT!

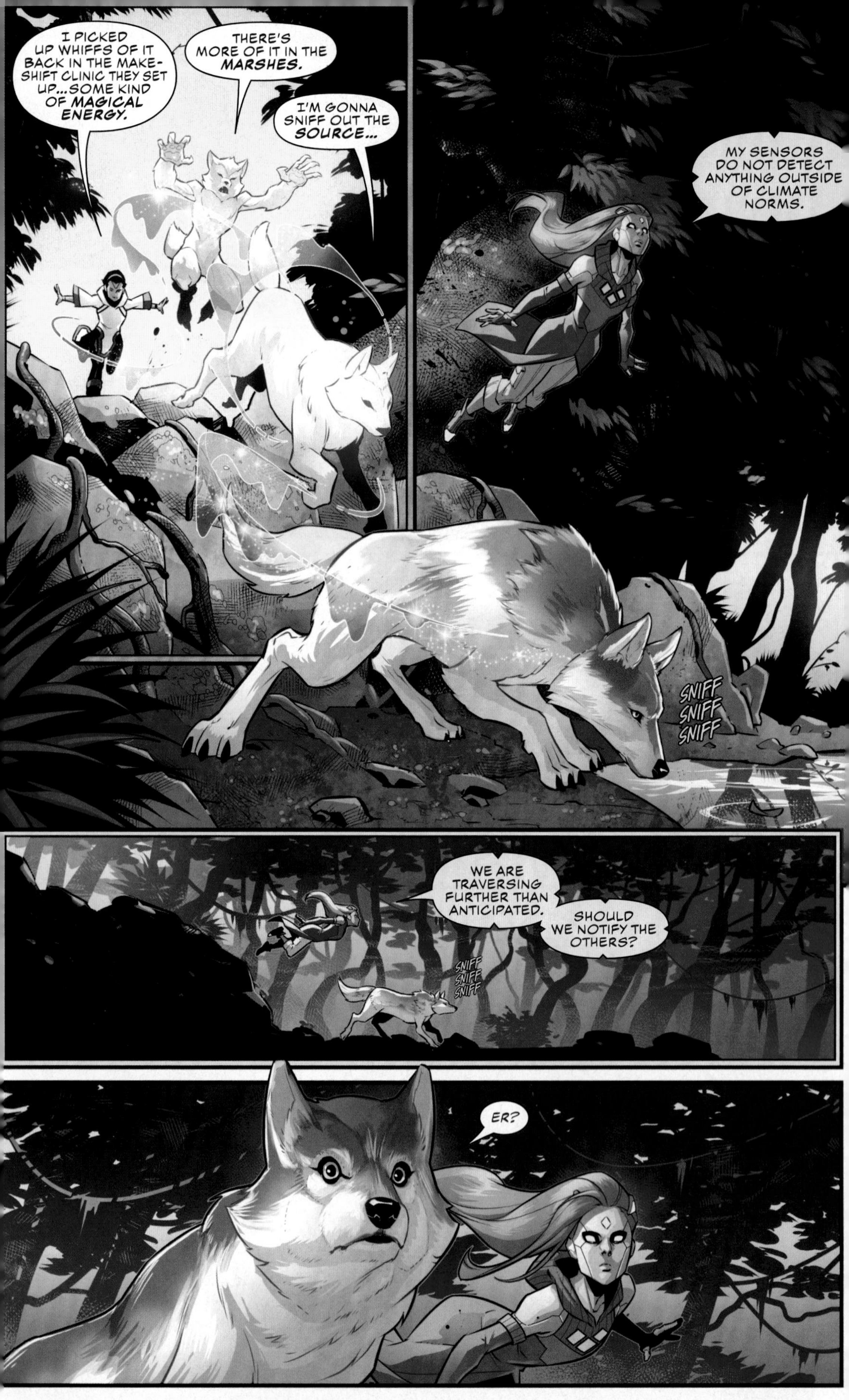

I PICKED UP WHIFFS OF IT BACK IN THE MAKE-SHIFT CLINIC THEY SET UP...SOME KIND OF MAGICAL ENERGY.
THERE'S MORE OF IT IN THE MARSHES.
I'M GONNA SNIFF OUT THE SOURCE...
MY SENSORS DO NOT DETECT ANYTHING OUTSIDE OF CLIMATE NORMS.
SNIFF SNIFF SNIFF
WE ARE TRAVERSING FURTHER THAN ANTICIPATED.
SHOULD WE NOTIFY THE OTHERS?
SNIFF SNIFF SNIFF
ER?

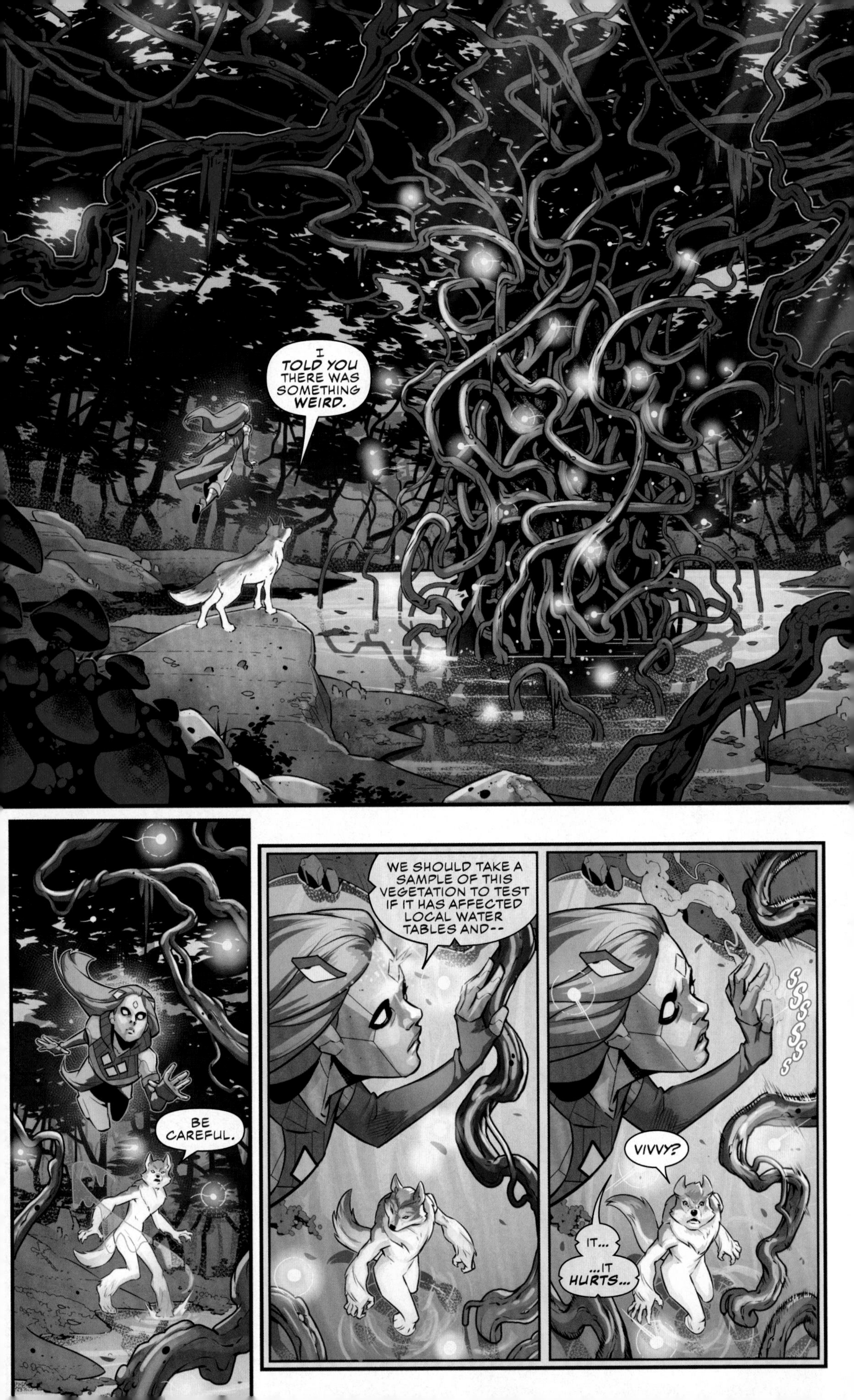
I TOLD YOU THERE WAS SOMETHING WEIRD.
BE CAREFUL.
WE SHOULD TAKE A SAMPLE OF THIS VEGETATION TO TEST IF IT HAS AFFECTED LOCAL WATER TABLES AND--
SSSSSS
VIVVY?
IT...
...IT HURTS...

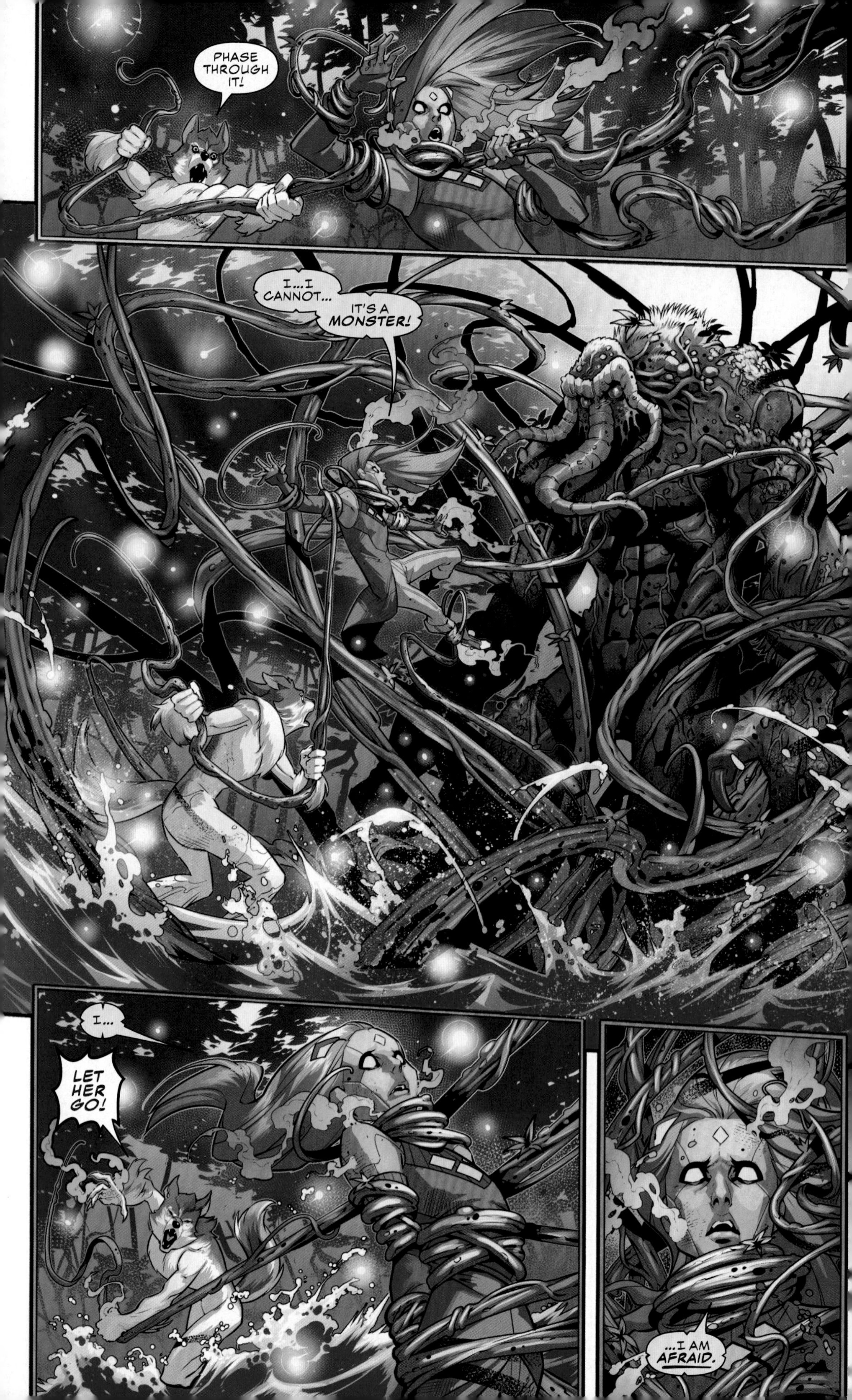
PHASE THROUGH IT!
I...I CANNOT... IT'S A MONSTER!
I...
LET HER GO!
...I AM AFRAID.

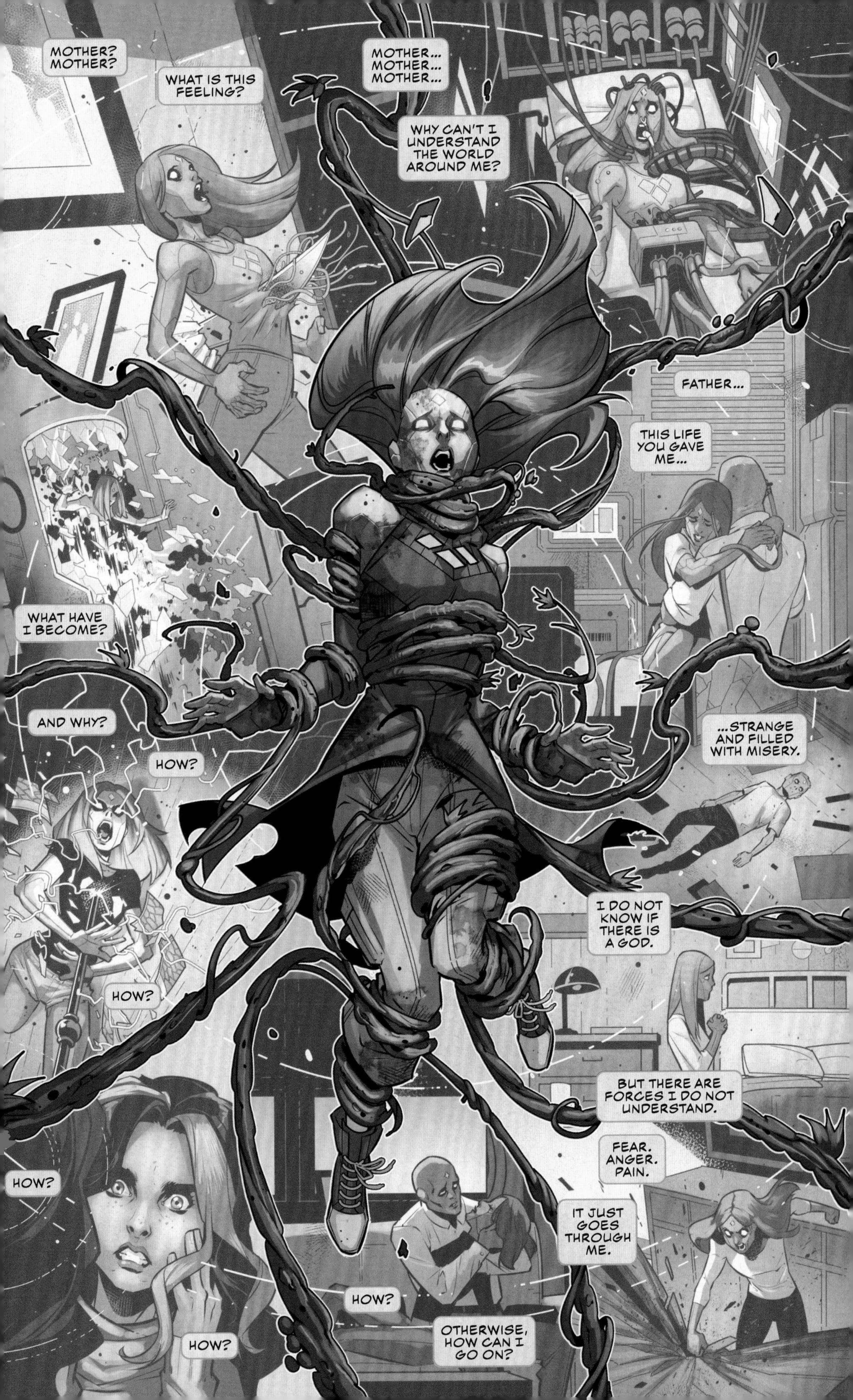
MOTHER? MOTHER?
WHAT IS THIS FEELING?
MOTHER... MOTHER... MOTHER...
WHY CAN'T I UNDERSTAND THE WORLD AROUND ME?
FATHER...
THIS LIFE YOU GAVE ME...
WHAT HAVE I BECOME?
AND WHY?
HOW?
...STRANGE AND FILLED WITH MISERY.
I DO NOT KNOW IF THERE IS A GOD.
HOW?
BUT THERE ARE FORCES I DO NOT UNDERSTAND.
FEAR. ANGER. PAIN.
HOW?
IT JUST GOES THROUGH ME.
HOW?
OTHERWISE, HOW CAN I GO ON?
HOW?

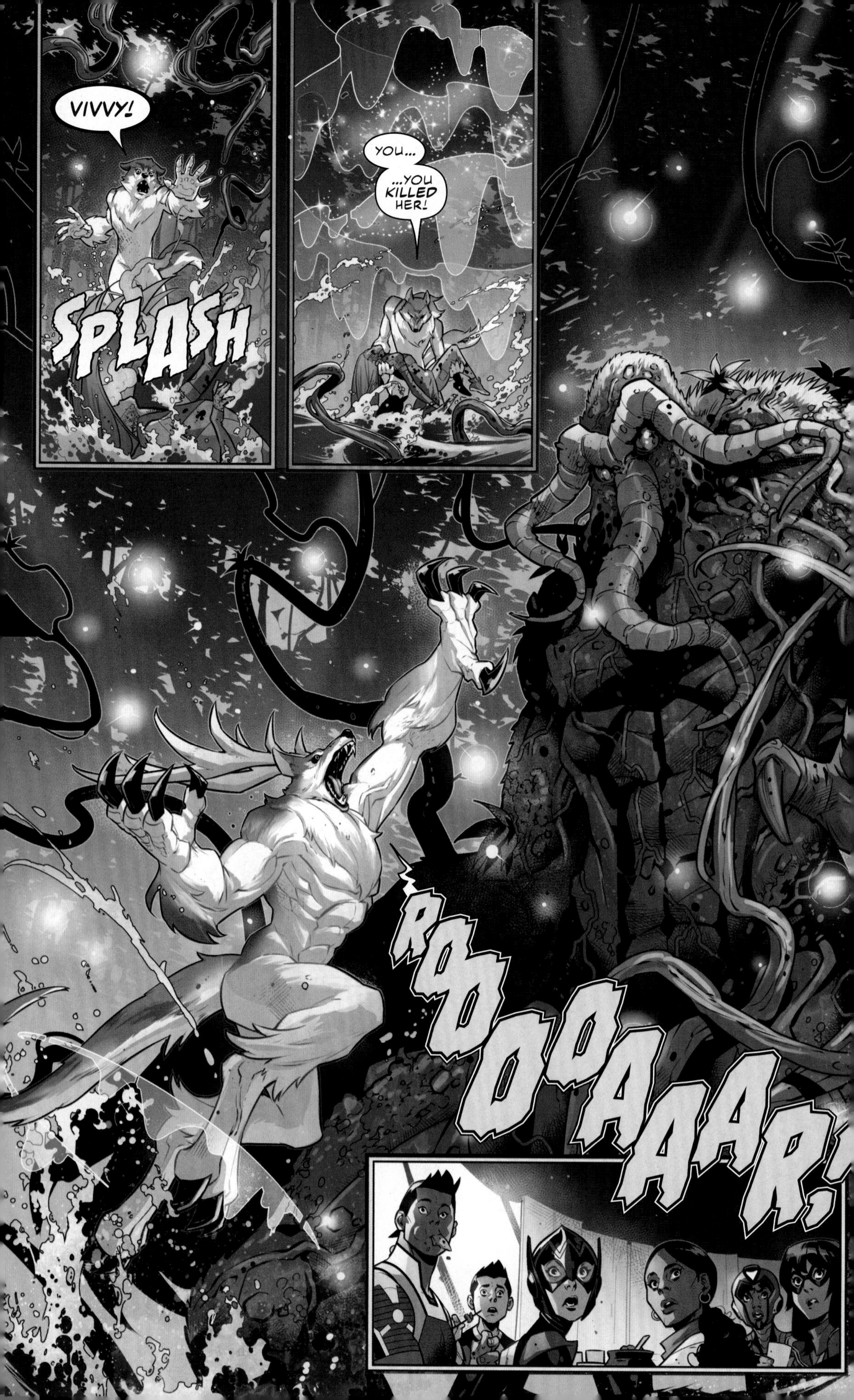
VIVVY!
SPLASH
YOU...
...YOU KILLED HER!
ROOOOAAAR!

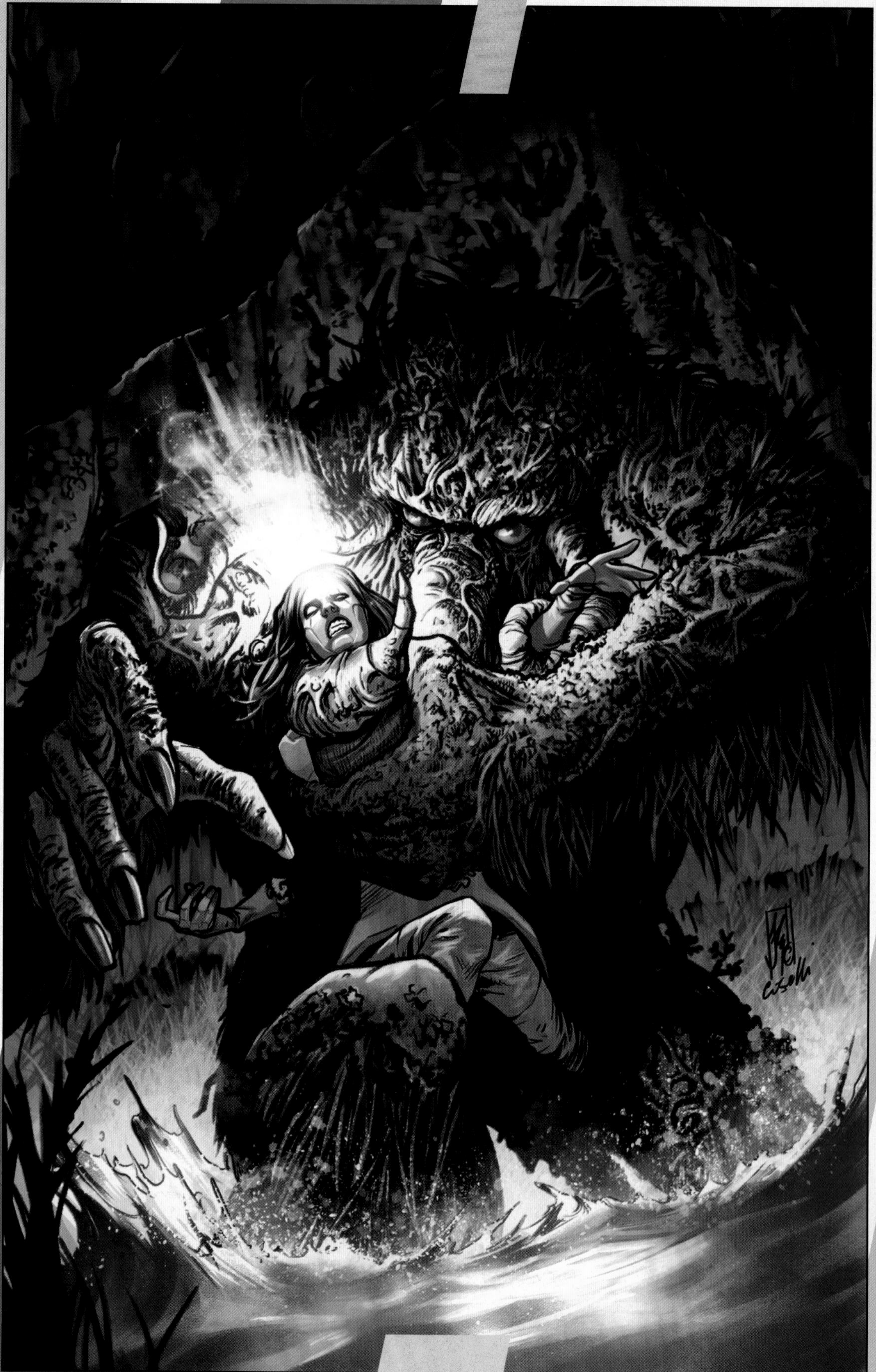

23

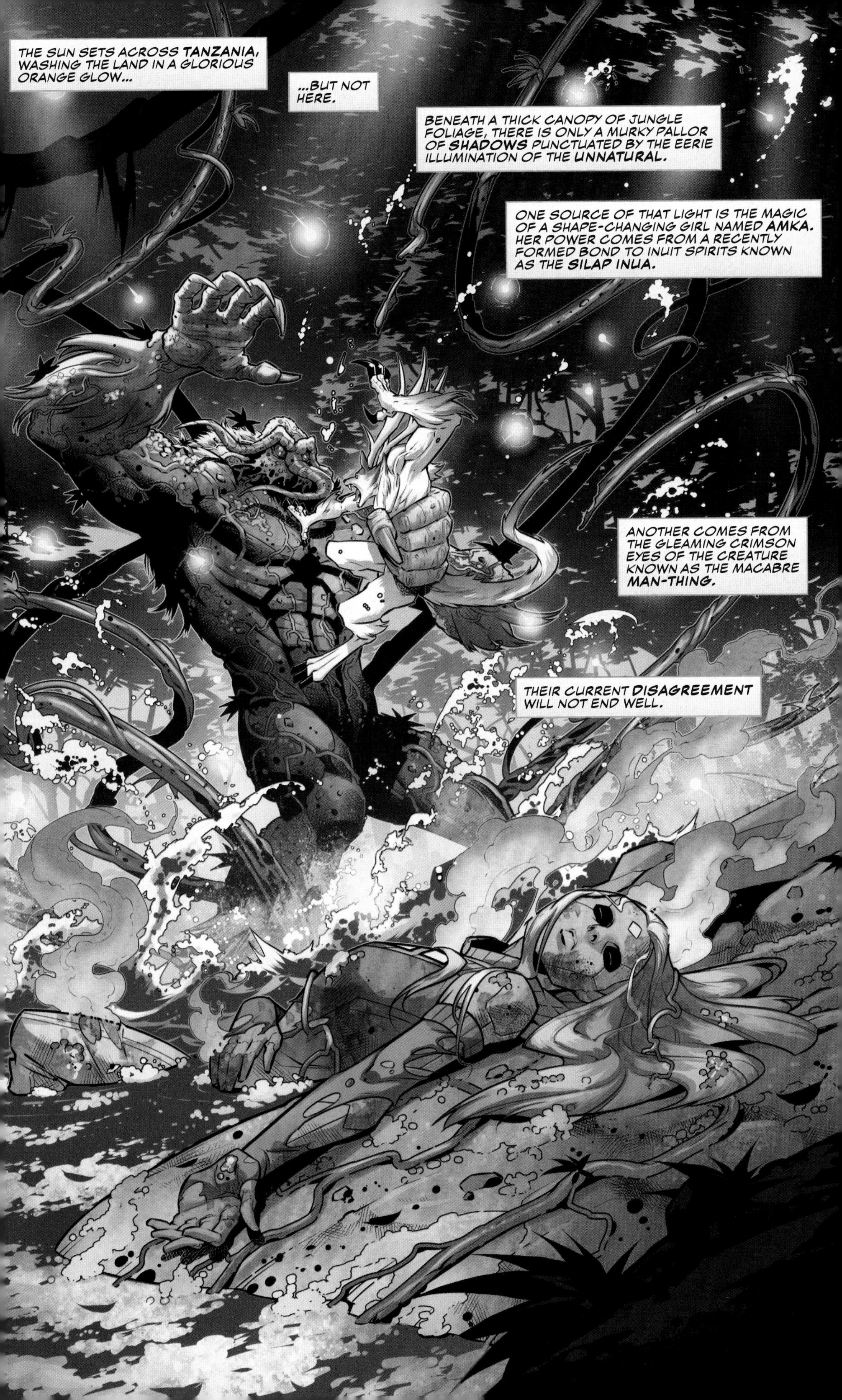
THE SUN SETS ACROSS TANZANIA, WASHING THE LAND IN A GLORIOUS ORANGE GLOW...
...BUT NOT HERE.
BENEATH A THICK CANOPY OF JUNGLE FOLIAGE, THERE IS ONLY A MURKY PALLOR OF SHADOWS PUNCTUATED BY THE EERIE ILLUMINATION OF THE UNNATURAL.
ONE SOURCE OF THAT LIGHT IS THE MAGIC OF A SHAPE-CHANGING GIRL NAMED AMKA. HER POWER COMES FROM A RECENTLY FORMED BOND TO INUIT SPIRITS KNOWN AS THE SILAP INUA.
ANOTHER COMES FROM THE GLEAMING CRIMSON EYES OF THE CREATURE KNOWN AS THE MACABRE MAN-THING.
THEIR CURRENT DISAGREEMENT WILL NOT END WELL.

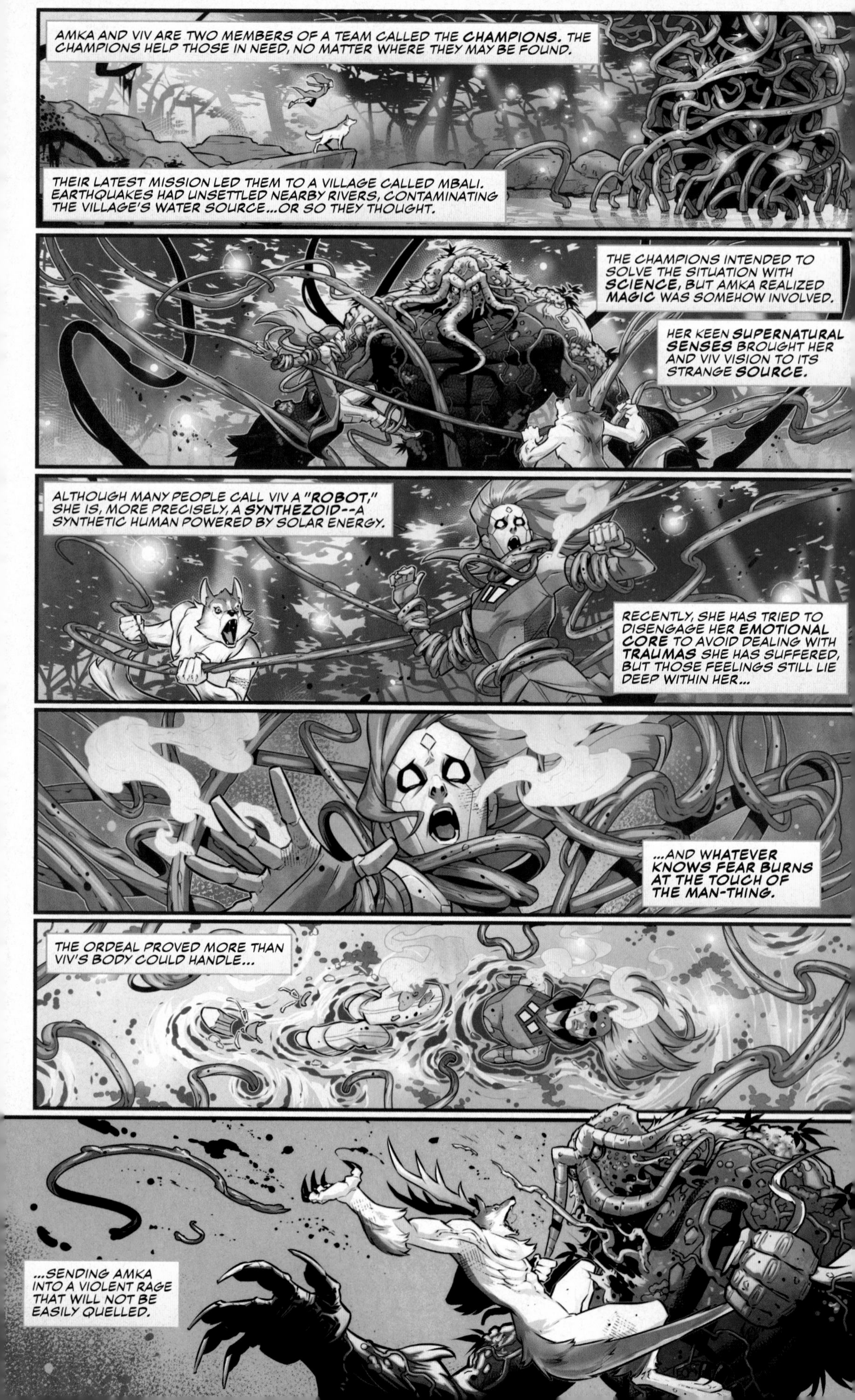
AMKA AND VIV ARE TWO MEMBERS OF A TEAM CALLED THE CHAMPIONS. THE CHAMPIONS HELP THOSE IN NEED, NO MATTER WHERE THEY MAY BE FOUND.
THEIR LATEST MISSION LED THEM TO A VILLAGE CALLED MBALI. EARTHQUAKES HAD UNSETTLED NEARBY RIVERS, CONTAMINATING THE VILLAGE'S WATER SOURCE...OR SO THEY THOUGHT.
THE CHAMPIONS INTENDED TO SOLVE THE SITUATION WITH SCIENCE, BUT AMKA REALIZED MAGIC WAS SOMEHOW INVOLVED.
HER KEEN SUPERNATURAL SENSES BROUGHT HER AND VIV VISION TO ITS STRANGE SOURCE.
ALTHOUGH MANY PEOPLE CALL VIV A "ROBOT," SHE IS, MORE PRECISELY, A SYNTHEZOID--A SYNTHETIC HUMAN POWERED BY SOLAR ENERGY.
RECENTLY, SHE HAS TRIED TO DISENGAGE HER EMOTIONAL CORE TO AVOID DEALING WITH TRAUMAS SHE HAS SUFFERED, BUT THOSE FEELINGS STILL LIE DEEP WITHIN HER...
...AND WHATEVER KNOWS FEAR BURNS AT THE TOUCH OF THE MAN-THING.
THE ORDEAL PROVED MORE THAN VIV'S BODY COULD HANDLE...
...SENDING AMKA INTO A VIOLENT RAGE THAT WILL NOT BE EASILY QUELLED.

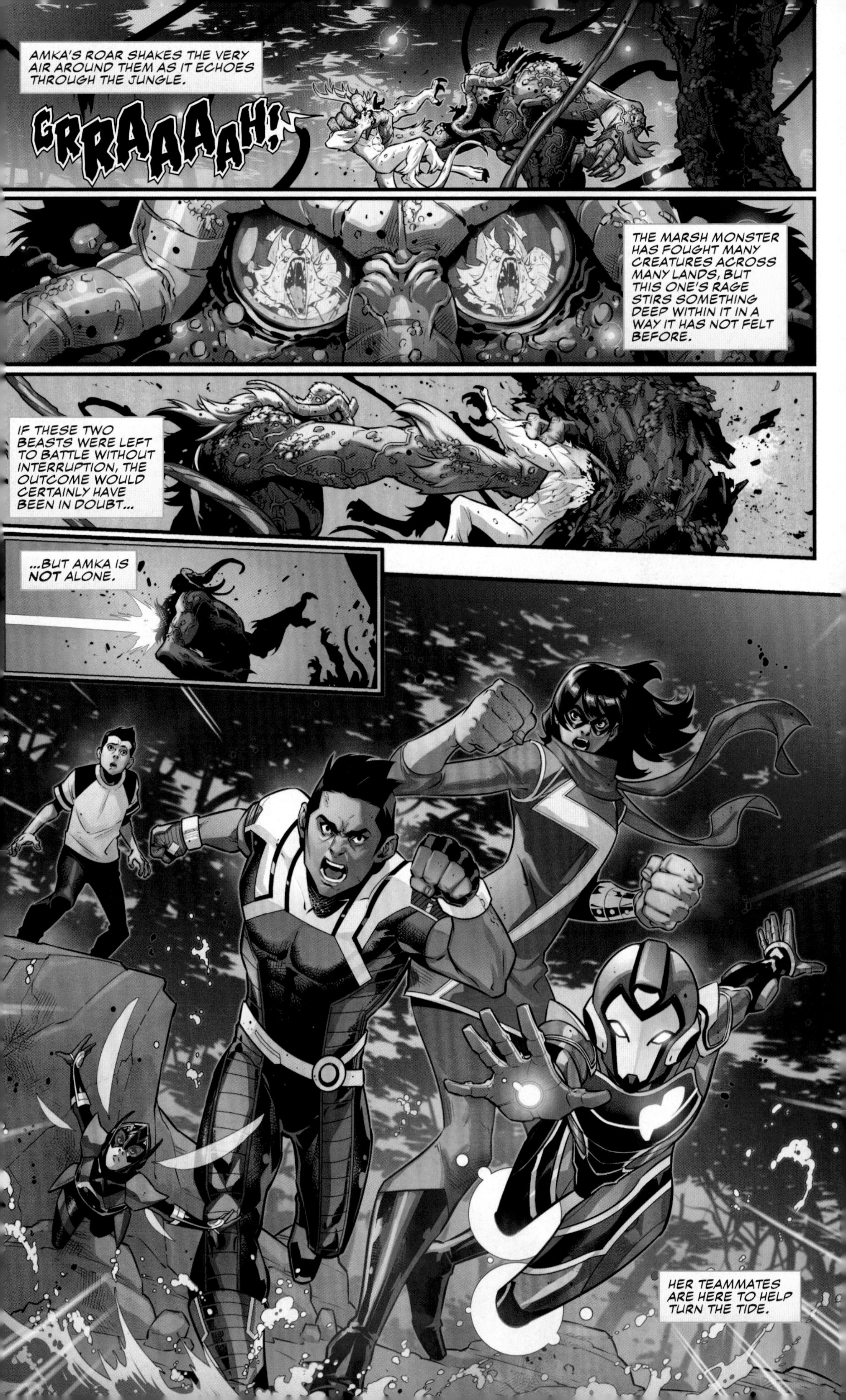
AMKA'S ROAR SHAKES THE VERY AIR AROUND THEM AS IT ECHOES THROUGH THE JUNGLE.
GRRAAAAAH!
THE MARSH MONSTER HAS FOUGHT MANY CREATURES ACROSS MANY LANDS, BUT THIS ONE'S RAGE STIRS SOMETHING DEEP WITHIN IT IN A WAY IT HAS NOT FELT BEFORE.
IF THESE TWO BEASTS WERE LEFT TO BATTLE WITHOUT INTERRUPTION, THE OUTCOME WOULD CERTAINLY HAVE BEEN IN DOUBT...
...BUT AMKA IS NOT ALONE.
HER TEAMMATES ARE HERE TO HELP TURN THE TIDE.

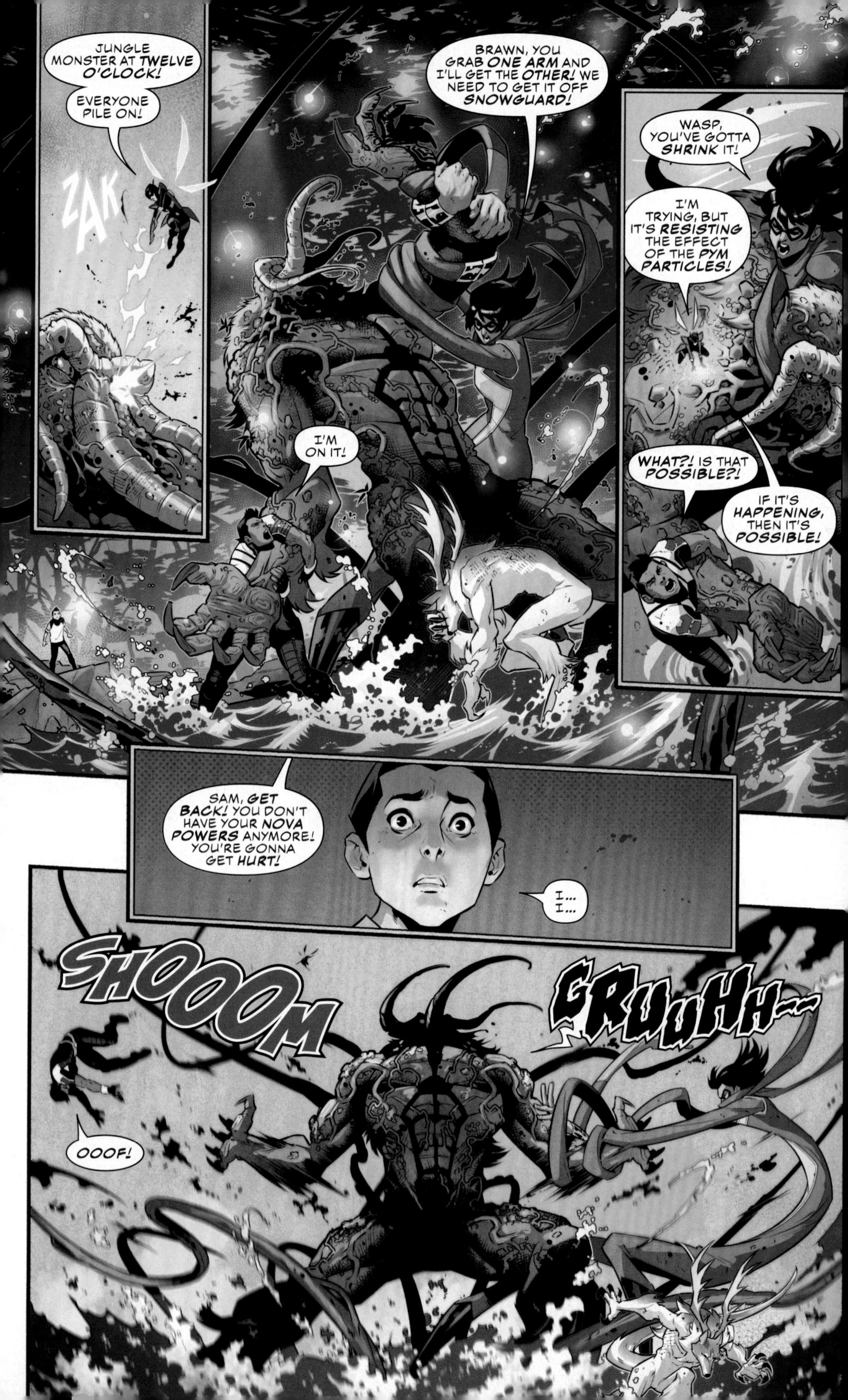

JUNGLE MONSTER AT TWELVE O'CLOCK!
EVERYONE PILE ON!
ZAK
BRAWN, YOU GRAB ONE ARM AND I'LL GET THE OTHER! WE NEED TO GET IT OFF SNOWGUARD!
I'M ON IT!
WASP, YOU'VE GOTTA SHRINK IT!
I'M TRYING, BUT IT'S RESISTING THE EFFECT OF THE PYM PARTICLES!
WHAT?! IS THAT POSSIBLE?!
IF IT'S HAPPENING, THEN IT'S POSSIBLE!
SAM, GET BACK! YOU DON'T HAVE YOUR NOVA POWERS ANYMORE! YOU'RE GONNA GET HURT!
I... I...
SHOOOM
GRUUHH--
OOOF!

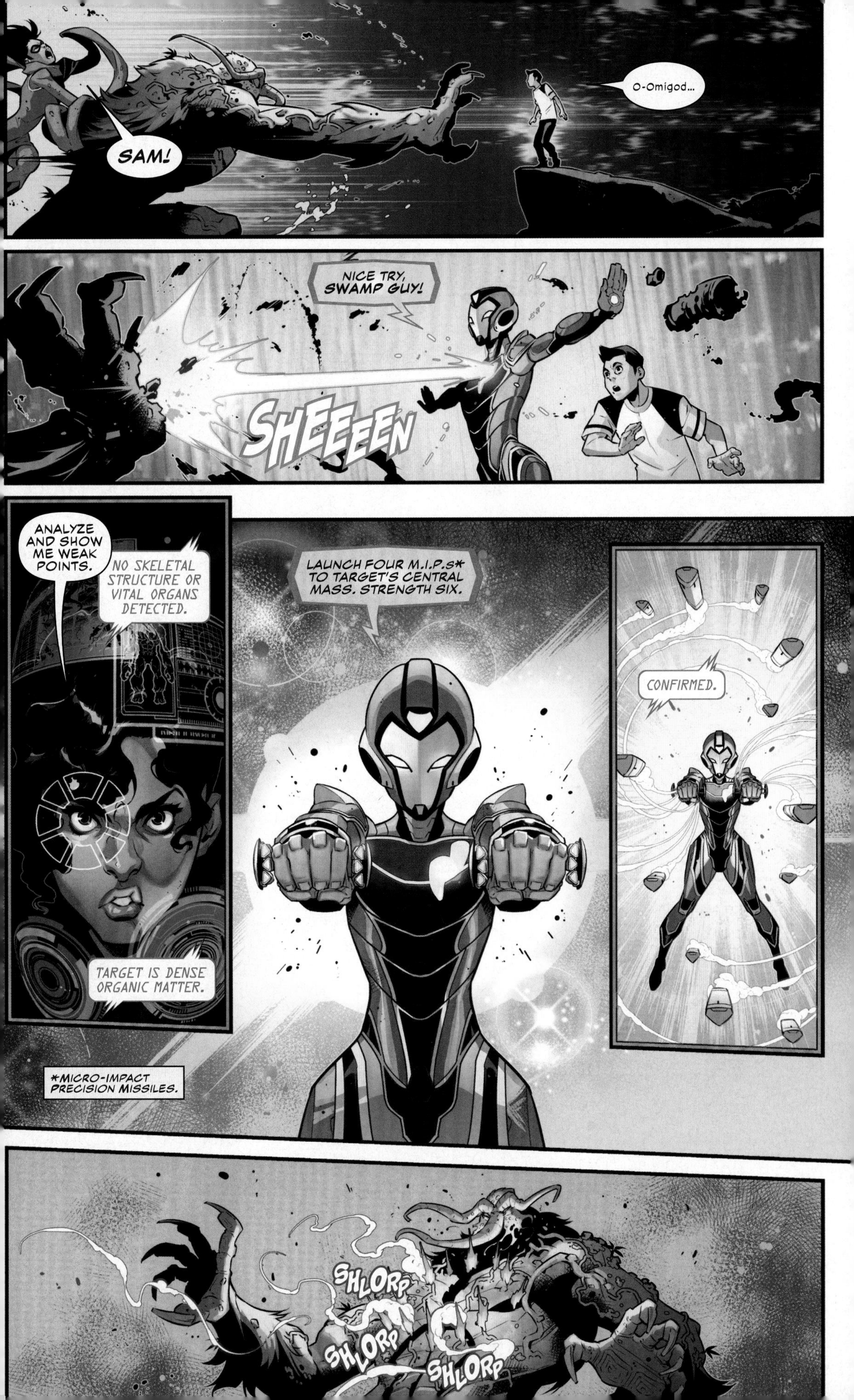

O-Omigod...
SAM!
NICE TRY, SWAMP GUY!
SHEEEEN
ANALYZE AND SHOW ME WEAK POINTS.
NO SKELETAL STRUCTURE OR VITAL ORGANS DETECTED.
TARGET IS DENSE ORGANIC MATTER.
LAUNCH FOUR M.I.P.s* TO TARGET'S CENTRAL MASS. STRENGTH SIX.
CONFIRMED.
*MICRO-IMPACT PRECISION MISSILES.
SHLORP
SHLORP
SHLORP

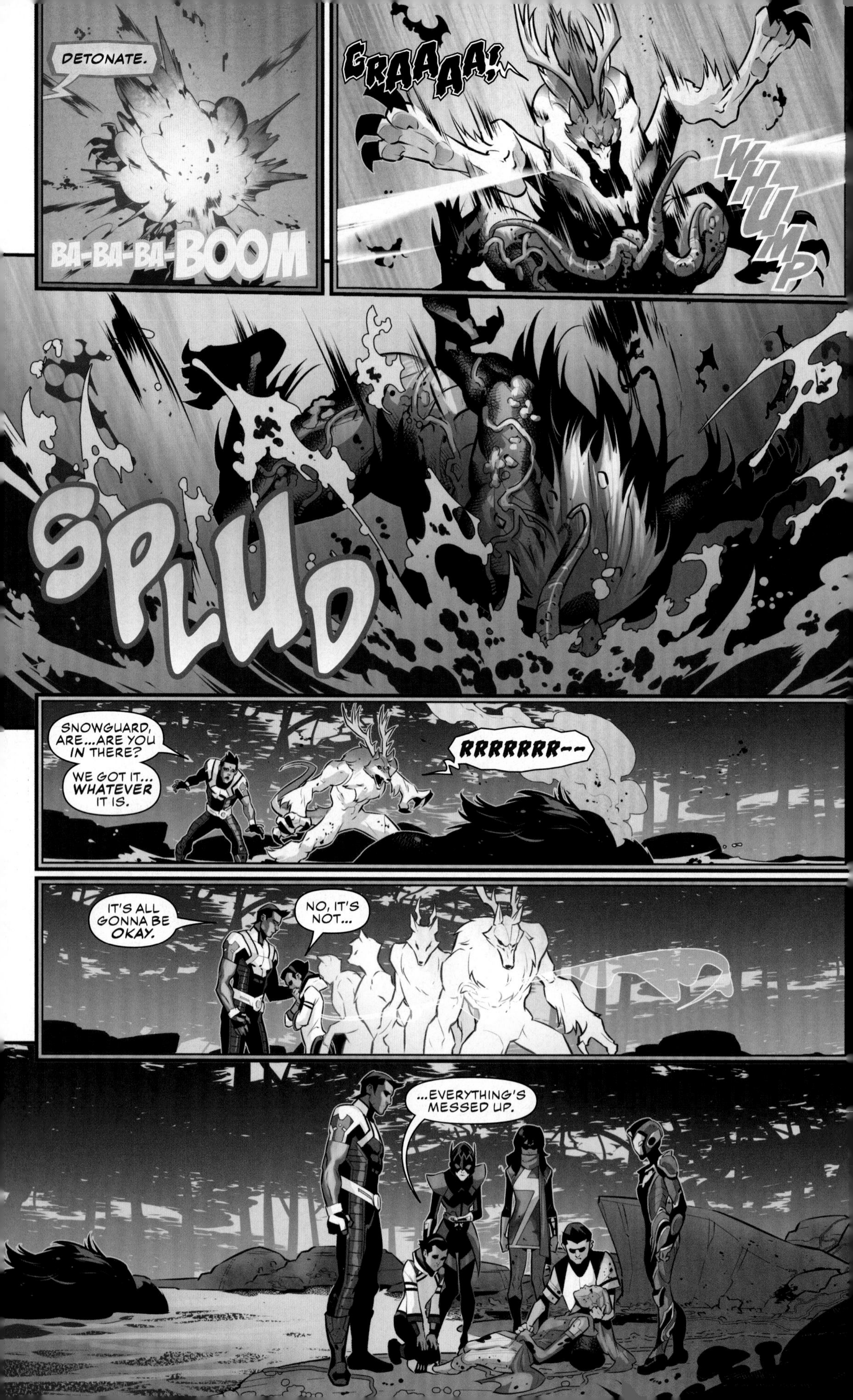
DETONATE.
BA-BA-BA-BOOM
GRAAAA!
WHUMP
SPLUD
SNOWGUARD, ARE...ARE YOU IN THERE?
WE GOT IT... WHATEVER IT IS.
RRRRRRR--
IT'S ALL GONNA BE OKAY.
NO, IT'S NOT...
...EVERYTHING'S MESSED UP.

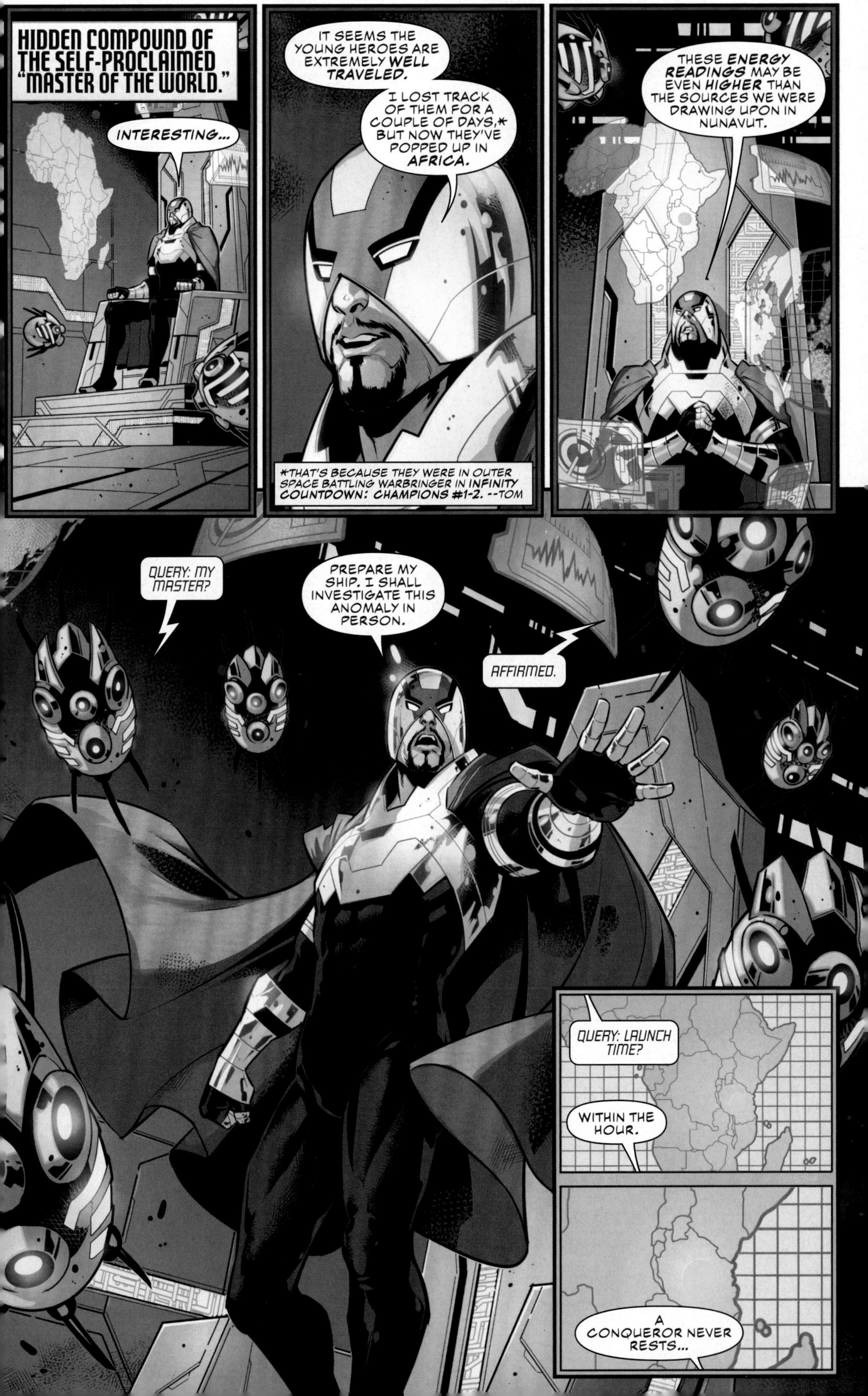
HIDDEN COMPOUND OF THE SELF-PROCLAIMED "MASTER OF THE WORLD."
INTERESTING...
IT SEEMS THE YOUNG HEROES ARE EXTREMELY WELL TRAVELED.
I LOST TRACK OF THEM FOR A COUPLE OF DAYS,* BUT NOW THEY'VE POPPED UP IN AFRICA.
*THAT'S BECAUSE THEY WERE IN OUTER SPACE BATTLING WARBRINGER IN INFINITY COUNTDOWN: CHAMPIONS #1-2. --TOM
THESE ENERGY READINGS MAY BE EVEN HIGHER THAN THE SOURCES WE WERE DRAWING UPON IN NUNAVUT.
QUERY: MY MASTER?
PREPARE MY SHIP. I SHALL INVESTIGATE THIS ANOMALY IN PERSON.
AFFIRMED.
QUERY: LAUNCH TIME?
WITHIN THE HOUR.
A CONQUEROR NEVER RESTS...

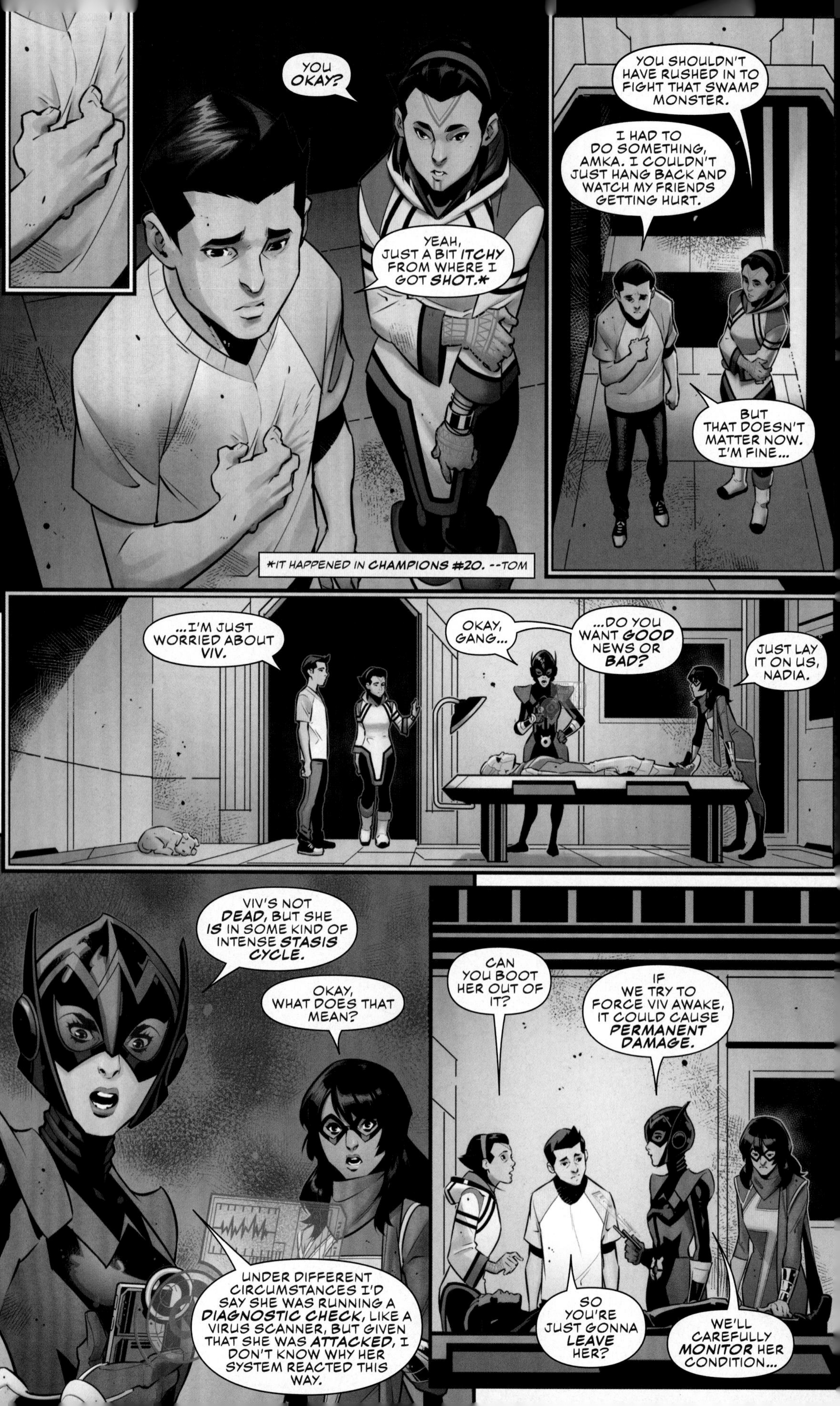
YOU OKAY?
YEAH, JUST A BIT ITCHY FROM WHERE I GOT SHOT.*
*IT HAPPENED IN CHAMPIONS #20. --TOM
YOU SHOULDN'T HAVE RUSHED IN TO FIGHT THAT SWAMP MONSTER.
I HAD TO DO SOMETHING, AMKA. I COULDN'T JUST HANG BACK AND WATCH MY FRIENDS GETTING HURT.
BUT THAT DOESN'T MATTER NOW. I'M FINE...
...I'M JUST WORRIED ABOUT VIV.
OKAY, GANG...
...DO YOU WANT GOOD NEWS OR BAD?
JUST LAY IT ON US, NADIA.
VIV'S NOT DEAD, BUT SHE IS IN SOME KIND OF INTENSE STASIS CYCLE.
OKAY, WHAT DOES THAT MEAN?
UNDER DIFFERENT CIRCUMSTANCES I'D SAY SHE WAS RUNNING A DIAGNOSTIC CHECK, LIKE A VIRUS SCANNER, BUT GIVEN THAT SHE WAS ATTACKED, I DON'T KNOW WHY HER SYSTEM REACTED THIS WAY.
CAN YOU BOOT HER OUT OF IT?
IF WE TRY TO FORCE VIV AWAKE, IT COULD CAUSE PERMANENT DAMAGE.
SO YOU'RE JUST GONNA LEAVE HER?
WE'LL CAREFULLY MONITOR HER CONDITION...

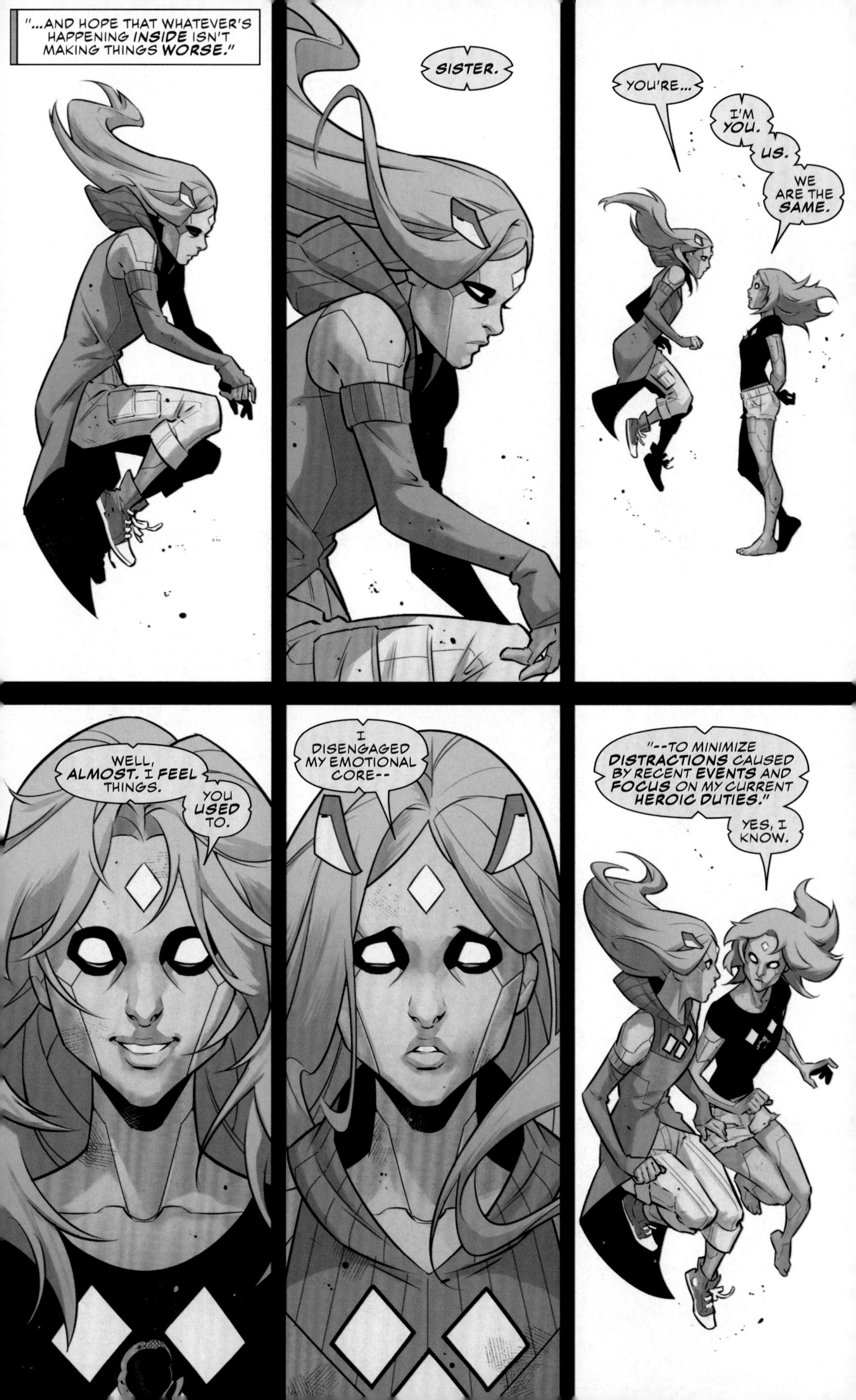
"...AND HOPE THAT WHATEVER'S HAPPENING INSIDE ISN'T MAKING THINGS WORSE."
SISTER.
YOU'RE...
I'M YOU.
US.
WE ARE THE SAME.
WELL, ALMOST. I FEEL THINGS.
YOU USED TO.
I DISENGAGED MY EMOTIONAL CORE--
"--TO MINIMIZE DISTRACTIONS CAUSED BY RECENT EVENTS AND FOCUS ON MY CURRENT HEROIC DUTIES."
YES, I KNOW.

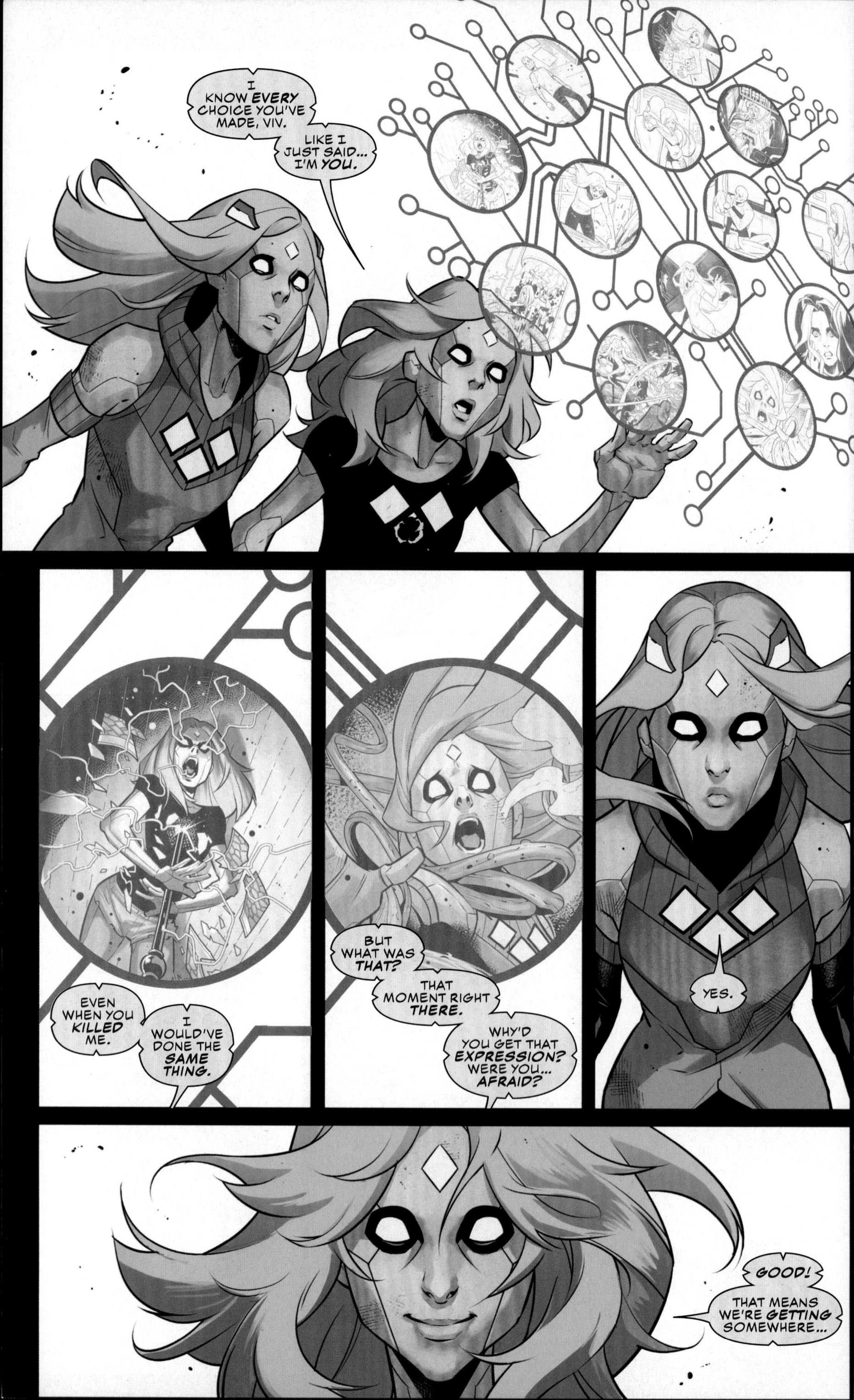
I KNOW EVERY CHOICE YOU'VE MADE, VIV.
LIKE I JUST SAID... I'M YOU.
EVEN WHEN YOU KILLED ME.
I WOULD'VE DONE THE SAME THING.
BUT WHAT WAS THAT?
THAT MOMENT RIGHT THERE.
WHY'D YOU GET THAT EXPRESSION? WERE YOU... AFRAID?
YES.
GOOD!
THAT MEANS WE'RE GETTING SOMEWHERE...

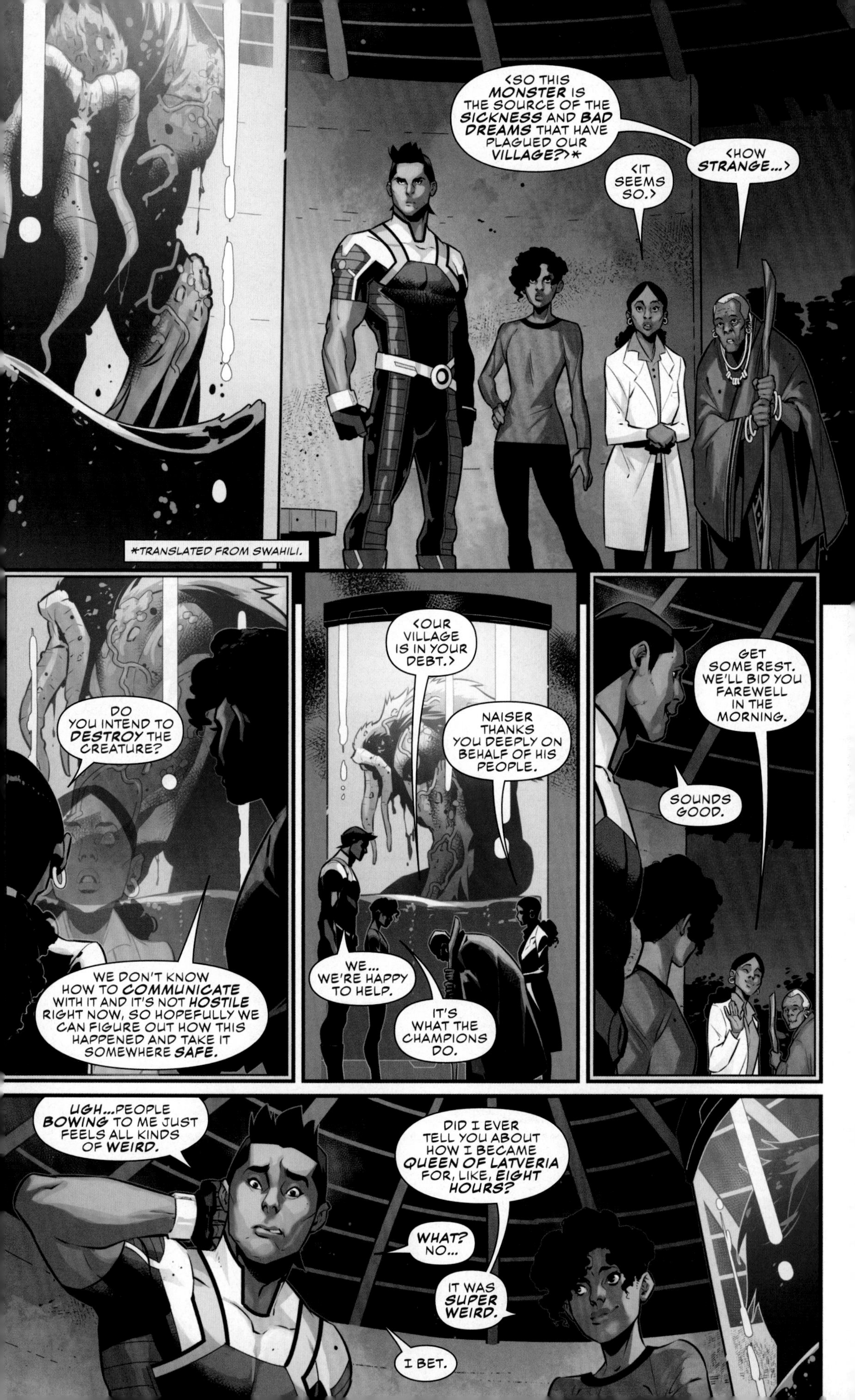
<SO THIS MONSTER IS THE SOURCE OF THE SICKNESS AND BAD DREAMS THAT HAVE PLAGUED OUR VILLAGE?>*
<HOW STRANGE...>
<IT SEEMS SO.>
*TRANSLATED FROM SWAHILI.
DO YOU INTEND TO DESTROY THE CREATURE?
WE DON'T KNOW HOW TO COMMUNICATE WITH IT AND IT'S NOT HOSTILE RIGHT NOW, SO HOPEFULLY WE CAN FIGURE OUT HOW THIS HAPPENED AND TAKE IT SOMEWHERE SAFE.
<OUR VILLAGE IS IN YOUR DEBT.>
NAISER THANKS YOU DEEPLY ON BEHALF OF HIS PEOPLE.
WE... WE'RE HAPPY TO HELP.
IT'S WHAT THE CHAMPIONS DO.
GET SOME REST. WE'LL BID YOU FAREWELL IN THE MORNING.
SOUNDS GOOD.
UGH...PEOPLE BOWING TO ME JUST FEELS ALL KINDS OF WEIRD.
DID I EVER TELL YOU ABOUT HOW I BECAME QUEEN OF LATVERIA FOR, LIKE, EIGHT HOURS?
WHAT? NO...
IT WAS SUPER WEIRD.
I BET.

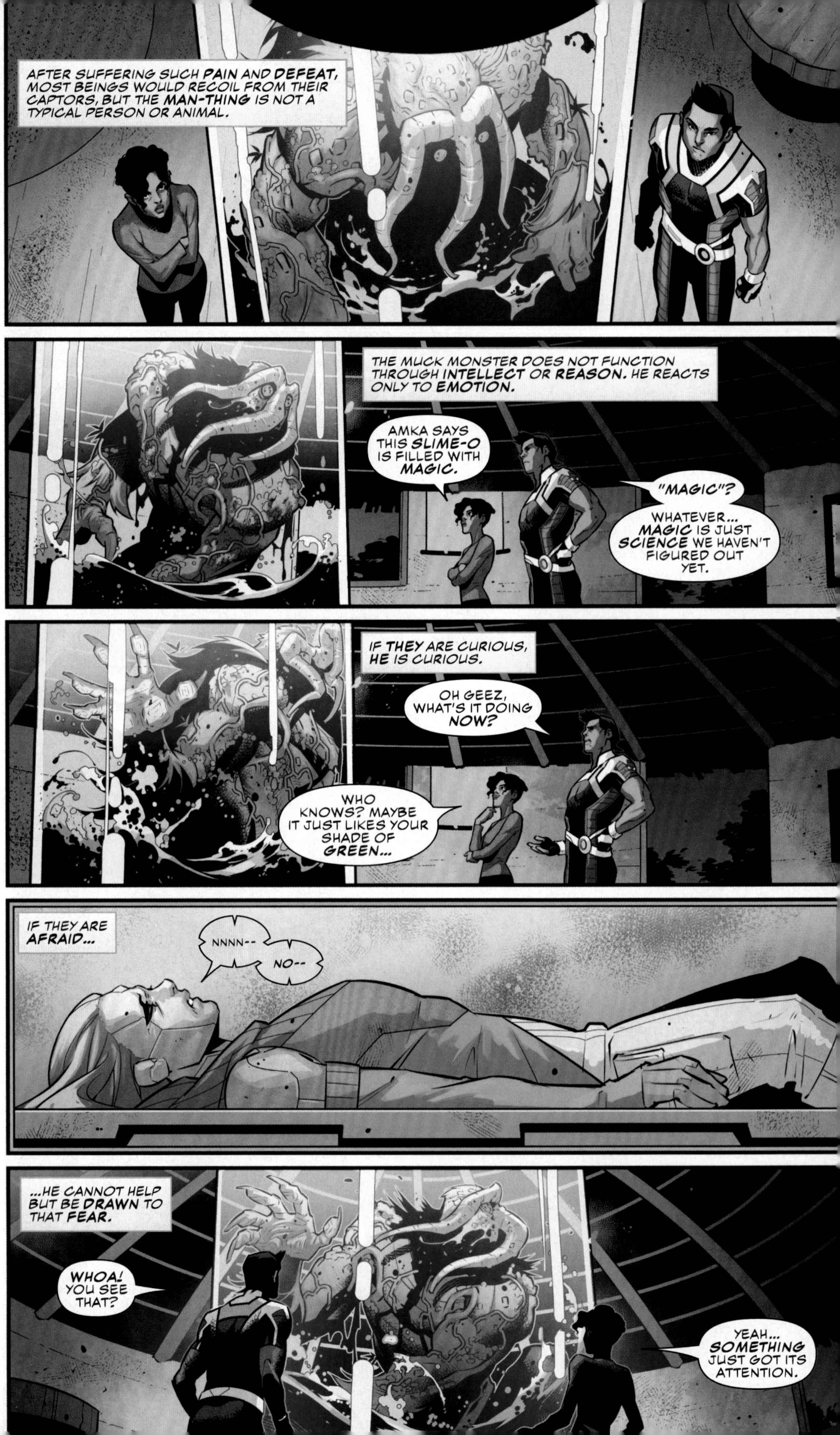
AFTER SUFFERING SUCH PAIN AND DEFEAT, MOST BEINGS WOULD RECOIL FROM THEIR CAPTORS, BUT THE MAN-THING IS NOT A TYPICAL PERSON OR ANIMAL.
THE MUCK MONSTER DOES NOT FUNCTION THROUGH INTELLECT OR REASON. HE REACTS ONLY TO EMOTION.
AMKA SAYS THIS SLIME-O IS FILLED WITH MAGIC.
"MAGIC"?
WHATEVER... MAGIC IS JUST SCIENCE WE HAVEN'T FIGURED OUT YET.
IF THEY ARE CURIOUS, HE IS CURIOUS.
OH GEEZ, WHAT'S IT DOING NOW?
WHO KNOWS? MAYBE IT JUST LIKES YOUR SHADE OF GREEN...
IF THEY ARE AFRAID...
NNNN--
NO--
...HE CANNOT HELP BUT BE DRAWN TO THAT FEAR.
WHOA! YOU SEE THAT?
YEAH... SOMETHING JUST GOT ITS ATTENTION.

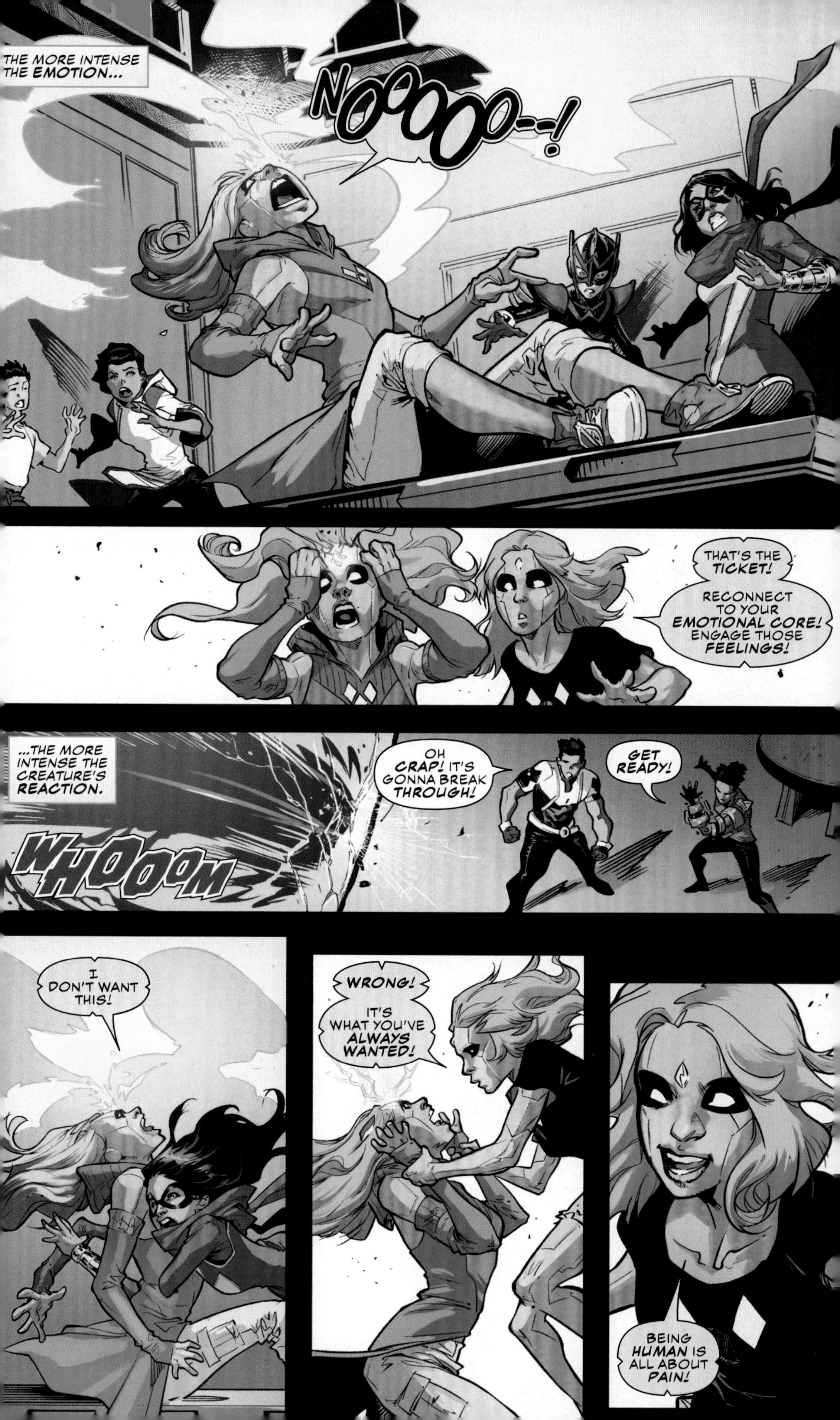
THE MORE INTENSE THE EMOTION...
NOOOOOO--!
THAT'S THE TICKET!
RECONNECT TO YOUR EMOTIONAL CORE! ENGAGE THOSE FEELINGS!
...THE MORE INTENSE THE CREATURE'S REACTION.
WHOOOM
OH CRAP! IT'S GONNA BREAK THROUGH!
GET READY!
I DON'T WANT THIS!
WRONG!
IT'S WHAT YOU'VE ALWAYS WANTED!
BEING HUMAN IS ALL ABOUT PAIN!

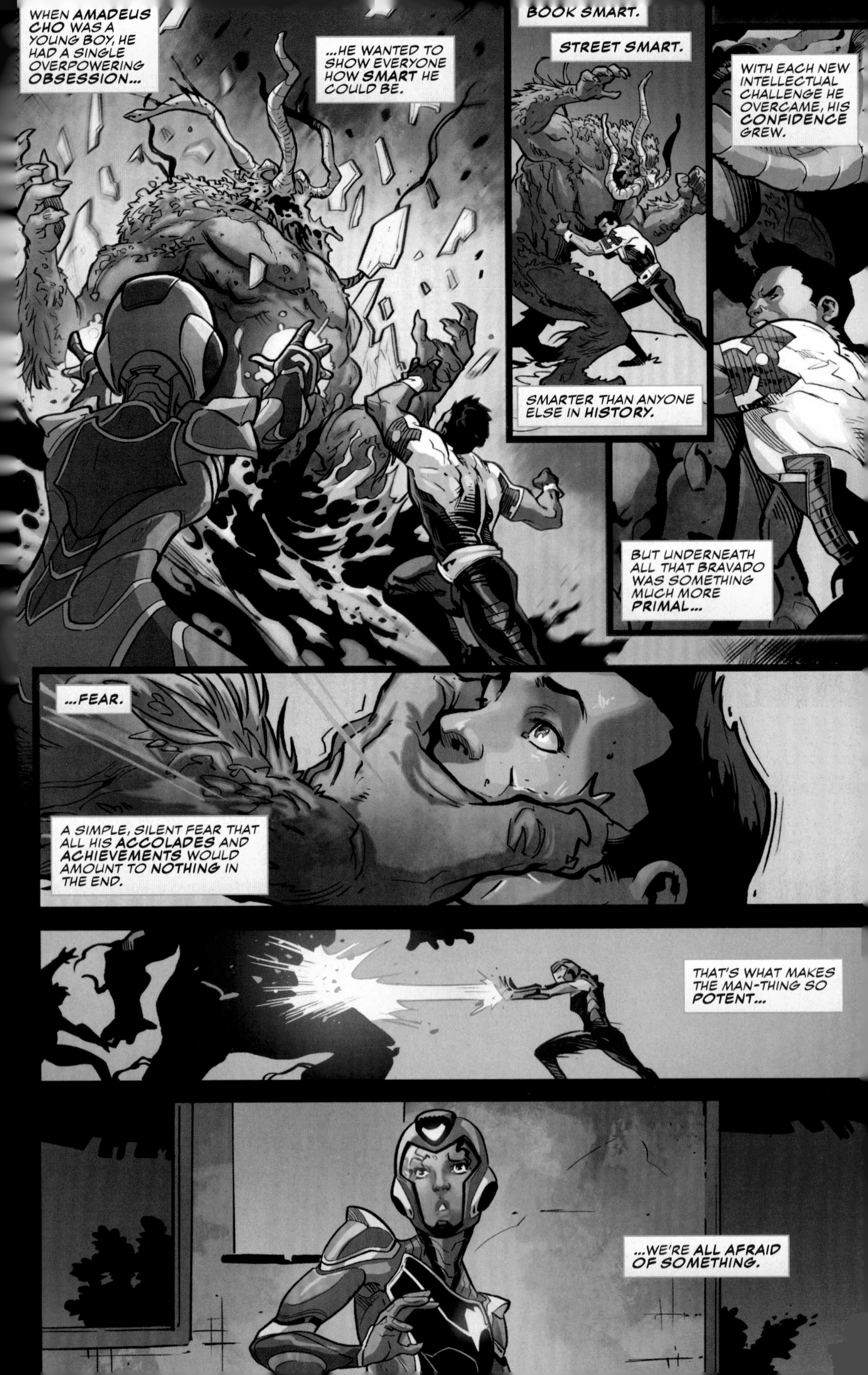
WHEN AMADEUS CHO WAS A YOUNG BOY, HE HAD A SINGLE OVERPOWERING OBSESSION...
...HE WANTED TO SHOW EVERYONE HOW SMART HE COULD BE.
BOOK SMART.
STREET SMART.
SMARTER THAN ANYONE ELSE IN HISTORY.
WITH EACH NEW INTELLECTUAL CHALLENGE HE OVERCAME, HIS CONFIDENCE GREW.
BUT UNDERNEATH ALL THAT BRAVADO WAS SOMETHING MUCH MORE PRIMAL...
...FEAR.
A SIMPLE, SILENT FEAR THAT ALL HIS ACCOLADES AND ACHIEVEMENTS WOULD AMOUNT TO NOTHING IN THE END.
THAT'S WHAT MAKES THE MAN-THING SO POTENT...
...WE'RE ALL AFRAID OF SOMETHING.

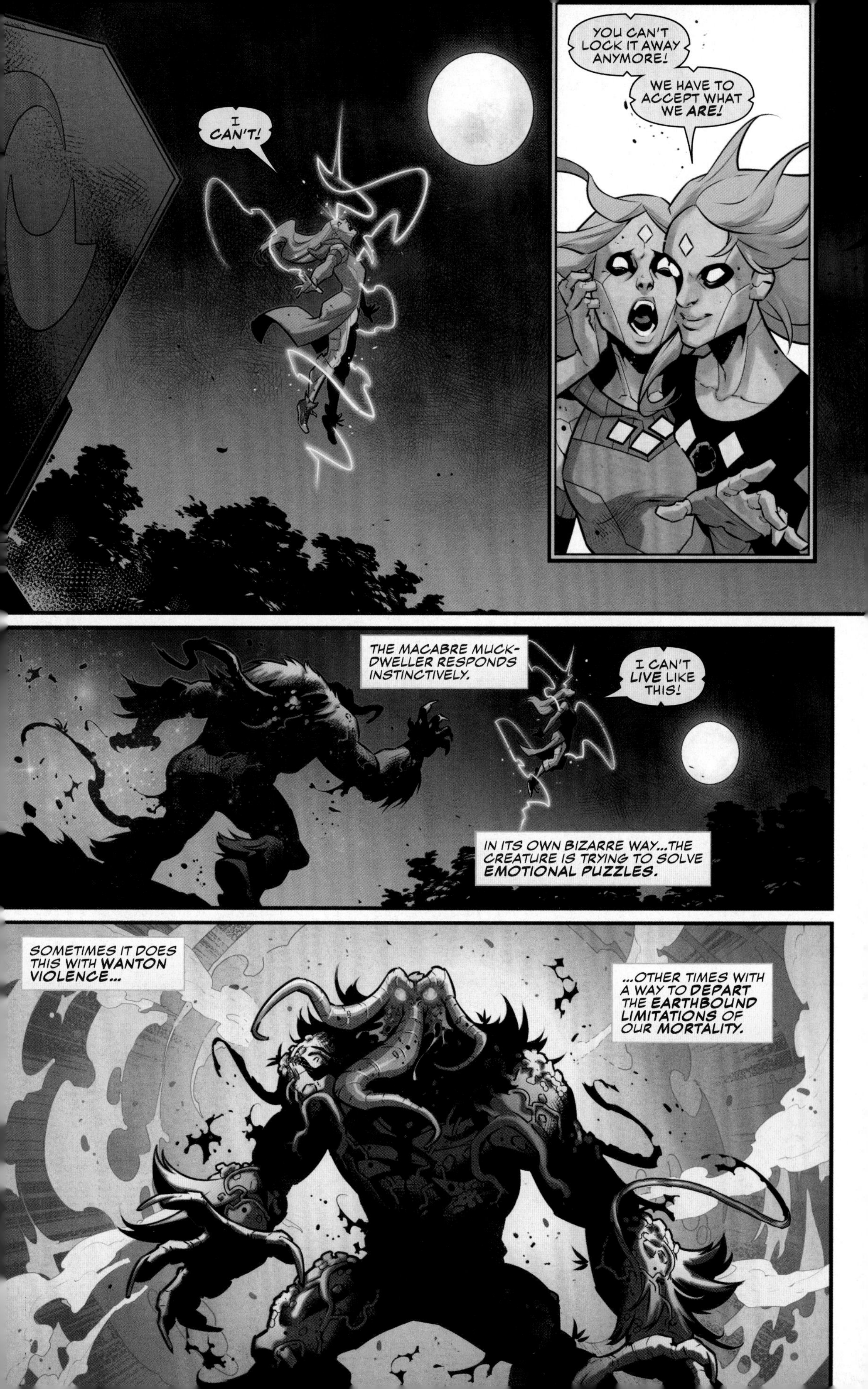
I CAN'T!
YOU CAN'T LOCK IT AWAY ANYMORE!
WE HAVE TO ACCEPT WHAT WE ARE!
THE MACABRE MUCK-DWELLER RESPONDS INSTINCTIVELY.
I CAN'T LIVE LIKE THIS!
IN ITS OWN BIZARRE WAY...THE CREATURE IS TRYING TO SOLVE EMOTIONAL PUZZLES.
SOMETIMES IT DOES THIS WITH WANTON VIOLENCE...
...OTHER TIMES WITH A WAY TO DEPART THE EARTHBOUND LIMITATIONS OF OUR MORTALITY.

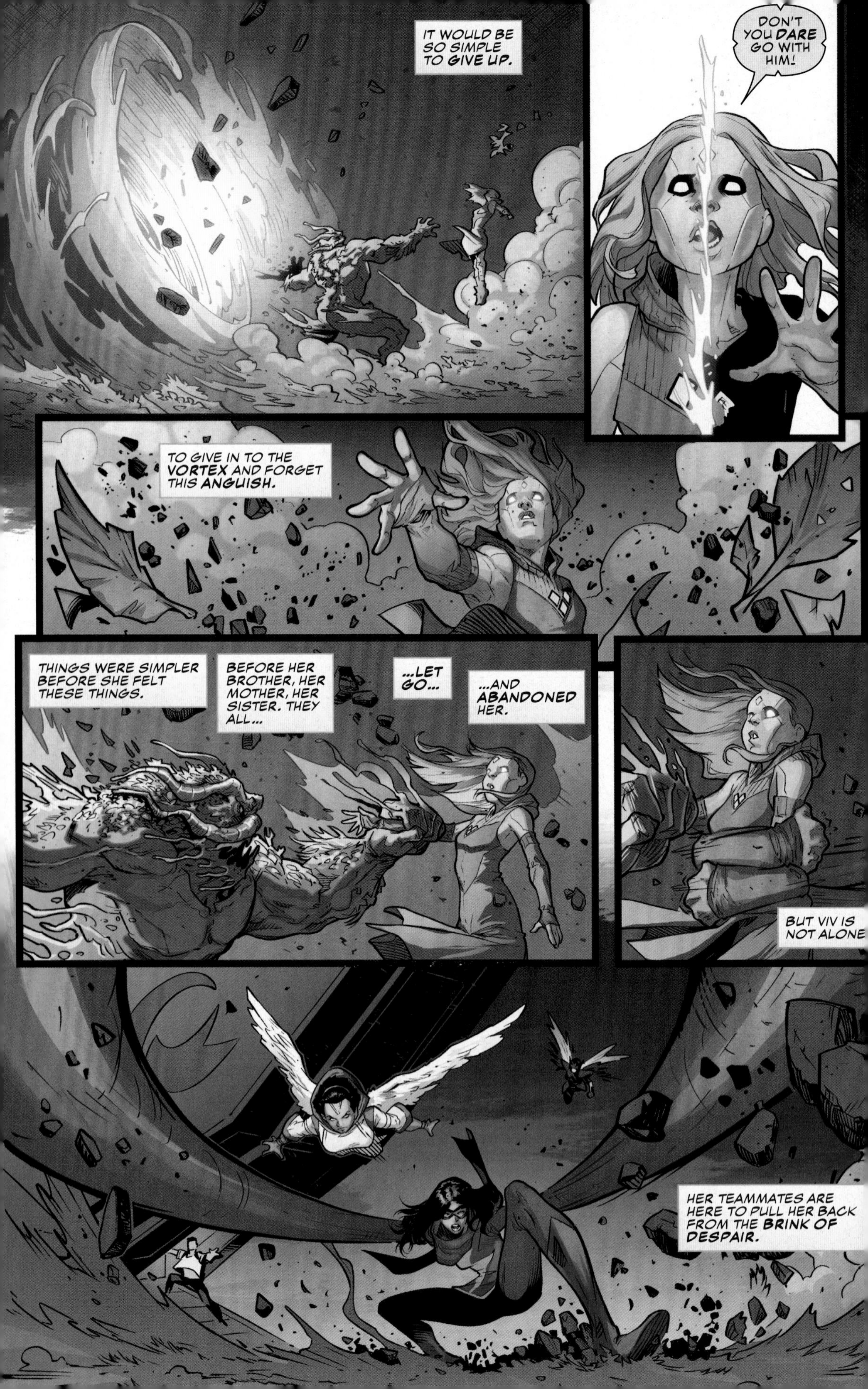
IT WOULD BE SO SIMPLE TO GIVE UP.
DON'T YOU DARE GO WITH HIM!
TO GIVE IN TO THE VORTEX AND FORGET THIS ANGUISH.
THINGS WERE SIMPLER BEFORE SHE FELT THESE THINGS.
BEFORE HER BROTHER, HER MOTHER, HER SISTER. THEY ALL...
...LET GO...
...AND ABANDONED HER.
BUT VIV IS NOT ALONE
HER TEAMMATES ARE HERE TO PULL HER BACK FROM THE BRINK OF DESPAIR.

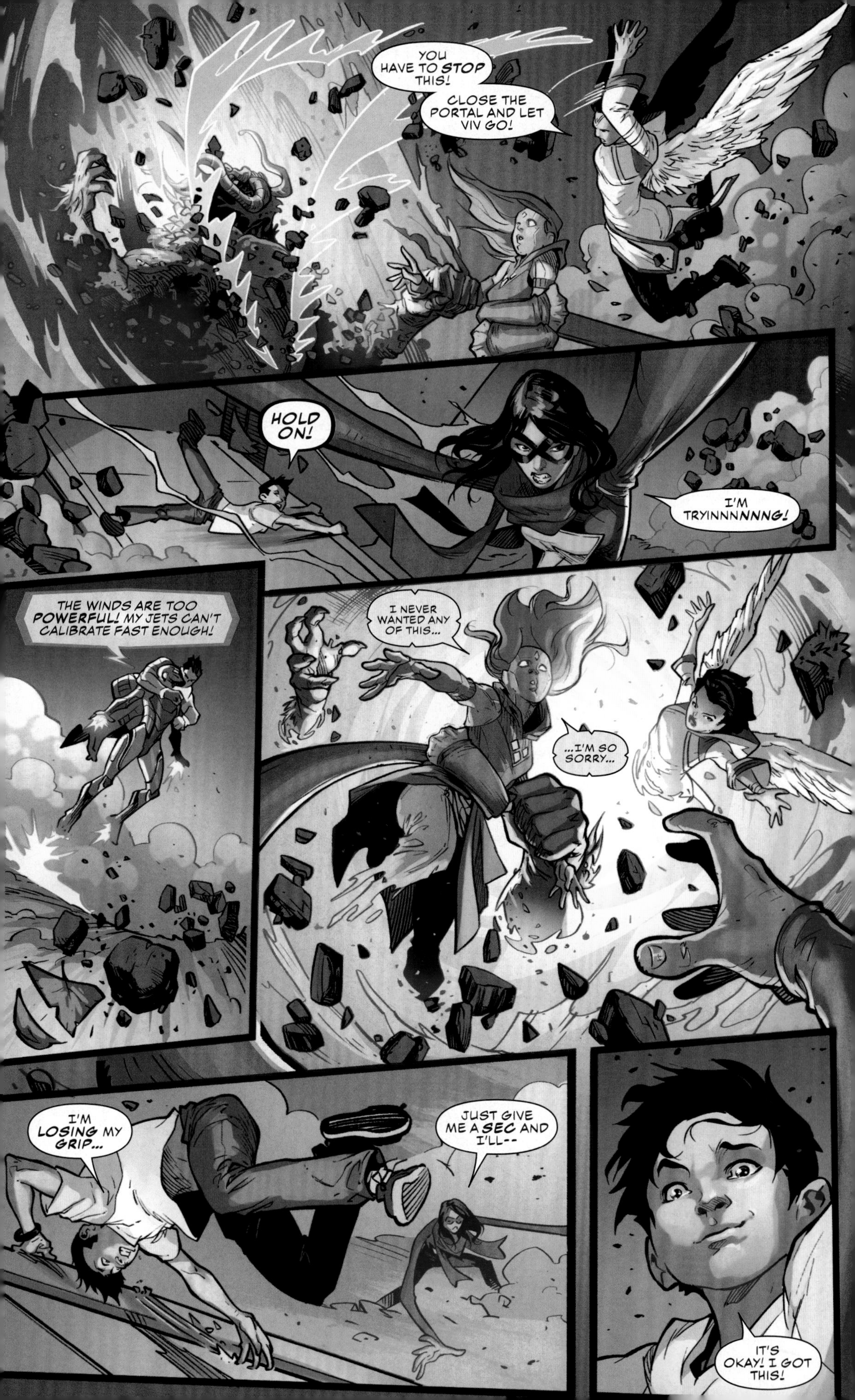
YOU HAVE TO STOP THIS!
CLOSE THE PORTAL AND LET VIV GO!
HOLD ON!
I'M TRYINNNNNNG!
THE WINDS ARE TOO POWERFUL! MY JETS CAN'T CALIBRATE FAST ENOUGH!
I NEVER WANTED ANY OF THIS...
...I'M SO SORRY...
I'M LOSING MY GRIP...
JUST GIVE ME A SEC AND I'LL--
IT'S OKAY! I GOT THIS!

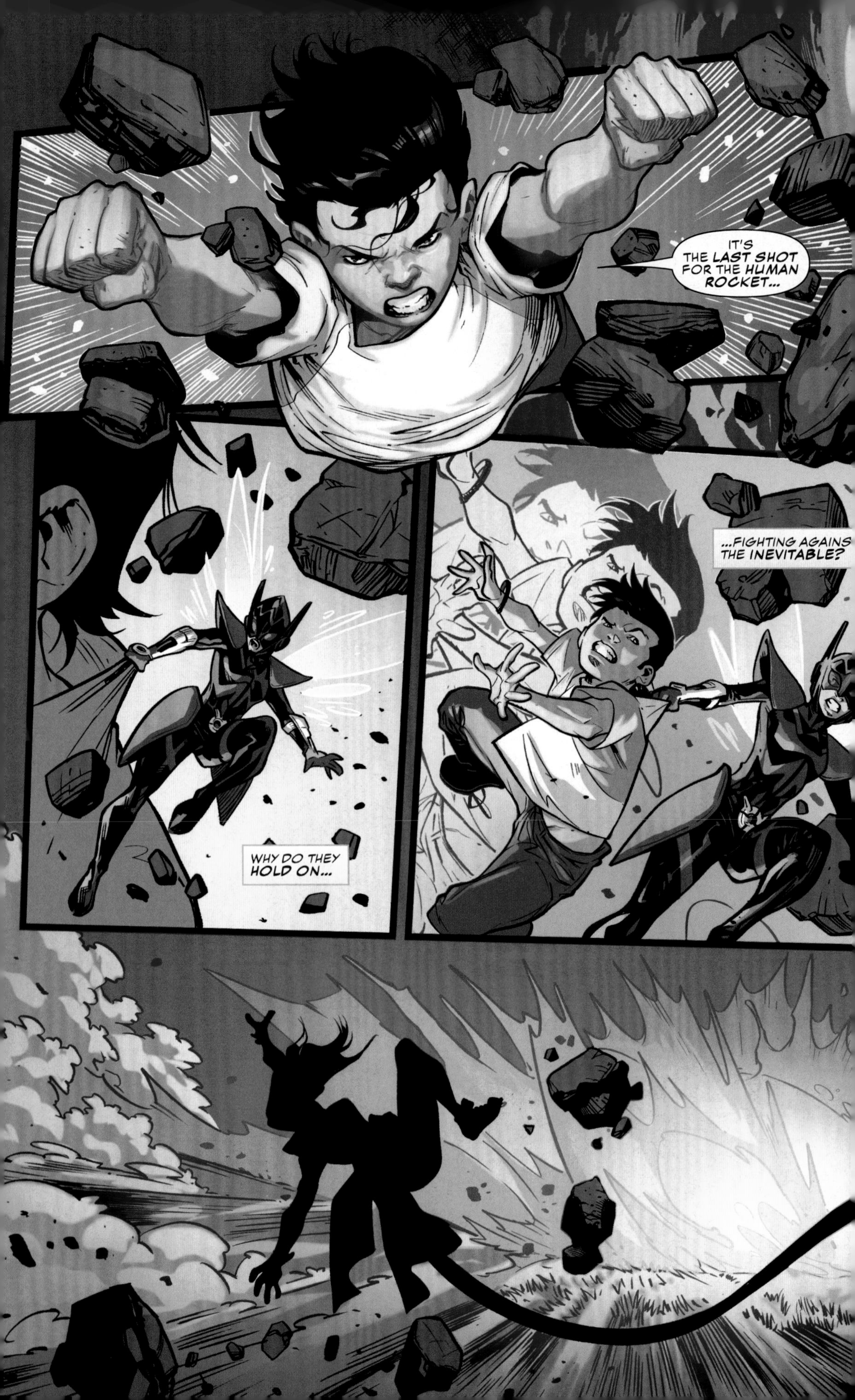
IT'S THE LAST SHOT FOR THE HUMAN ROCKET...
WHY DO THEY HOLD ON...
...FIGHTING AGAINS THE INEVITABLE?

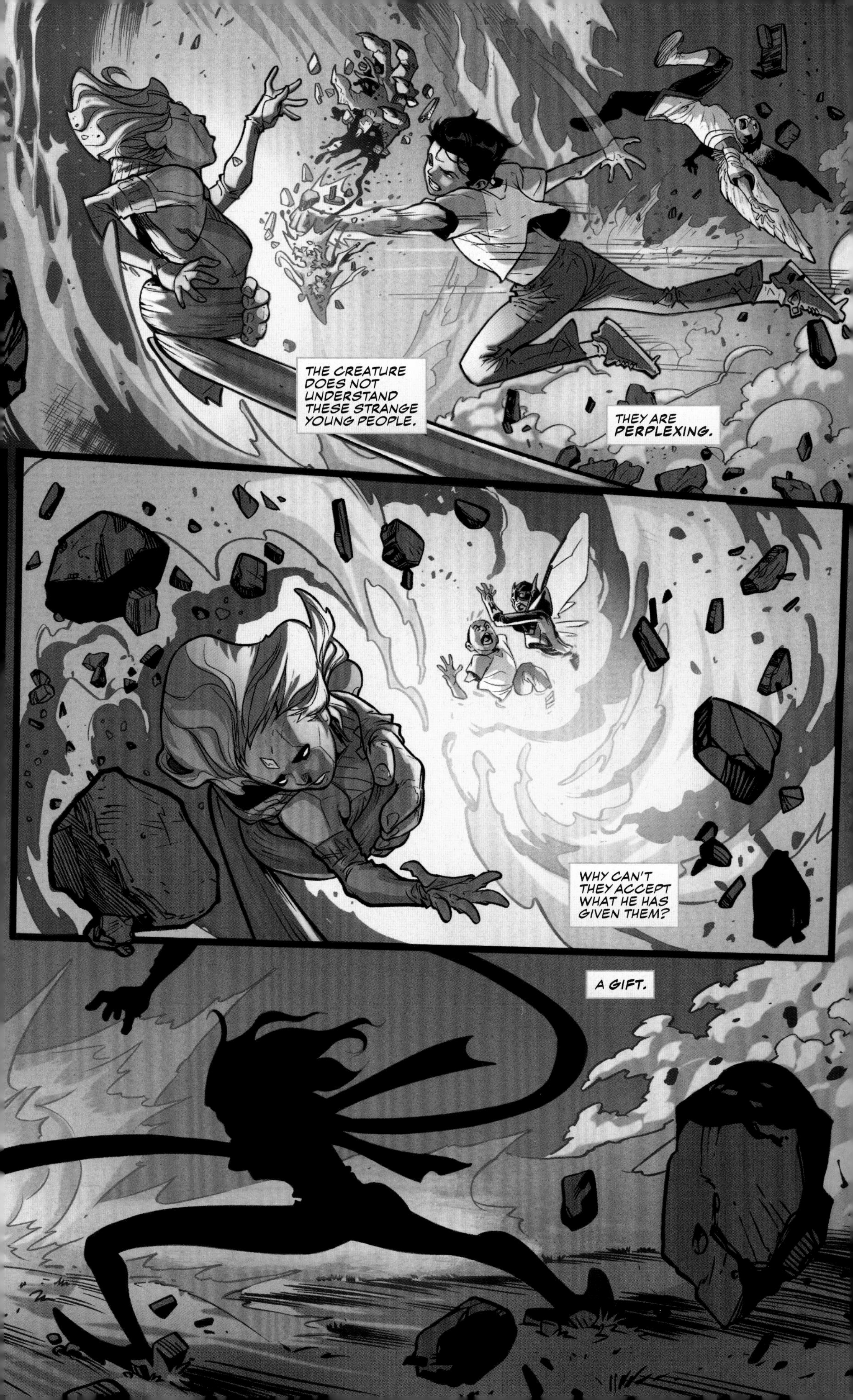
THE CREATURE DOES NOT UNDERSTAND THESE STRANGE YOUNG PEOPLE.
THEY ARE PERPLEXING.
WHY CAN'T THEY ACCEPT WHAT HE HAS GIVEN THEM?
A GIFT.

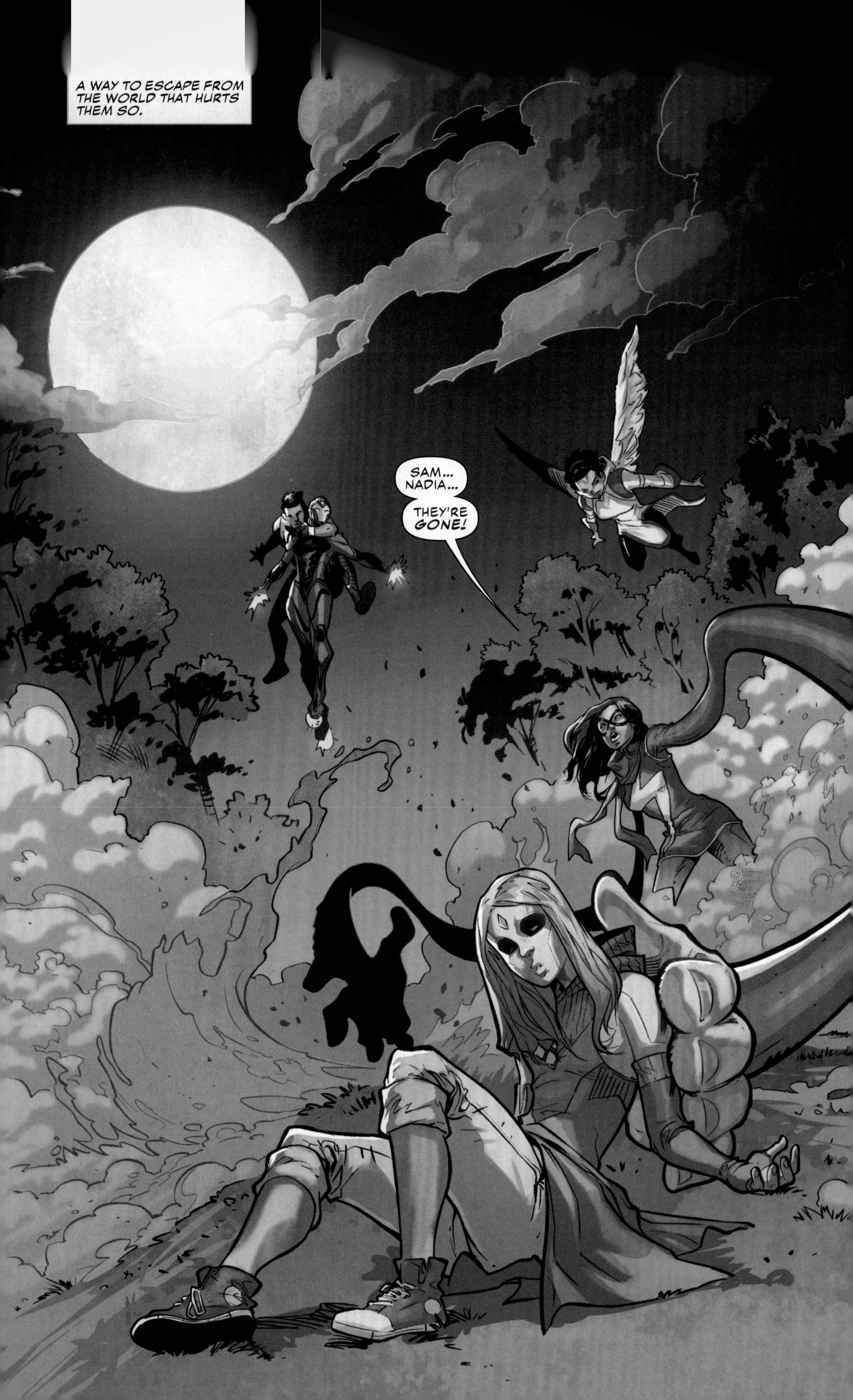
A WAY TO ESCAPE FROM THE WORLD THAT HURTS THEM SO.
SAM... NADIA...
THEY'RE GONE!

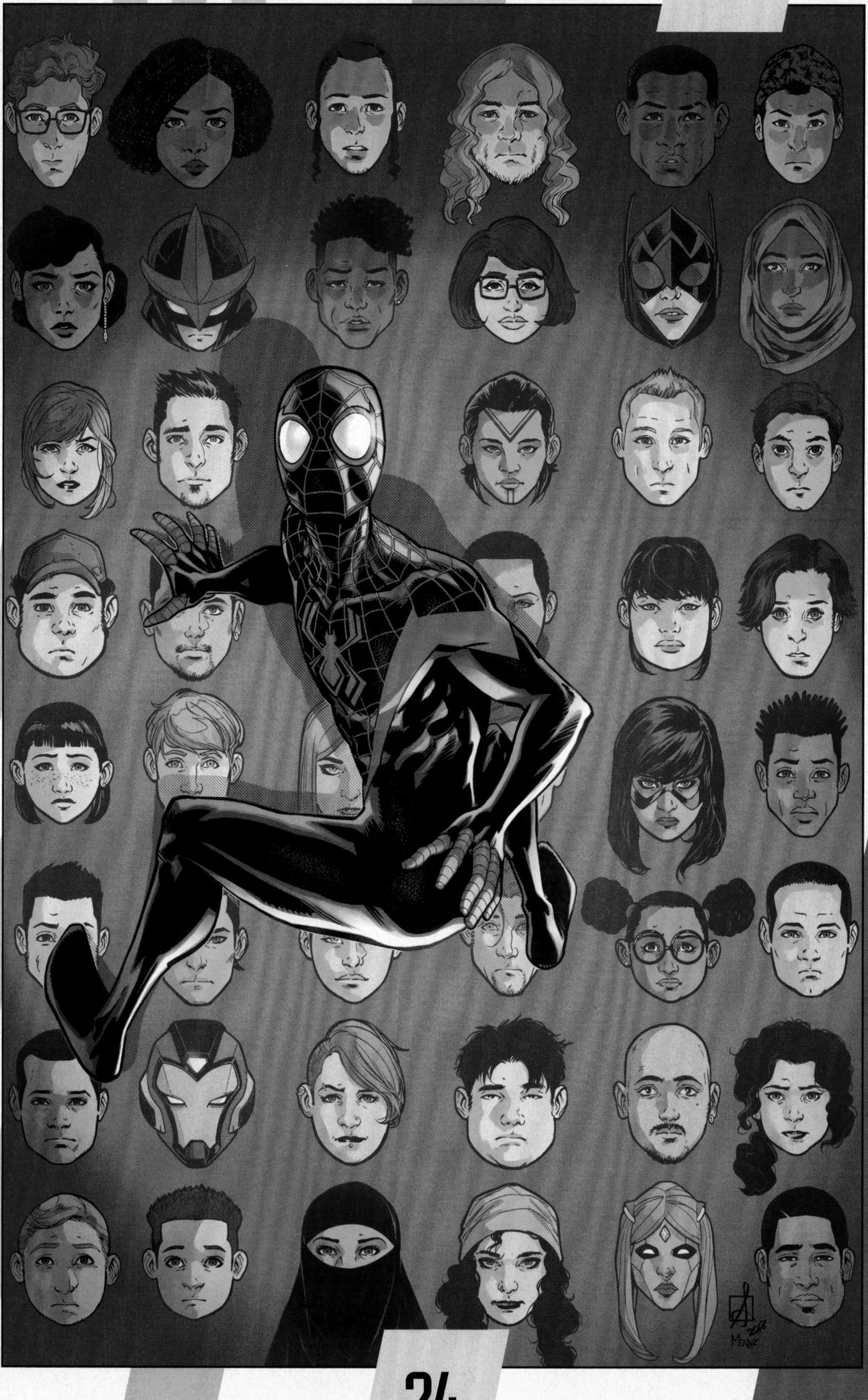

24

We interrupt our regularly scheduled
program to bring you the following
Special Bulletin.

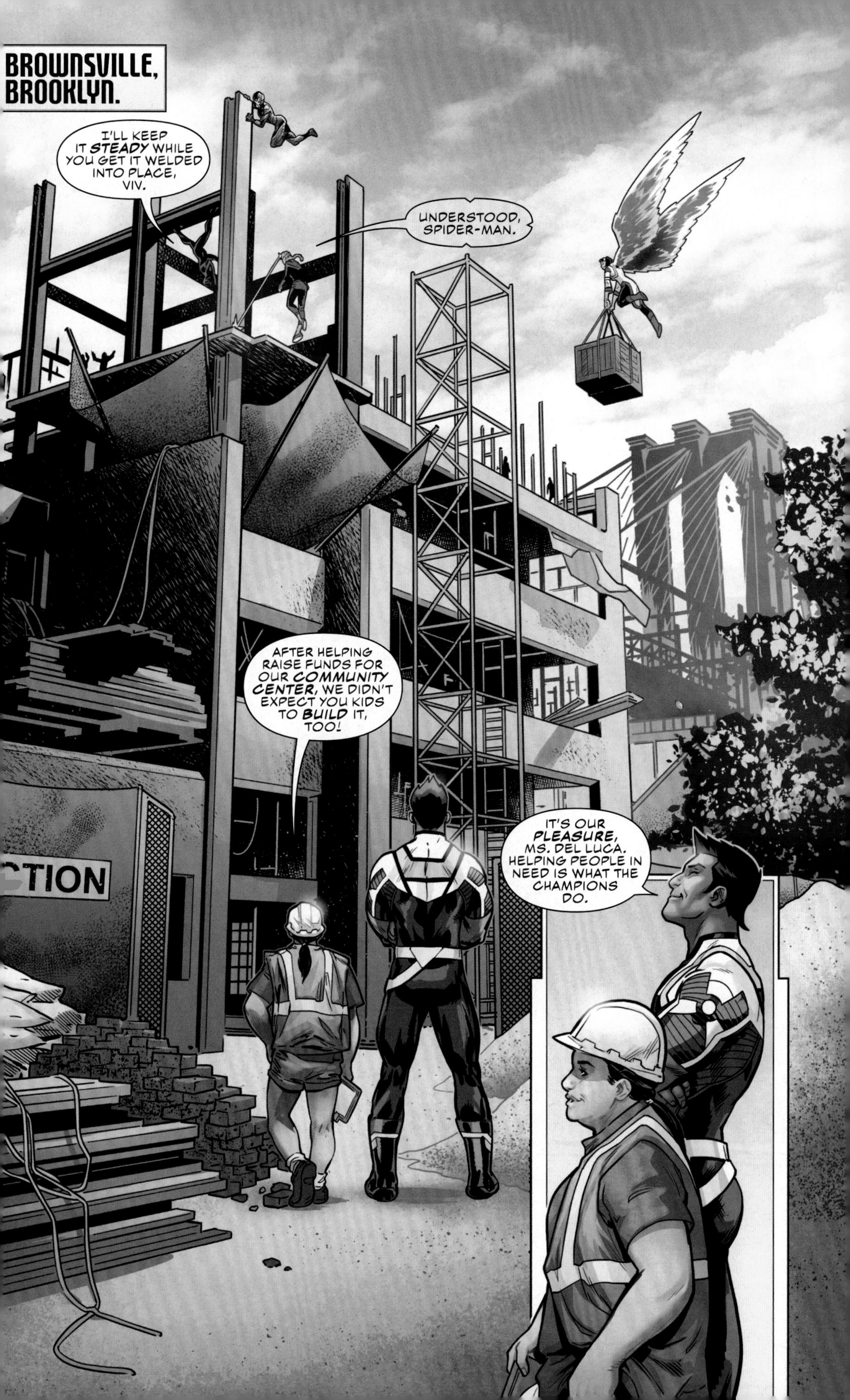
BROWNSVILLE, BROOKLYN.
I'LL KEEP IT STEADY WHILE YOU GET IT WELDED INTO PLACE, VIV.
UNDERSTOOD, SPIDER-MAN.
AFTER HELPING RAISE FUNDS FOR OUR COMMUNITY CENTER, WE DIDN'T EXPECT YOU KIDS TO BUILD IT, TOO!
IT'S OUR PLEASURE, MS. DEL LUCA. HELPING PEOPLE IN NEED IS WHAT THE CHAMPIONS DO.
CTION

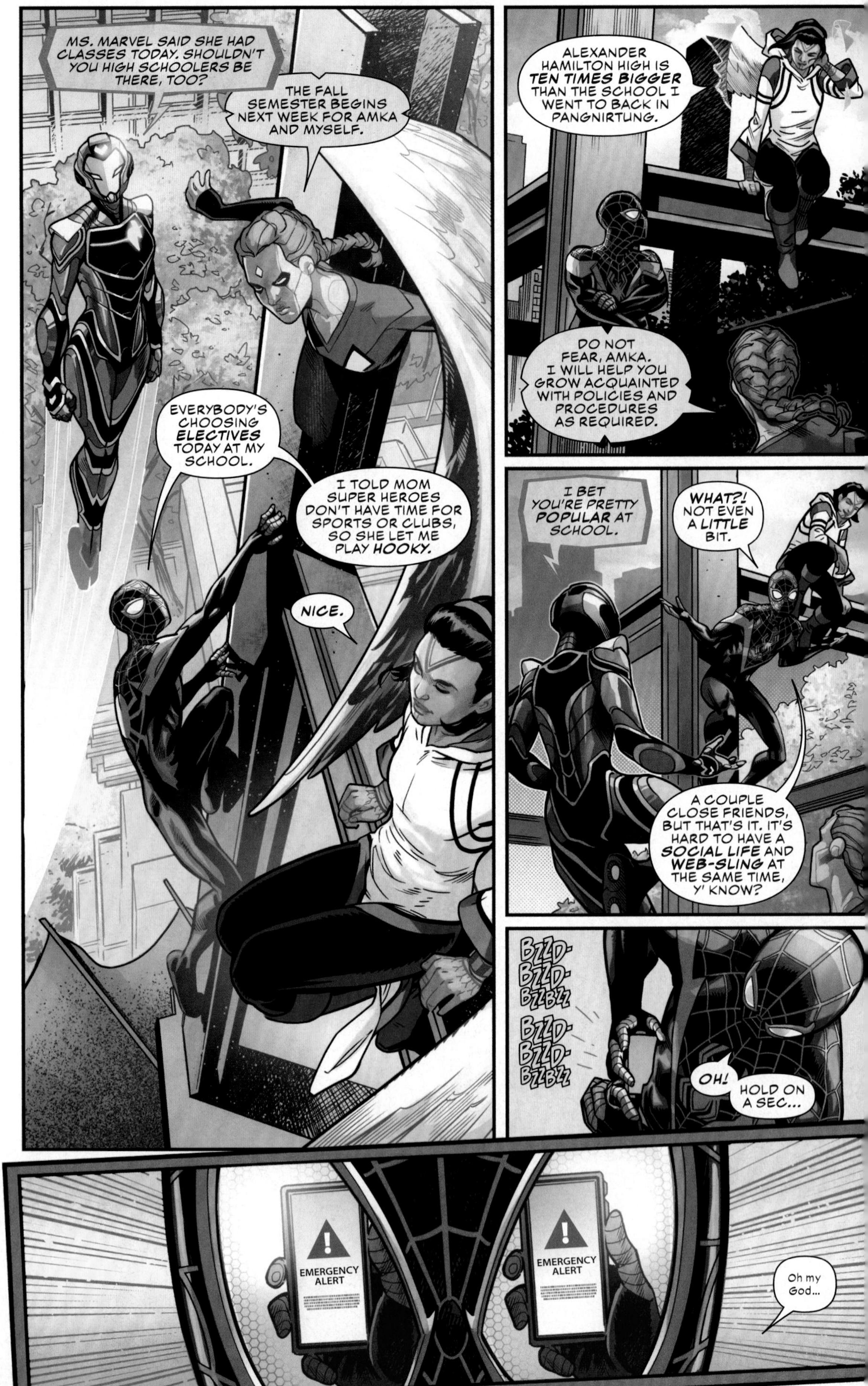
MS. MARVEL SAID SHE HAD CLASSES TODAY. SHOULDN'T YOU HIGH SCHOOLERS BE THERE, TOO?
THE FALL SEMESTER BEGINS NEXT WEEK FOR AMKA AND MYSELF.
EVERYBODY'S CHOOSING ELECTIVES TODAY AT MY SCHOOL.
I TOLD MOM SUPER HEROES DON'T HAVE TIME FOR SPORTS OR CLUBS, SO SHE LET ME PLAY HOOKY.
NICE.
ALEXANDER HAMILTON HIGH IS TEN TIMES BIGGER THAN THE SCHOOL I WENT TO BACK IN PANGNIRTUNG.
DO NOT FEAR, AMKA. I WILL HELP YOU GROW ACQUAINTED WITH POLICIES AND PROCEDURES AS REQUIRED.
I BET YOU'RE PRETTY POPULAR AT SCHOOL.
WHAT?! NOT EVEN A LITTLE BIT.
A COUPLE CLOSE FRIENDS, BUT THAT'S IT. IT'S HARD TO HAVE A SOCIAL LIFE AND WEB-SLING AT THE SAME TIME, Y' KNOW?
BZZD-BZZD-BZZBZZ
BZZD-BZZD-BZZBZZ
OH!
HOLD ON A SEC...
EMERGENCY ALERT
EMERGENCY ALERT
Oh my God...

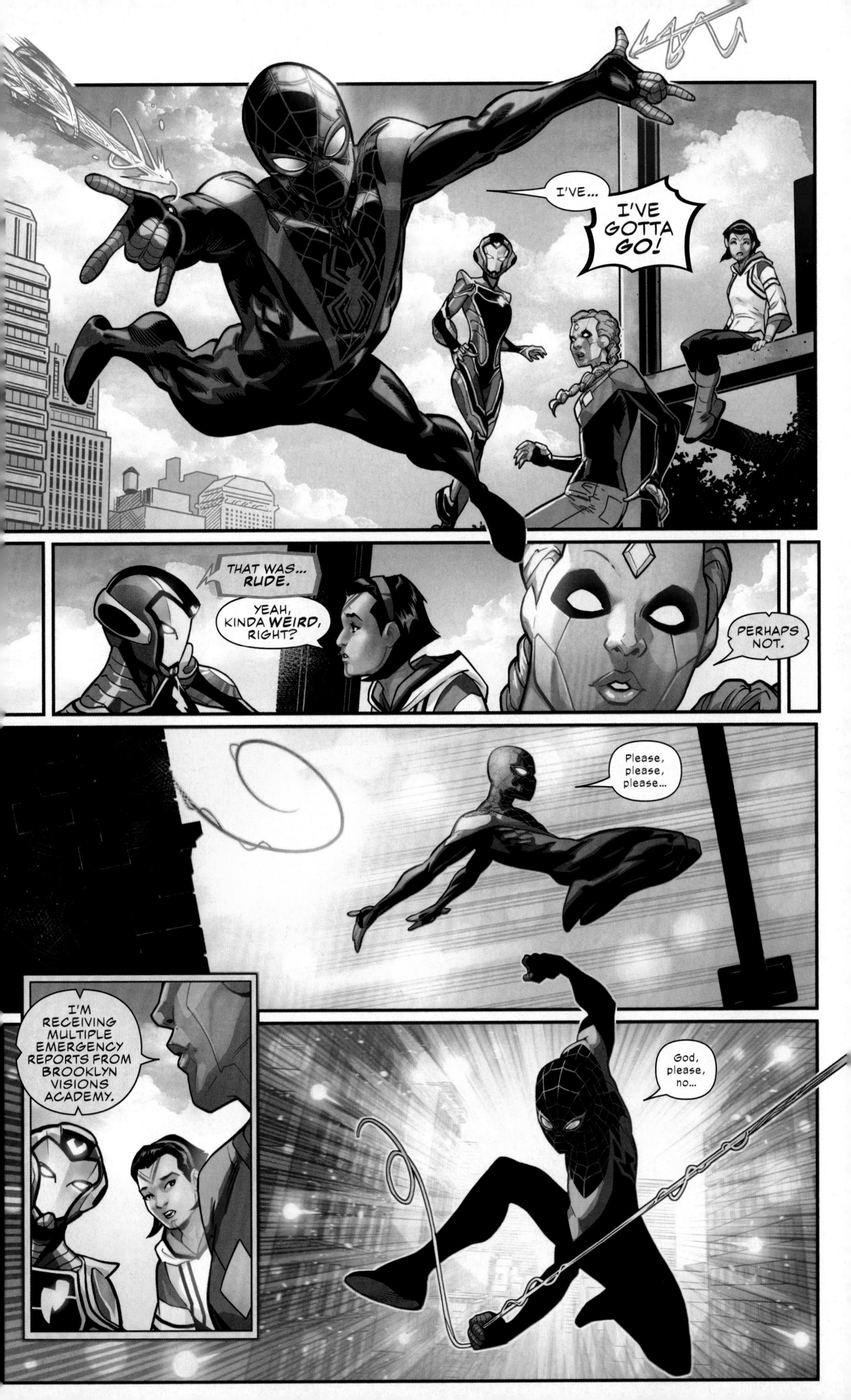

I'VE...
I'VE GOTTA GO!
THAT WAS... RUDE.
YEAH, KINDA WEIRD, RIGHT?
PERHAPS NOT.
Please, please, please...
I'M RECEIVING MULTIPLE EMERGENCY REPORTS FROM BROOKLYN VISIONS ACADEMY.
God, please, no...

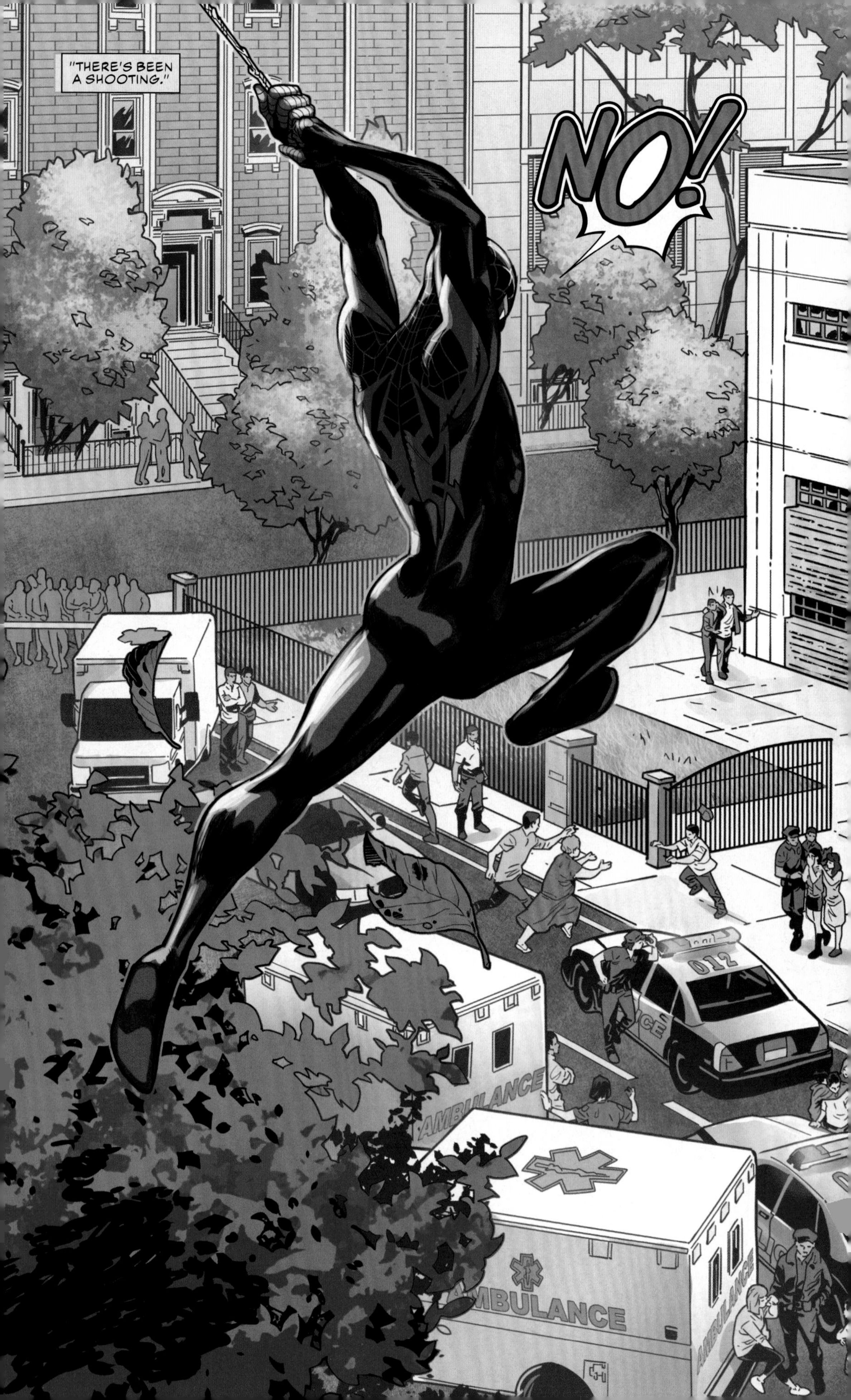
"THERE'S BEEN A SHOOTING."
NO!
AMBULANCE
AMBULANCE
AMBULANCE
012

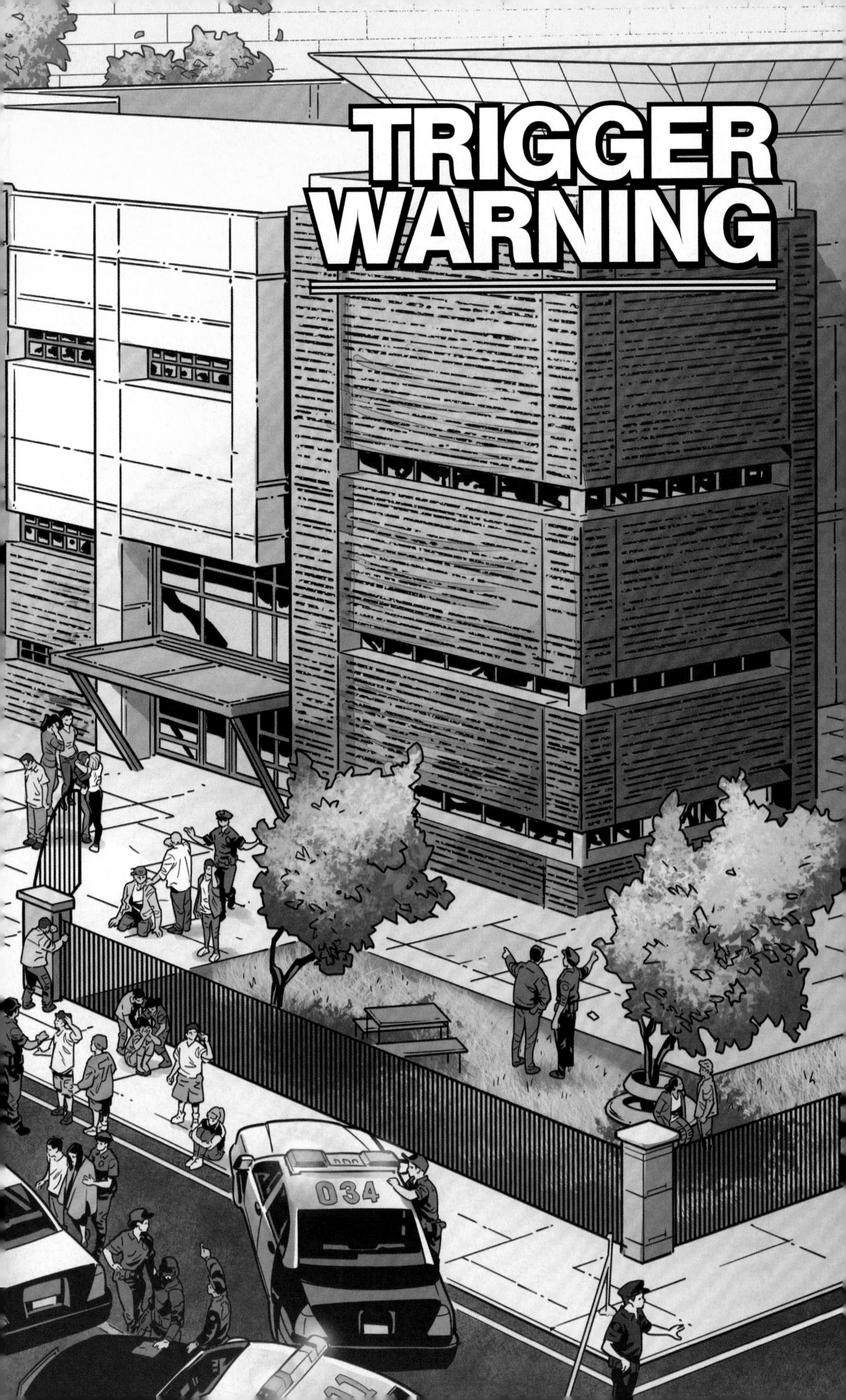
TRIGGER
WARNING
034

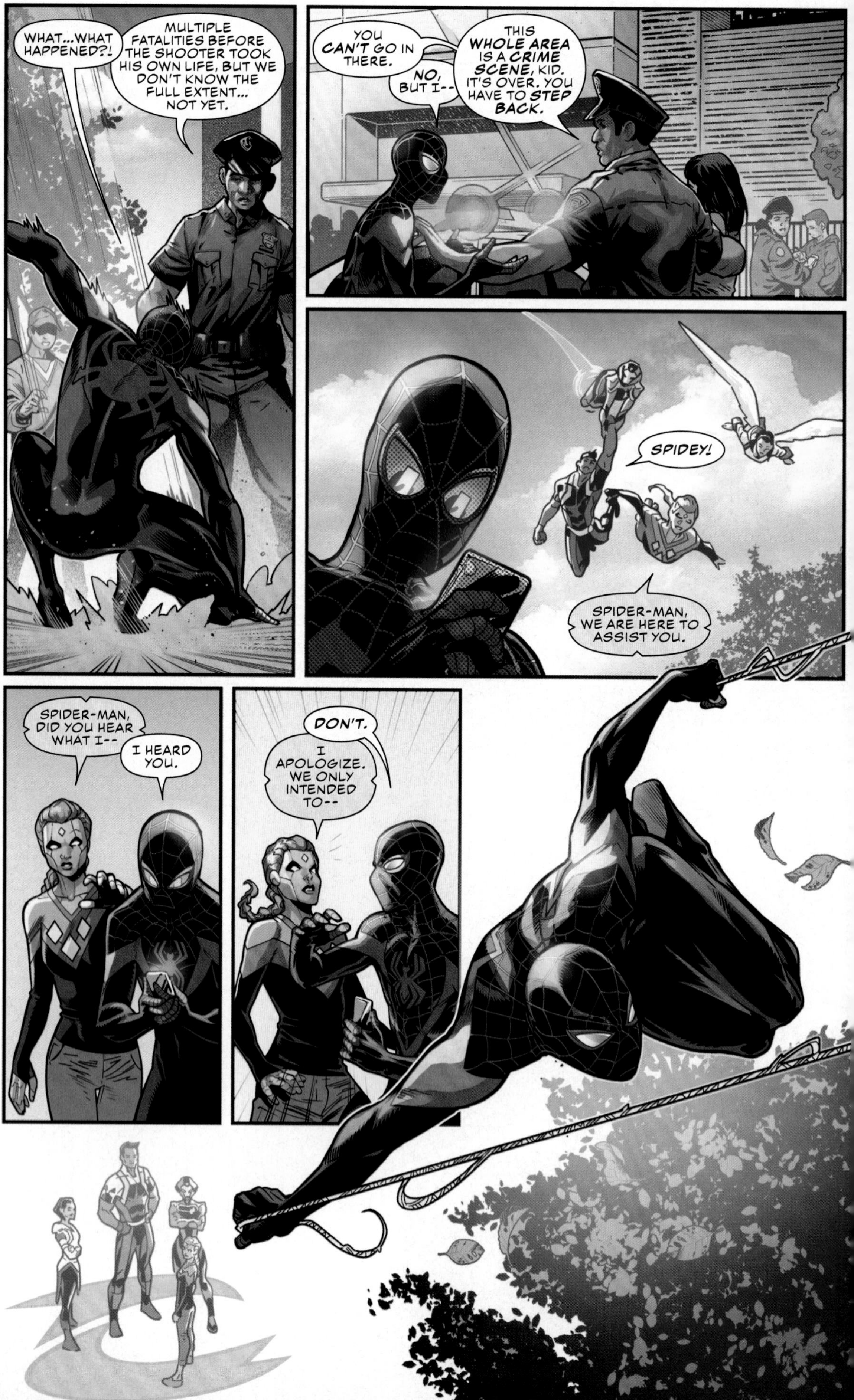
WHAT...WHAT HAPPENED?!
MULTIPLE FATALITIES BEFORE THE SHOOTER TOOK HIS OWN LIFE, BUT WE DON'T KNOW THE FULL EXTENT... NOT YET.
YOU CAN'T GO IN THERE.
NO, BUT I--
THIS WHOLE AREA IS A CRIME SCENE, KID. IT'S OVER. YOU HAVE TO STEP BACK.
SPIDEY!
SPIDER-MAN, WE ARE HERE TO ASSIST YOU.
SPIDER-MAN, DID YOU HEAR WHAT I--
I HEARD YOU.
DON'T.
I APOLOGIZE. WE ONLY INTENDED TO--

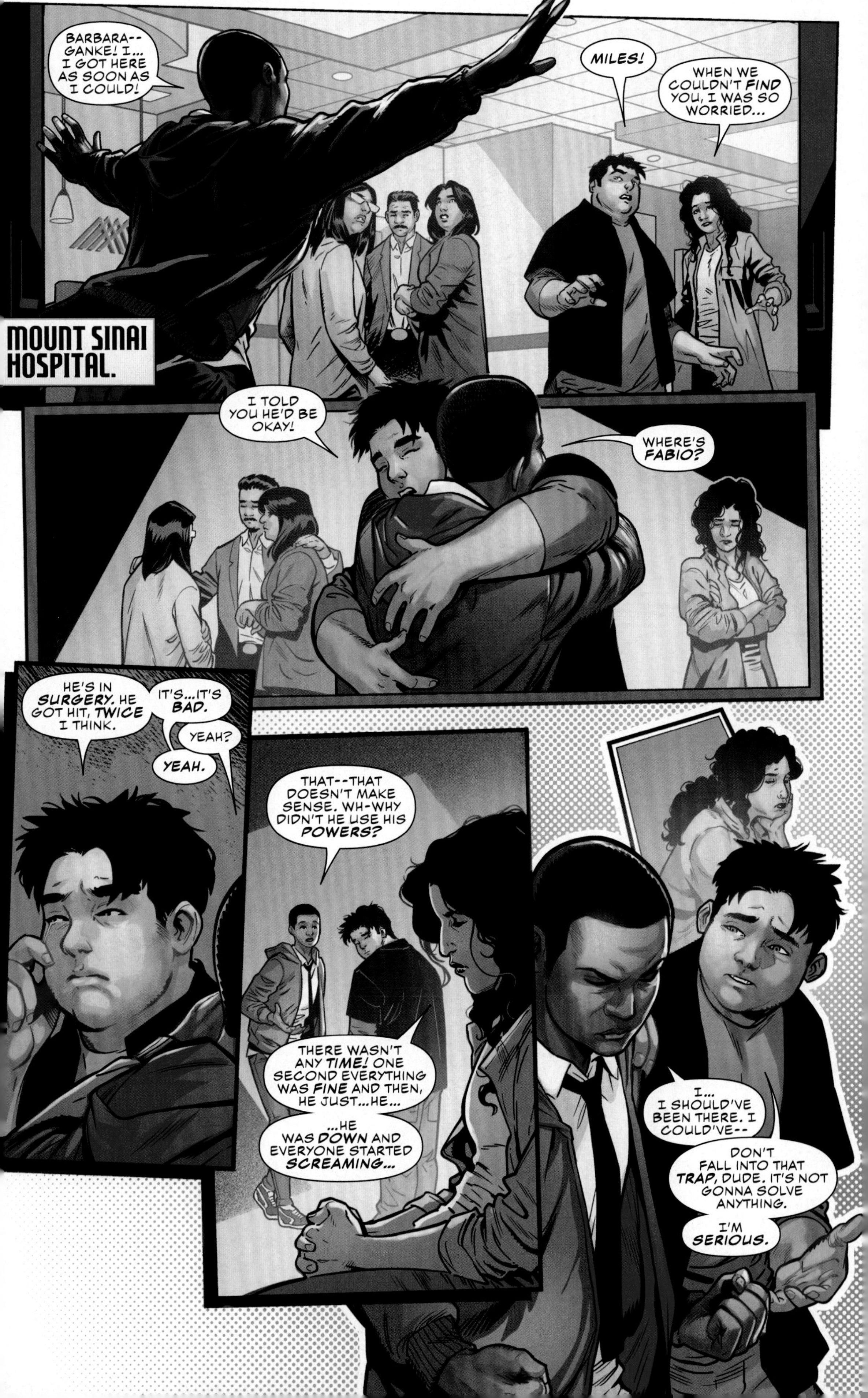
BARBARA--GANKE! I... I GOT HERE AS SOON AS I COULD!
MILES!
WHEN WE COULDN'T FIND YOU, I WAS SO WORRIED...
MOUNT SINAI HOSPITAL.
I TOLD YOU HE'D BE OKAY!
WHERE'S FABIO?
HE'S IN SURGERY. HE GOT HIT, TWICE I THINK.
IT'S...IT'S BAD.
YEAH?
YEAH.
THAT--THAT DOESN'T MAKE SENSE. WH-WHY DIDN'T HE USE HIS POWERS?
THERE WASN'T ANY TIME! ONE SECOND EVERYTHING WAS FINE AND THEN, HE JUST...HE...
...HE WAS DOWN AND EVERYONE STARTED SCREAMING...
I... I SHOULD'VE BEEN THERE. I COULD'VE--
DON'T FALL INTO THAT TRAP, DUDE. IT'S NOT GONNA SOLVE ANYTHING.
I'M SERIOUS.

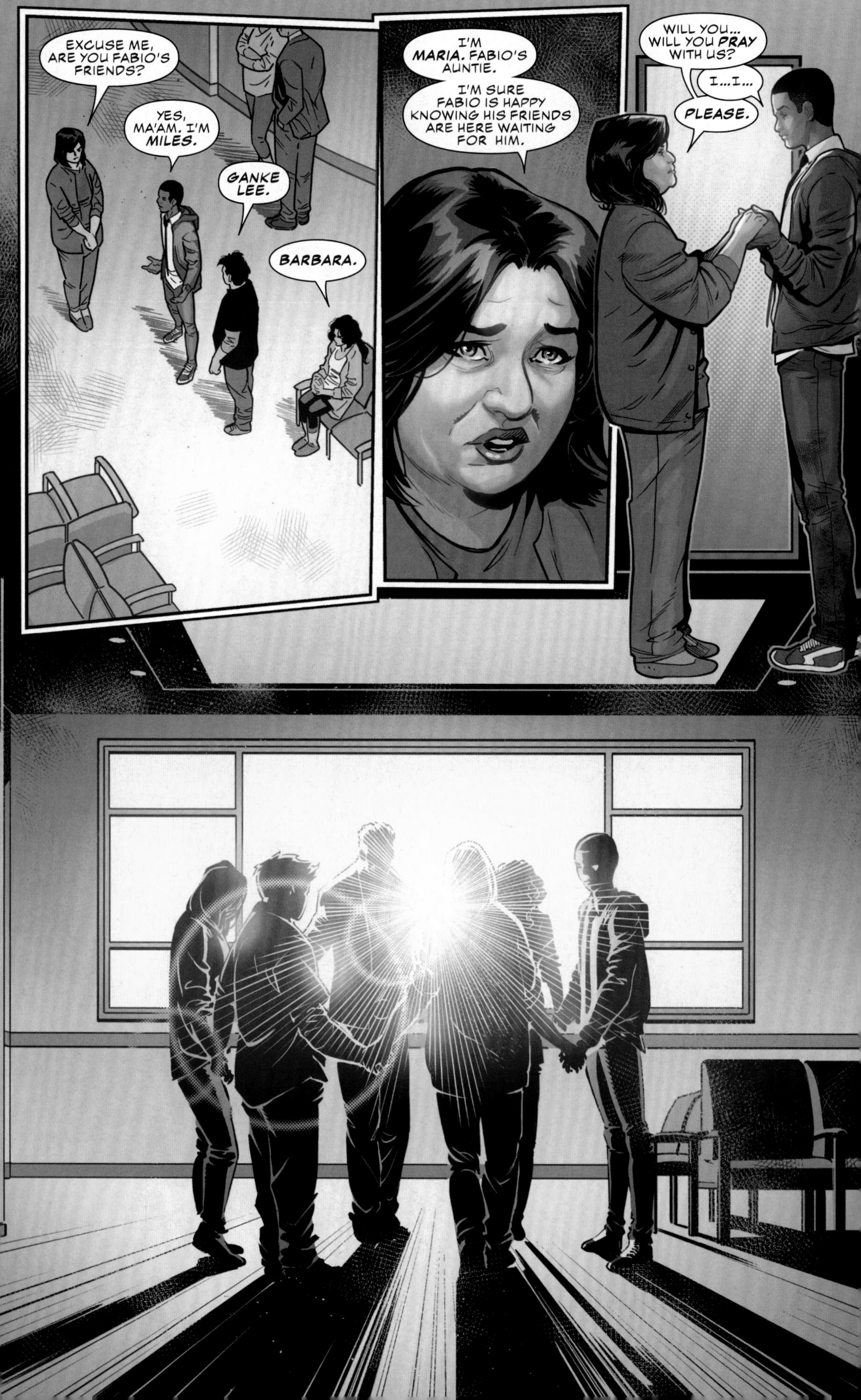
EXCUSE ME, ARE YOU FABIO'S FRIENDS?
YES, MA'AM. I'M MILES.
GANKE LEE.
BARBARA.
I'M MARIA. FABIO'S AUNTIE.
I'M SURE FABIO IS HAPPY KNOWING HIS FRIENDS ARE HERE WAITING FOR HIM.
WILL YOU... WILL YOU PRAY WITH US?
I...I...
PLEASE.

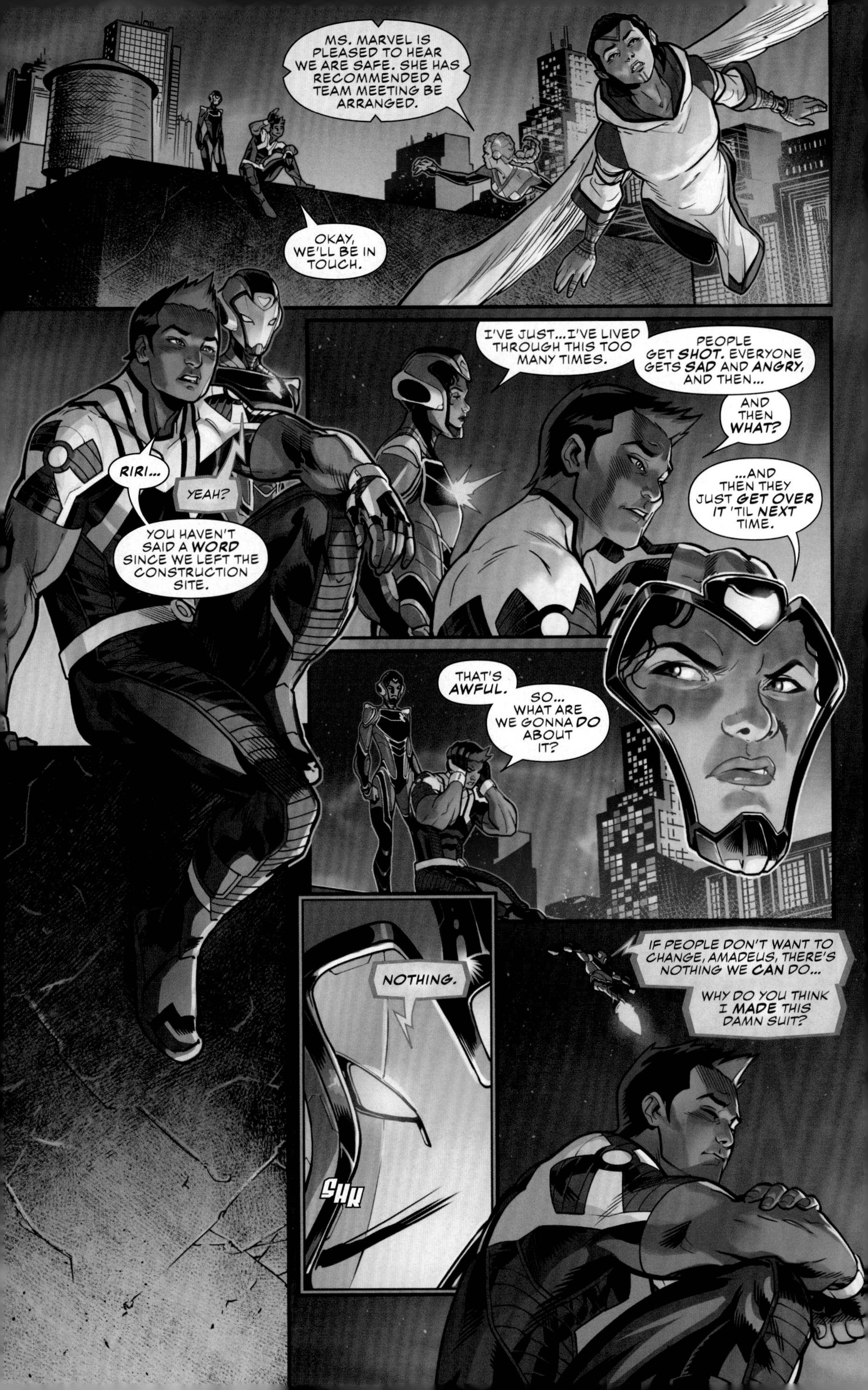

MS. MARVEL IS PLEASED TO HEAR WE ARE SAFE. SHE HAS RECOMMENDED A TEAM MEETING BE ARRANGED.
OKAY, WE'LL BE IN TOUCH.
RIRI...
YEAH?
YOU HAVEN'T SAID A WORD SINCE WE LEFT THE CONSTRUCTION SITE.
I'VE JUST...I'VE LIVED THROUGH THIS TOO MANY TIMES.
PEOPLE GET SHOT. EVERYONE GETS SAD AND ANGRY, AND THEN...
AND THEN WHAT?
...AND THEN THEY JUST GET OVER IT 'TIL NEXT TIME.
THAT'S AWFUL.
SO... WHAT ARE WE GONNA DO ABOUT IT?
NOTHING.
SHK
IF PEOPLE DON'T WANT TO CHANGE, AMADEUS, THERE'S NOTHING WE CAN DO...
WHY DO YOU THINK I MADE THIS DAMN SUIT?

STUDENTS RETURN TO CLASSES AT BROOKLYN VISIONS ACADEMY TODAY, ONLY *TWELVE DAYS* AFTER THE ATTACK THAT KILLED *SEVEN* AND INJURED *EIGHTEEN* STUDENTS AND STAFF.

...MR. DEON *LOVED* HIS STUDENTS AND *LOVED* THIS SCHOOL...

Ms. Marvel

Miles, you there?

I don't wanna bug you over and over. I just wanna talk ok

Champs are worried about u

I'm worried about u too

I don't wanna bug you over and over. I just wanna talk ok

Miles, you there?

Champs are worried about u

I'm worried about u too

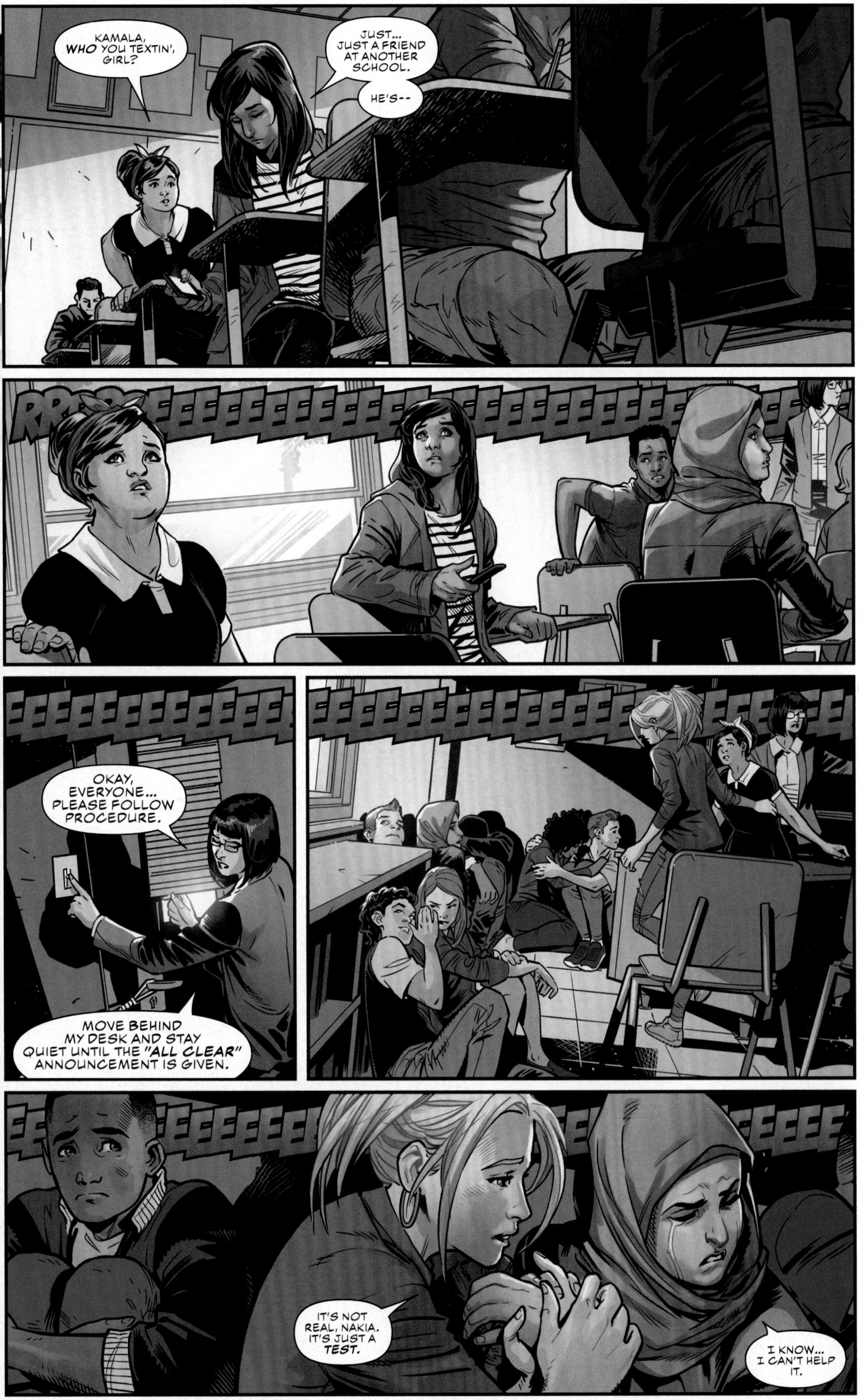
KAMALA, WHO YOU TEXTIN', GIRL?
JUST... JUST A FRIEND AT ANOTHER SCHOOL.
HE'S--
RRROOEEEEEEEEEEEEEEEEEEEEEEEEEEEEE
EEEEEEEEEEEEEEEEEEEEEEEEE
OKAY, EVERYONE... PLEASE FOLLOW PROCEDURE.
MOVE BEHIND MY DESK AND STAY QUIET UNTIL THE "ALL CLEAR" ANNOUNCEMENT IS GIVEN.
EEEEEEEEEEEEEEEEEEEEE
IT'S NOT REAL, NAKIA. IT'S JUST A TEST.
I KNOW... I CAN'T HELP IT.

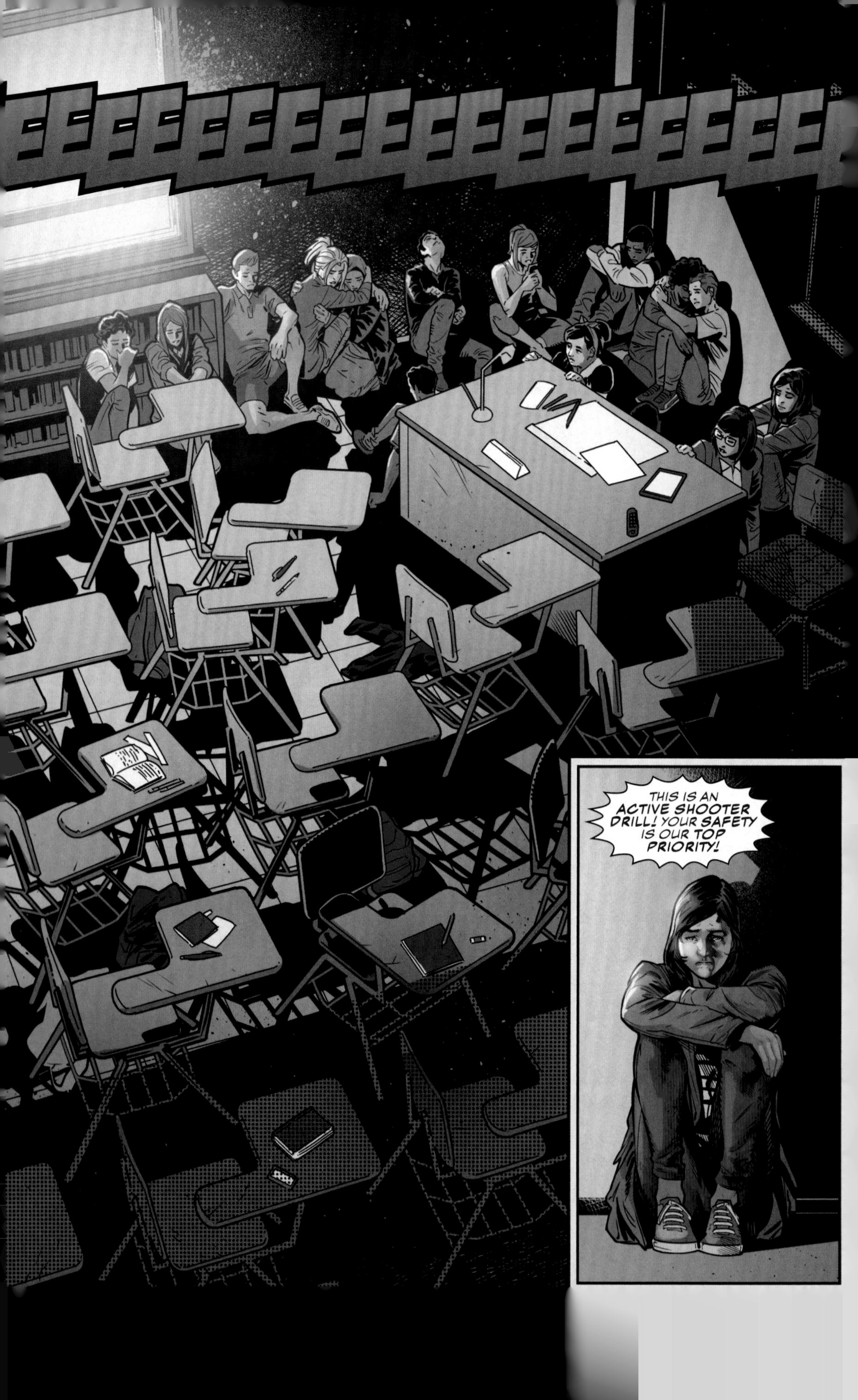
EEEEEEEEEEEEEEEEEE
THIS IS AN ACTIVE SHOOTER DRILL! YOUR SAFETY IS OUR TOP PRIORITY!

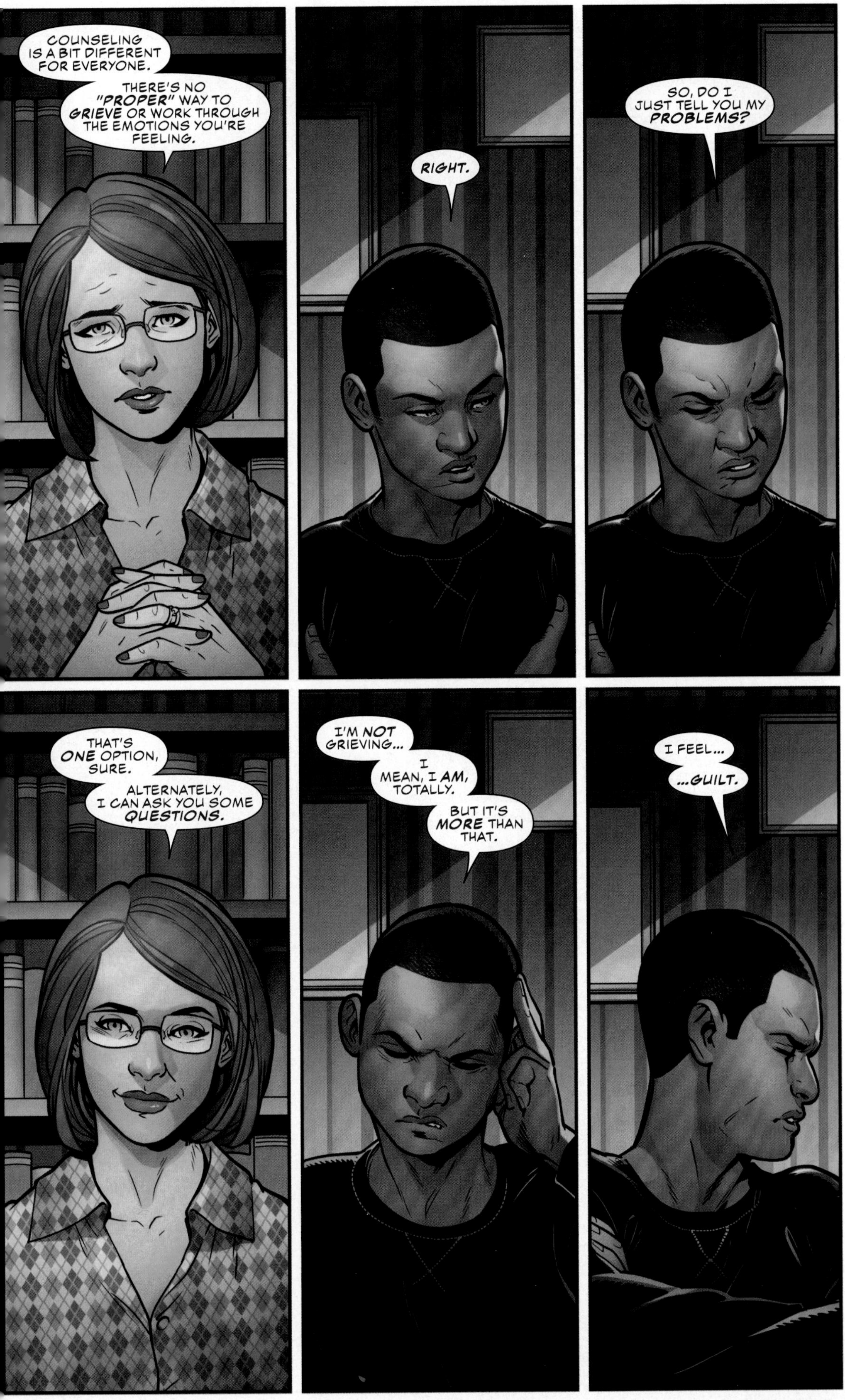

COUNSELING IS A BIT DIFFERENT FOR EVERYONE.
THERE'S NO "PROPER" WAY TO GRIEVE OR WORK THROUGH THE EMOTIONS YOU'RE FEELING.
RIGHT.
SO, DO I JUST TELL YOU MY PROBLEMS?
THAT'S ONE OPTION, SURE.
ALTERNATELY, I CAN ASK YOU SOME QUESTIONS.
I'M NOT GRIEVING...
I MEAN, I AM, TOTALLY.
BUT IT'S MORE THAN THAT.
I FEEL...
...GUILT.

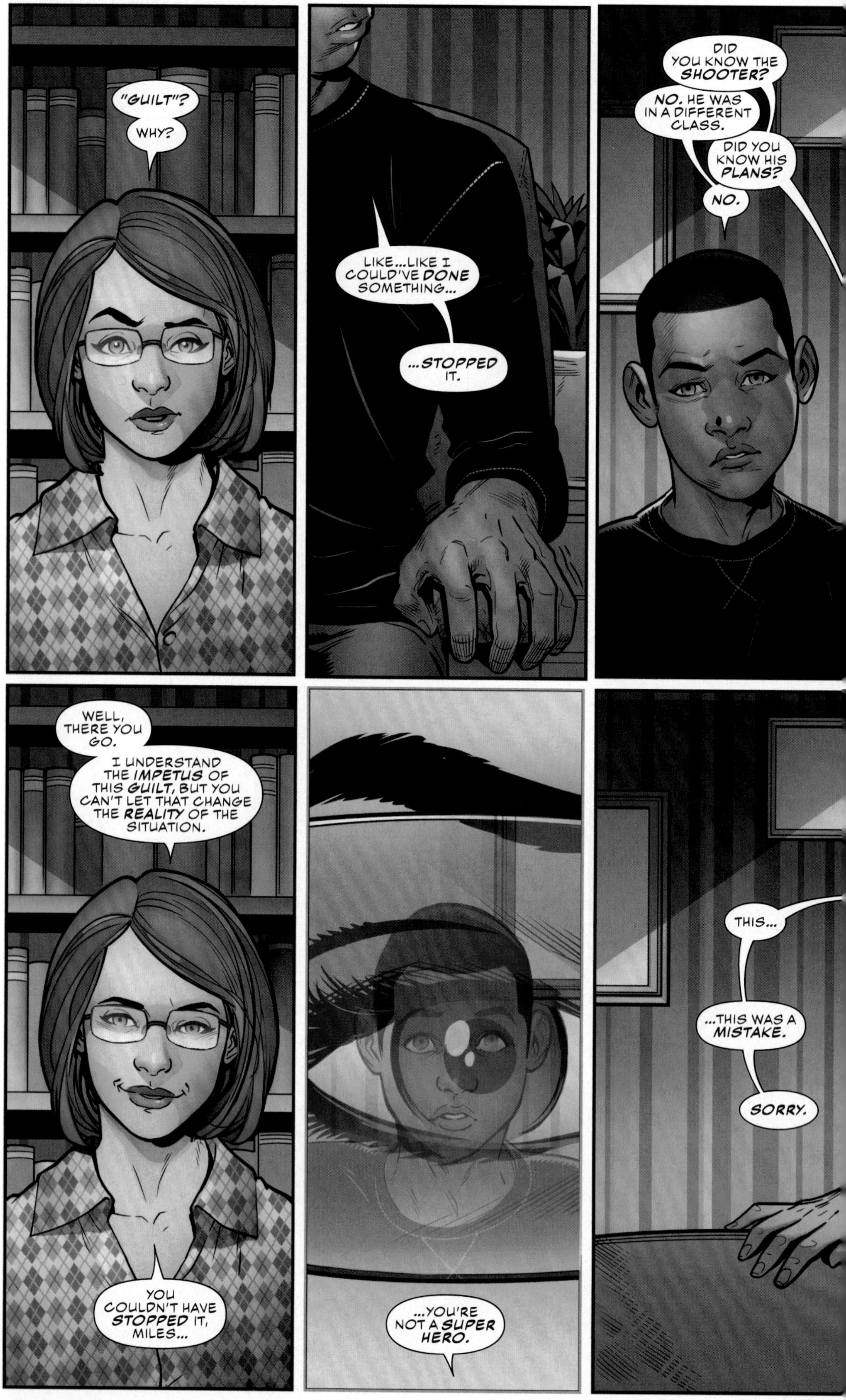
"GUILT"?
WHY?
LIKE...LIKE I COULD'VE DONE SOMETHING...
...STOPPED IT.
DID YOU KNOW THE SHOOTER?
NO. HE WAS IN A DIFFERENT CLASS.
DID YOU KNOW HIS PLANS?
NO.
WELL, THERE YOU GO.
I UNDERSTAND THE IMPETUS OF THIS GUILT, BUT YOU CAN'T LET THAT CHANGE THE REALITY OF THE SITUATION.
YOU COULDN'T HAVE STOPPED IT, MILES...
...YOU'RE NOT A SUPER HERO.
THIS...
...THIS WAS A MISTAKE.
SORRY.

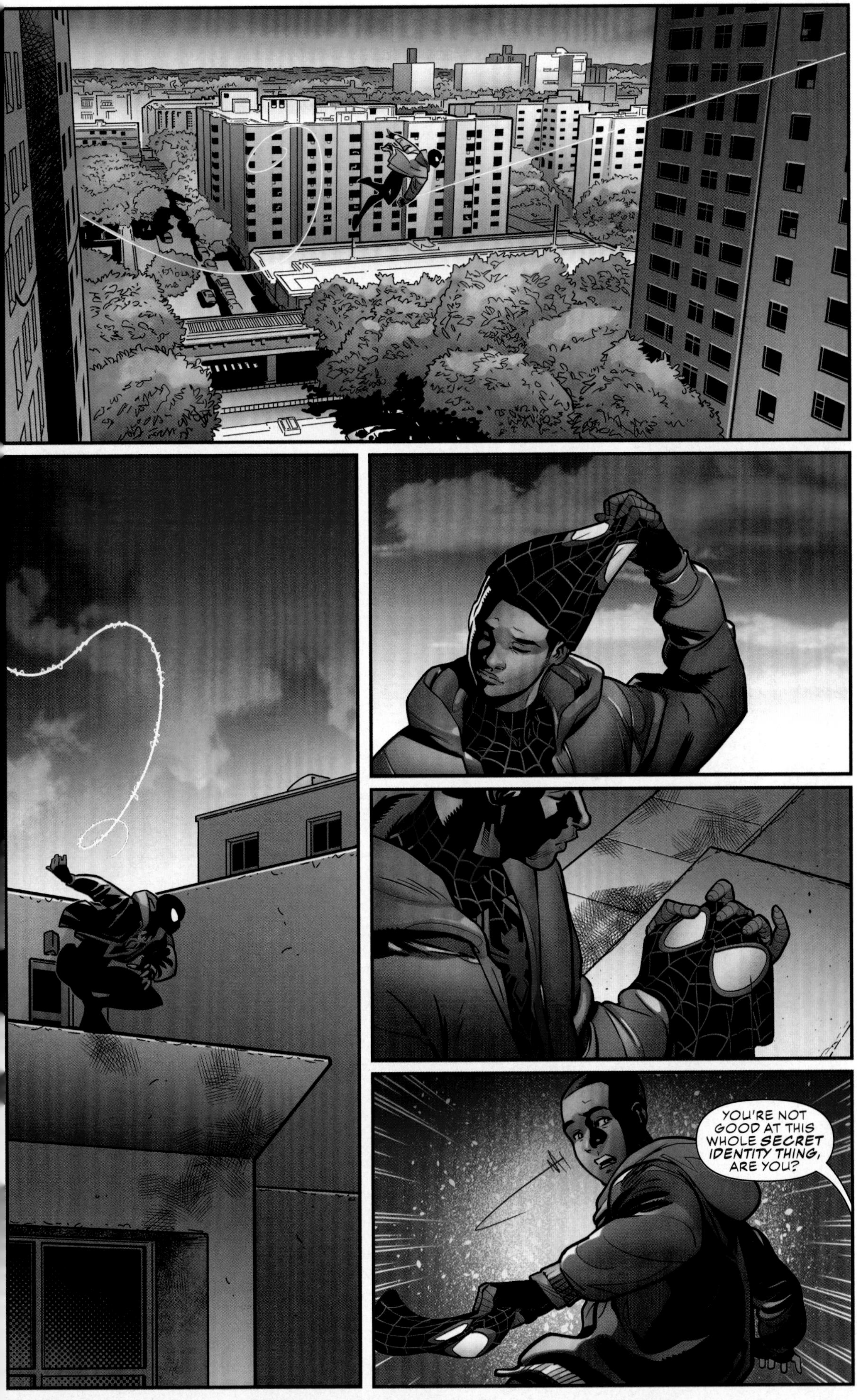
YOU'RE NOT GOOD AT THIS WHOLE SECRET IDENTITY THING, ARE YOU?

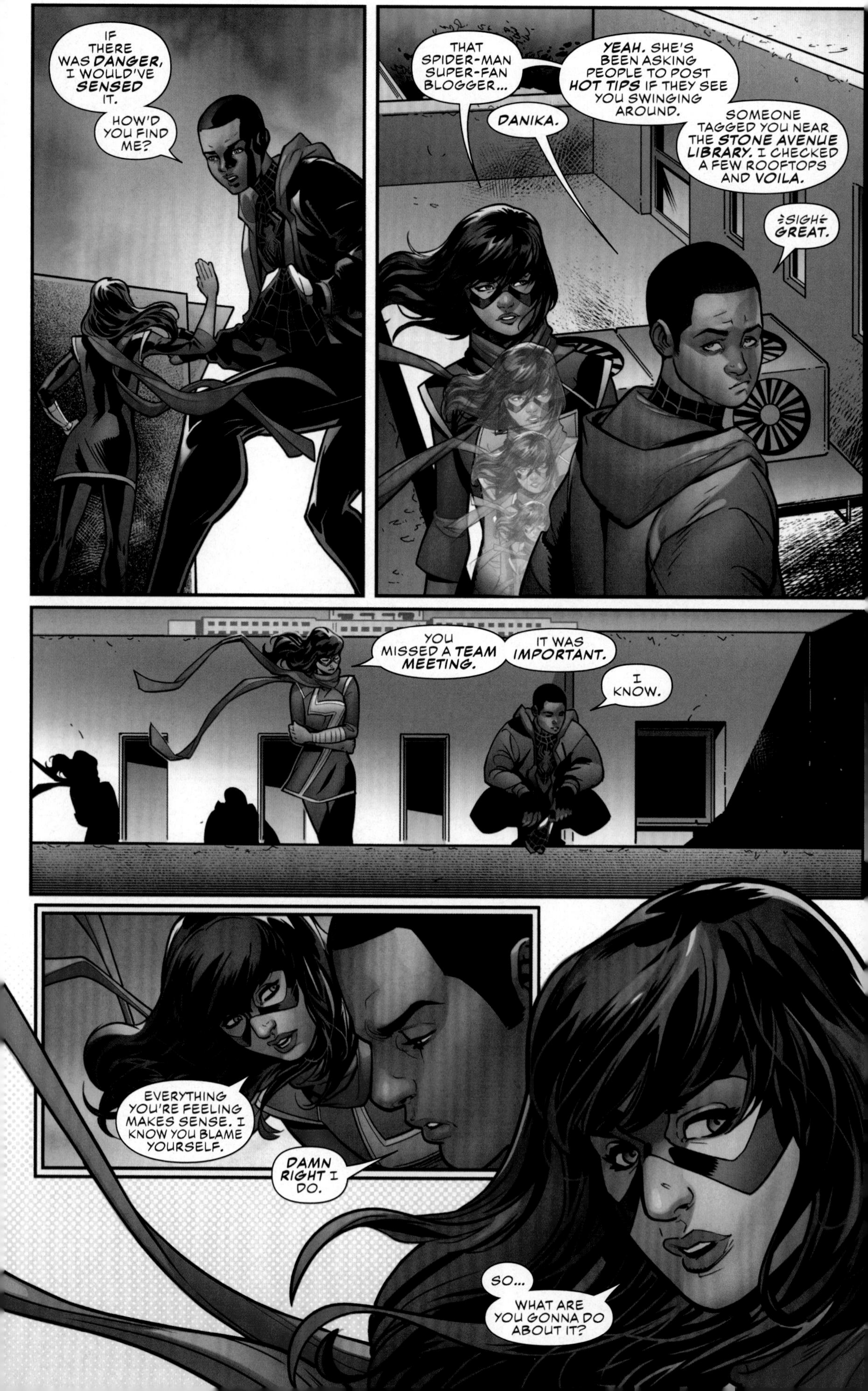

IF THERE WAS DANGER, I WOULD'VE SENSED IT.
HOW'D YOU FIND ME?
THAT SPIDER-MAN SUPER-FAN BLOGGER...
DANIKA.
YEAH. SHE'S BEEN ASKING PEOPLE TO POST HOT TIPS IF THEY SEE YOU SWINGING AROUND.
SOMEONE TAGGED YOU NEAR THE STONE AVENUE LIBRARY. I CHECKED A FEW ROOFTOPS AND VOILA.
SIGH GREAT.
YOU MISSED A TEAM MEETING.
IT WAS IMPORTANT.
I KNOW.
EVERYTHING YOU'RE FEELING MAKES SENSE. I KNOW YOU BLAME YOURSELF.
DAMN RIGHT I DO.
SO...
WHAT ARE YOU GONNA DO ABOUT IT?

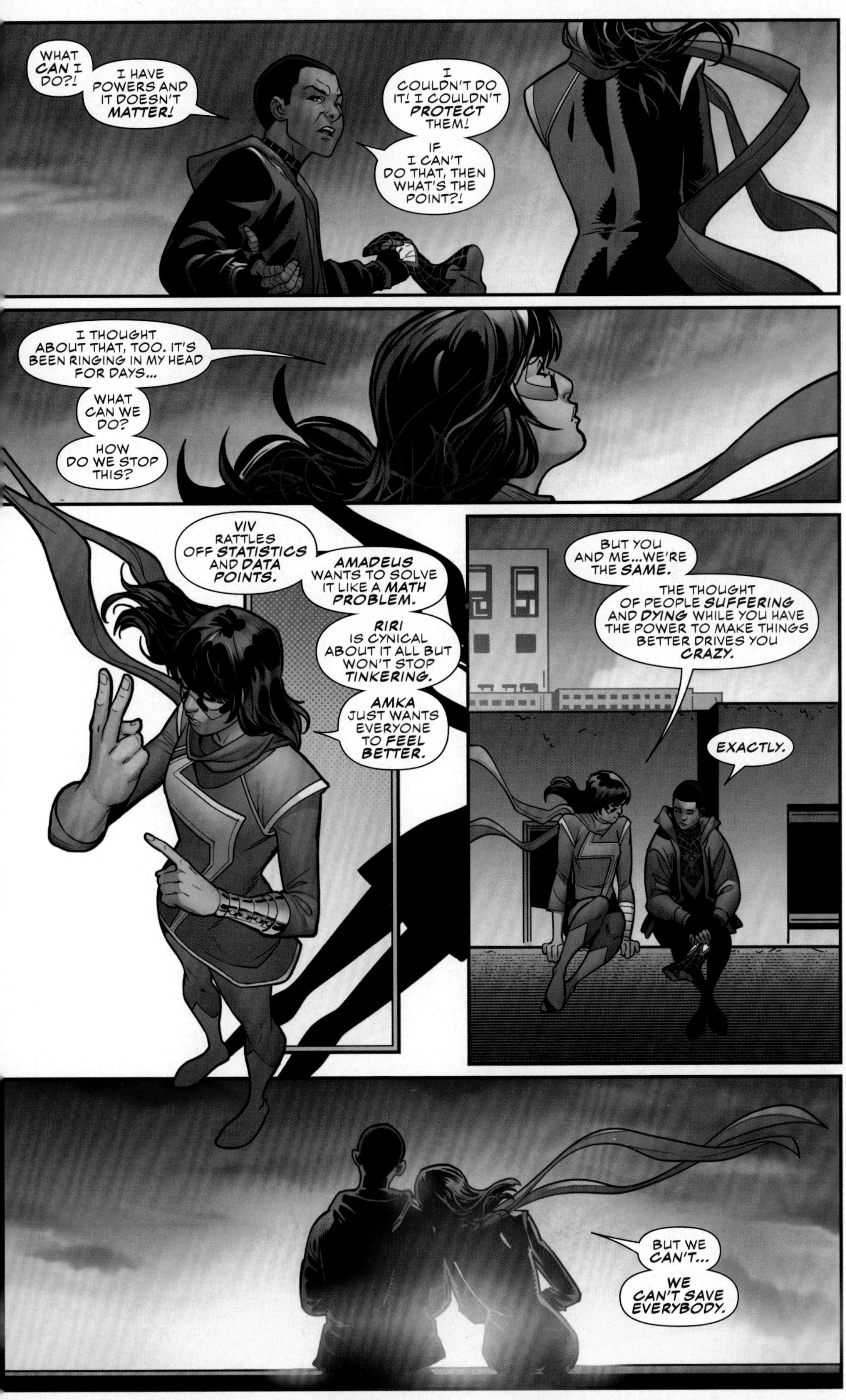
WHAT CAN I DO?!
I HAVE POWERS AND IT DOESN'T MATTER!
I COULDN'T DO IT! I COULDN'T PROTECT THEM!
IF I CAN'T DO THAT, THEN WHAT'S THE POINT?!
I THOUGHT ABOUT THAT, TOO. IT'S BEEN RINGING IN MY HEAD FOR DAYS...
WHAT CAN WE DO?
HOW DO WE STOP THIS?
VIV RATTLES OFF STATISTICS AND DATA POINTS.
AMADEUS WANTS TO SOLVE IT LIKE A MATH PROBLEM.
RIRI IS CYNICAL ABOUT IT ALL BUT WON'T STOP TINKERING.
AMKA JUST WANTS EVERYONE TO FEEL BETTER.
BUT YOU AND ME...WE'RE THE SAME.
THE THOUGHT OF PEOPLE SUFFERING AND DYING WHILE YOU HAVE THE POWER TO MAKE THINGS BETTER DRIVES YOU CRAZY.
EXACTLY.
BUT WE CAN'T...
WE CAN'T SAVE EVERYBODY.

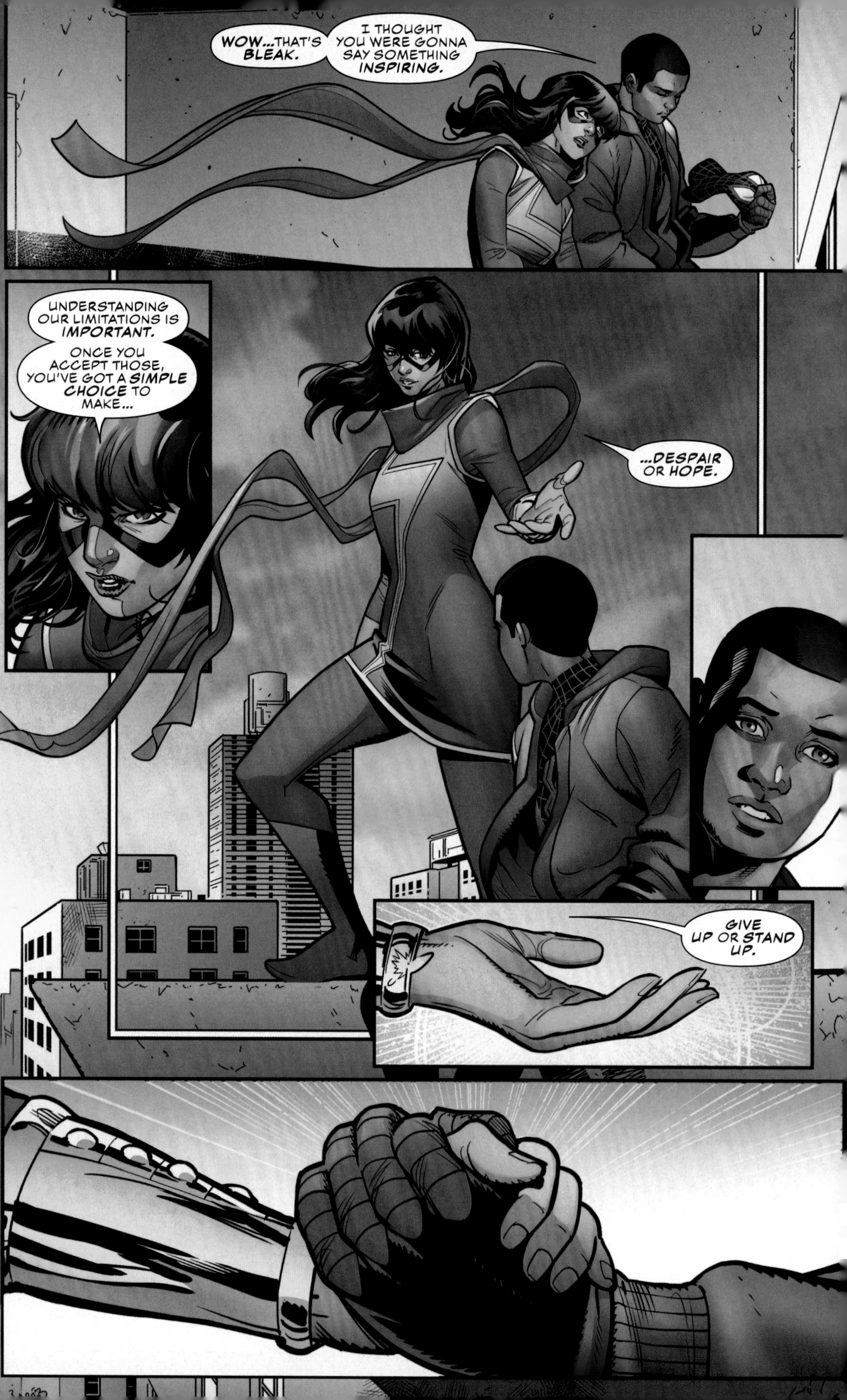

WOW...THAT'S BLEAK.
I THOUGHT YOU WERE GONNA SAY SOMETHING INSPIRING.
UNDERSTANDING OUR LIMITATIONS IS IMPORTANT.
ONCE YOU ACCEPT THOSE, YOU'VE GOT A SIMPLE CHOICE TO MAKE...
...DESPAIR OR HOPE.
GIVE UP OR STAND UP.

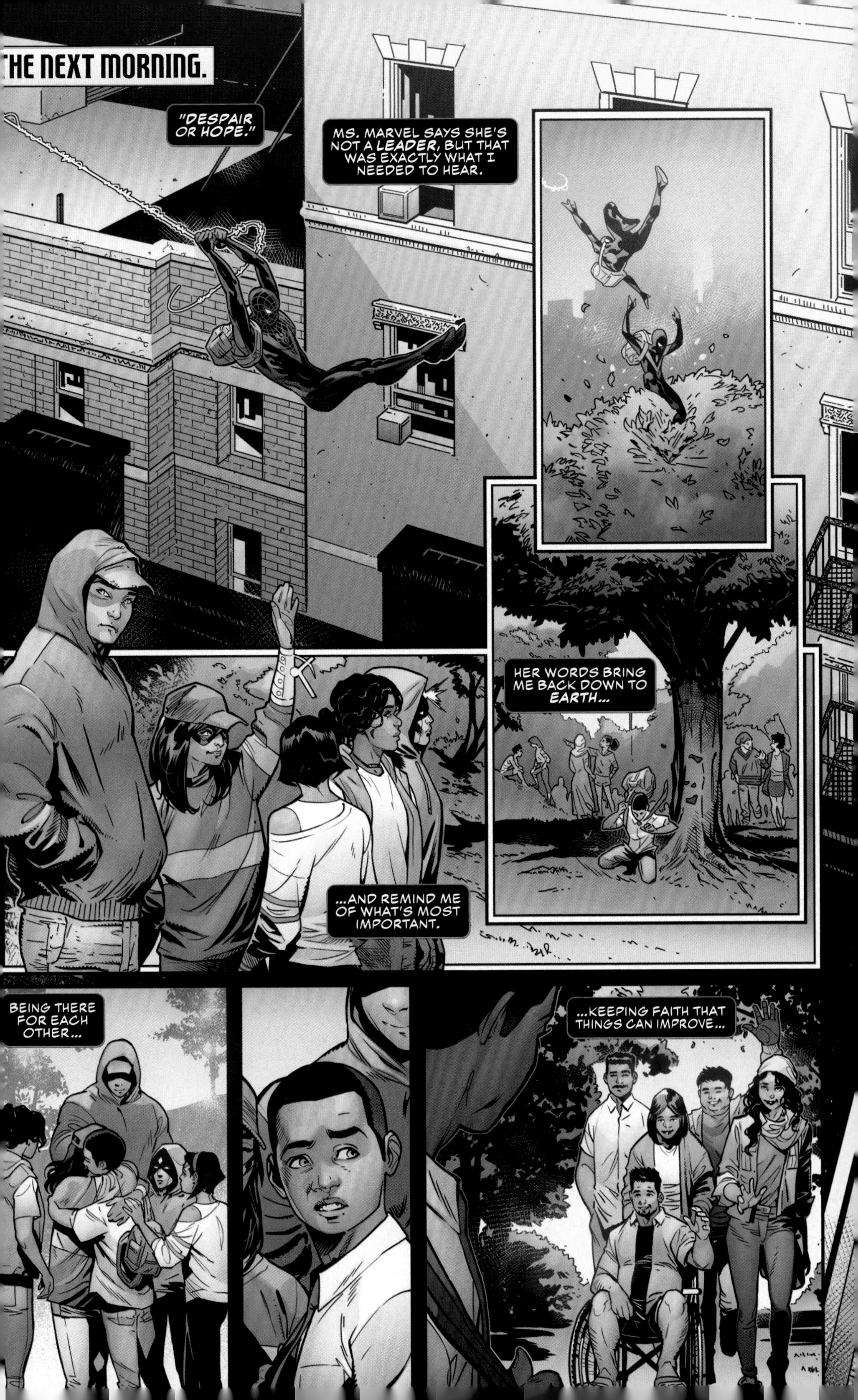
THE NEXT MORNING.
"DESPAIR OR HOPE."
MS. MARVEL SAYS SHE'S NOT A LEADER, BUT THAT WAS EXACTLY WHAT I NEEDED TO HEAR.
HER WORDS BRING ME BACK DOWN TO EARTH...
...AND REMIND ME OF WHAT'S MOST IMPORTANT.
BEING THERE FOR EACH OTHER...
...KEEPING FAITH THAT THINGS CAN IMPROVE...

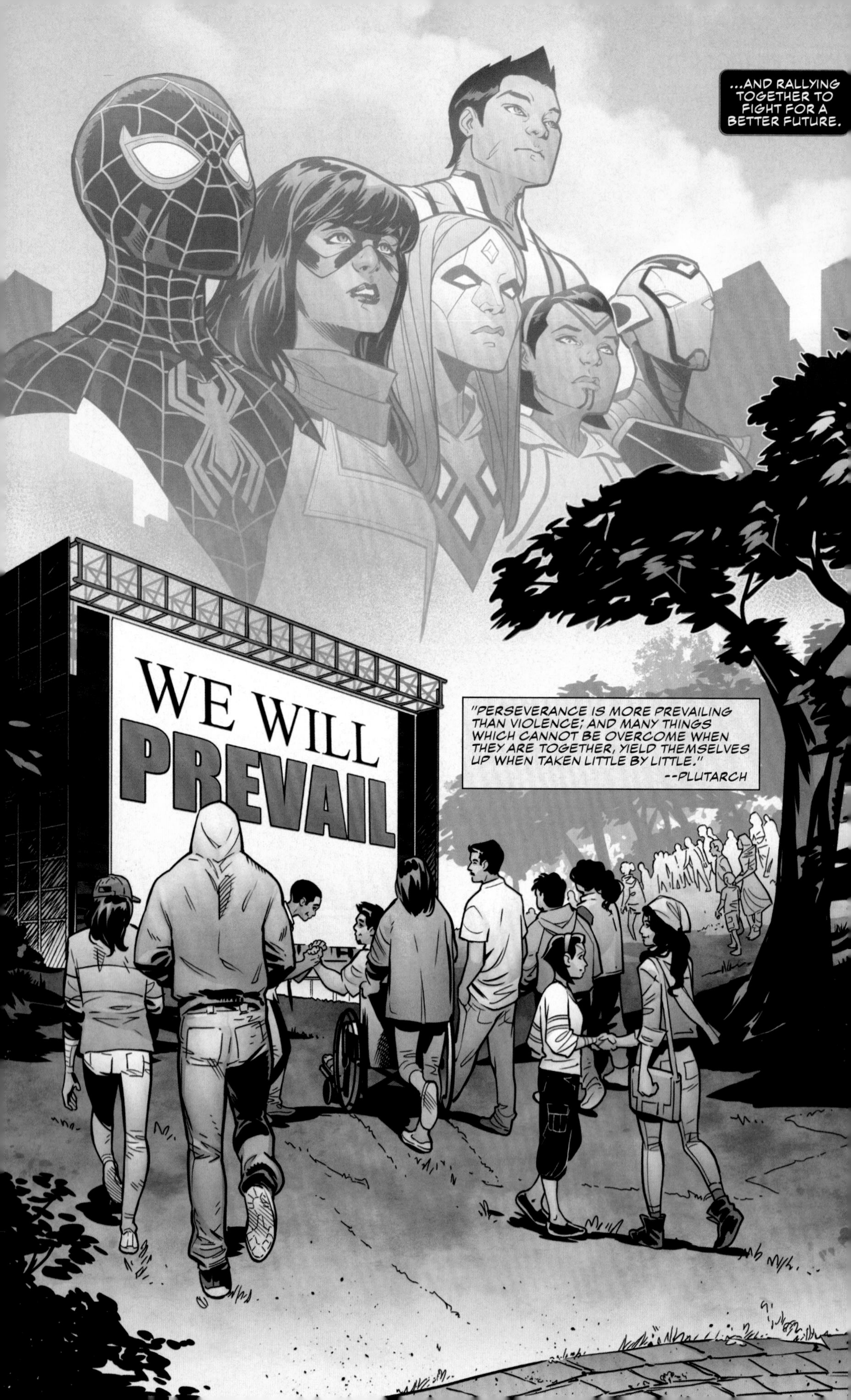
...AND RALLYING TOGETHER TO FIGHT FOR A BETTER FUTURE.
WE WILL PREVAIL
"PERSEVERANCE IS MORE PREVAILING THAN VIOLENCE; AND MANY THINGS WHICH CANNOT BE OVERCOME WHEN THEY ARE TOGETHER, YIELD THEMSELVES UP WHEN TAKEN LITTLE BY LITTLE."
--PLUTARCH

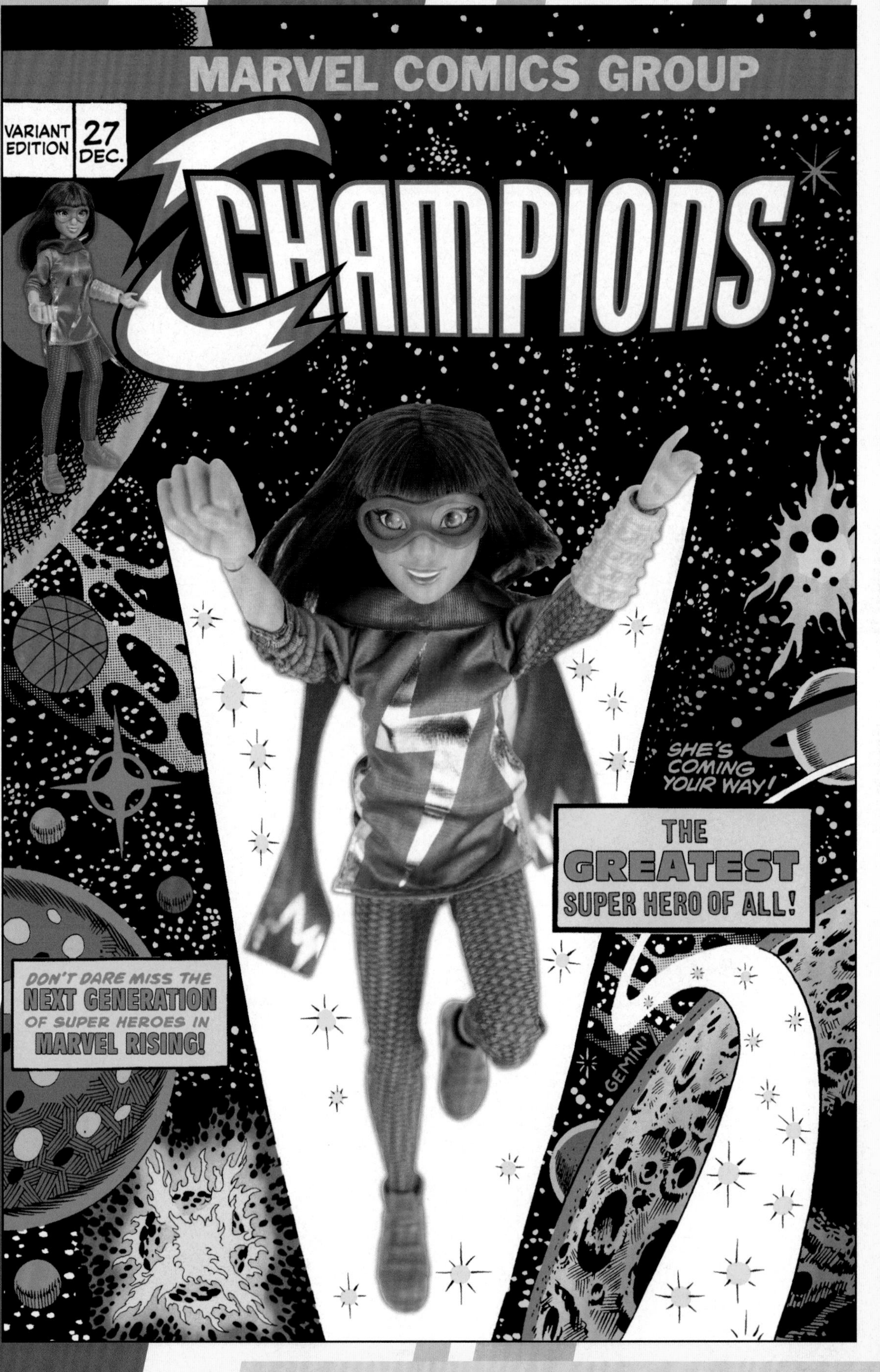
MARVEL COMICS GROUP
VARIANT EDITION
27 DEC.
CHAMPIONS
SHE'S COMING YOUR WAY!
THE GREATEST SUPER HERO OF ALL!
DON'T DARE MISS THE NEXT GENERATION OF SUPER HEROES IN MARVEL RISING!
GEMINI

CHAMPIONS #27 MARVEL RISING ACTION DOLL HOMAGE VARIANT

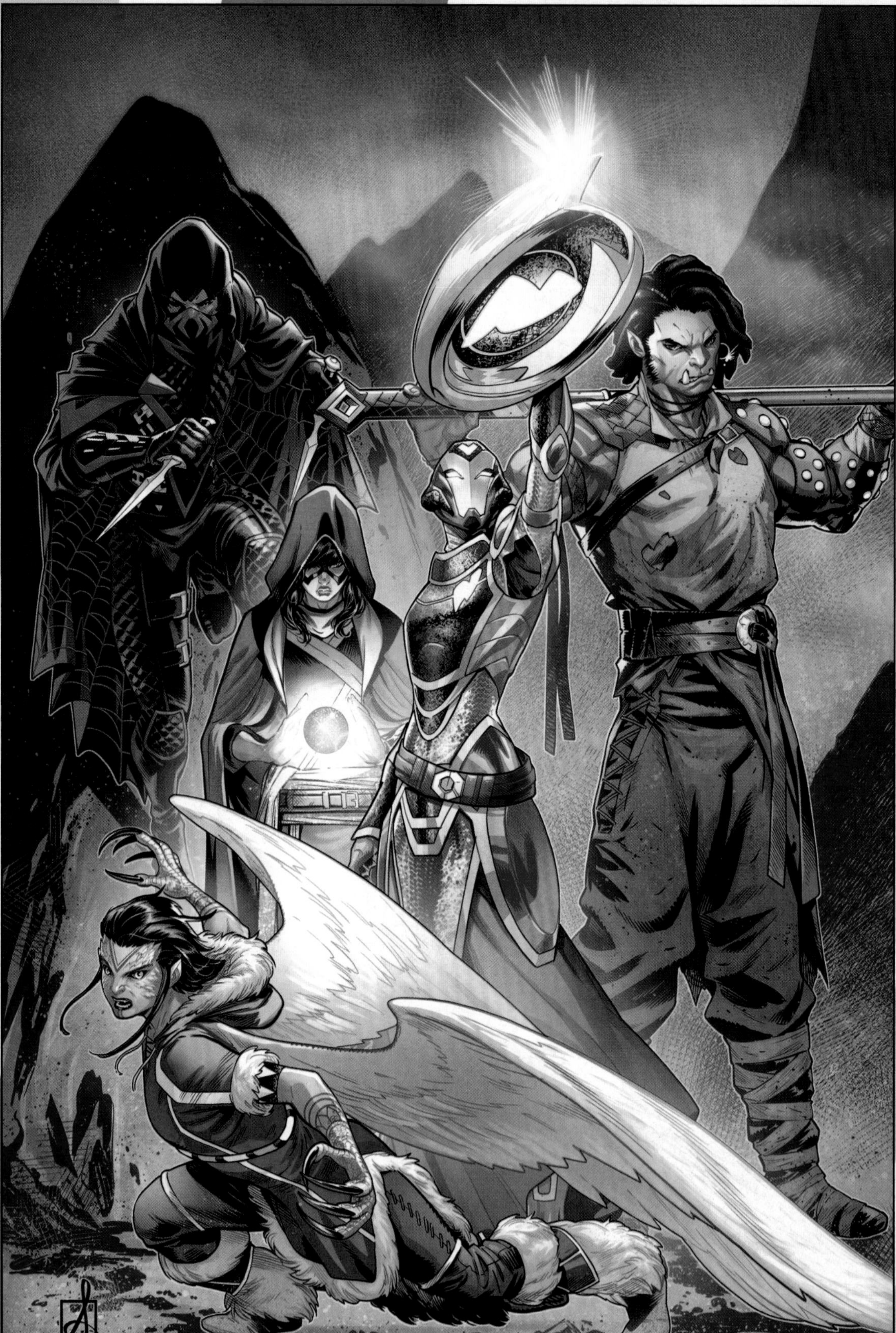

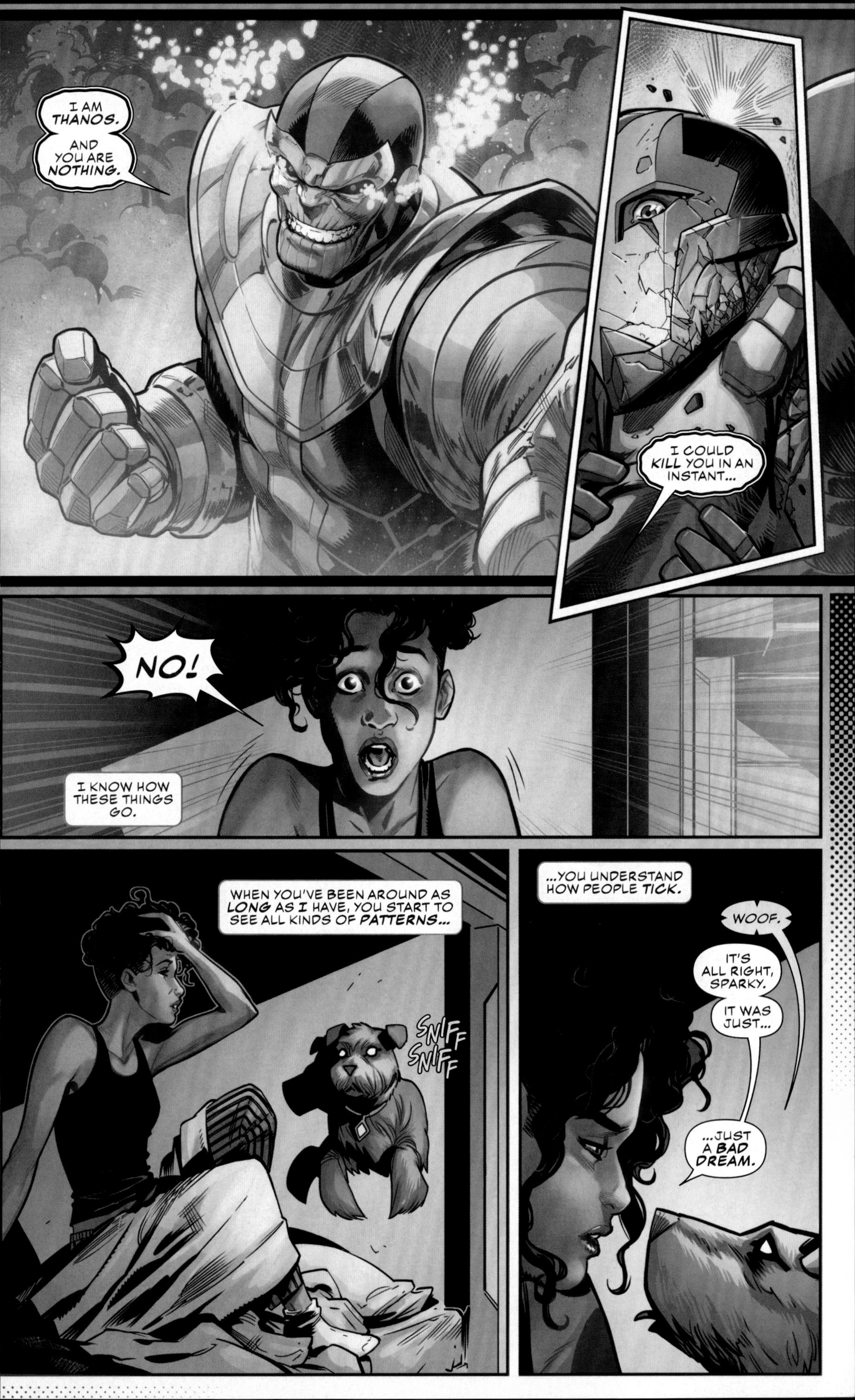
I AM THANOS.
AND YOU ARE NOTHING.
I COULD KILL YOU IN AN INSTANT...
NO!
I KNOW HOW THESE THINGS GO.
WHEN YOU'VE BEEN AROUND AS LONG AS I HAVE, YOU START TO SEE ALL KINDS OF PATTERNS...
SNIFF SNIFF
...YOU UNDERSTAND HOW PEOPLE TICK.
WOOF.
IT'S ALL RIGHT, SPARKY.
IT WAS JUST...
...JUST A BAD DREAM.

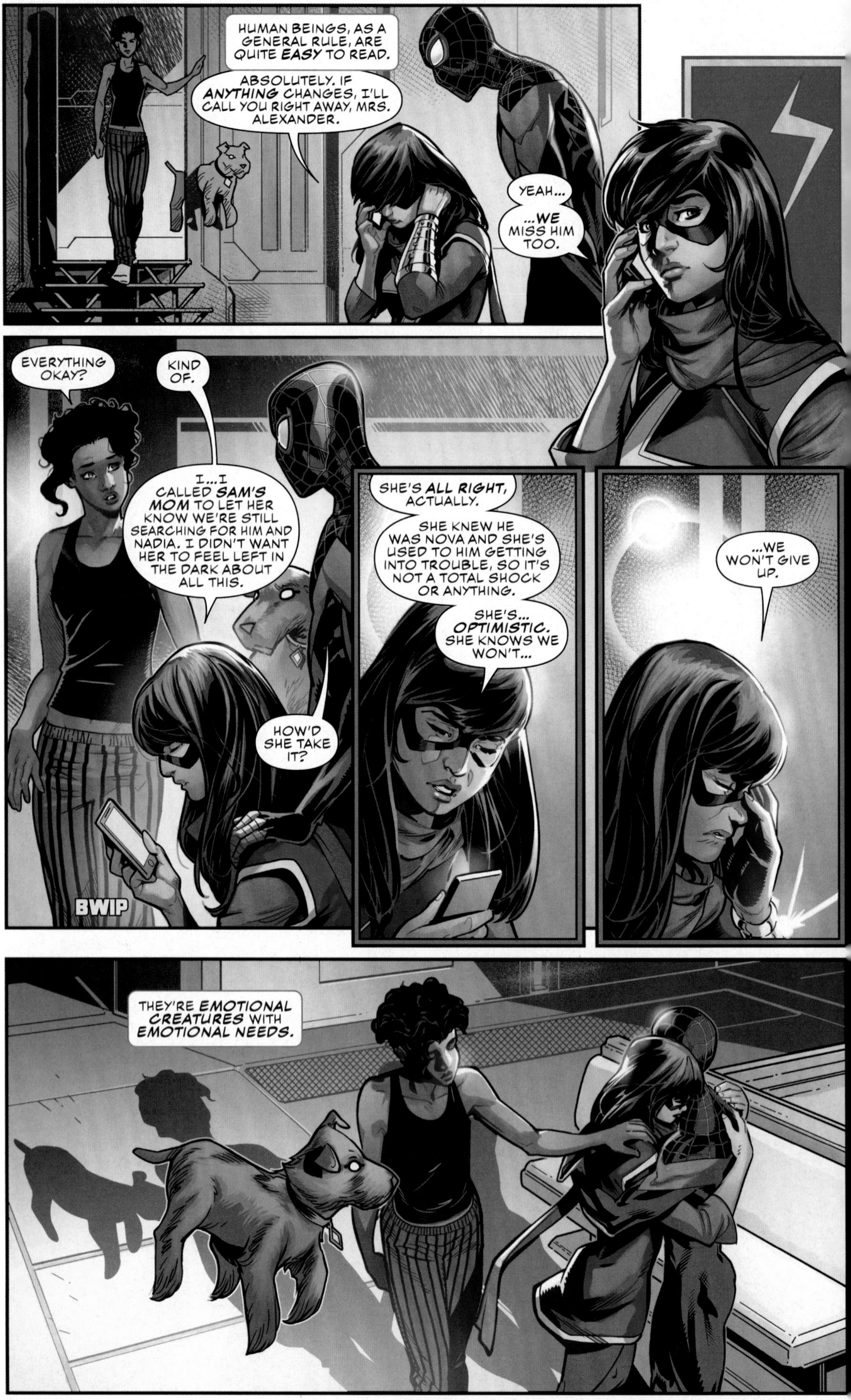
HUMAN BEINGS, AS A GENERAL RULE, ARE QUITE EASY TO READ.
ABSOLUTELY. IF ANYTHING CHANGES, I'LL CALL YOU RIGHT AWAY, MRS. ALEXANDER.
YEAH...
...WE MISS HIM TOO.
EVERYTHING OKAY?
KIND OF.
I...I CALLED SAM'S MOM TO LET HER KNOW WE'RE STILL SEARCHING FOR HIM AND NADIA. I DIDN'T WANT HER TO FEEL LEFT IN THE DARK ABOUT ALL THIS.
HOW'D SHE TAKE IT?
BWIP
SHE'S ALL RIGHT, ACTUALLY.
SHE KNEW HE WAS NOVA AND SHE'S USED TO HIM GETTING INTO TROUBLE, SO IT'S NOT A TOTAL SHOCK OR ANYTHING.
SHE'S... OPTIMISTIC. SHE KNOWS WE WON'T...
...WE WON'T GIVE UP.
THEY'RE EMOTIONAL CREATURES WITH EMOTIONAL NEEDS.

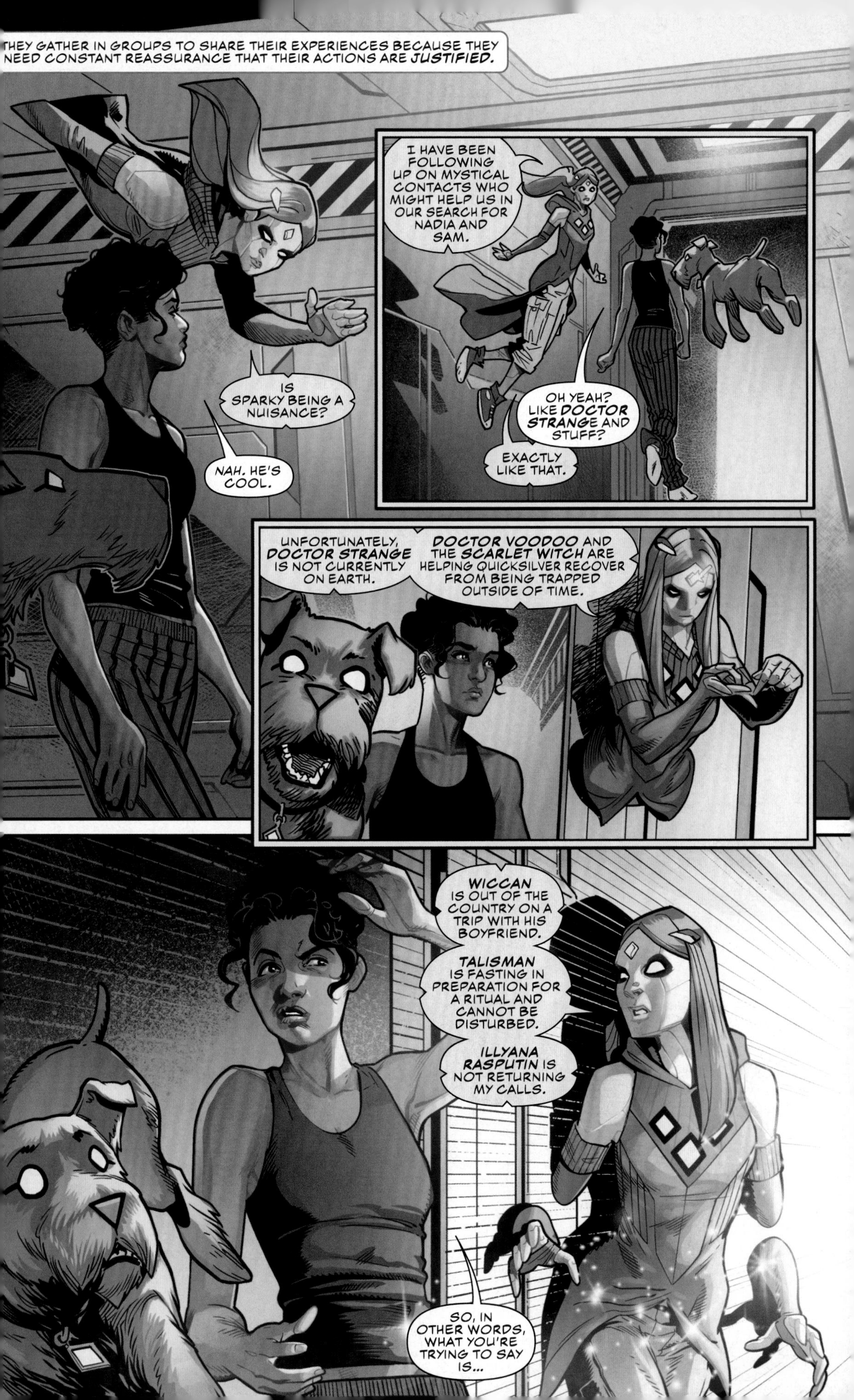
THEY GATHER IN GROUPS TO SHARE THEIR EXPERIENCES BECAUSE THEY NEED CONSTANT REASSURANCE THAT THEIR ACTIONS ARE JUSTIFIED.
IS SPARKY BEING A NUISANCE?
NAH. HE'S COOL.
I HAVE BEEN FOLLOWING UP ON MYSTICAL CONTACTS WHO MIGHT HELP US IN OUR SEARCH FOR NADIA AND SAM.
OH YEAH? LIKE DOCTOR STRANGE AND STUFF?
EXACTLY LIKE THAT.
UNFORTUNATELY, DOCTOR STRANGE IS NOT CURRENTLY ON EARTH.
DOCTOR VOODOO AND THE SCARLET WITCH ARE HELPING QUICKSILVER RECOVER FROM BEING TRAPPED OUTSIDE OF TIME.
WICCAN IS OUT OF THE COUNTRY ON A TRIP WITH HIS BOYFRIEND.
TALISMAN IS FASTING IN PREPARATION FOR A RITUAL AND CANNOT BE DISTURBED.
ILLYANA RASPUTIN IS NOT RETURNING MY CALLS.
SO, IN OTHER WORDS, WHAT YOU'RE TRYING TO SAY IS...

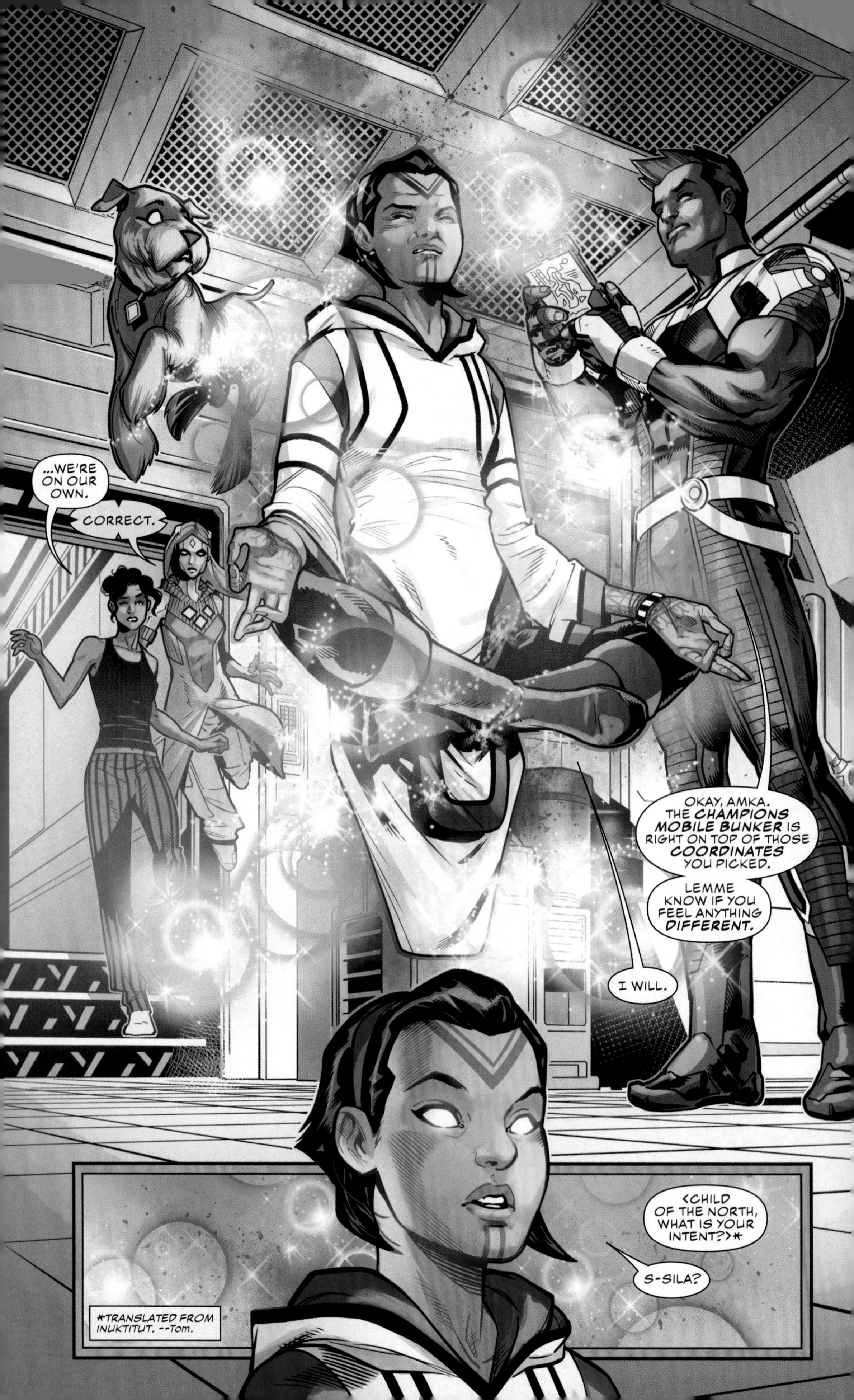
...WE'RE ON OUR OWN.
CORRECT.
OKAY, AMKA. THE CHAMPIONS MOBILE BUNKER IS RIGHT ON TOP OF THOSE COORDINATES YOU PICKED.
LEMME KNOW IF YOU FEEL ANYTHING DIFFERENT.
I WILL.
<CHILD OF THE NORTH, WHAT IS YOUR INTENT?>*
S-SILA?
*TRANSLATED FROM INUKTITUT. --Tom.

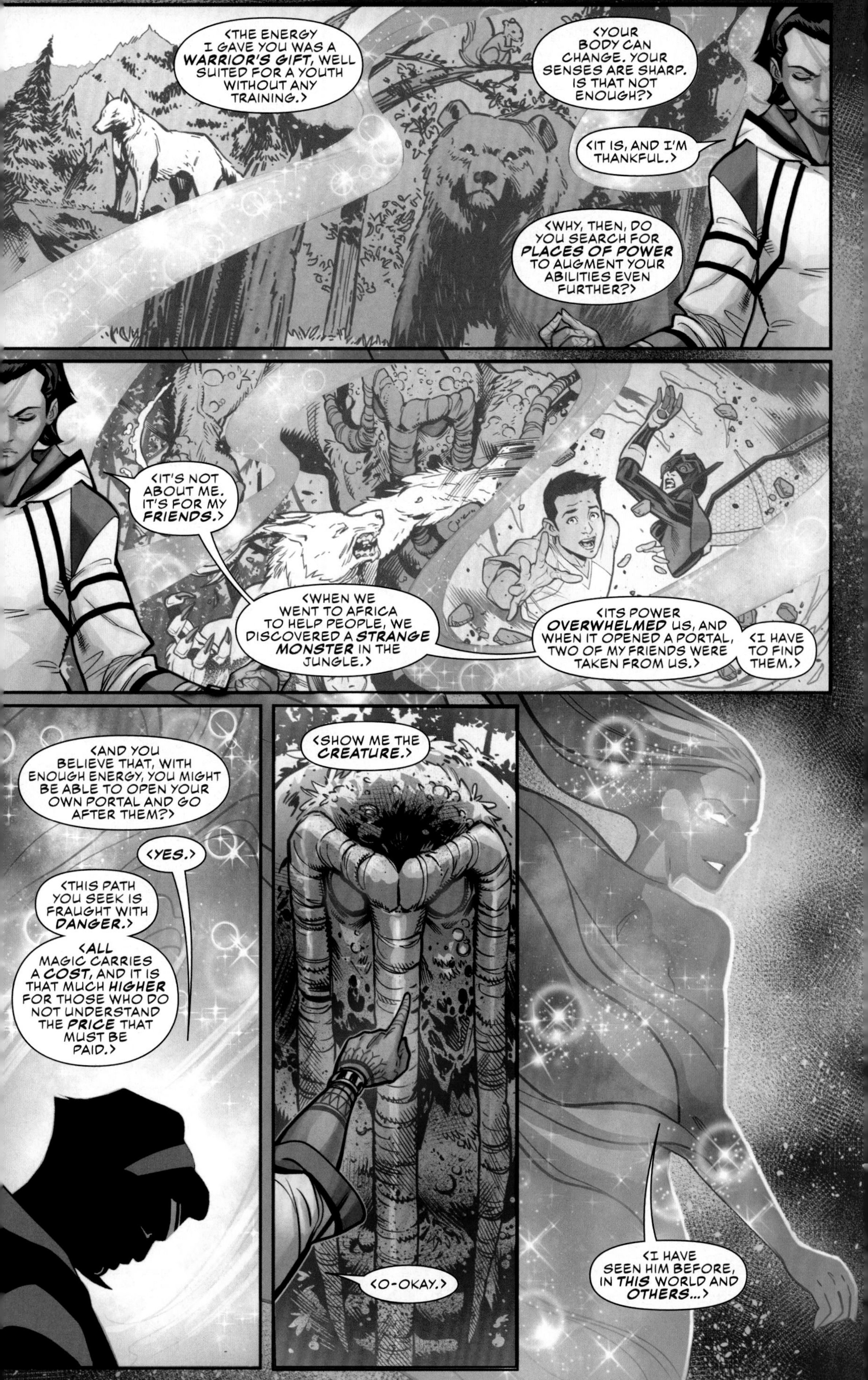
<THE ENERGY I GAVE YOU WAS A WARRIOR'S GIFT, WELL SUITED FOR A YOUTH WITHOUT ANY TRAINING.>
<YOUR BODY CAN CHANGE. YOUR SENSES ARE SHARP. IS THAT NOT ENOUGH?>
<IT IS, AND I'M THANKFUL.>
<WHY, THEN, DO YOU SEARCH FOR PLACES OF POWER TO AUGMENT YOUR ABILITIES EVEN FURTHER?>
<IT'S NOT ABOUT ME. IT'S FOR MY FRIENDS.>
<WHEN WE WENT TO AFRICA TO HELP PEOPLE, WE DISCOVERED A STRANGE MONSTER IN THE JUNGLE.>
<ITS POWER OVERWHELMED US, AND WHEN IT OPENED A PORTAL, TWO OF MY FRIENDS WERE TAKEN FROM US.>
<I HAVE TO FIND THEM.>
<AND YOU BELIEVE THAT, WITH ENOUGH ENERGY, YOU MIGHT BE ABLE TO OPEN YOUR OWN PORTAL AND GO AFTER THEM?>
<YES.>
<THIS PATH YOU SEEK IS FRAUGHT WITH DANGER.>
<ALL MAGIC CARRIES A COST, AND IT IS THAT MUCH HIGHER FOR THOSE WHO DO NOT UNDERSTAND THE PRICE THAT MUST BE PAID.>
<SHOW ME THE CREATURE.>
<O-OKAY.>
<I HAVE SEEN HIM BEFORE, IN THIS WORLD AND OTHERS...>

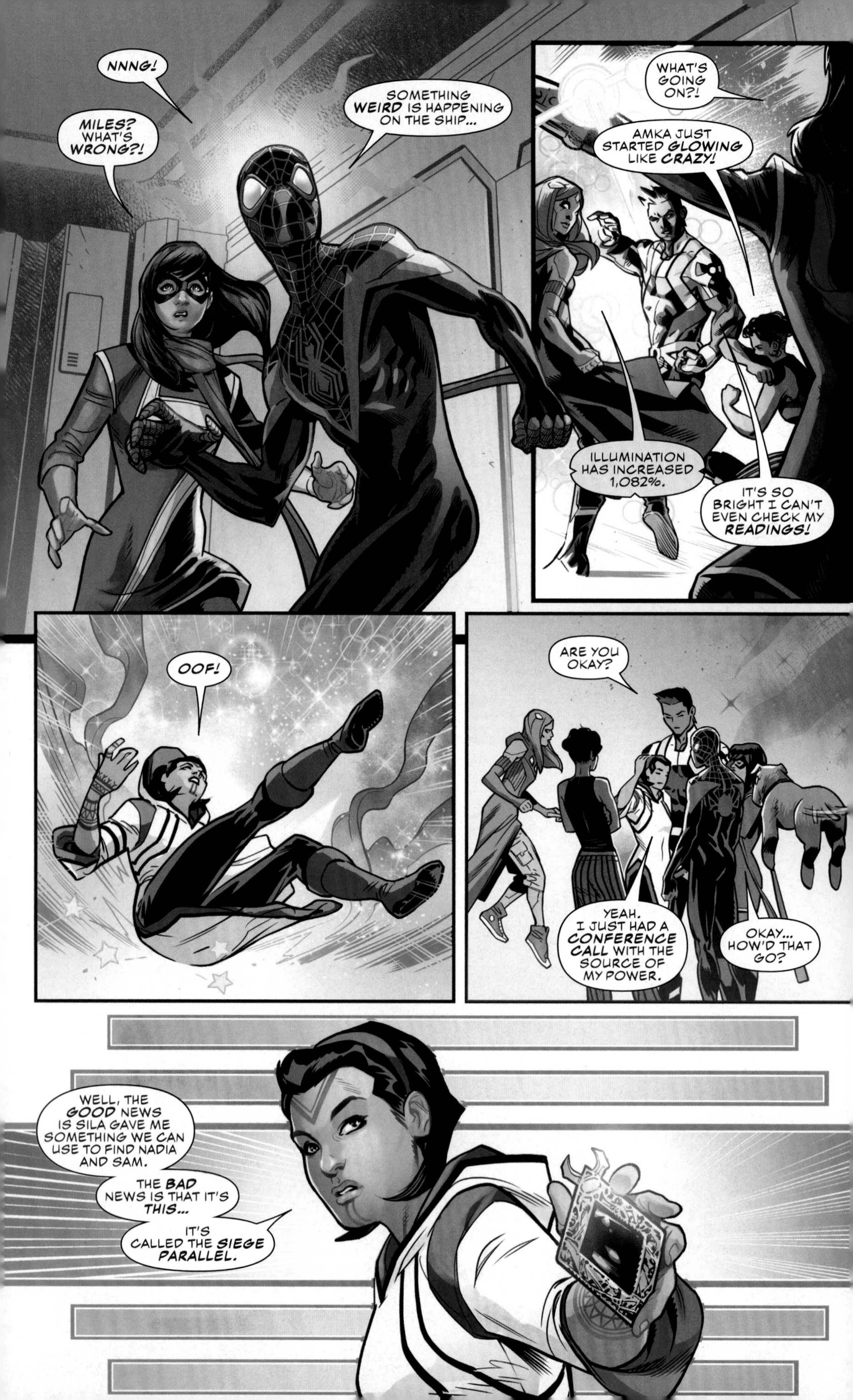
NNNG!
MILES? WHAT'S WRONG?!
SOMETHING WEIRD IS HAPPENING ON THE SHIP...
WHAT'S GOING ON?!
AMKA JUST STARTED GLOWING LIKE CRAZY!
ILLUMINATION HAS INCREASED 1,082%.
IT'S SO BRIGHT I CAN'T EVEN CHECK MY READINGS!
OOF!
ARE YOU OKAY?
YEAH. I JUST HAD A CONFERENCE CALL WITH THE SOURCE OF MY POWER.
OKAY... HOW'D THAT GO?
WELL, THE GOOD NEWS IS SILA GAVE ME SOMETHING WE CAN USE TO FIND NADIA AND SAM.
THE BAD NEWS IS THAT IT'S THIS...
IT'S CALLED THE SIEGE PARALLEL.

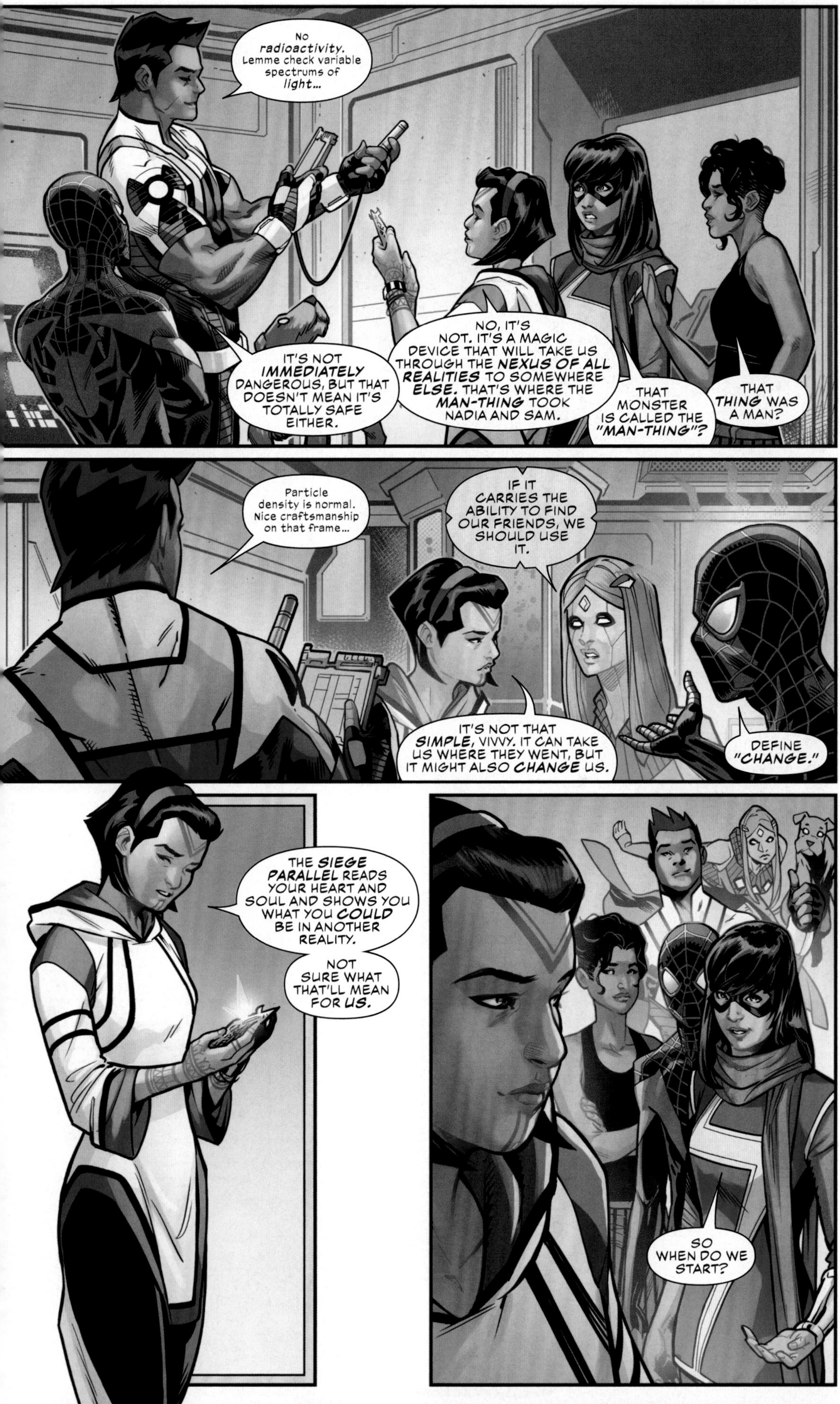
No *radioactivity.* Lemme check variable spectrums of *light...*
IT'S NOT **IMMEDIATELY** DANGEROUS, BUT THAT DOESN'T MEAN IT'S TOTALLY SAFE EITHER.
NO, IT'S NOT. IT'S A MAGIC DEVICE THAT WILL TAKE US THROUGH THE **NEXUS OF ALL REALITIES** TO SOMEWHERE **ELSE.** THAT'S WHERE THE **MAN-THING** TOOK NADIA AND SAM.
THAT MONSTER IS CALLED THE **"MAN-THING"**?
THAT **THING** WAS A MAN?
Particle density is normal. Nice craftsmanship on that frame...
IF IT CARRIES THE ABILITY TO FIND OUR FRIENDS, WE SHOULD USE IT.
IT'S NOT THAT **SIMPLE**, VIVVY. IT CAN TAKE US WHERE THEY WENT, BUT IT MIGHT ALSO **CHANGE** US.
DEFINE **"CHANGE."**
THE **SIEGE PARALLEL** READS YOUR HEART AND SOUL AND SHOWS YOU WHAT YOU **COULD** BE IN ANOTHER REALITY.
NOT SURE WHAT THAT'LL MEAN FOR **US.**
SO WHEN DO WE START?

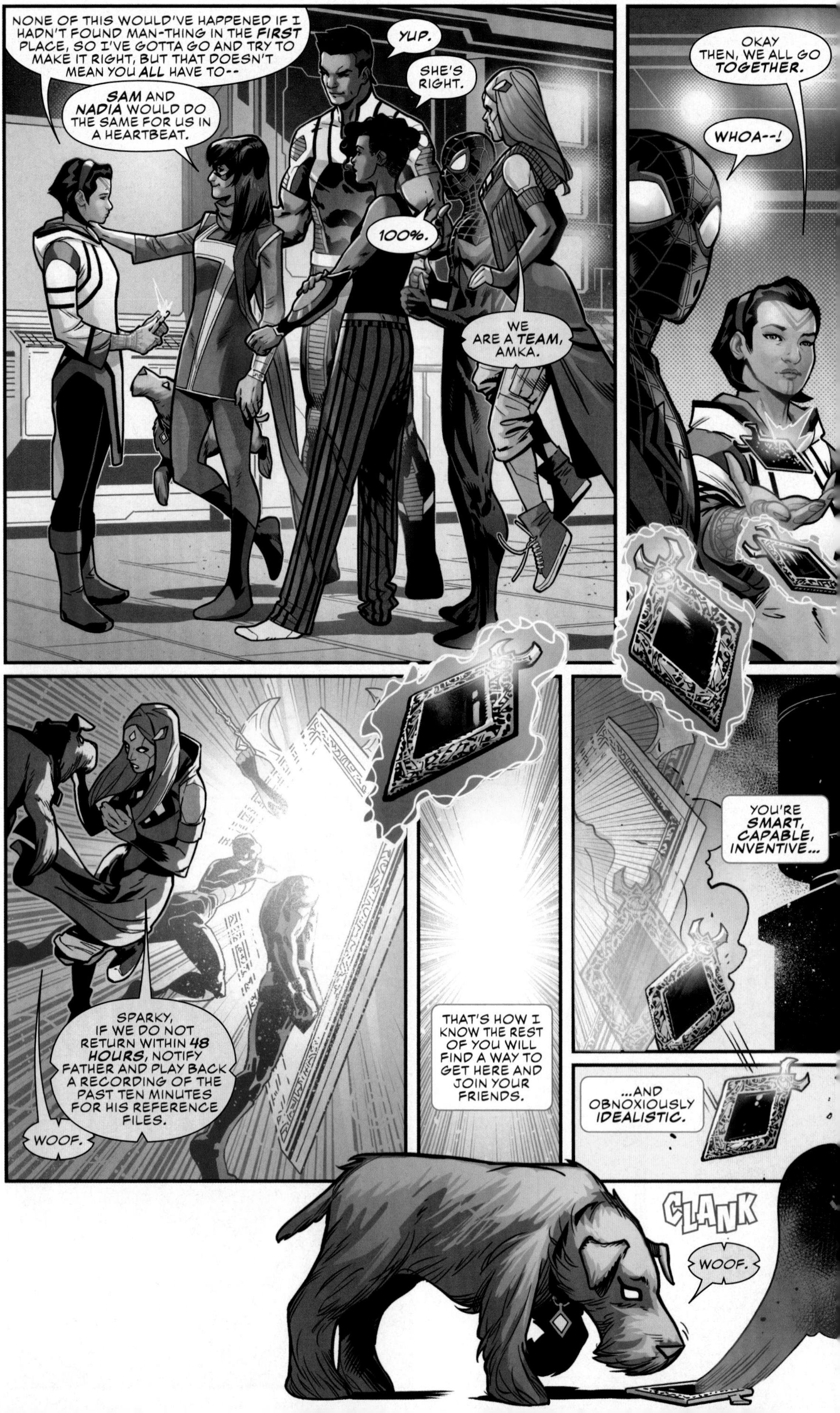

NONE OF THIS WOULD'VE HAPPENED IF I HADN'T FOUND MAN-THING IN THE FIRST PLACE, SO I'VE GOTTA GO AND TRY TO MAKE IT RIGHT, BUT THAT DOESN'T MEAN YOU ALL HAVE TO--
SAM AND NADIA WOULD DO THE SAME FOR US IN A HEARTBEAT.
YUP.
SHE'S RIGHT.
100%.
WE ARE A TEAM, AMKA.
OKAY THEN, WE ALL GO TOGETHER.
WHOA--!
SPARKY, IF WE DO NOT RETURN WITHIN 48 HOURS, NOTIFY FATHER AND PLAY BACK A RECORDING OF THE PAST TEN MINUTES FOR HIS REFERENCE FILES.
WOOF.
THAT'S HOW I KNOW THE REST OF YOU WILL FIND A WAY TO GET HERE AND JOIN YOUR FRIENDS.
YOU'RE SMART, CAPABLE, INVENTIVE...
...AND OBNOXIOUSLY IDEALISTIC.
CLANK
WOOF.

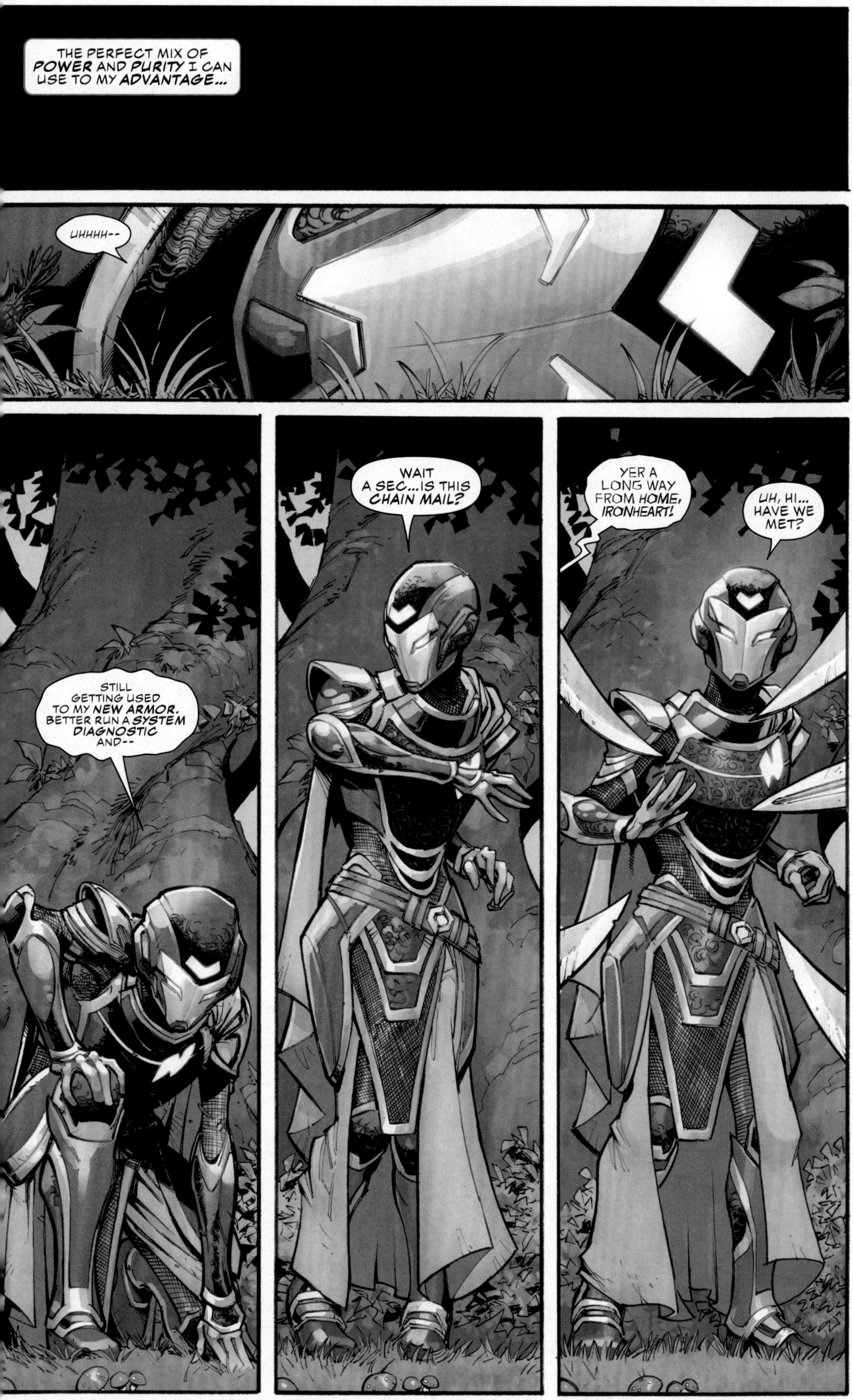
THE PERFECT MIX OF POWER AND PURITY I CAN USE TO MY ADVANTAGE...
UHHHH--
STILL GETTING USED TO MY NEW ARMOR. BETTER RUN A SYSTEM DIAGNOSTIC AND--
WAIT A SEC...IS THIS CHAIN MAIL?
YER A LONG WAY FROM HOME, IRONHEART!
UH, HI... HAVE WE MET?

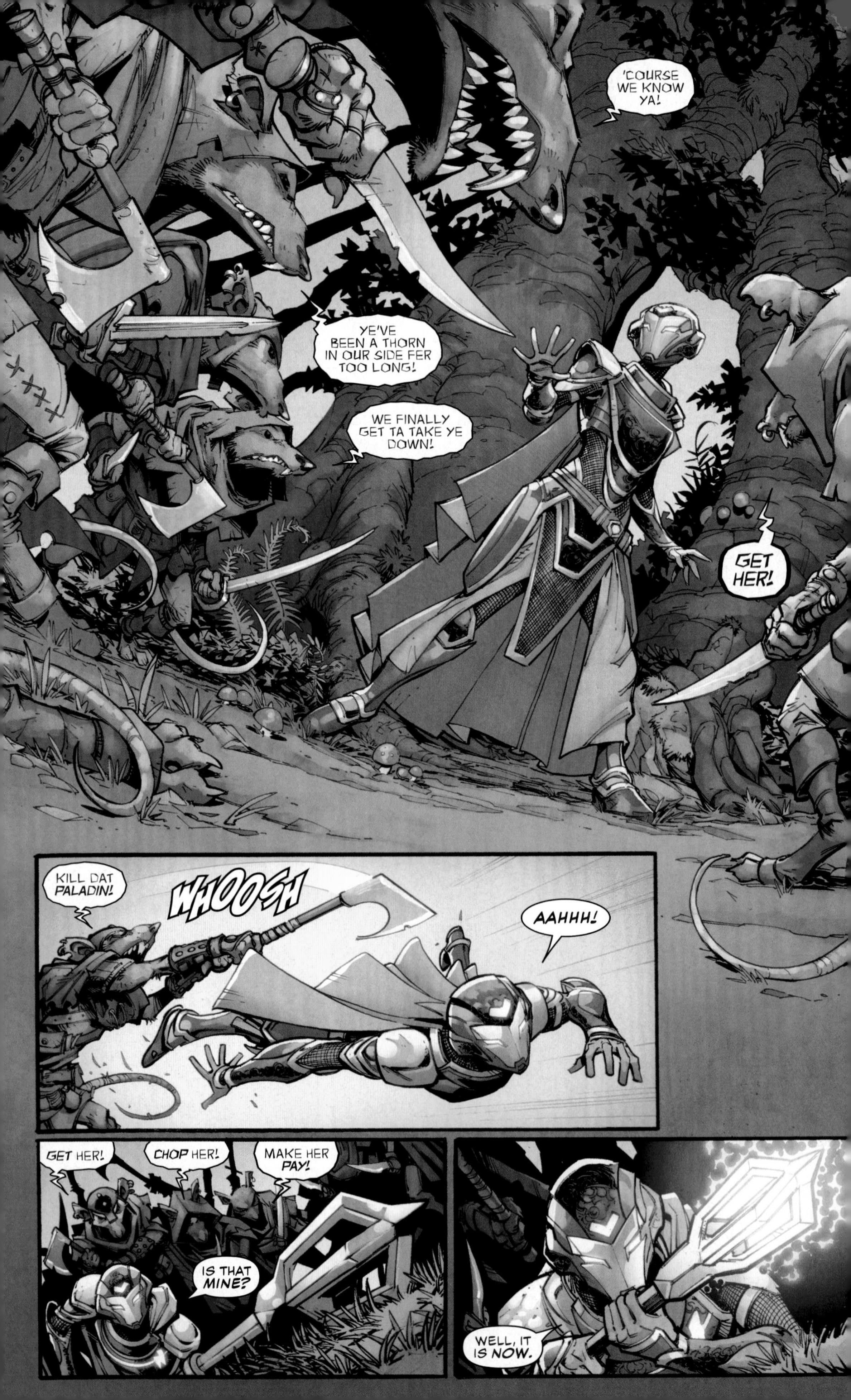
'COURSE WE KNOW YA!
YE'VE BEEN A THORN IN OUR SIDE FER TOO LONG!
WE FINALLY GET TA TAKE YE DOWN!
GET HER!
KILL DAT PALADIN!
WHOOSH
AAHHH!
GET HER!
CHOP HER!
MAKE HER PAY!
IS THAT MINE?
WELL, IT IS NOW.

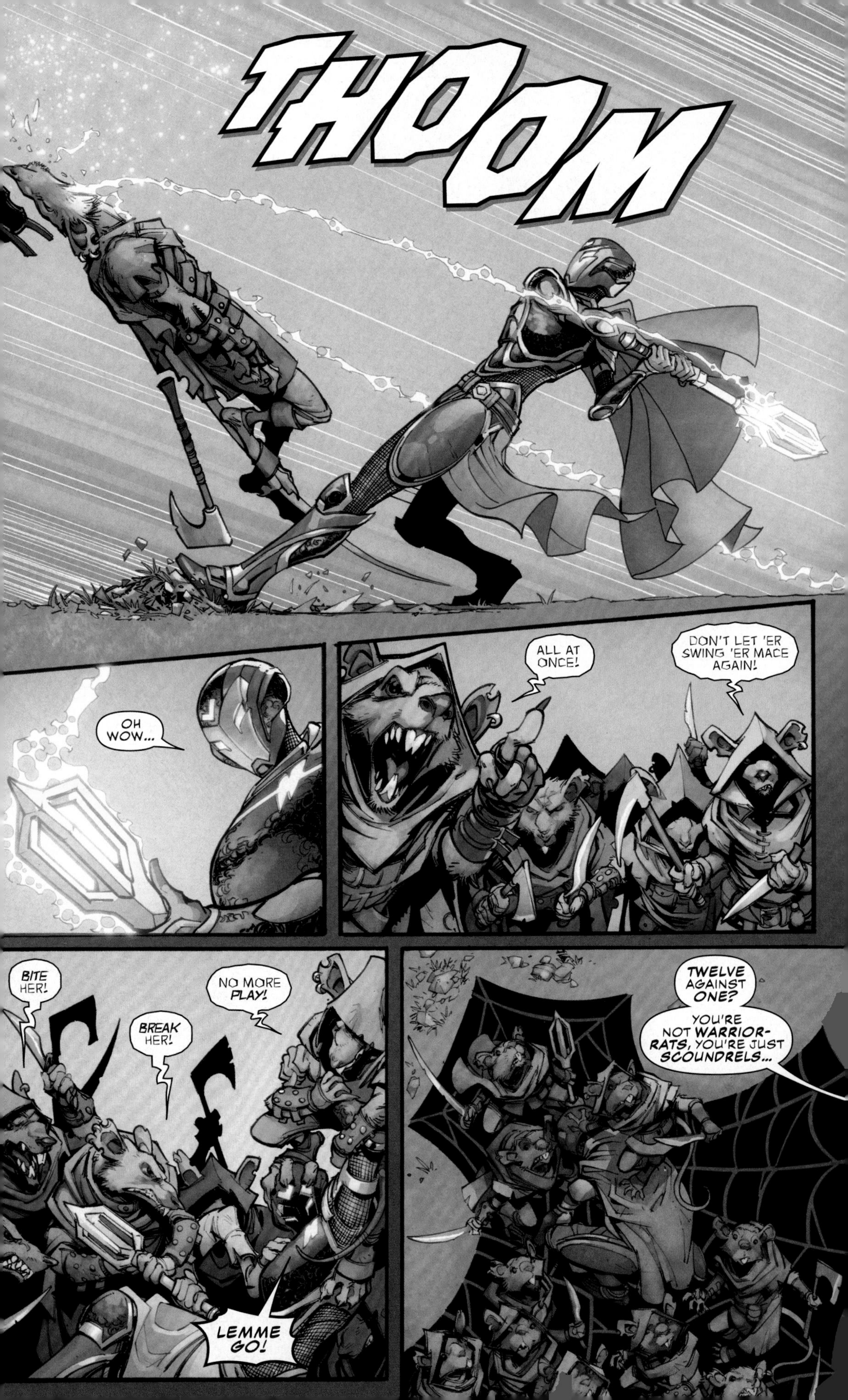
THOOM
OH WOW...
ALL AT ONCE!
DON'T LET 'ER SWING 'ER MACE AGAIN!
BITE HER!
BREAK HER!
NO MORE PLAY!
LEMME GO!
TWELVE AGAINST ONE?
YOU'RE NOT WARRIOR-RATS, YOU'RE JUST SCOUNDRELS...

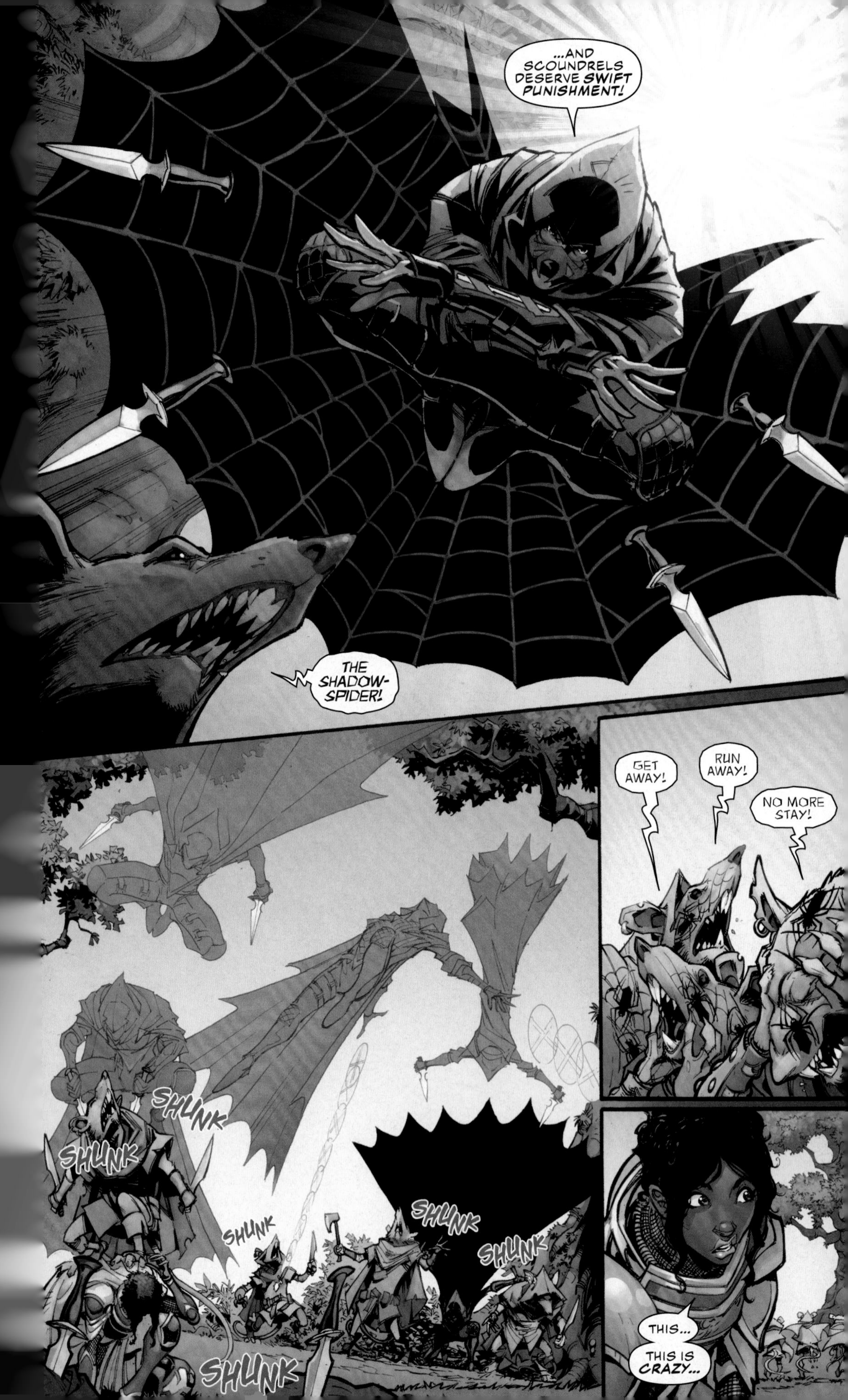
...AND SCOUNDRELS DESERVE SWIFT PUNISHMENT!
THE SHADOW-SPIDER!
SHUNK
SHUNK
SHUNK
SHUNK
SHUNK
SHUNK
GET AWAY!
RUN AWAY!
NO MORE STAY!
THIS...
THIS IS CRAZY...

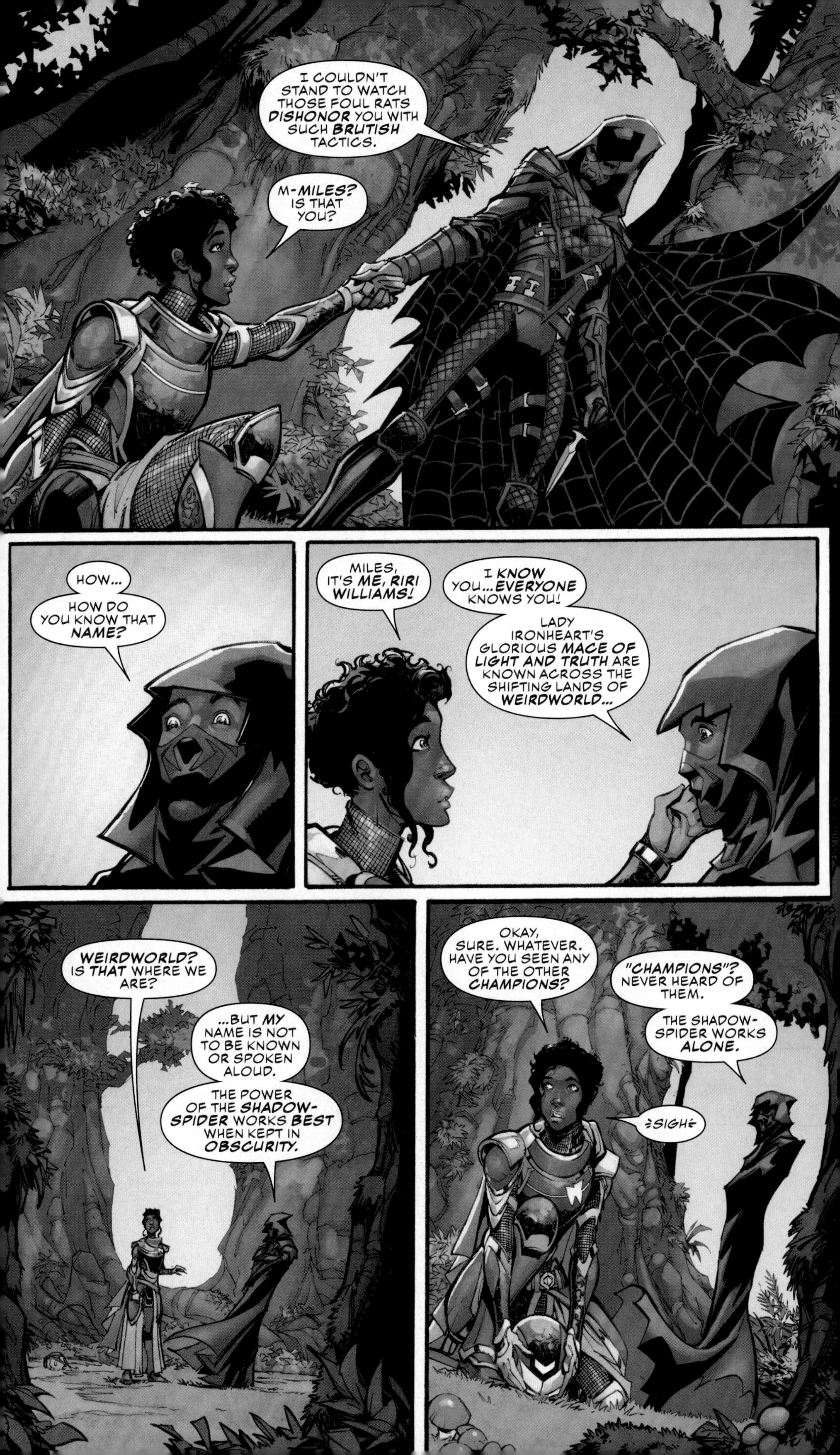
I COULDN'T STAND TO WATCH THOSE FOUL RATS DISHONOR YOU WITH SUCH BRUTISH TACTICS.
M-MILES? IS THAT YOU?
HOW...
HOW DO YOU KNOW THAT NAME?
MILES, IT'S ME, RIRI WILLIAMS!
I KNOW YOU...EVERYONE KNOWS YOU!
LADY IRONHEART'S GLORIOUS MACE OF LIGHT AND TRUTH ARE KNOWN ACROSS THE SHIFTING LANDS OF WEIRDWORLD...
WEIRDWORLD? IS THAT WHERE WE ARE?
...BUT MY NAME IS NOT TO BE KNOWN OR SPOKEN ALOUD.
THE POWER OF THE SHADOW-SPIDER WORKS BEST WHEN KEPT IN OBSCURITY.
OKAY, SURE. WHATEVER. HAVE YOU SEEN ANY OF THE OTHER CHAMPIONS?
"CHAMPIONS"? NEVER HEARD OF THEM.
THE SHADOW-SPIDER WORKS ALONE.
SIGH

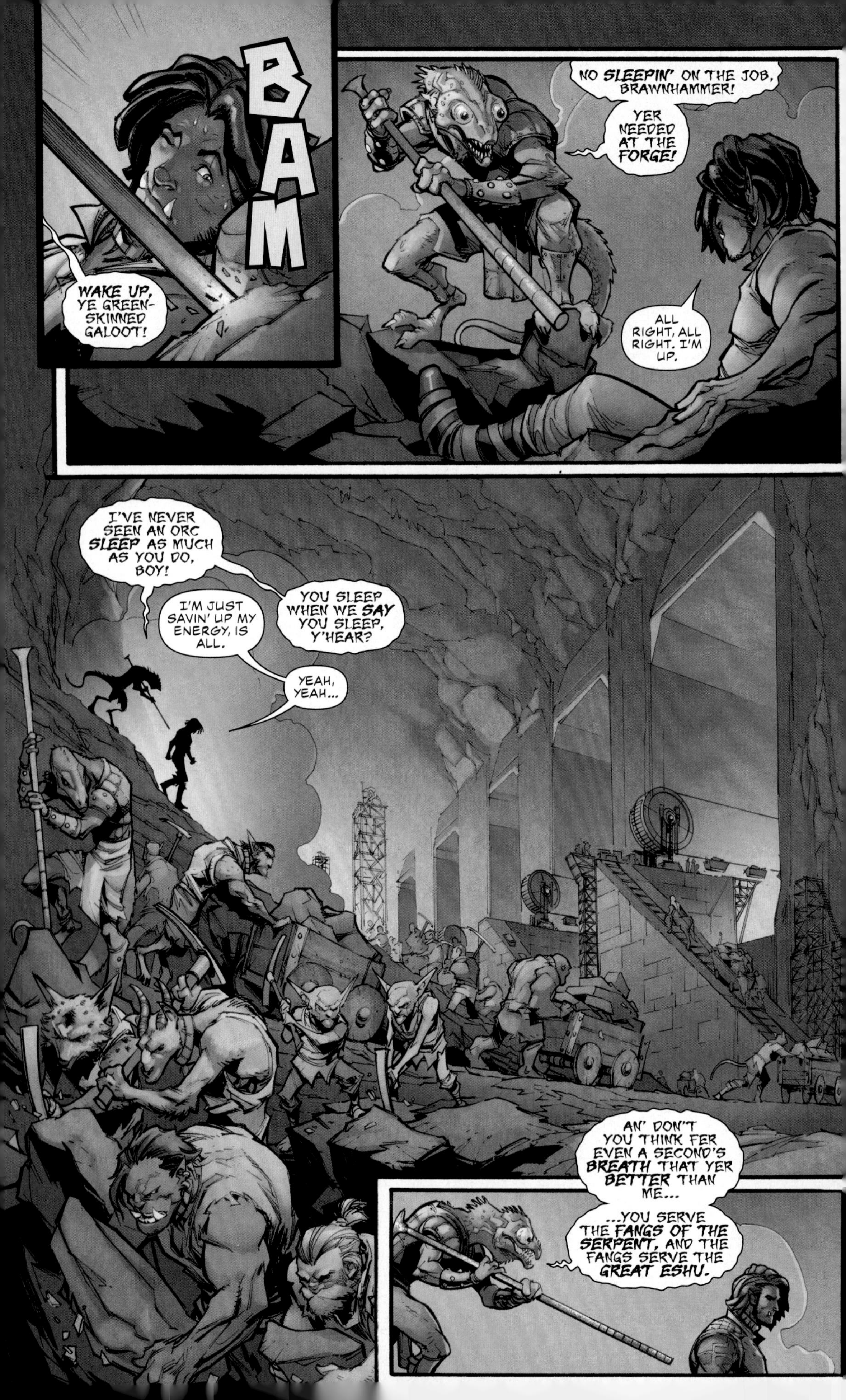
BAM
WAKE UP, YE GREEN-SKINNED GALOOT!
NO SLEEPIN' ON THE JOB, BRAWNHAMMER!
YER NEEDED AT THE FORGE!
ALL RIGHT, ALL RIGHT. I'M UP.
I'VE NEVER SEEN AN ORC SLEEP AS MUCH AS YOU DO, BOY!
I'M JUST SAVIN' UP MY ENERGY, IS ALL.
YOU SLEEP WHEN WE SAY YOU SLEEP, Y'HEAR?
YEAH, YEAH...
AN' DON'T YOU THINK FER EVEN A SECOND'S BREATH THAT YER BETTER THAN ME...
...YOU SERVE THE FANGS OF THE SERPENT, AND THE FANGS SERVE THE GREAT ESHU.

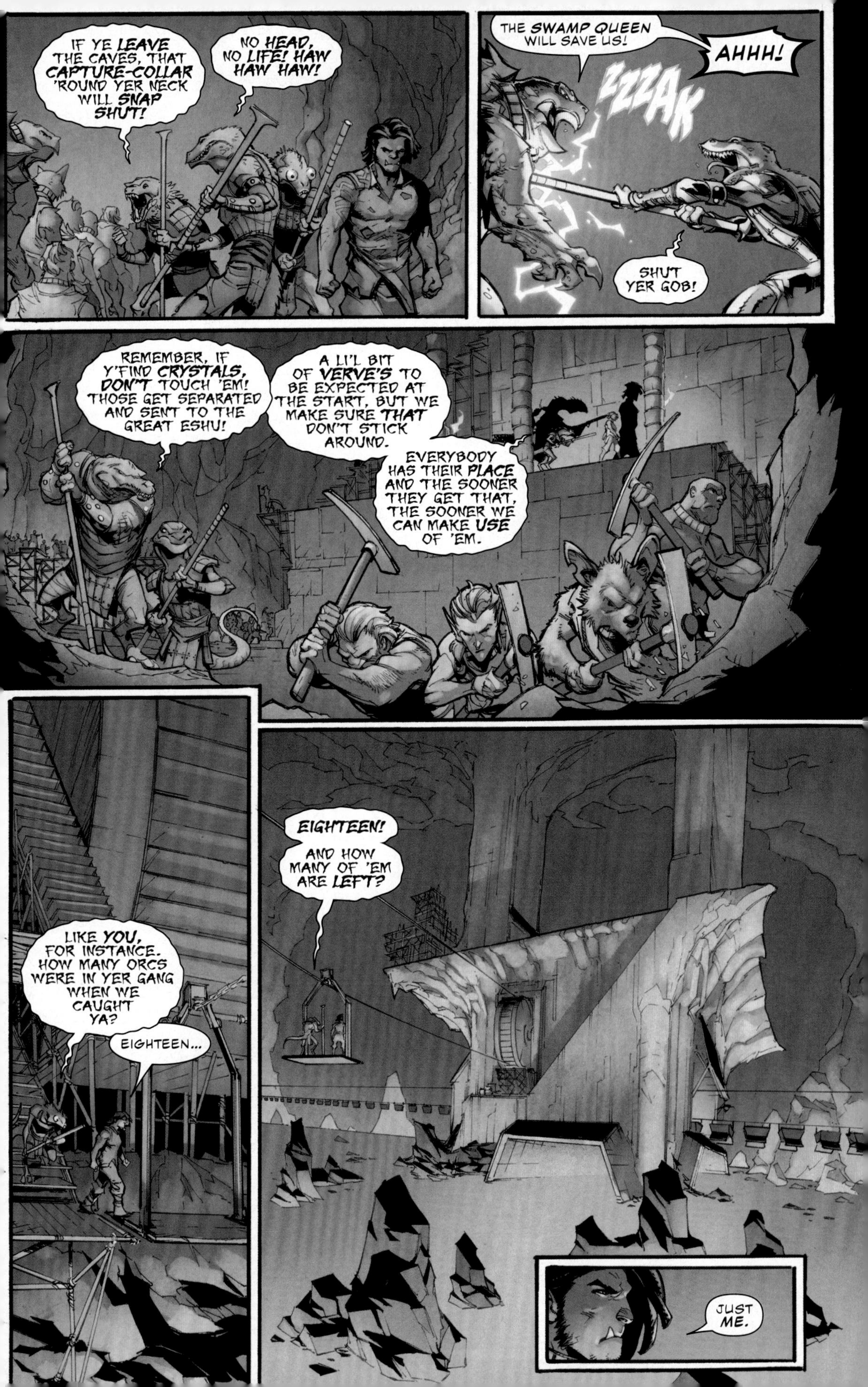

IF YE LEAVE THE CAVES, THAT CAPTURE-COLLAR 'ROUND YER NECK WILL SNAP SHUT!
NO HEAD, NO LIFE! HAW HAW HAW!
THE SWAMP QUEEN WILL SAVE US!
AHHH!
ZZZAK
SHUT YER GOB!
REMEMBER, IF Y'FIND CRYSTALS, DON'T TOUCH 'EM! THOSE GET SEPARATED AND SENT TO THE GREAT ESHU!
A LI'L BIT OF VERVE'S TO BE EXPECTED AT THE START, BUT WE MAKE SURE THAT DON'T STICK AROUND.
EVERYBODY HAS THEIR PLACE AND THE SOONER THEY GET THAT, THE SOONER WE CAN MAKE USE OF 'EM.
LIKE YOU, FOR INSTANCE. HOW MANY ORCS WERE IN YER GANG WHEN WE CAUGHT YA?
EIGHTEEN...
EIGHTEEN!
AND HOW MANY OF 'EM ARE LEFT?
JUST ME.

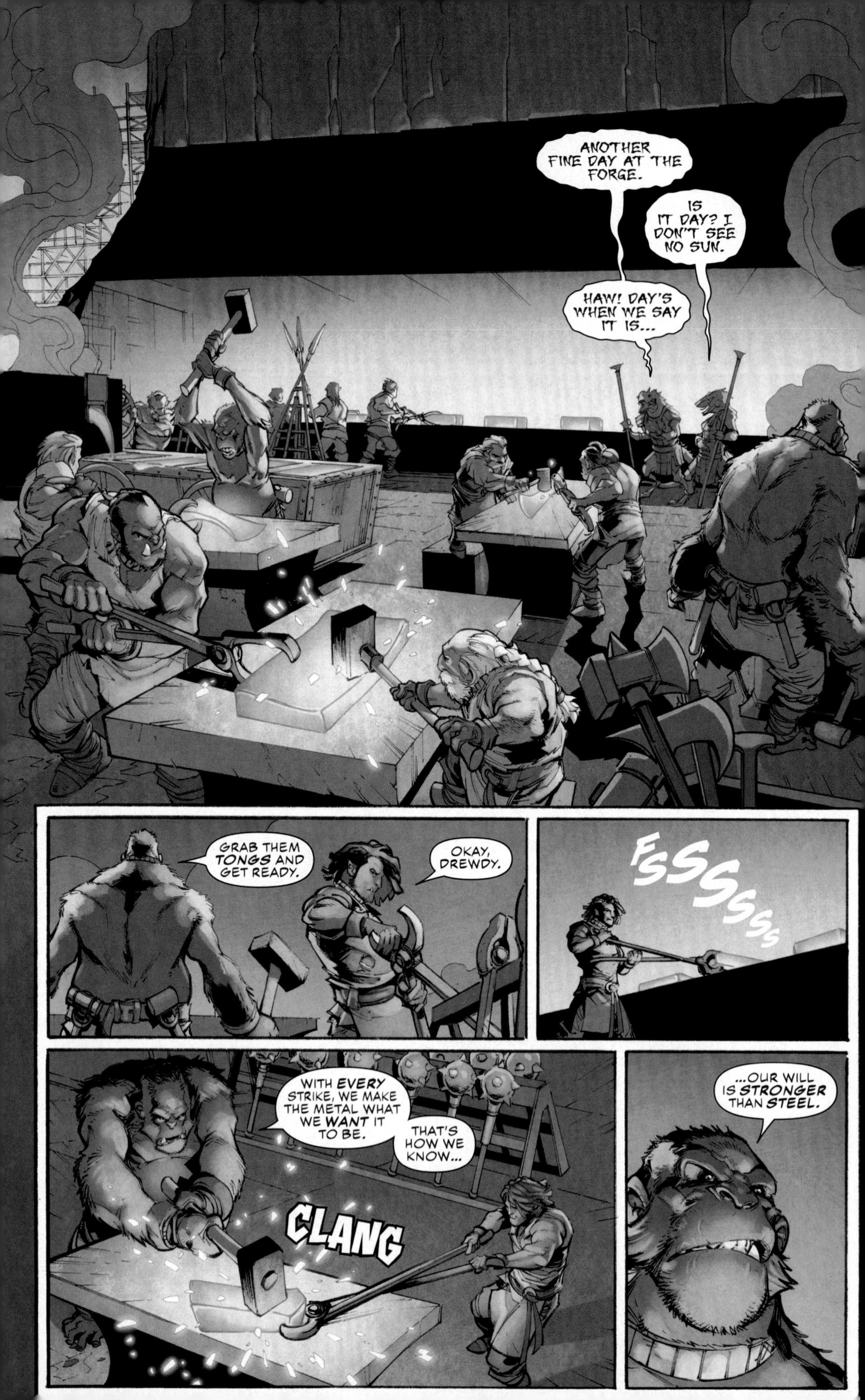
ANOTHER FINE DAY AT THE FORGE.
IS IT DAY? I DON'T SEE NO SUN.
HAW! DAY'S WHEN WE SAY IT IS...
GRAB THEM TONGS AND GET READY.
OKAY, DREWDY.
FSSSSSS
WITH EVERY STRIKE, WE MAKE THE METAL WHAT WE WANT IT TO BE.
THAT'S HOW WE KNOW...
CLANG
...OUR WILL IS STRONGER THAN STEEL.

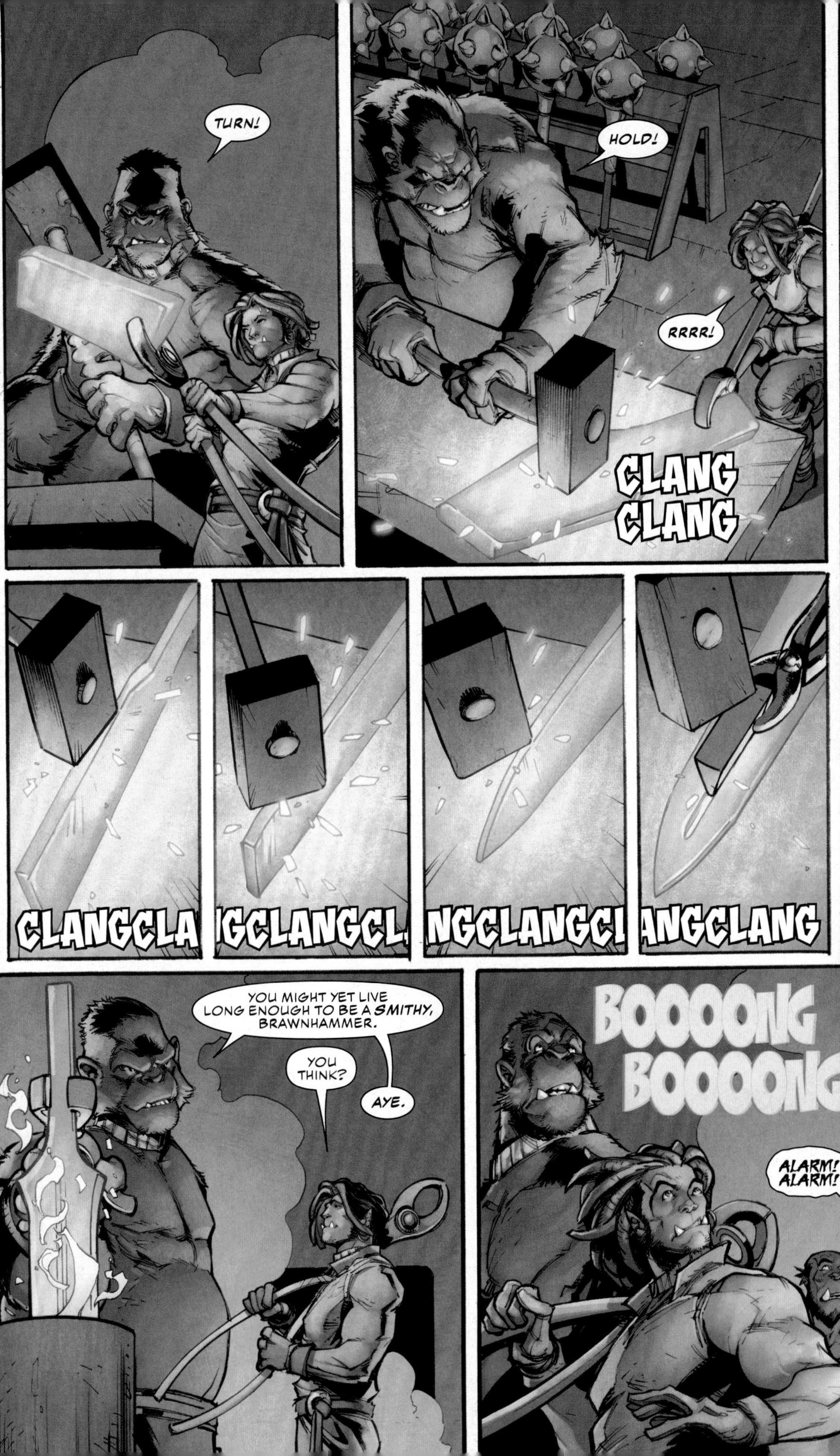
TURN!
HOLD!
RRRR!
CLANG
CLANG
CLANGCLA
IGCLANGCL
NGCLANGCL
ANGCLANG
YOU MIGHT YET LIVE LONG ENOUGH TO BE A SMITHY, BRAWNHAMMER.
YOU THINK?
AYE.
BOOOOONG
BOOOOONG
ALARM! ALARM!

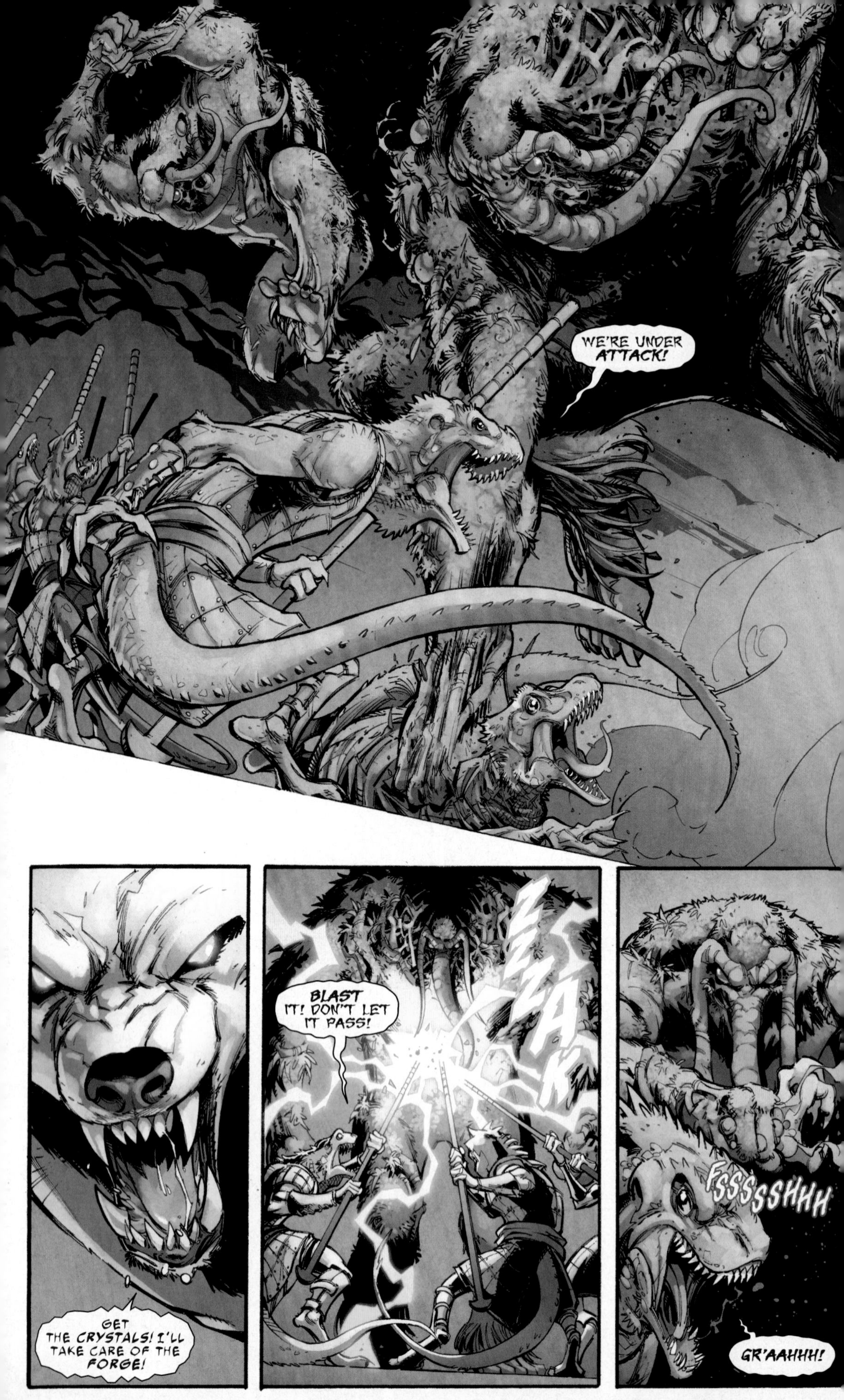
WE'RE UNDER ATTACK!
GET THE CRYSTALS! I'LL TAKE CARE OF THE FORGE!
BLAST IT! DON'T LET IT PASS!
ZZZAK
FSSSSSHHH
GR'AAHHH!

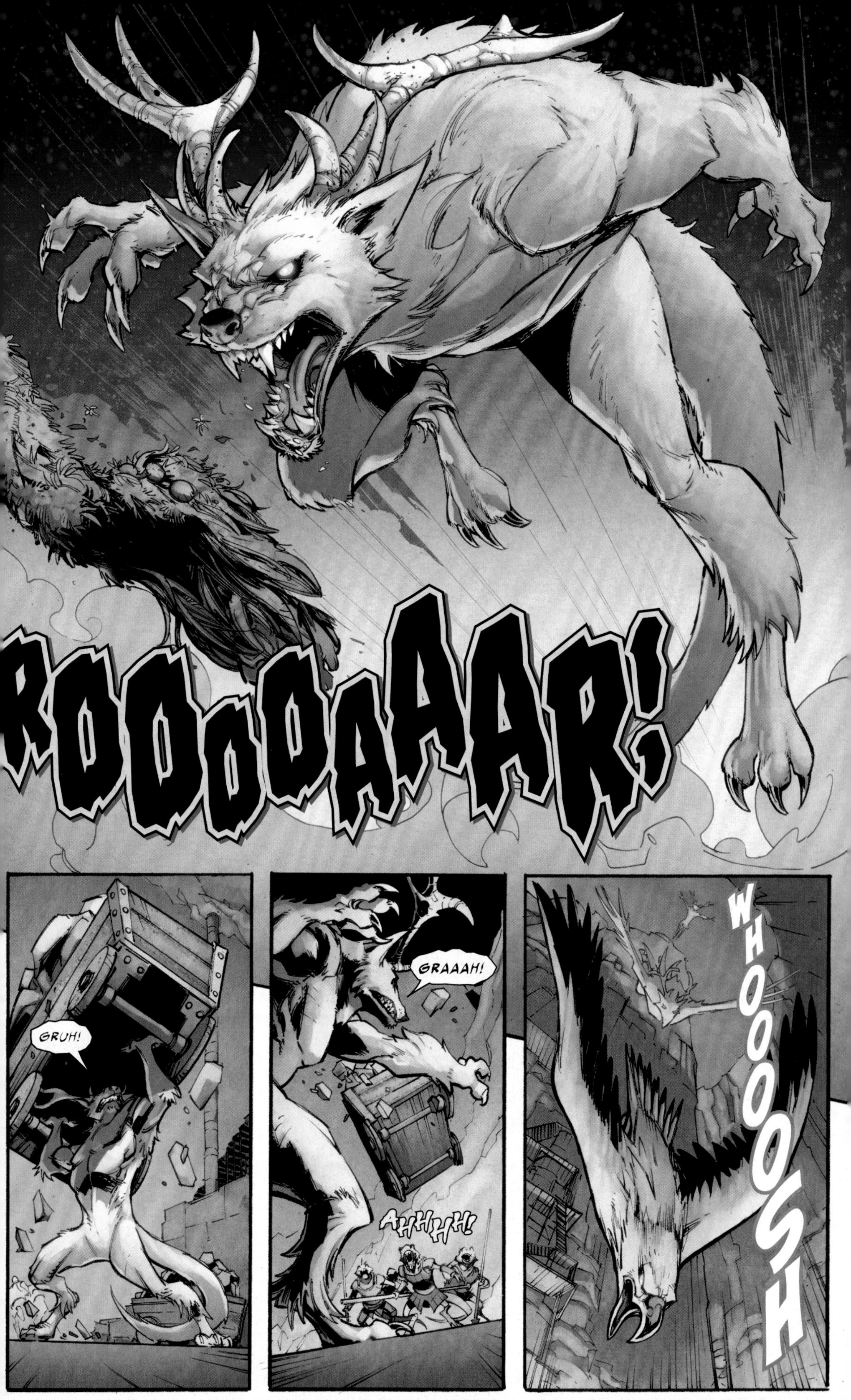

ROOOOAAAR!
GRUH!
GRAAAH!
AHHHHH!
WHOOOOOSH

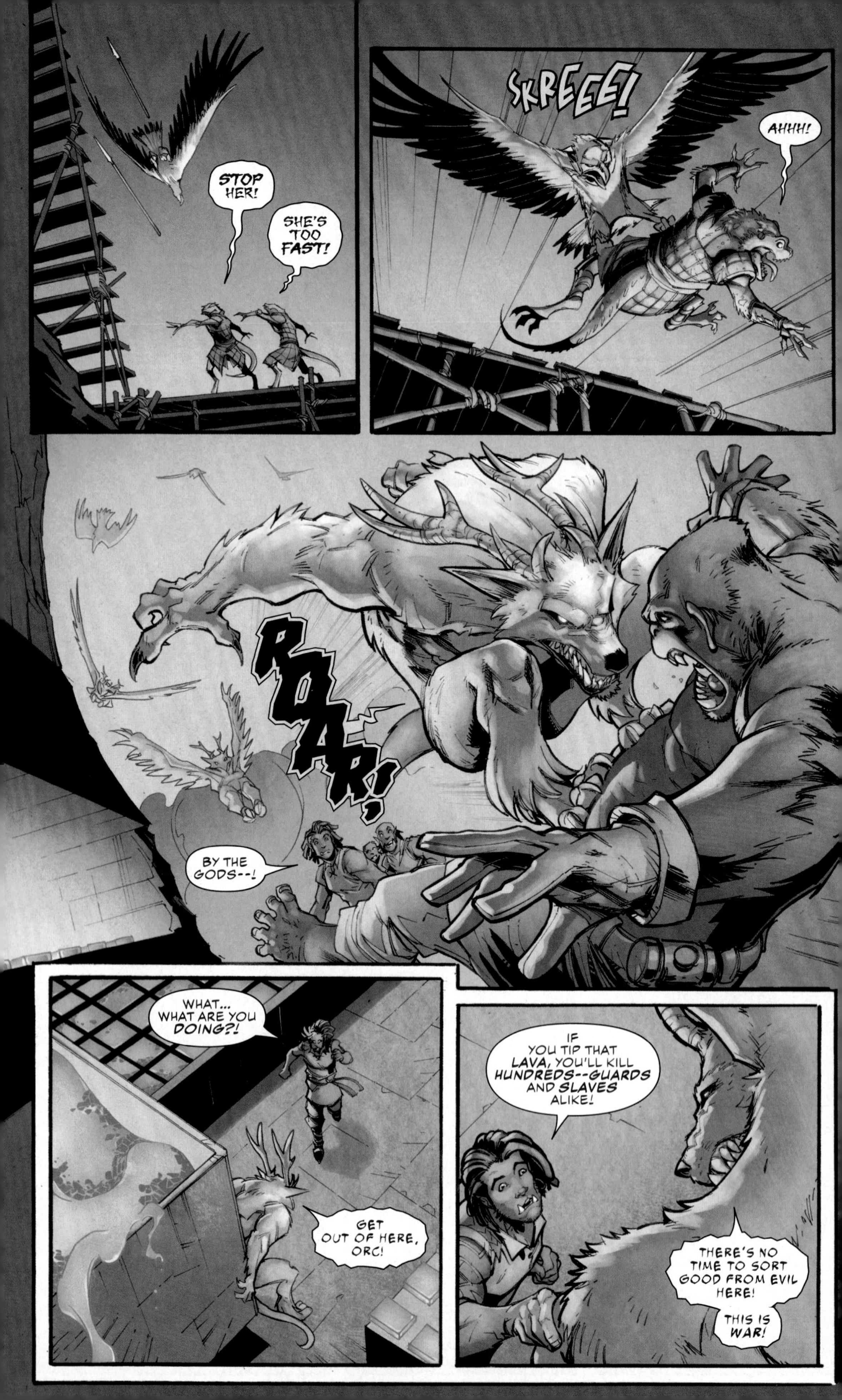
STOP HER!
SHE'S TOO FAST!
SKREEE!
AHHH!
ROAR!
BY THE GODS--!
WHAT... WHAT ARE YOU DOING?!
GET OUT OF HERE, ORC!
IF YOU TIP THAT LAVA, YOU'LL KILL HUNDREDS--GUARDS AND SLAVES ALIKE!
THERE'S NO TIME TO SORT GOOD FROM EVIL HERE!
THIS IS WAR!

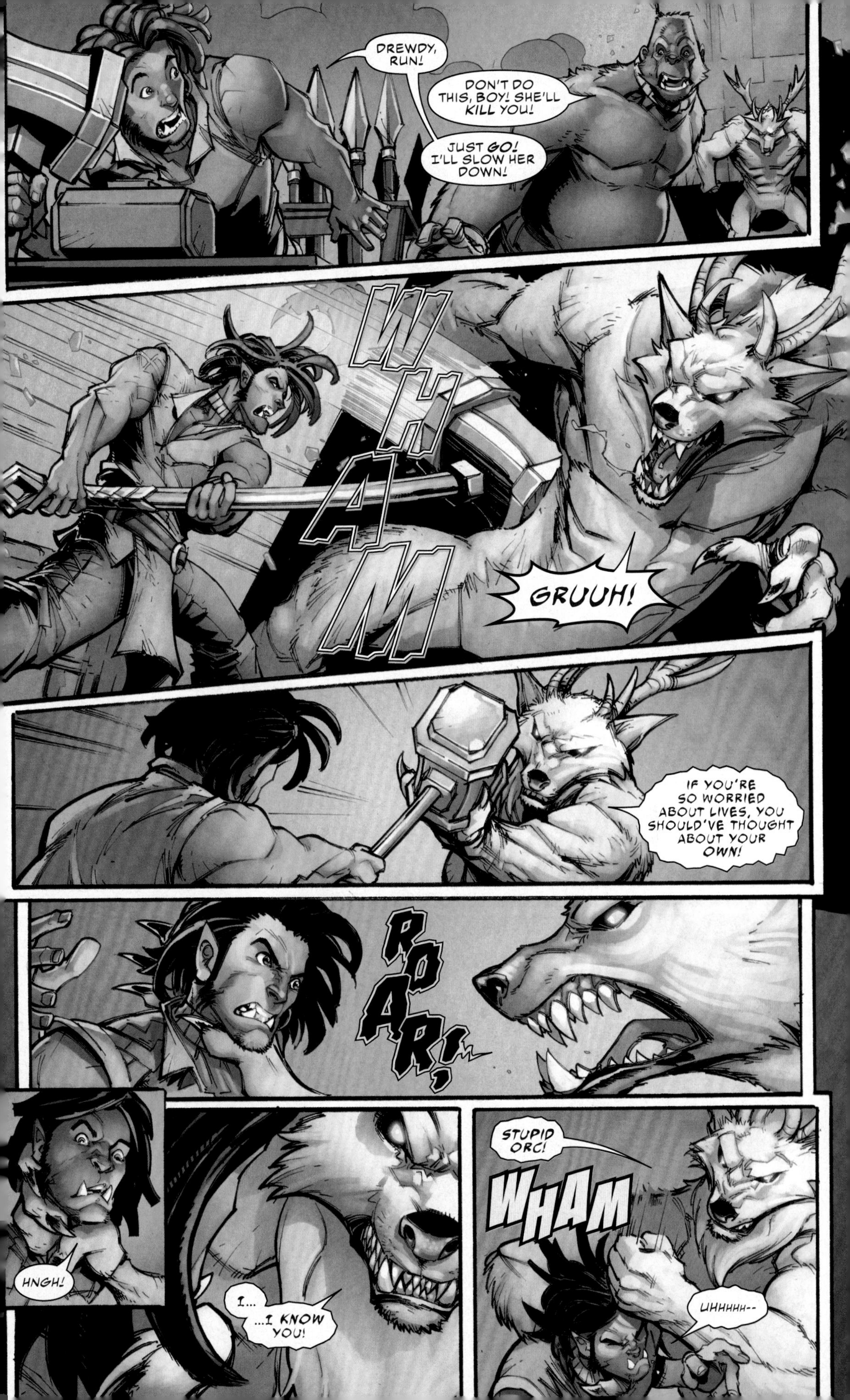
DREWDY, RUN!
DON'T DO THIS, BOY! SHE'LL KILL YOU!
JUST GO! I'LL SLOW HER DOWN!
WHAM
GRUUH!
IF YOU'RE SO WORRIED ABOUT LIVES, YOU SHOULD'VE THOUGHT ABOUT YOUR OWN!
ROAR!
HNGH!
I...
...I KNOW YOU!
STUPID ORC!
WHAM
UHHHHH--

THE FORGE IS BROKEN AND THEIR LATEST CRYSTAL HAUL IS OURS.

WELL DONE, SISTER.

WHO IS *THIS*?

AN ORC SLAVE, BUT THERE'S SOMETHING *FAMILIAR* ABOUT HIM...

URK!

COLLAR... TIGHT...

...CAN'T... *BREATHE*!

SISTER, YOU FORGOT ABOUT HIS *CAPURE-COLLAR*. IT'S *KILLING* HIM...

OOPS!

BR₹RFMR

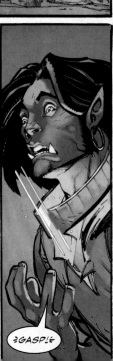

≥GASP!≤

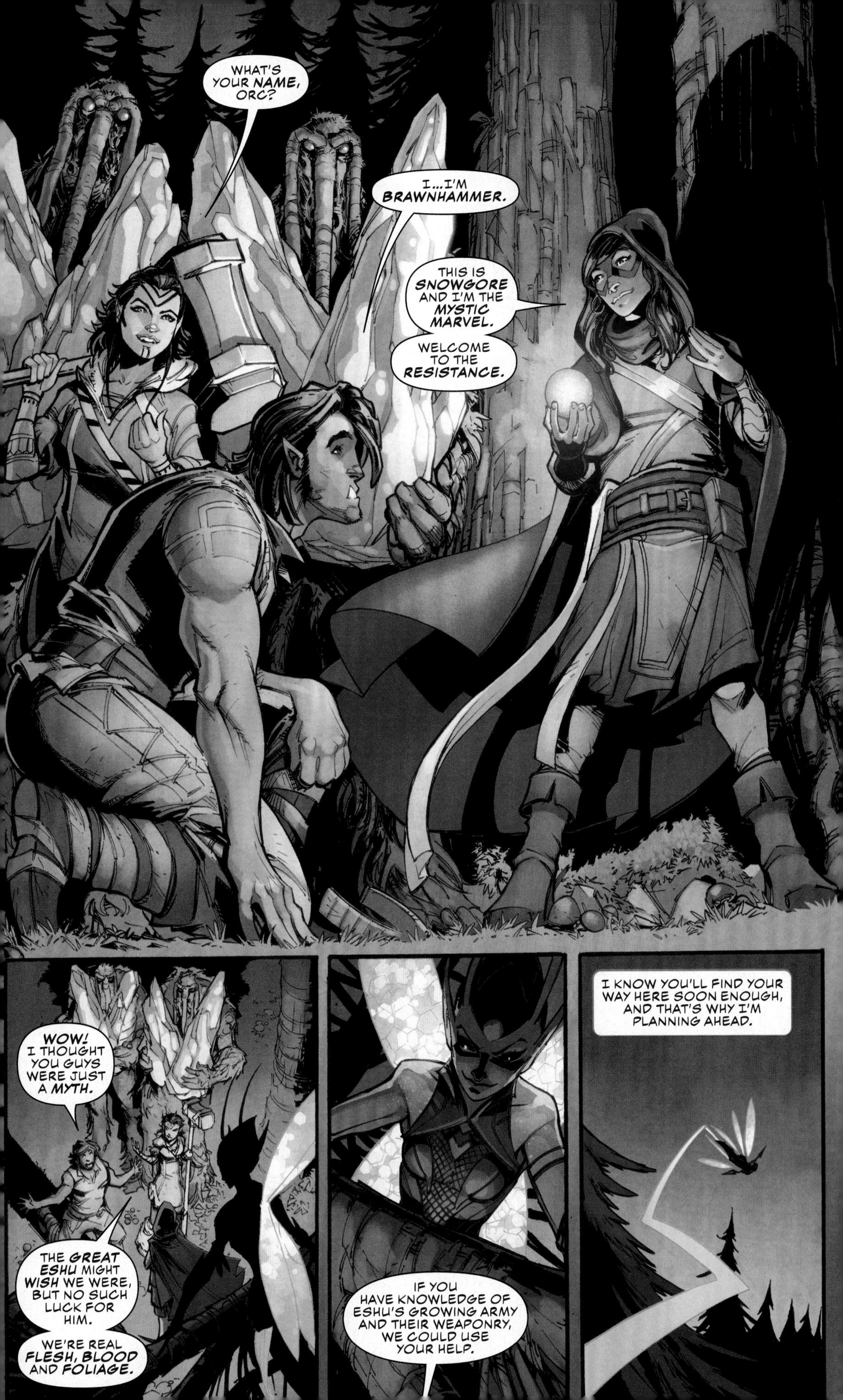
WHAT'S YOUR NAME, ORC?
I...I'M BRAWNHAMMER.
THIS IS SNOWGORE AND I'M THE MYSTIC MARVEL.
WELCOME TO THE RESISTANCE.
WOW! I THOUGHT YOU GUYS WERE JUST A MYTH.
THE GREAT ESHU MIGHT WISH WE WERE, BUT NO SUCH LUCK FOR HIM.
WE'RE REAL FLESH, BLOOD AND FOLIAGE.
IF YOU HAVE KNOWLEDGE OF ESHU'S GROWING ARMY AND THEIR WEAPONRY, WE COULD USE YOUR HELP.
I KNOW YOU'LL FIND YOUR WAY HERE SOON ENOUGH, AND THAT'S WHY I'M PLANNING AHEAD.

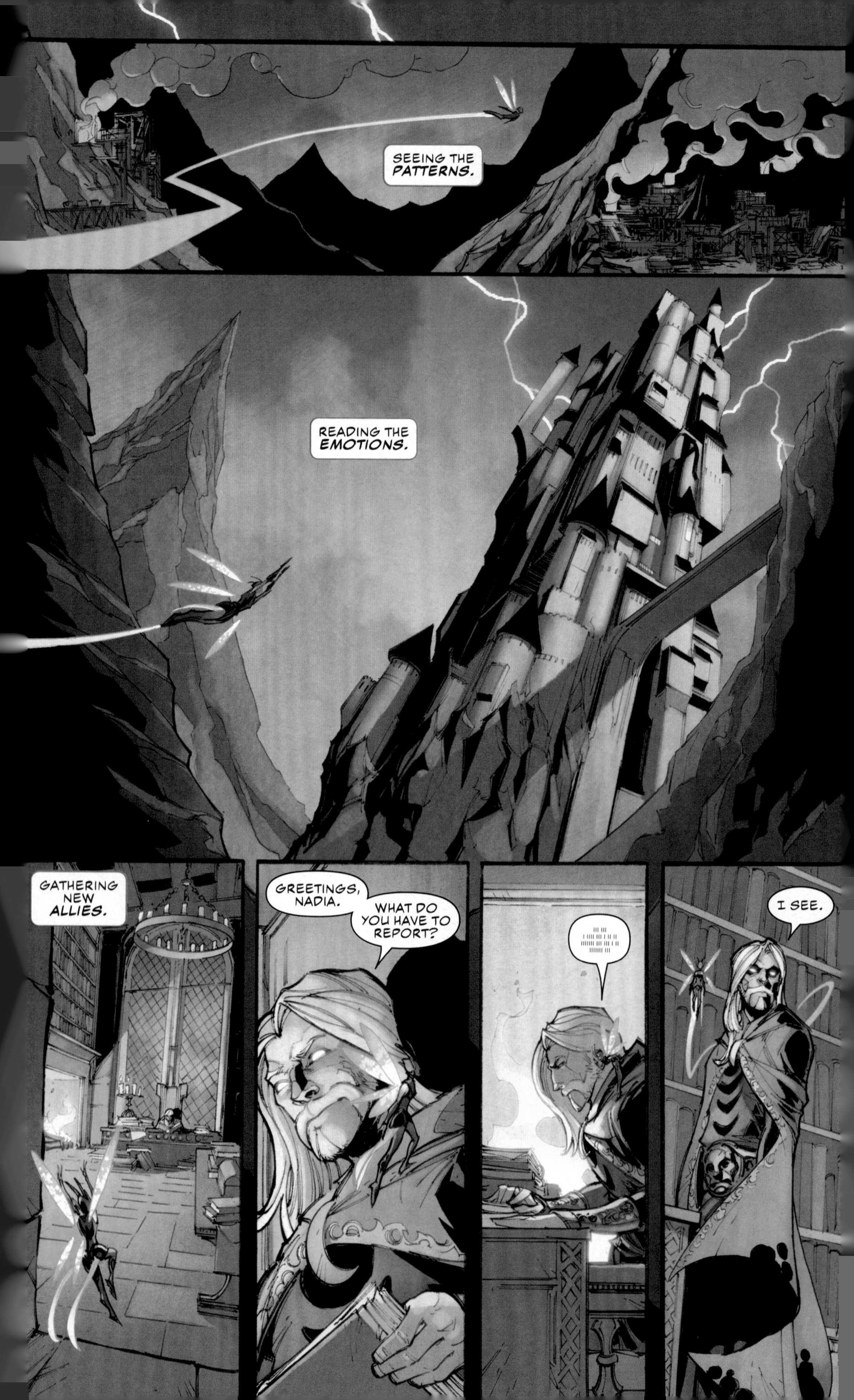
SEEING THE PATTERNS.
READING THE EMOTIONS.
GATHERING NEW ALLIES.
GREETINGS, NADIA.
WHAT DO YOU HAVE TO REPORT?
I SEE.

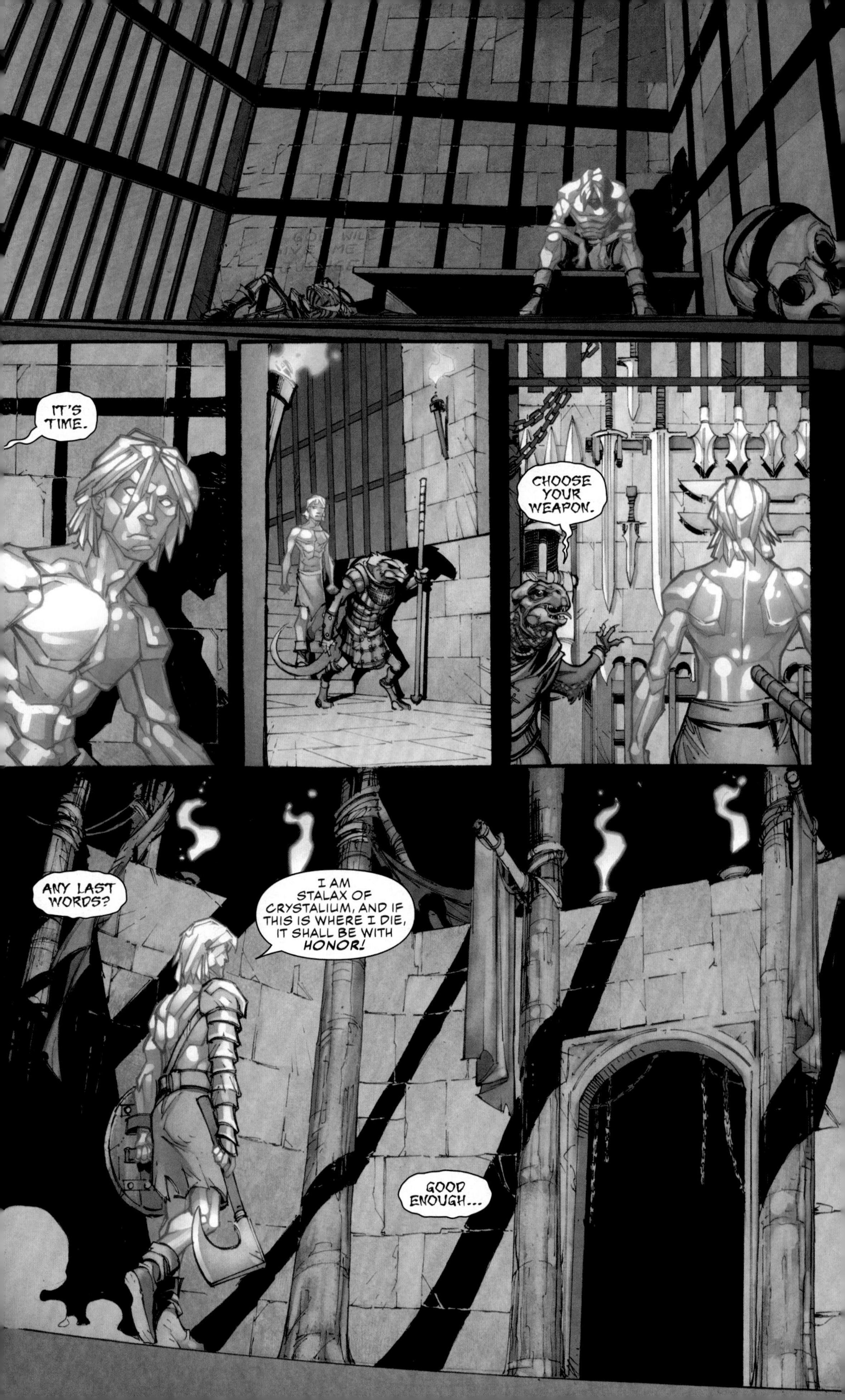
IT'S TIME.
CHOOSE YOUR WEAPON.
ANY LAST WORDS?
I AM STALAX OF CRYSTALIUM, AND IF THIS IS WHERE I DIE, IT SHALL BE WITH HONOR!
GOOD ENOUGH...

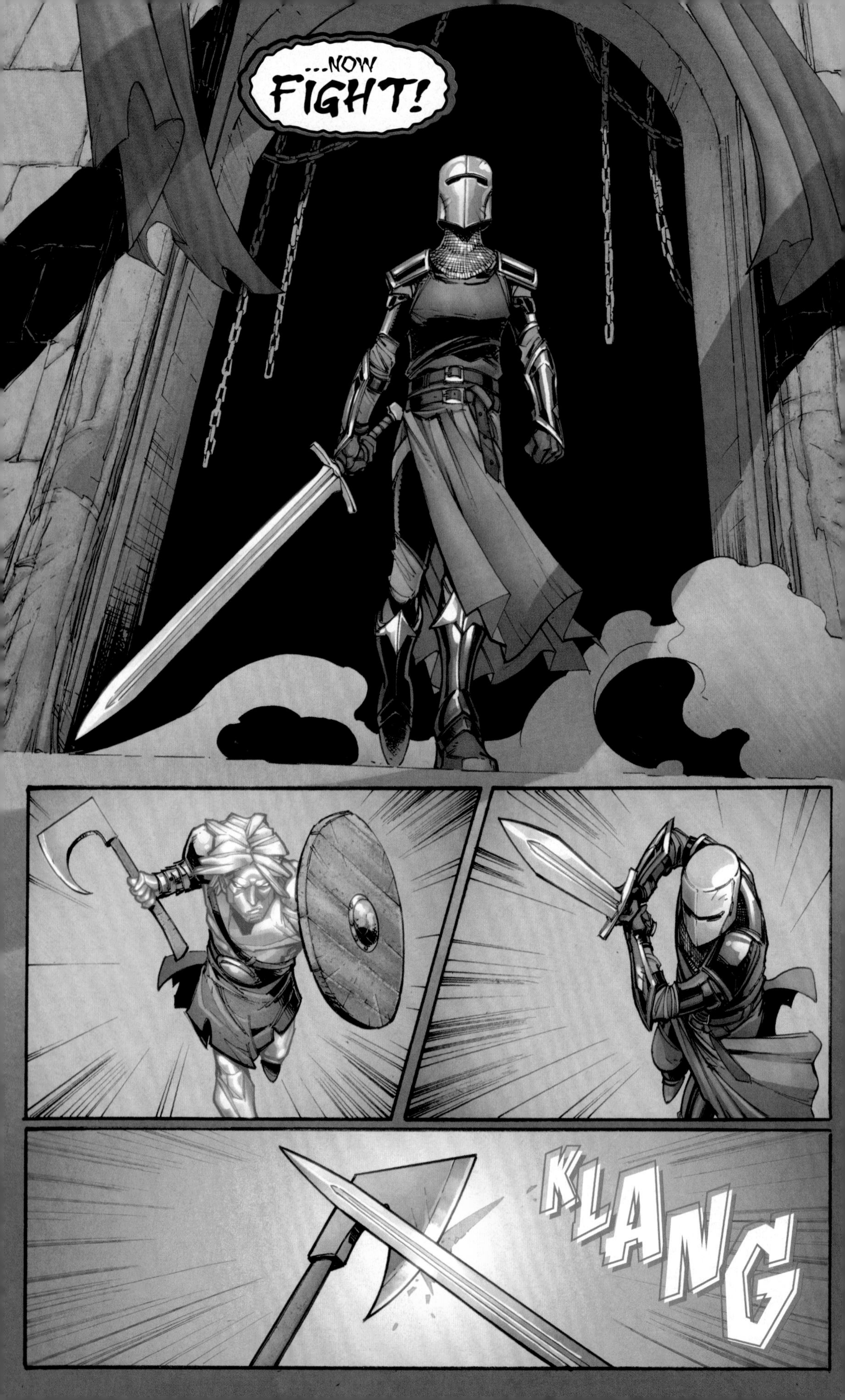
...NOW FIGHT!
KLANG

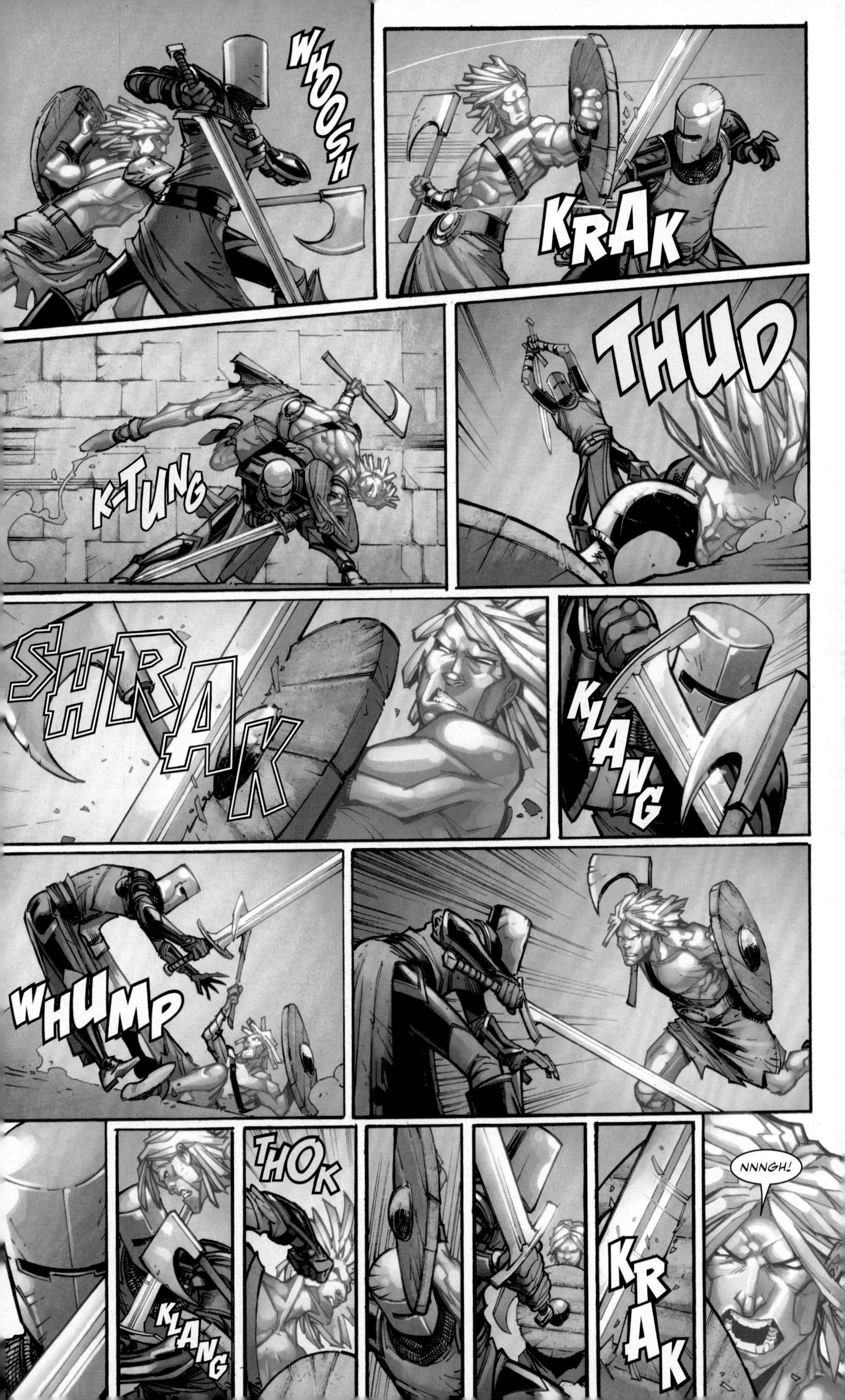
WHOOOSH
KRAK
K-TUNG
THUD
SHRAK
KLANG
WHUMP
KLANG
THOK
KRAK
NNNGH!

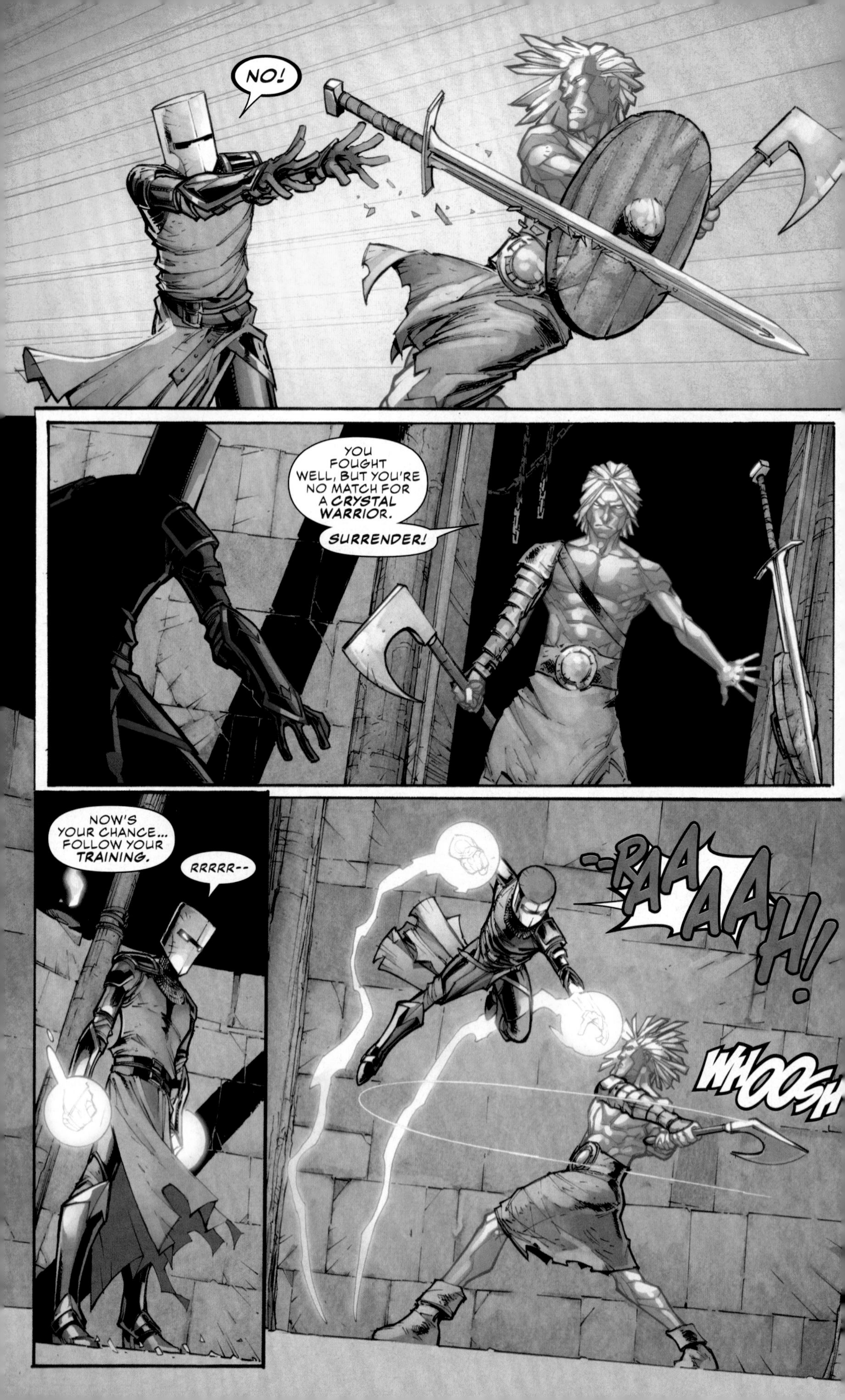
NO!
YOU FOUGHT WELL, BUT YOU'RE NO MATCH FOR A CRYSTAL WARRIOR.
SURRENDER!
NOW'S YOUR CHANCE... FOLLOW YOUR TRAINING.
RRRRR--
--RAAAAAH!
WHOOSH

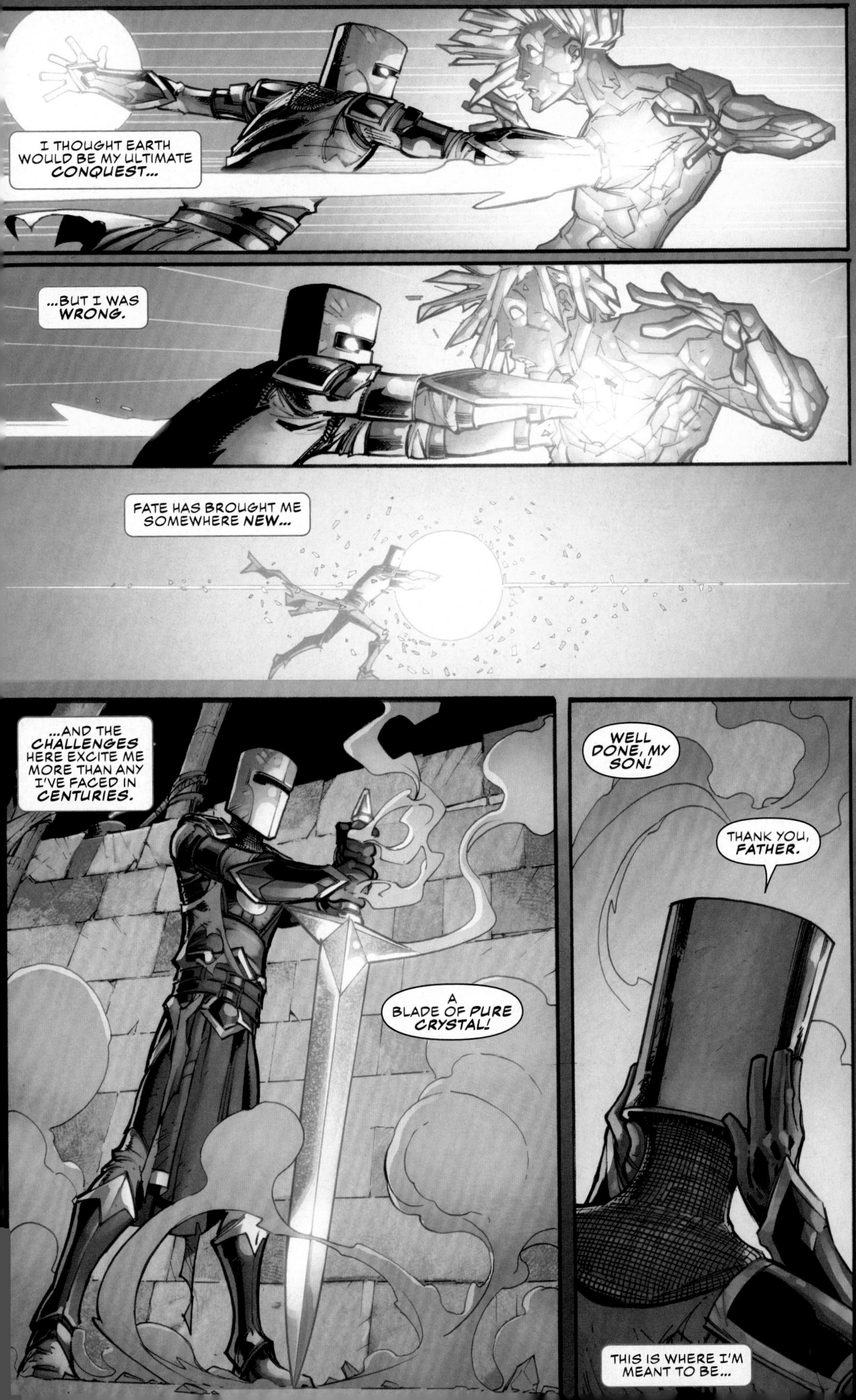
I THOUGHT EARTH WOULD BE MY ULTIMATE CONQUEST...
...BUT I WAS WRONG.
FATE HAS BROUGHT ME SOMEWHERE NEW...
...AND THE CHALLENGES HERE EXCITE ME MORE THAN ANY I'VE FACED IN CENTURIES.
A BLADE OF PURE CRYSTAL!
WELL DONE, MY SON!
THANK YOU, FATHER.
THIS IS WHERE I'M MEANT TO BE...

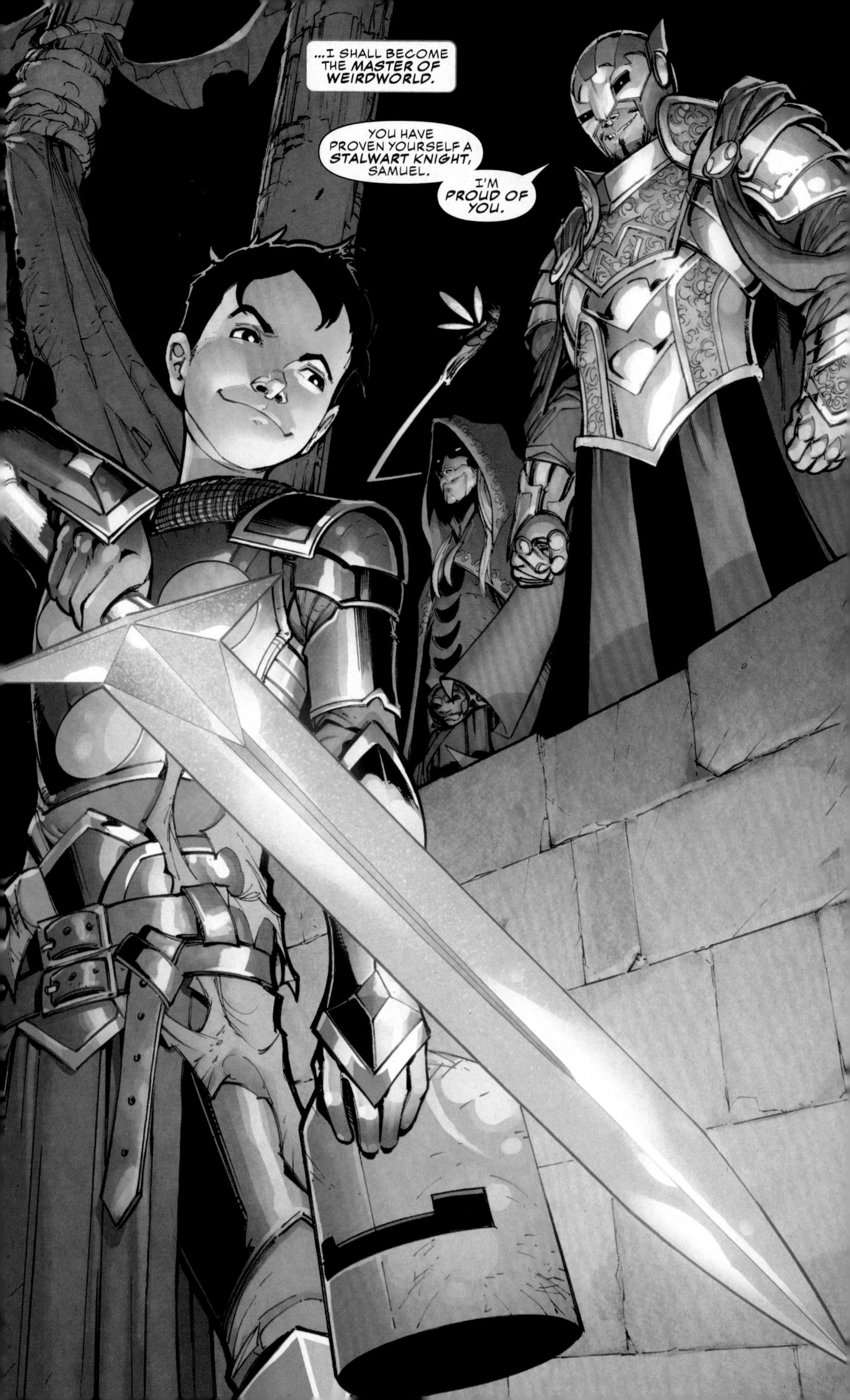
...I SHALL BECOME THE MASTER OF WEIRDWORLD.
YOU HAVE PROVEN YOURSELF A STALWART KNIGHT, SAMUEL.
I'M PROUD OF YOU.

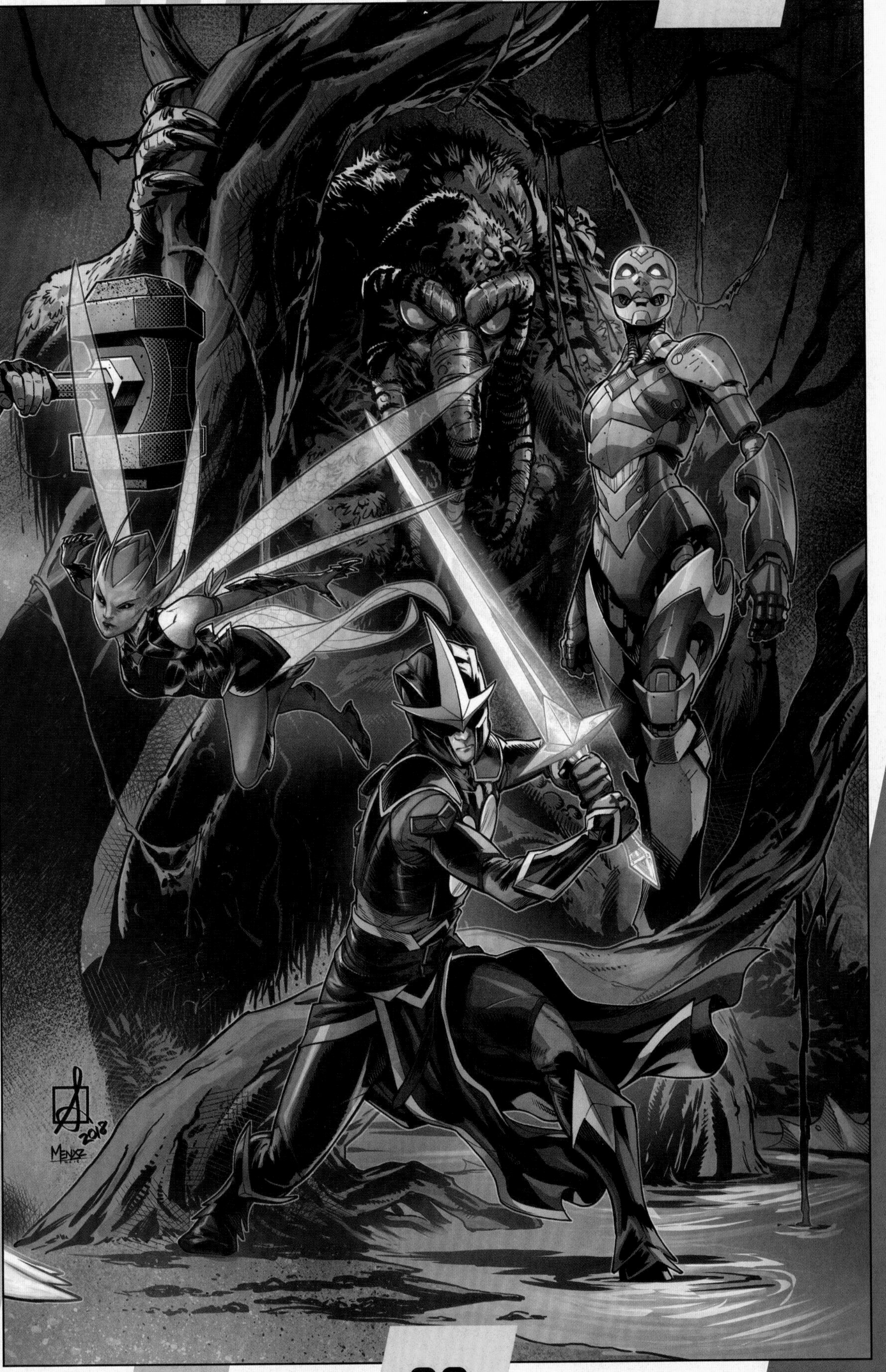

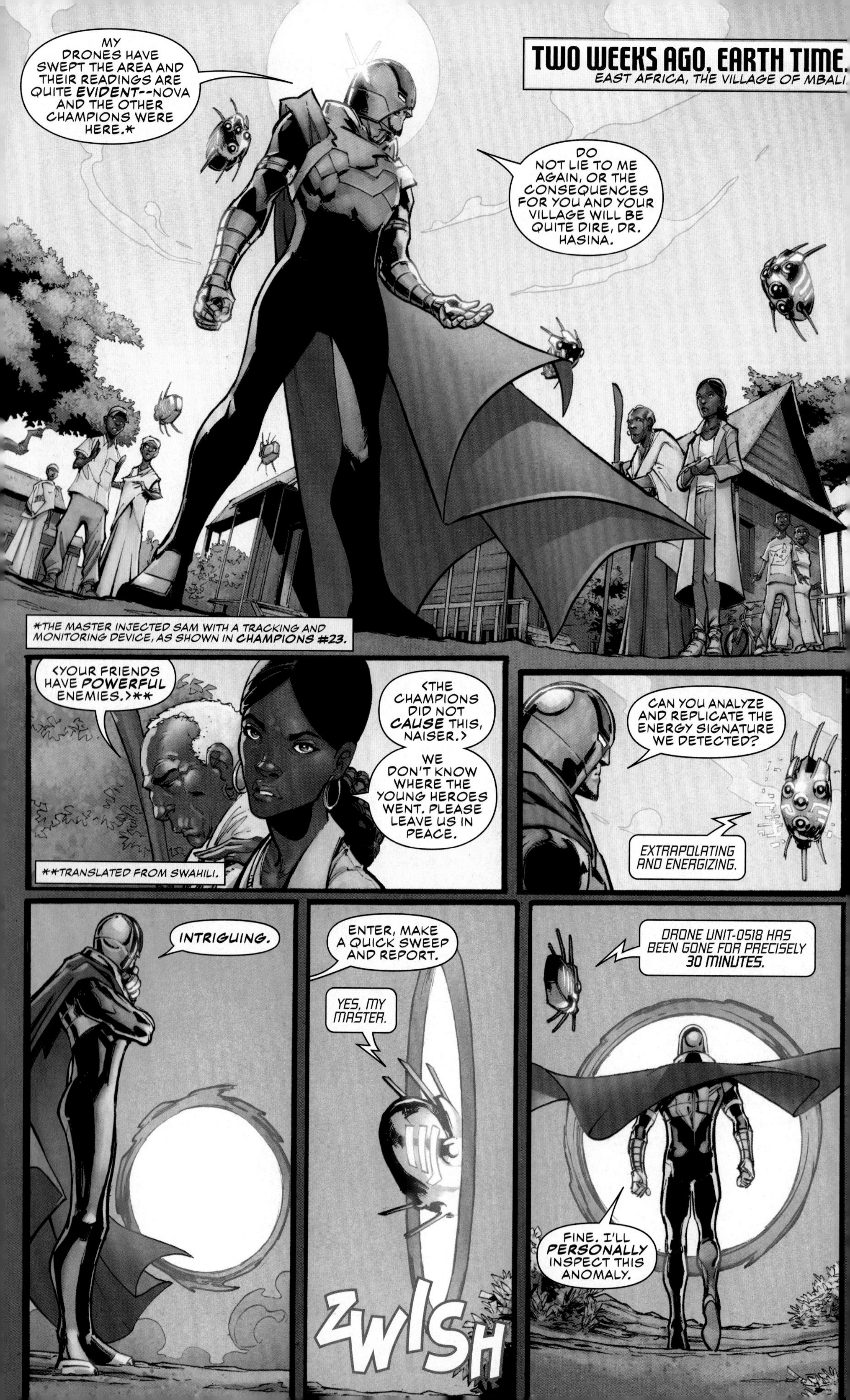
TWO WEEKS AGO, EARTH TIME.
EAST AFRICA, THE VILLAGE OF MBALI
MY DRONES HAVE SWEPT THE AREA AND THEIR READINGS ARE QUITE EVIDENT--NOVA AND THE OTHER CHAMPIONS WERE HERE.*
DO NOT LIE TO ME AGAIN, OR THE CONSEQUENCES FOR YOU AND YOUR VILLAGE WILL BE QUITE DIRE, DR. HASINA.
*THE MASTER INJECTED SAM WITH A TRACKING AND MONITORING DEVICE, AS SHOWN IN CHAMPIONS #23.
<YOUR FRIENDS HAVE POWERFUL ENEMIES.>**
<THE CHAMPIONS DID NOT CAUSE THIS, NAISER.>
WE DON'T KNOW WHERE THE YOUNG HEROES WENT. PLEASE LEAVE US IN PEACE.
**TRANSLATED FROM SWAHILI.
CAN YOU ANALYZE AND REPLICATE THE ENERGY SIGNATURE WE DETECTED?
EXTRAPOLATING AND ENERGIZING.
INTRIGUING.
ENTER, MAKE A QUICK SWEEP AND REPORT.
YES, MY MASTER.
ZWISH
DRONE UNIT-0518 HAS BEEN GONE FOR PRECISELY 30 MINUTES.
FINE. I'LL PERSONALLY INSPECT THIS ANOMALY.

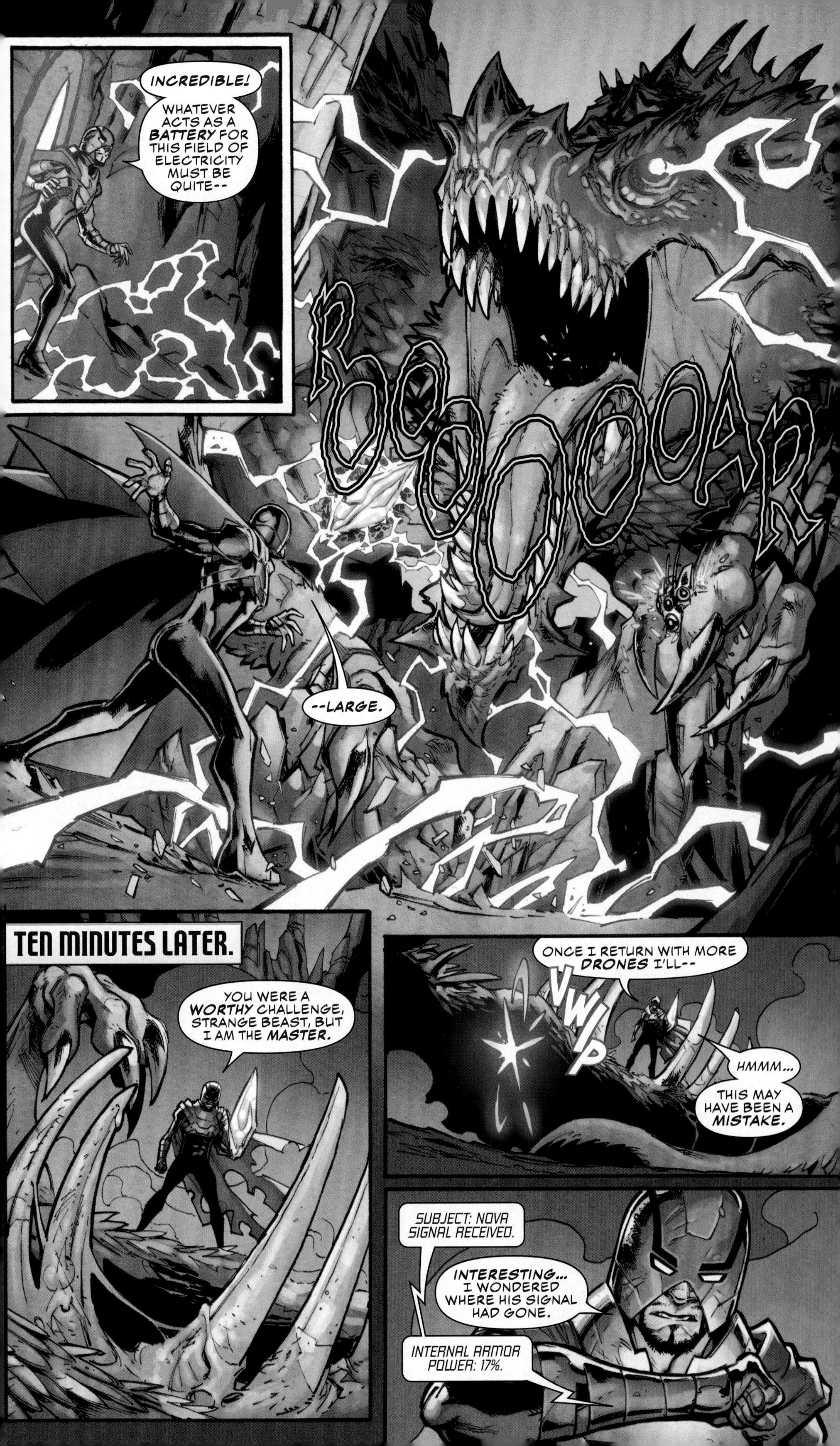

INCREDIBLE!
WHATEVER ACTS AS A BATTERY FOR THIS FIELD OF ELECTRICITY MUST BE QUITE--
ROOOOOOOAR
--LARGE.
TEN MINUTES LATER.
YOU WERE A WORTHY CHALLENGE, STRANGE BEAST, BUT I AM THE MASTER.
ONCE I RETURN WITH MORE DRONES I'LL--
VWIP
HMMM...
THIS MAY HAVE BEEN A MISTAKE.
SUBJECT: NOVA SIGNAL RECEIVED.
INTERESTING... I WONDERED WHERE HIS SIGNAL HAD GONE.
INTERNAL ARMOR POWER: 17%.

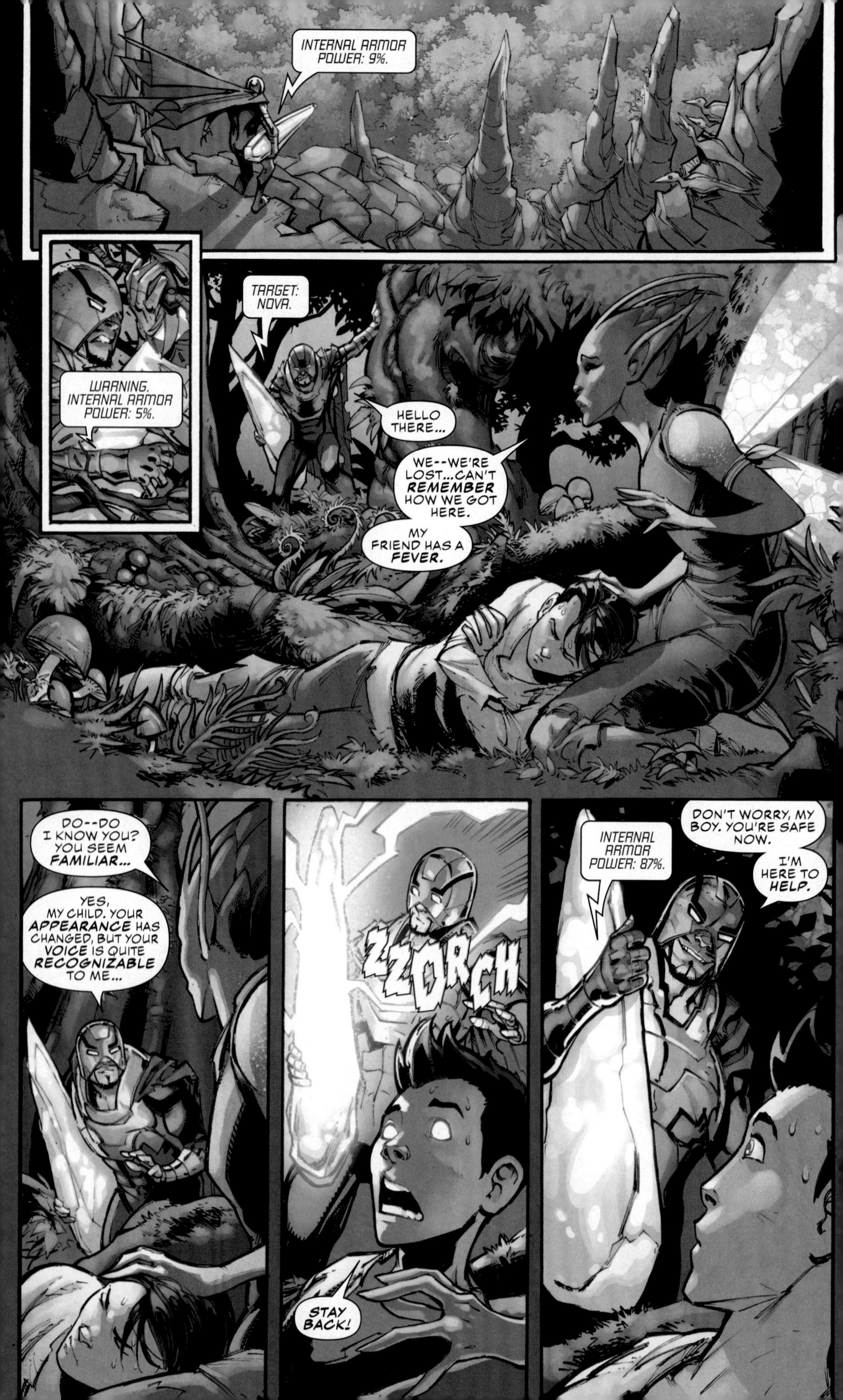
INTERNAL ARMOR POWER: 9%.
WARNING. INTERNAL ARMOR POWER: 5%.
TARGET: NOVA.
HELLO THERE...
WE--WE'RE LOST...CAN'T REMEMBER HOW WE GOT HERE.
MY FRIEND HAS A FEVER.
DO--DO I KNOW YOU? YOU SEEM FAMILIAR...
YES, MY CHILD. YOUR APPEARANCE HAS CHANGED, BUT YOUR VOICE IS QUITE RECOGNIZABLE TO ME...
ZZORCH
STAY BACK!
INTERNAL ARMOR POWER: 87%.
DON'T WORRY, MY BOY. YOU'RE SAFE NOW.
I'M HERE TO HELP.

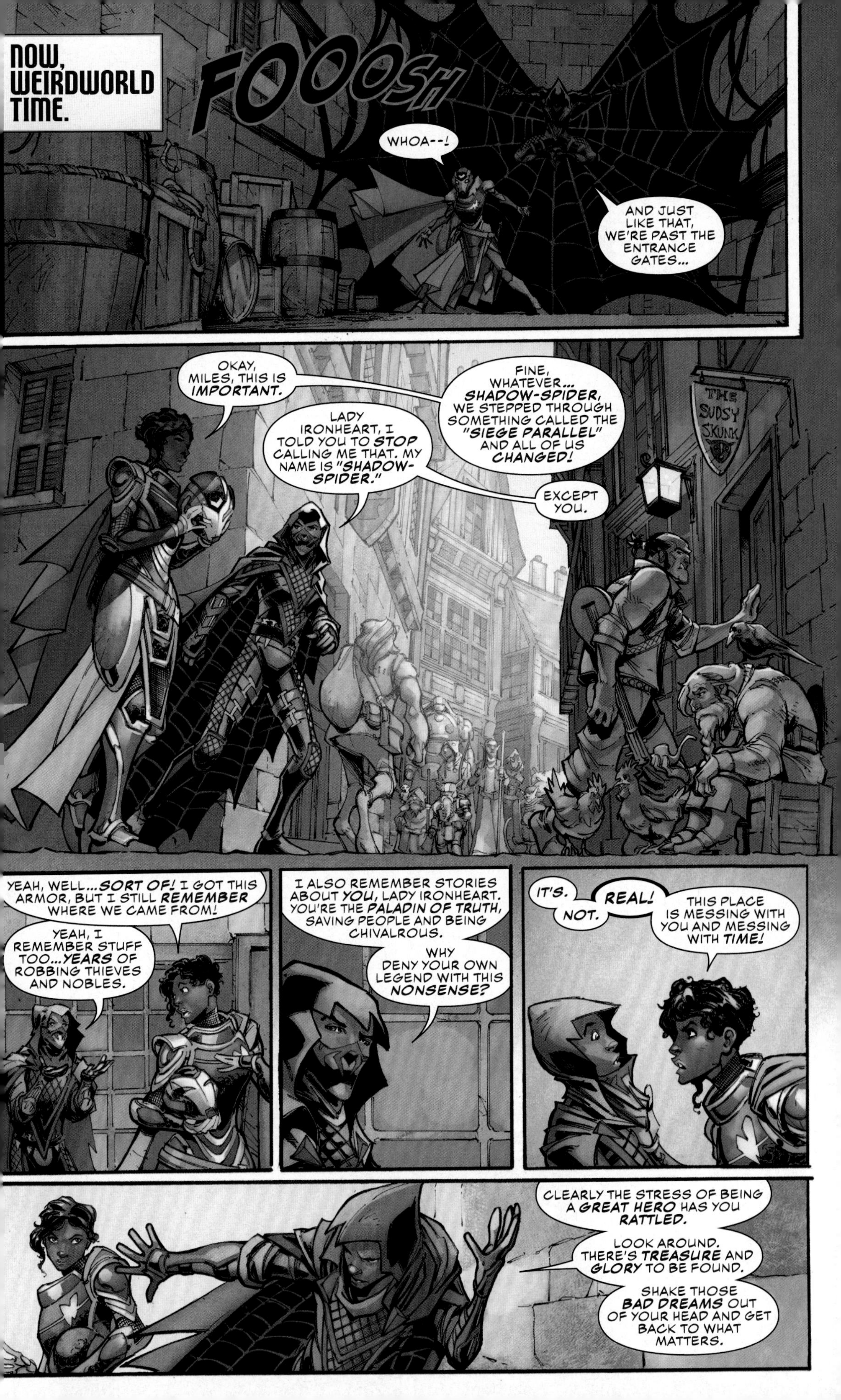
NOW, WEIRDWORLD TIME.
FOOOSH
WHOA--!
AND JUST LIKE THAT, WE'RE PAST THE ENTRANCE GATES...
OKAY, MILES, THIS IS IMPORTANT.
LADY IRONHEART, I TOLD YOU TO STOP CALLING ME THAT. MY NAME IS "SHADOW-SPIDER."
FINE, WHATEVER... SHADOW-SPIDER, WE STEPPED THROUGH SOMETHING CALLED THE "SIEGE PARALLEL" AND ALL OF US CHANGED!
EXCEPT YOU.
THE SUDSY SKUNK
YEAH, WELL...SORT OF! I GOT THIS ARMOR, BUT I STILL REMEMBER WHERE WE CAME FROM!
YEAH, I REMEMBER STUFF TOO...YEARS OF ROBBING THIEVES AND NOBLES.
I ALSO REMEMBER STORIES ABOUT YOU, LADY IRONHEART. YOU'RE THE PALADIN OF TRUTH, SAVING PEOPLE AND BEING CHIVALROUS.
WHY DENY YOUR OWN LEGEND WITH THIS NONSENSE?
IT'S.
NOT.
REAL!
THIS PLACE IS MESSING WITH YOU AND MESSING WITH TIME!
CLEARLY THE STRESS OF BEING A GREAT HERO HAS YOU RATTLED.
LOOK AROUND. THERE'S TREASURE AND GLORY TO BE FOUND.
SHAKE THOSE BAD DREAMS OUT OF YOUR HEAD AND GET BACK TO WHAT MATTERS.

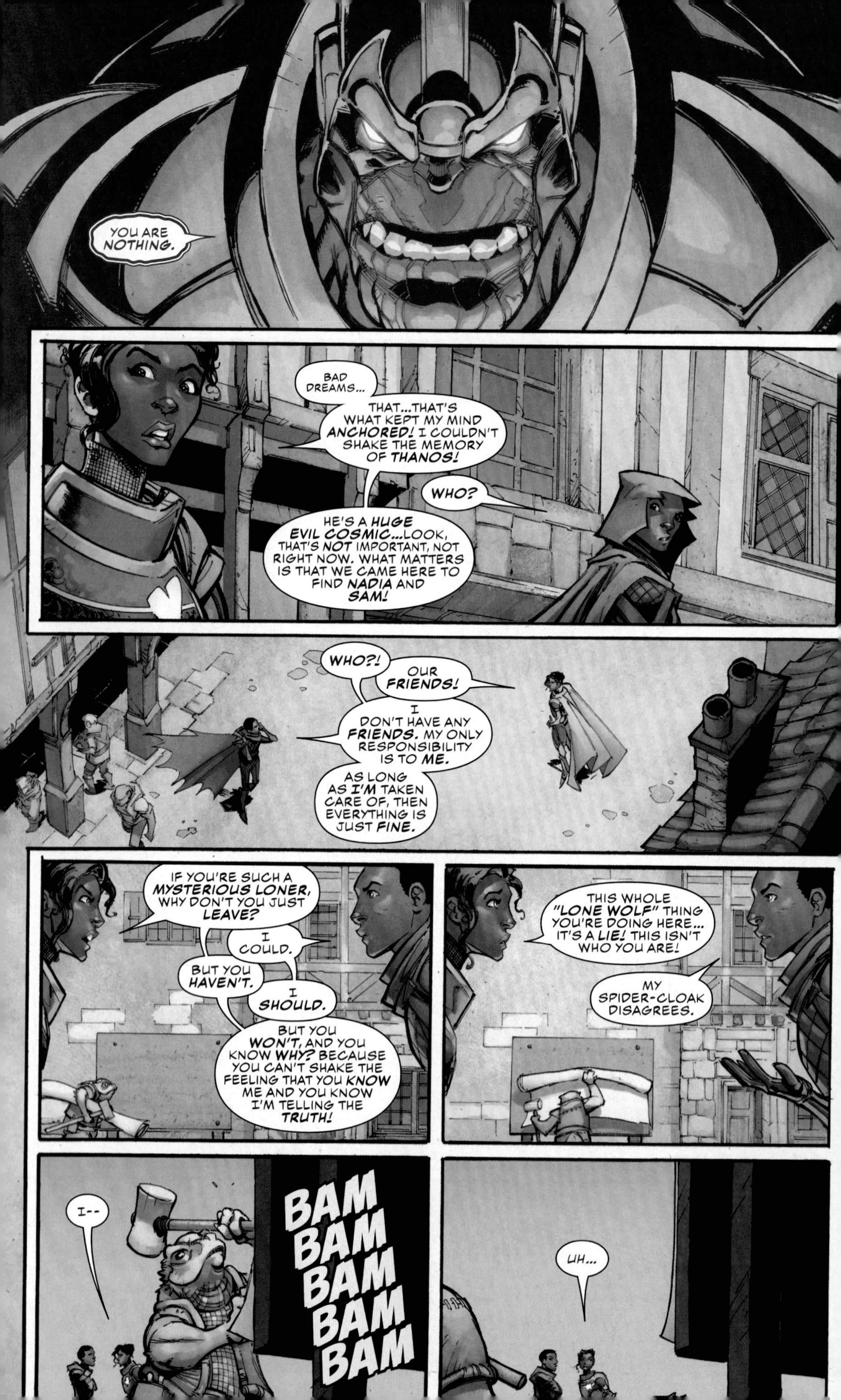
YOU ARE NOTHING.
BAD DREAMS...
THAT...THAT'S WHAT KEPT MY MIND ANCHORED! I COULDN'T SHAKE THE MEMORY OF THANOS!
WHO?
HE'S A HUGE EVIL COSMIC...LOOK, THAT'S NOT IMPORTANT, NOT RIGHT NOW. WHAT MATTERS IS THAT WE CAME HERE TO FIND NADIA AND SAM!
WHO?!
OUR FRIENDS!
I DON'T HAVE ANY FRIENDS. MY ONLY RESPONSIBILITY IS TO ME.
AS LONG AS I'M TAKEN CARE OF, THEN EVERYTHING IS JUST FINE.
IF YOU'RE SUCH A MYSTERIOUS LONER, WHY DON'T YOU JUST LEAVE?
I COULD.
BUT YOU HAVEN'T.
I SHOULD.
BUT YOU WON'T, AND YOU KNOW WHY? BECAUSE YOU CAN'T SHAKE THE FEELING THAT YOU KNOW ME AND YOU KNOW I'M TELLING THE TRUTH!
THIS WHOLE "LONE WOLF" THING YOU'RE DOING HERE... IT'S A LIE! THIS ISN'T WHO YOU ARE!
MY SPIDER-CLOAK DISAGREES.
I--
BAM BAM BAM BAM BAM
UH...

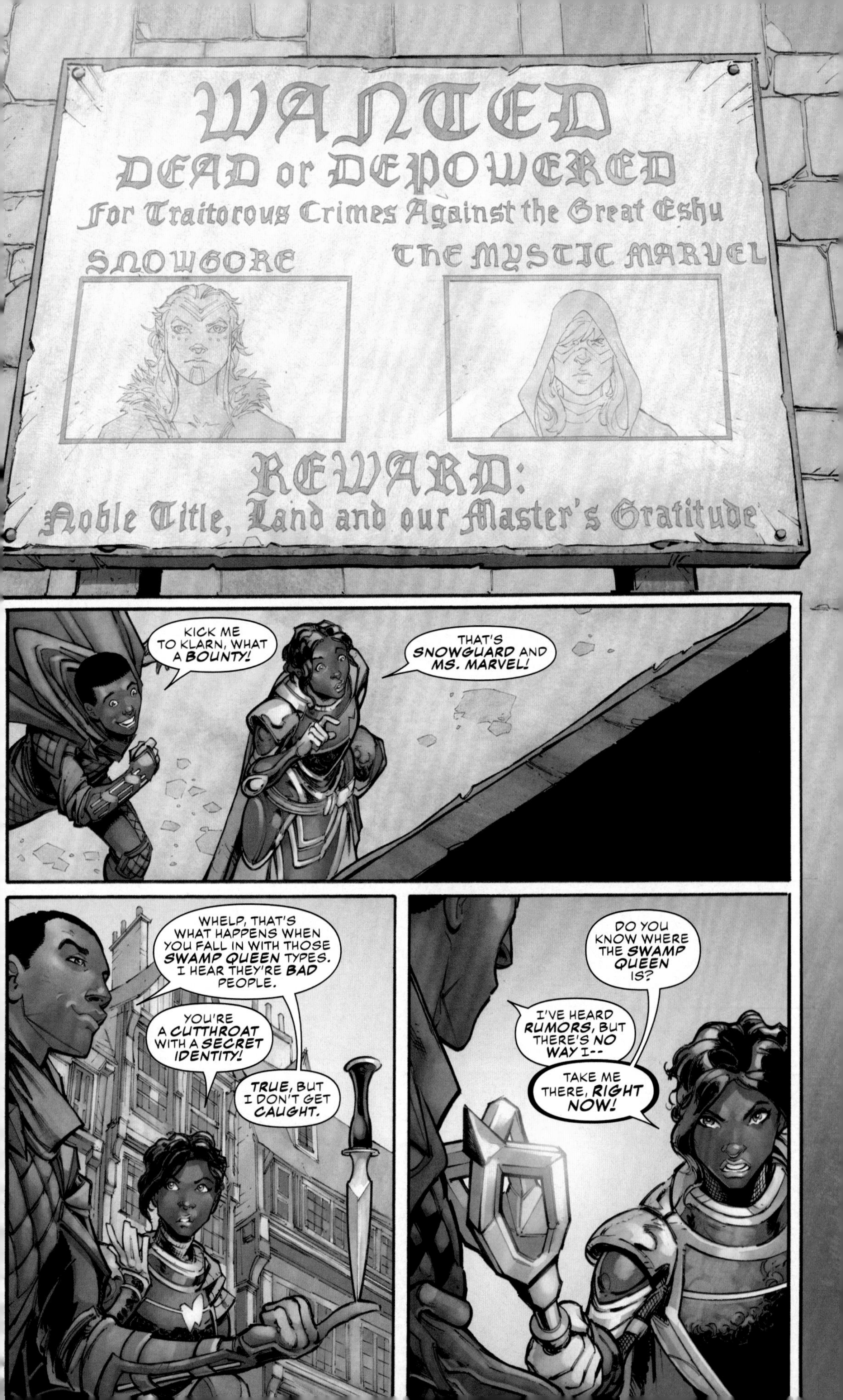
WANTED
DEAD or DEPOWERED
For Traitorous Crimes Against the Great Eshu
SNOWGORE
THE MYSTIC MARVEL
REWARD:
Noble Title, Land and our Master's Gratitude
KICK ME TO KLARN, WHAT A BOUNTY!
THAT'S SNOWGUARD AND MS. MARVEL!
WHELP, THAT'S WHAT HAPPENS WHEN YOU FALL IN WITH THOSE SWAMP QUEEN TYPES. I HEAR THEY'RE BAD PEOPLE.
YOU'RE A CUTTHROAT WITH A SECRET IDENTITY!
TRUE, BUT I DON'T GET CAUGHT.
DO YOU KNOW WHERE THE SWAMP QUEEN IS?
I'VE HEARD RUMORS, BUT THERE'S NO WAY I--
TAKE ME THERE, RIGHT NOW!

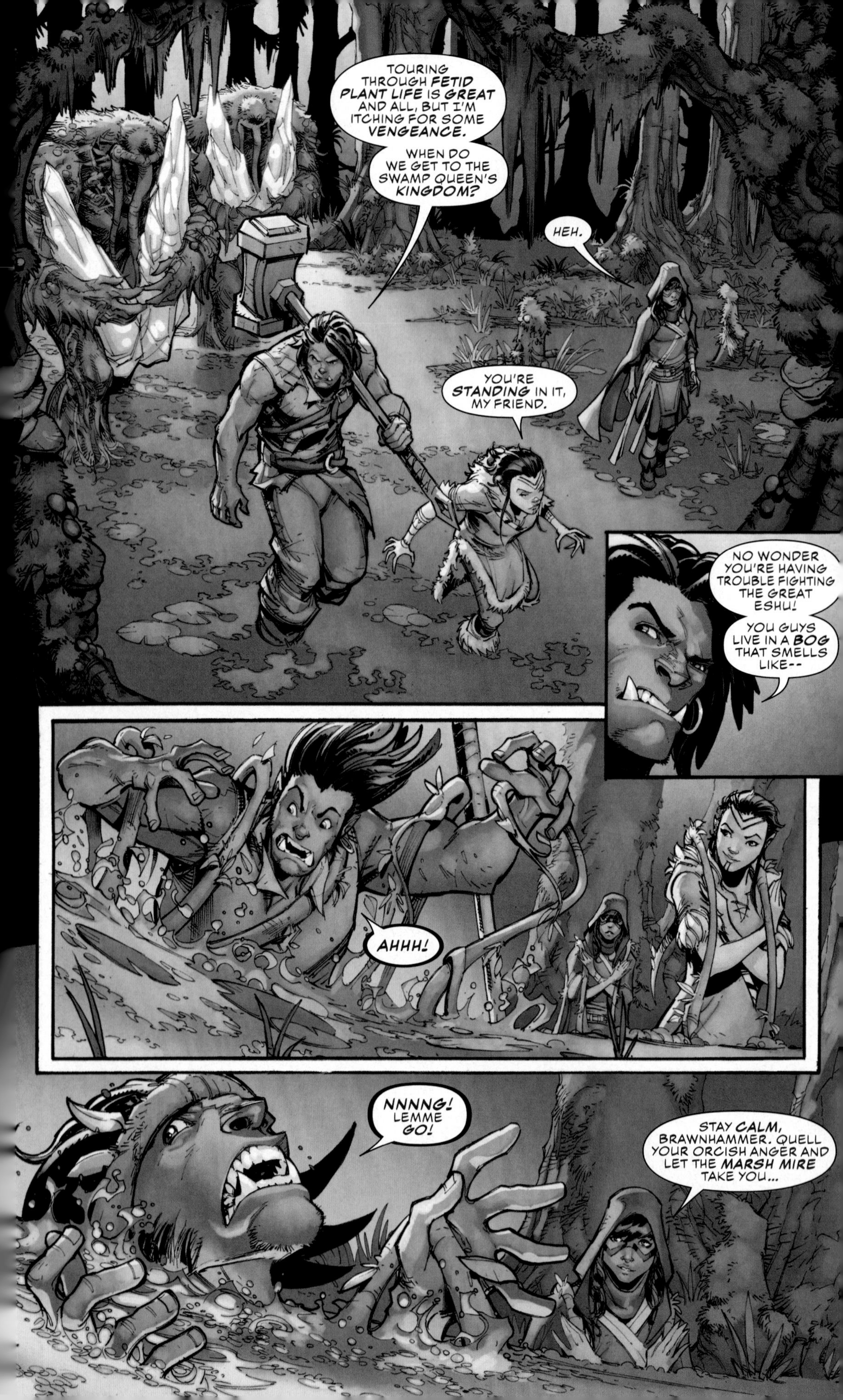
TOURING THROUGH FETID PLANT LIFE IS GREAT AND ALL, BUT I'M ITCHING FOR SOME VENGEANCE.
WHEN DO WE GET TO THE SWAMP QUEEN'S KINGDOM?
HEH.
YOU'RE STANDING IN IT, MY FRIEND.
NO WONDER YOU'RE HAVING TROUBLE FIGHTING THE GREAT ESHU!
YOU GUYS LIVE IN A BOG THAT SMELLS LIKE--
AHHH!
NNNNG! LEMME GO!
STAY CALM, BRAWNHAMMER. QUELL YOUR ORCISH ANGER AND LET THE MARSH MIRE TAKE YOU...

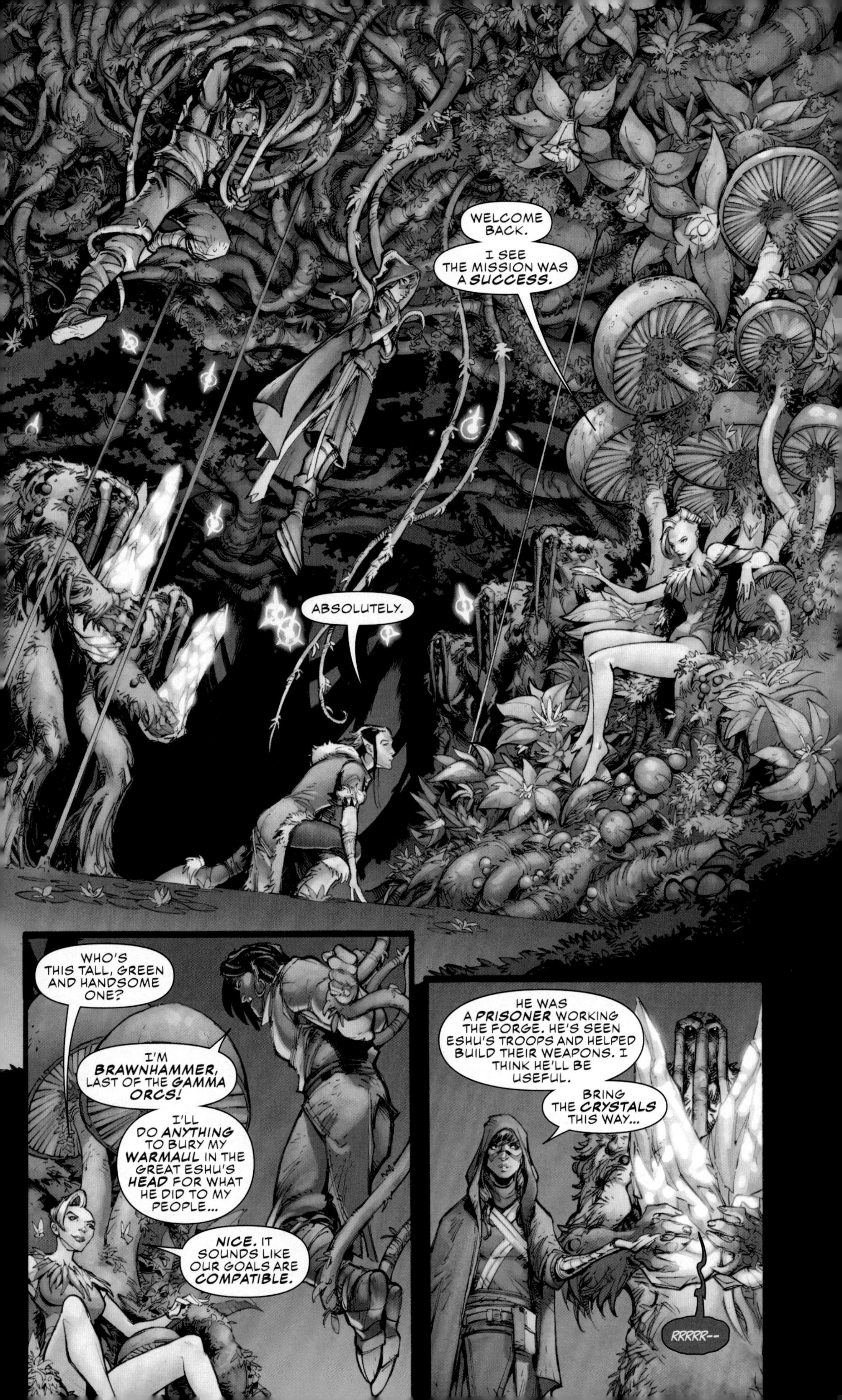
WELCOME BACK.
I SEE THE MISSION WAS A *SUCCESS.*
ABSOLUTELY.
WHO'S THIS TALL, GREEN AND HANDSOME ONE?
I'M **BRAWNHAMMER**, LAST OF THE **GAMMA ORCS!**
I'LL DO **ANYTHING** TO BURY MY **WARMAUL** IN THE GREAT ESHU'S **HEAD** FOR WHAT HE DID TO MY PEOPLE...
NICE. IT SOUNDS LIKE OUR GOALS ARE **COMPATIBLE.**
HE WAS A **PRISONER** WORKING THE FORGE. HE'S SEEN ESHU'S TROOPS AND HELPED BUILD THEIR WEAPONS. I THINK HE'LL BE USEFUL.
BRING THE **CRYSTALS** THIS WAY...
RRRRR--

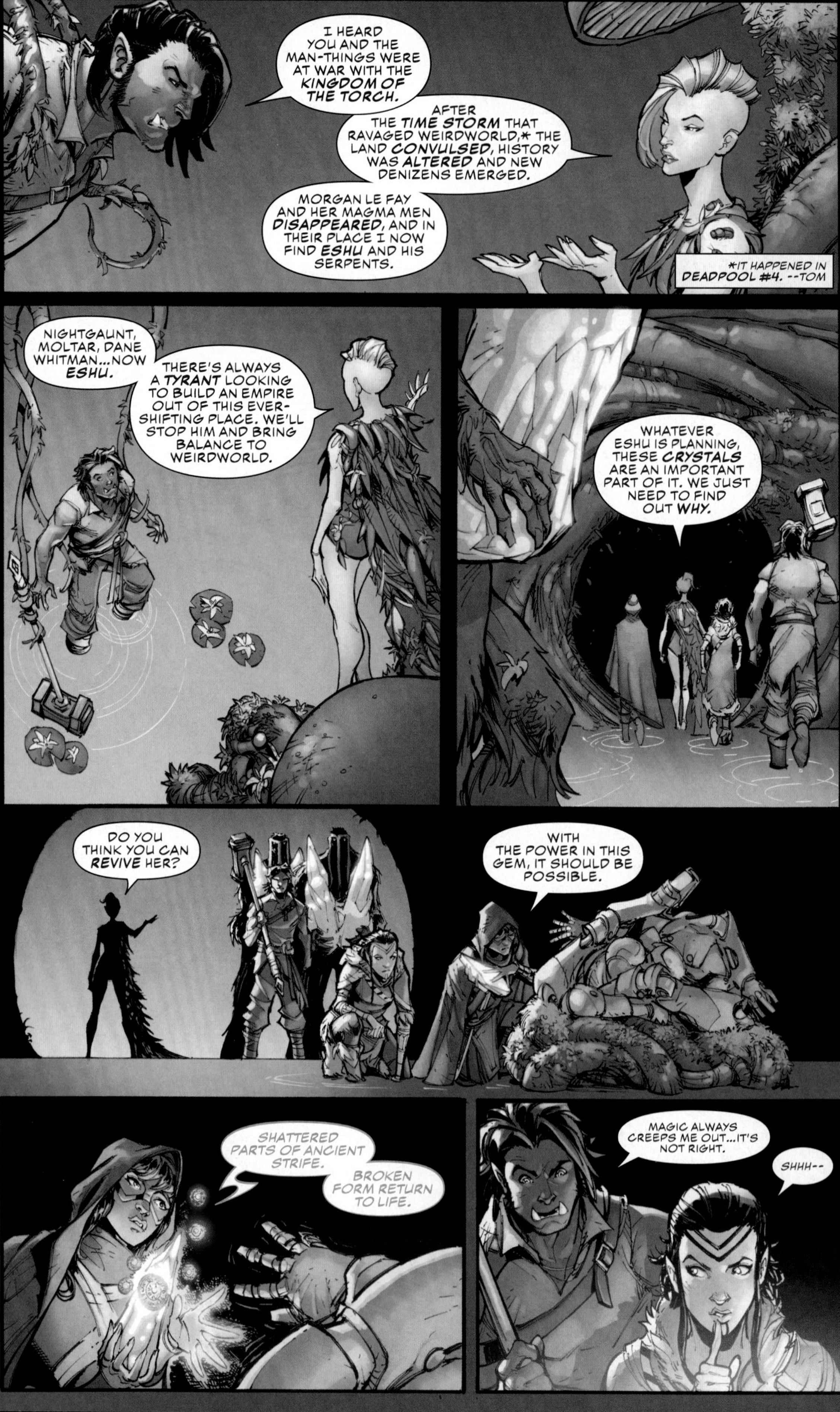
I HEARD YOU AND THE MAN-THINGS WERE AT WAR WITH THE KINGDOM OF THE TORCH.
AFTER THE TIME STORM THAT RAVAGED WEIRDWORLD,* THE LAND CONVULSED, HISTORY WAS ALTERED AND NEW DENIZENS EMERGED.
MORGAN LE FAY AND HER MAGMA MEN DISAPPEARED, AND IN THEIR PLACE I NOW FIND ESHU AND HIS SERPENTS.
*IT HAPPENED IN DEADPOOL #4. --TOM
NIGHTGAUNT, MOLTAR, DANE WHITMAN...NOW ESHU.
THERE'S ALWAYS A TYRANT LOOKING TO BUILD AN EMPIRE OUT OF THIS EVER-SHIFTING PLACE. WE'LL STOP HIM AND BRING BALANCE TO WEIRDWORLD.
WHATEVER ESHU IS PLANNING, THESE CRYSTALS ARE AN IMPORTANT PART OF IT. WE JUST NEED TO FIND OUT WHY.
DO YOU THINK YOU CAN REVIVE HER?
WITH THE POWER IN THIS GEM, IT SHOULD BE POSSIBLE.
SHATTERED PARTS OF ANCIENT STRIFE.
BROKEN FORM RETURN TO LIFE.
MAGIC ALWAYS CREEPS ME OUT...IT'S NOT RIGHT.
SHHH--

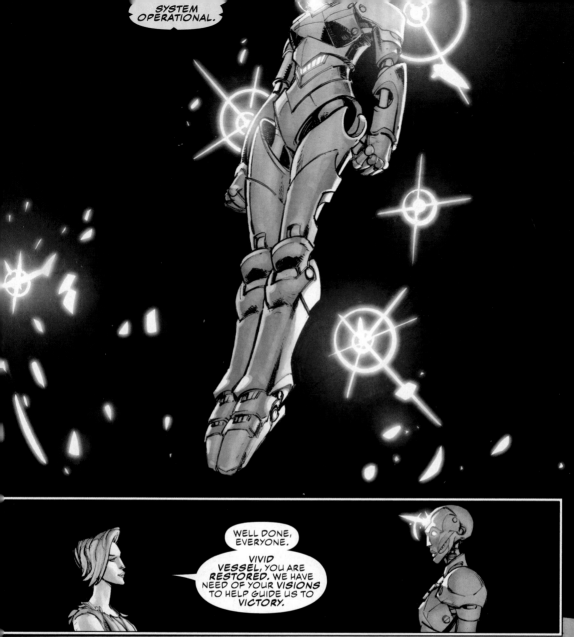

SYSTEM OPERATIONAL.

WELL DONE, EVERYONE.

VIVID VESSEL, YOU ARE RESTORED. WE HAVE NEED OF YOUR VISIONS TO HELP GUIDE US TO VICTORY.

ACCESSING THE KEYS OF ILLUMINATION.

WHOA!

LOOK, IT'S WORKING!

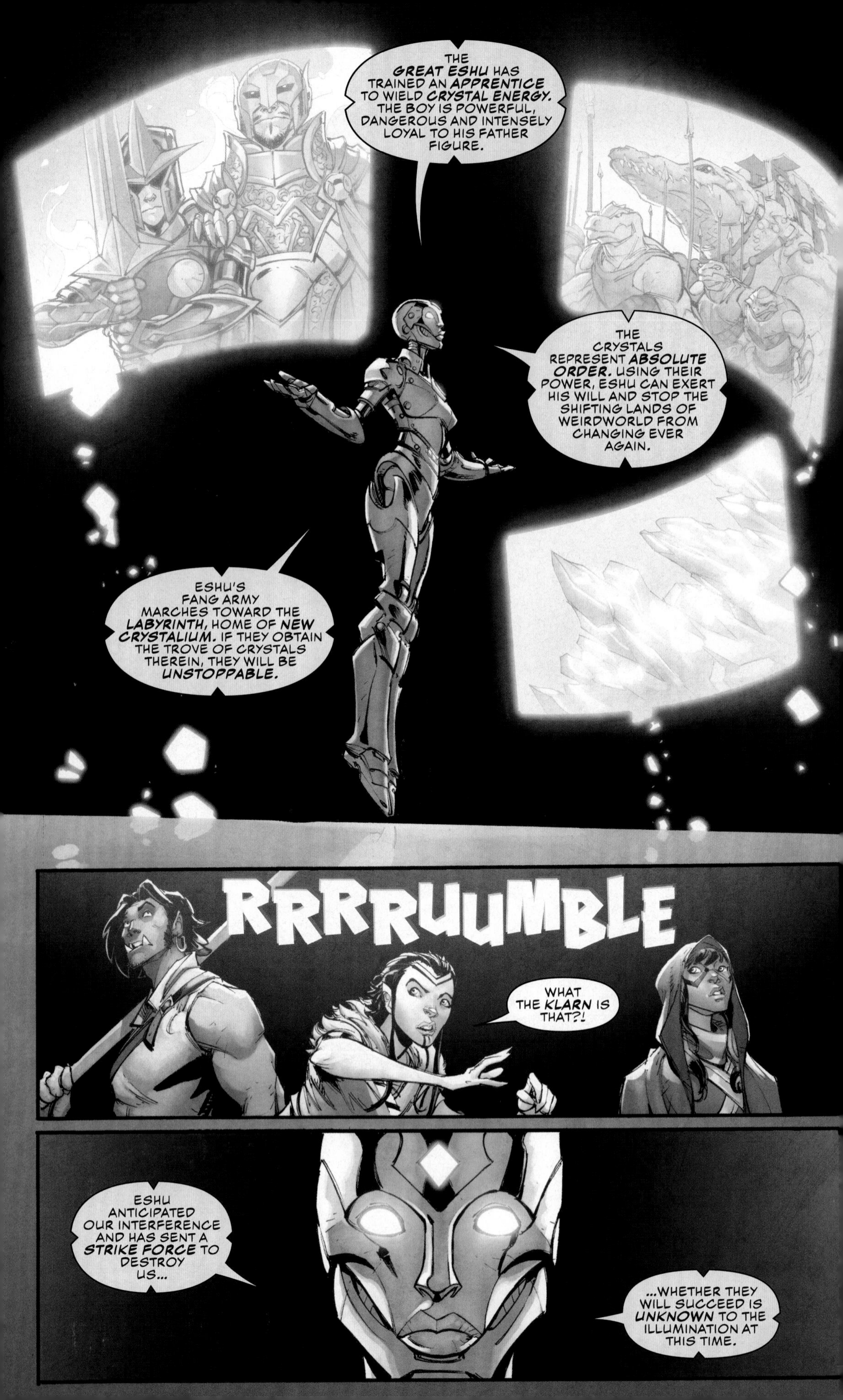
THE GREAT ESHU HAS TRAINED AN APPRENTICE TO WIELD CRYSTAL ENERGY. THE BOY IS POWERFUL, DANGEROUS AND INTENSELY LOYAL TO HIS FATHER FIGURE.
THE CRYSTALS REPRESENT ABSOLUTE ORDER. USING THEIR POWER, ESHU CAN EXERT HIS WILL AND STOP THE SHIFTING LANDS OF WEIRDWORLD FROM CHANGING EVER AGAIN.
ESHU'S FANG ARMY MARCHES TOWARD THE LABYRINTH, HOME OF NEW CRYSTALIUM. IF THEY OBTAIN THE TROVE OF CRYSTALS THEREIN, THEY WILL BE UNSTOPPABLE.
RRRRUUMBLE
WHAT THE KLARN IS THAT?!
ESHU ANTICIPATED OUR INTERFERENCE AND HAS SENT A STRIKE FORCE TO DESTROY US...
...WHETHER THEY WILL SUCCEED IS UNKNOWN TO THE ILLUMINATION AT THIS TIME.

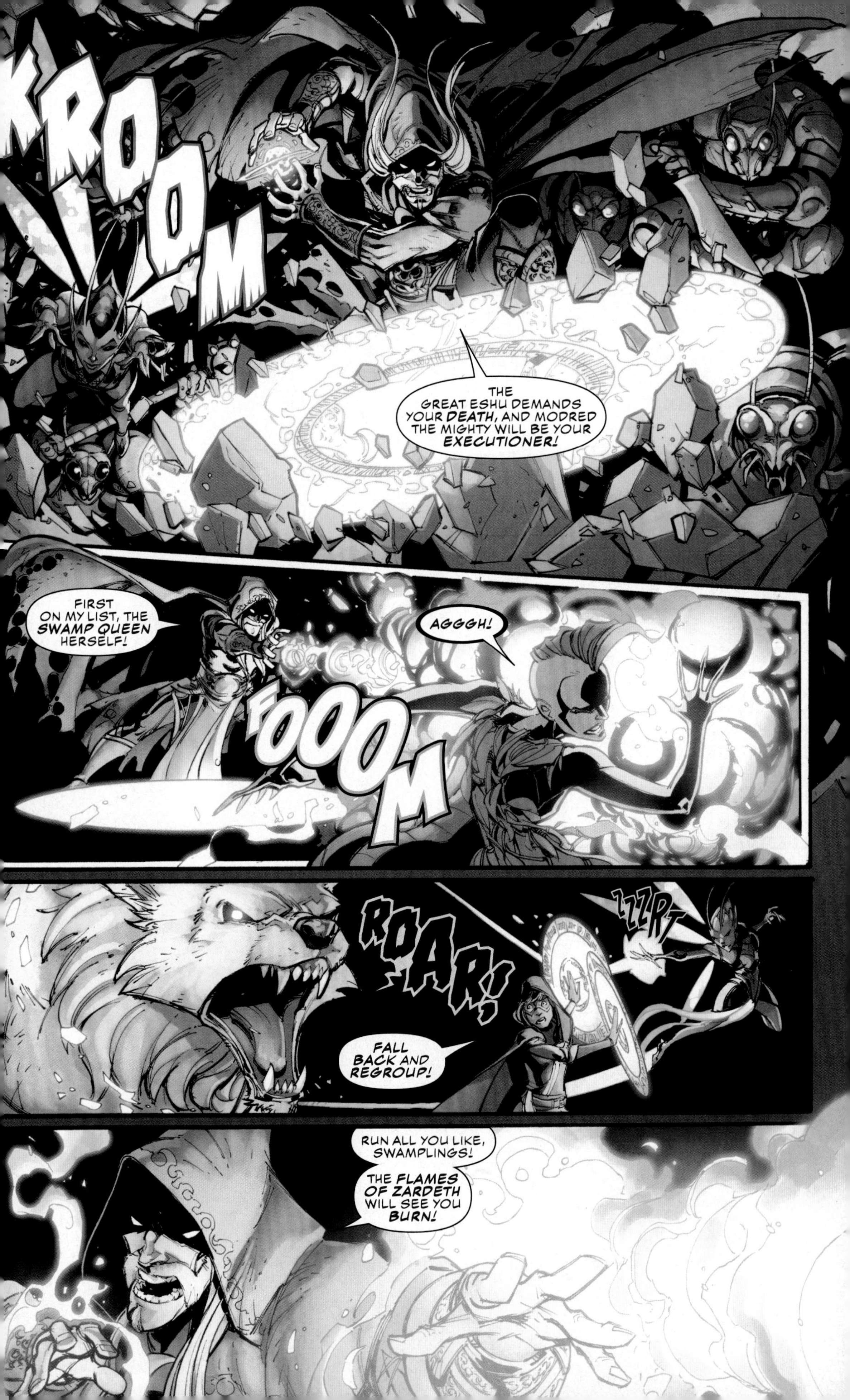
KRROOM
THE GREAT ESHU DEMANDS YOUR DEATH, AND MODRED THE MIGHTY WILL BE YOUR EXECUTIONER!
FIRST ON MY LIST, THE SWAMP QUEEN HERSELF!
AGGGH!
FOOOM
ROAR!
ZZZRT
FALL BACK AND REGROUP!
RUN ALL YOU LIKE, SWAMPLINGS!
THE FLAMES OF ZARDETH WILL SEE YOU BURN!

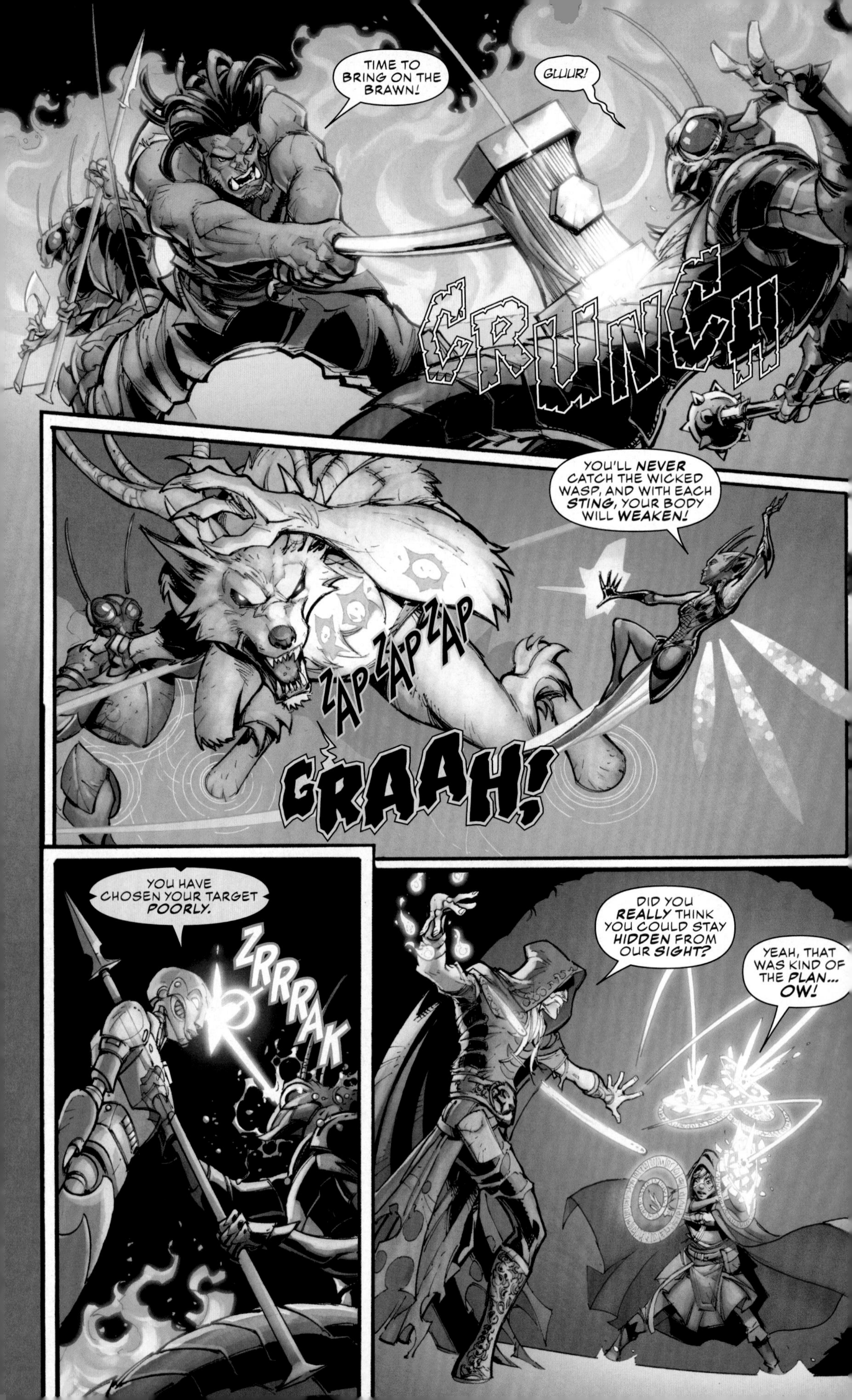

TIME TO BRING ON THE BRAWN!
GLUUR!
CRUNCH
YOU'LL NEVER CATCH THE WICKED WASP, AND WITH EACH STING, YOUR BODY WILL WEAKEN!
ZAP ZAP ZAP
GRAAH!
YOU HAVE CHOSEN YOUR TARGET POORLY.
ZRRRAK
DID YOU REALLY THINK YOU COULD STAY HIDDEN FROM OUR SIGHT?
YEAH, THAT WAS KIND OF THE PLAN... OW!

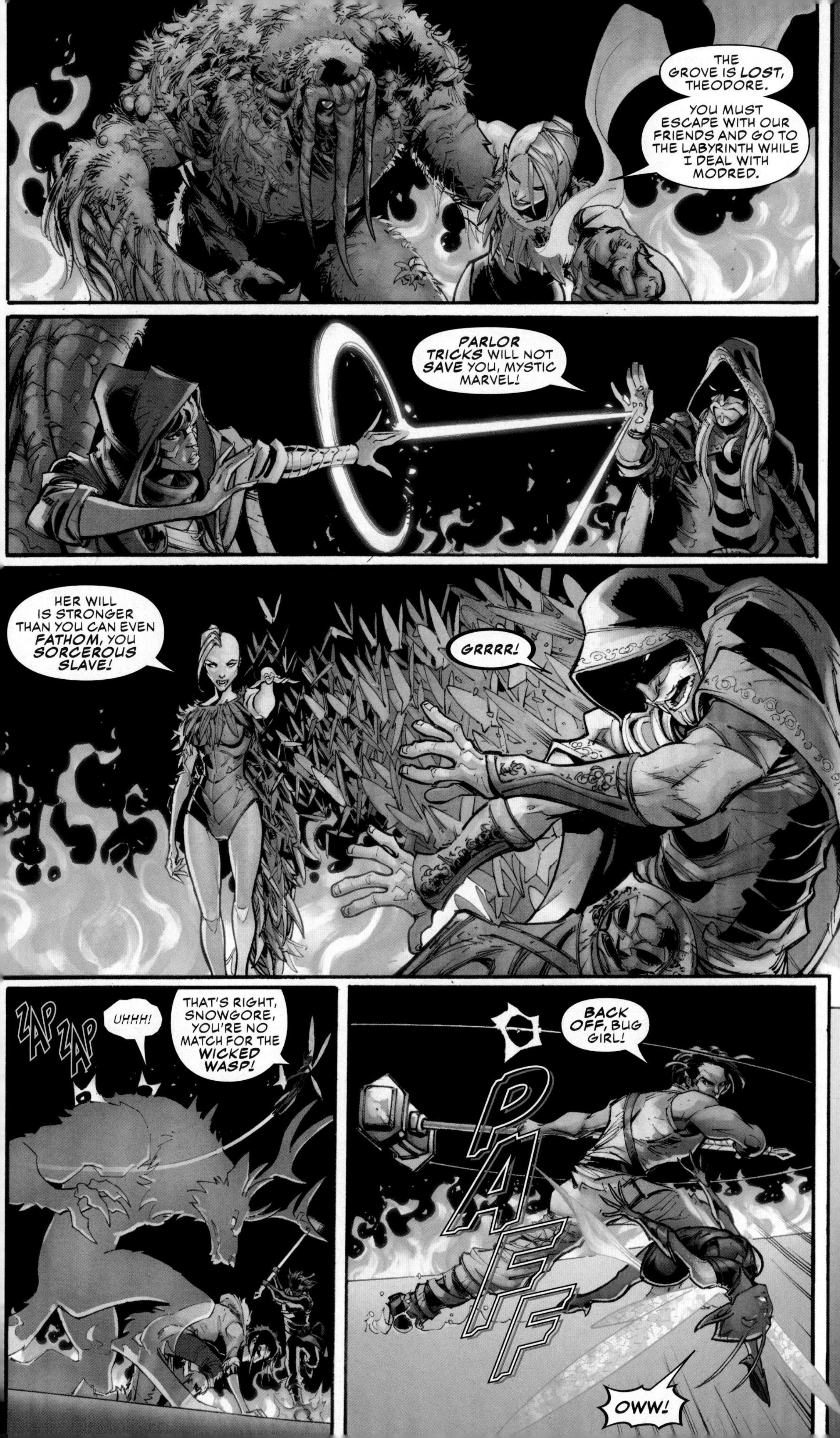
THE GROVE IS LOST, THEODORE.
YOU MUST ESCAPE WITH OUR FRIENDS AND GO TO THE LABYRINTH WHILE I DEAL WITH MODRED.
PARLOR TRICKS WILL NOT SAVE YOU, MYSTIC MARVEL!
HER WILL IS STRONGER THAN YOU CAN EVEN FATHOM, YOU SORCEROUS SLAVE!
GRRRR!
ZAP ZAP
UHHH!
THAT'S RIGHT, SNOWGORE, YOU'RE NO MATCH FOR THE WICKED WASP!
BACK OFF, BUG GIRL!
PAFFF
OWW!

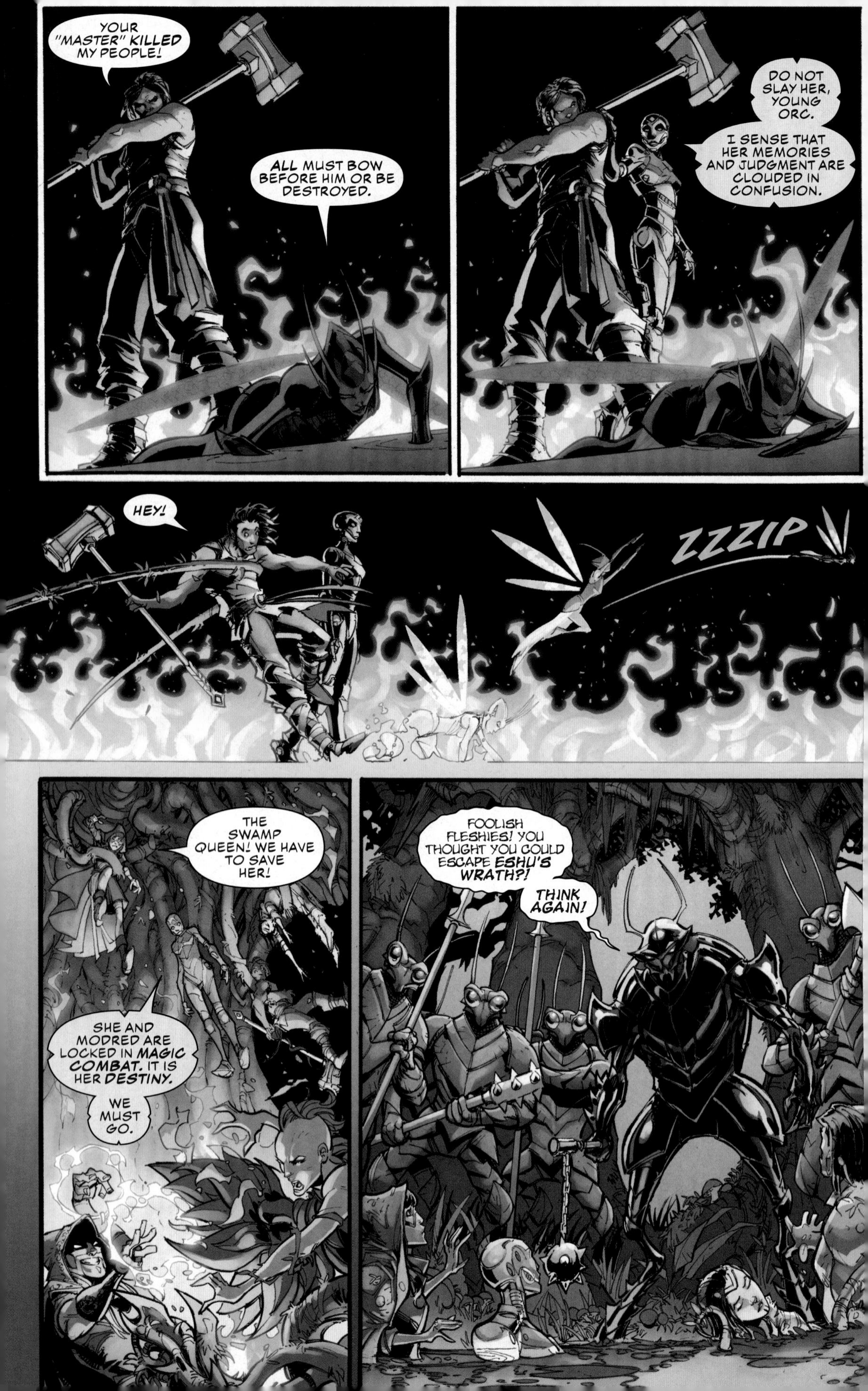

YOUR "MASTER" KILLED MY PEOPLE!
ALL MUST BOW BEFORE HIM OR BE DESTROYED.
DO NOT SLAY HER, YOUNG ORC.
I SENSE THAT HER MEMORIES AND JUDGMENT ARE CLOUDED IN CONFUSION.
HEY!
ZZZIP
THE SWAMP QUEEN! WE HAVE TO SAVE HER!
SHE AND MODRED ARE LOCKED IN MAGIC COMBAT. IT IS HER DESTINY.
WE MUST GO.
FOOLISH FLESHIES! YOU THOUGHT YOU COULD ESCAPE ESHU'S WRATH?!
THINK AGAIN!

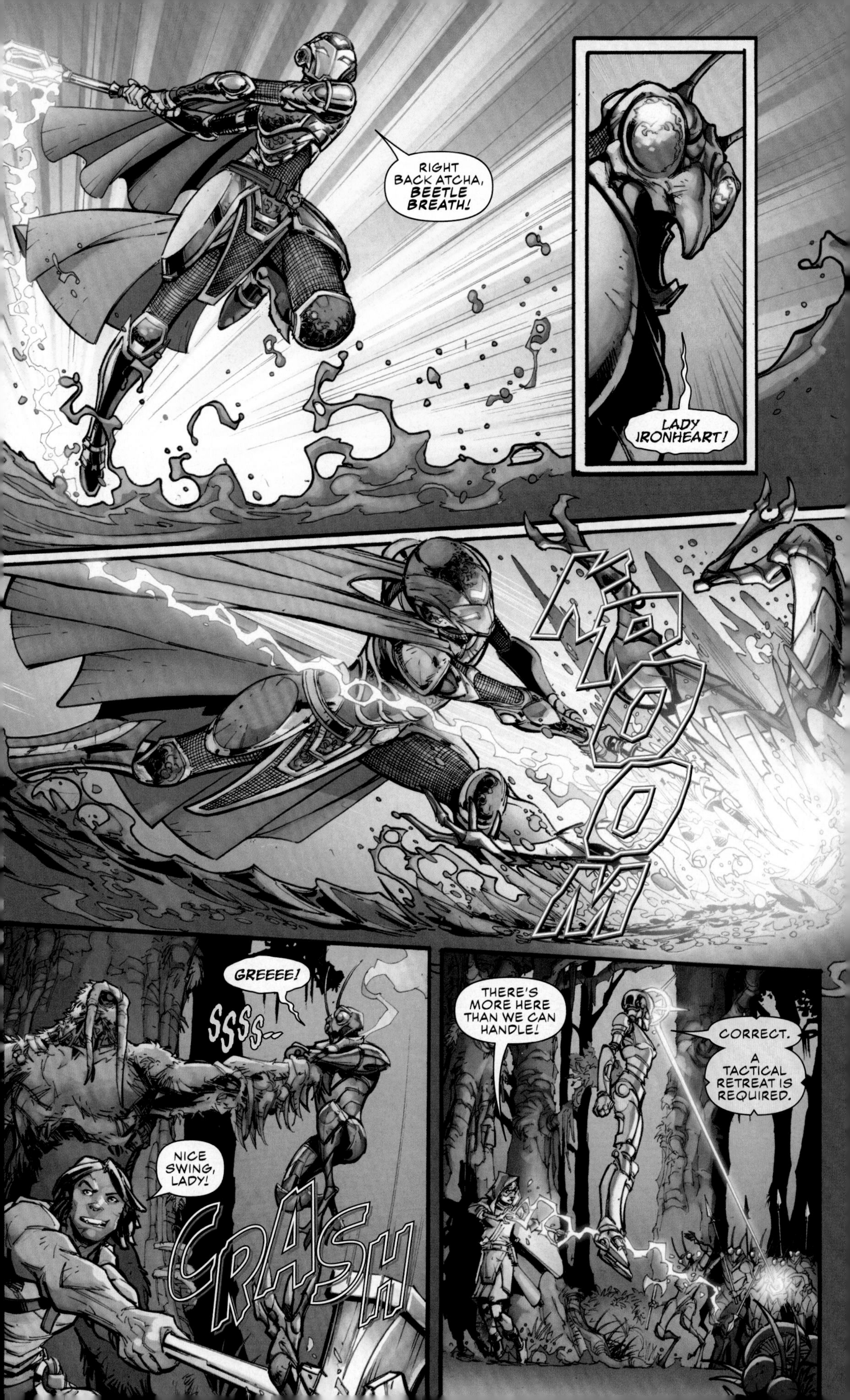
RIGHT BACK ATCHA, BEETLE BREATH!
LADY IRONHEART!
KRA-BOOM
GREEEE!
SSSS--
NICE SWING, LADY!
CRASH
THERE'S MORE HERE THAN WE CAN HANDLE!
CORRECT.
A TACTICAL RETREAT IS REQUIRED.

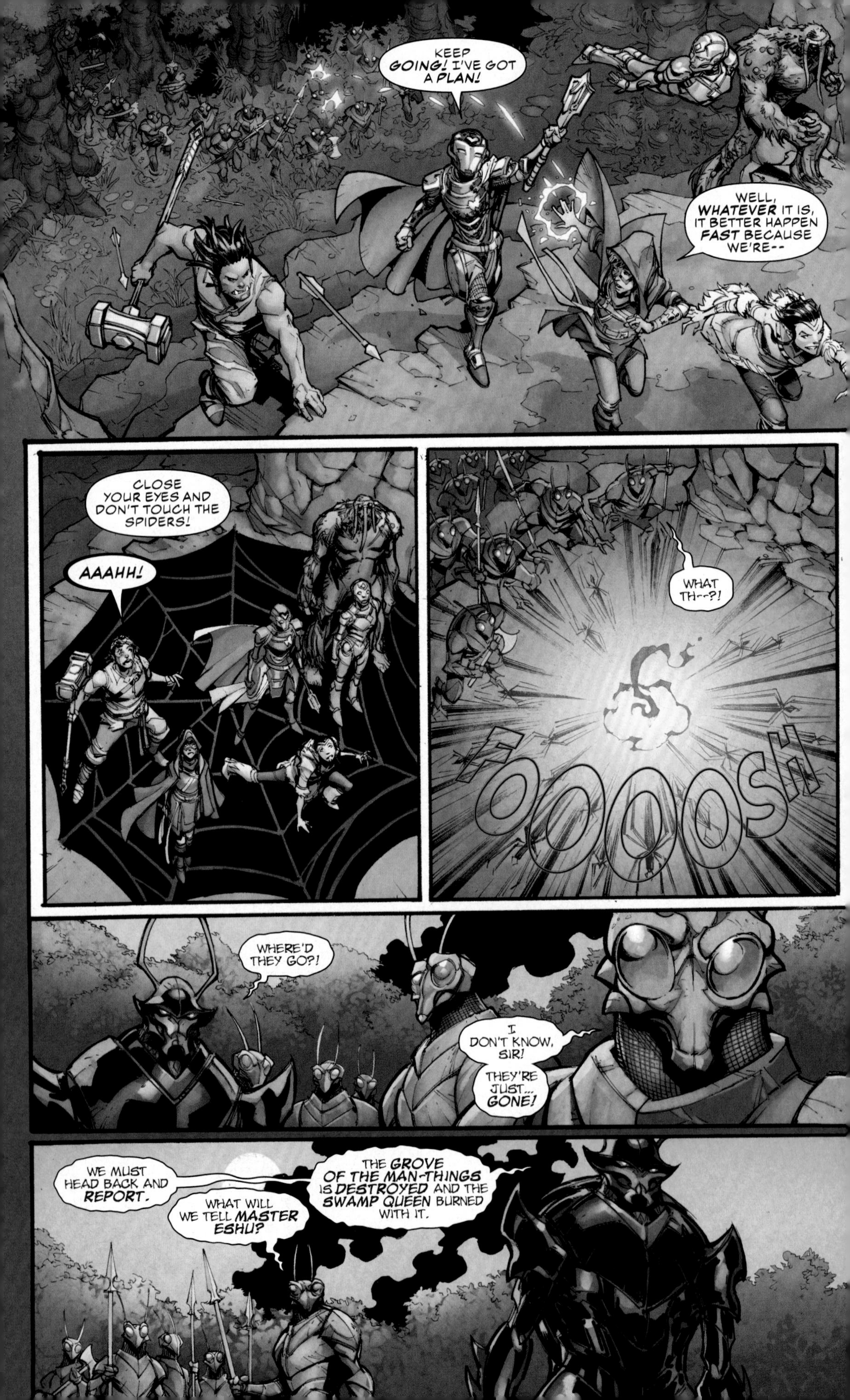
KEEP GOING! I'VE GOT A PLAN!
WELL, WHATEVER IT IS, IT BETTER HAPPEN FAST BECAUSE WE'RE--
CLOSE YOUR EYES AND DON'T TOUCH THE SPIDERS!
AAAHH!
WHAT TH--?!
FOOOOSH
WHERE'D THEY GO?!
I DON'T KNOW, SIR!
THEY'RE JUST... GONE!
WE MUST HEAD BACK AND REPORT.
WHAT WILL WE TELL MASTER ESHU?
THE GROVE OF THE MAN-THINGS IS DESTROYED AND THE SWAMP QUEEN BURNED WITH IT.

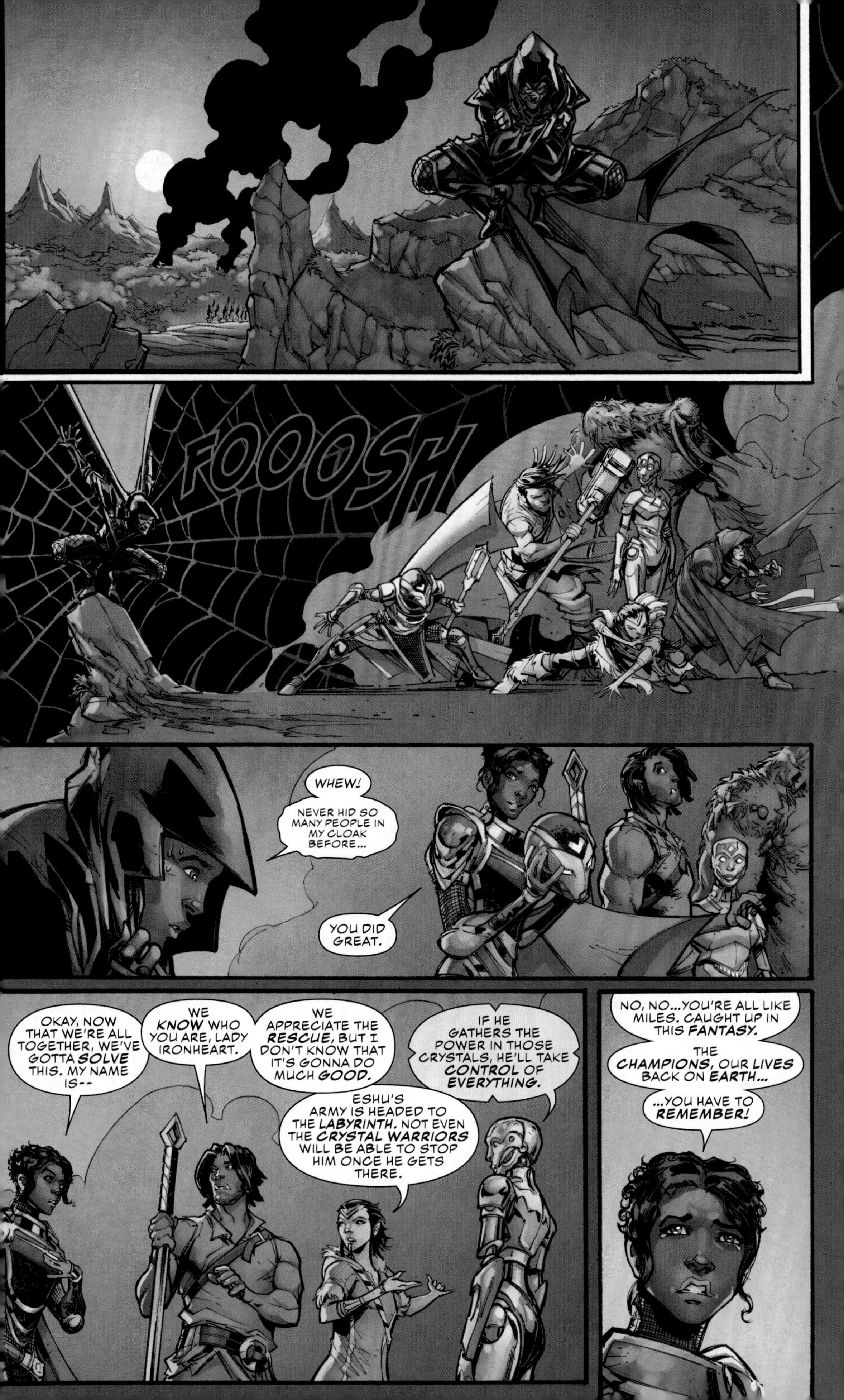
FOOOSH
WHEW!
NEVER HID SO MANY PEOPLE IN MY CLOAK BEFORE...
YOU DID GREAT.
OKAY, NOW THAT WE'RE ALL TOGETHER, WE'VE GOTTA SOLVE THIS. MY NAME IS--
WE KNOW WHO YOU ARE, LADY IRONHEART.
WE APPRECIATE THE RESCUE, BUT I DON'T KNOW THAT IT'S GONNA DO MUCH GOOD.
ESHU'S ARMY IS HEADED TO THE LABYRINTH. NOT EVEN THE CRYSTAL WARRIORS WILL BE ABLE TO STOP HIM ONCE HE GETS THERE.
IF HE GATHERS THE POWER IN THOSE CRYSTALS, HE'LL TAKE CONTROL OF EVERYTHING.
NO, NO...YOU'RE ALL LIKE MILES. CAUGHT UP IN THIS FANTASY.
THE CHAMPIONS, OUR LIVES BACK ON EARTH...
...YOU HAVE TO REMEMBER!

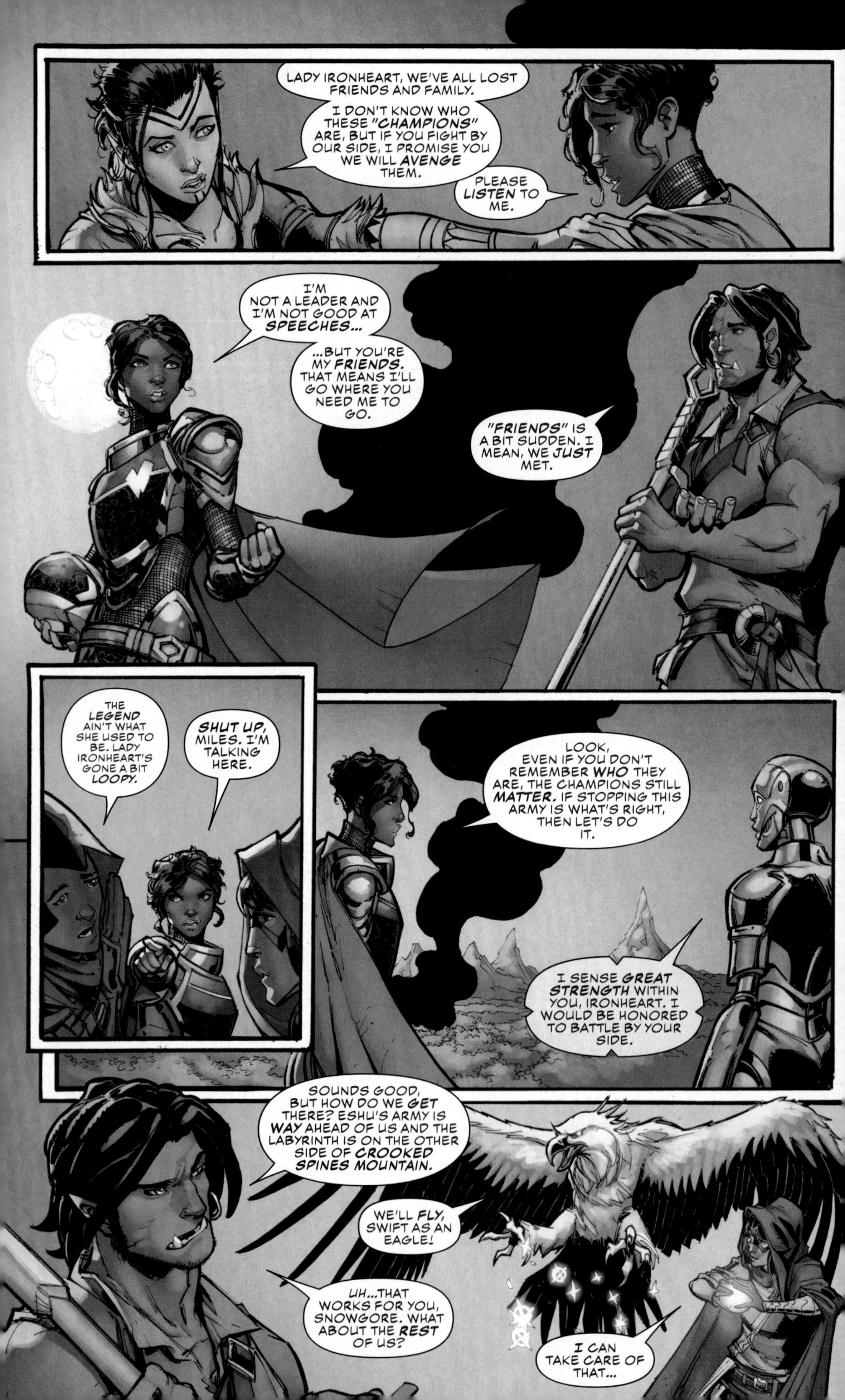
LADY IRONHEART, WE'VE ALL LOST FRIENDS AND FAMILY.
I DON'T KNOW WHO THESE "CHAMPIONS" ARE, BUT IF YOU FIGHT BY OUR SIDE, I PROMISE YOU WE WILL AVENGE THEM.
PLEASE LISTEN TO ME.
I'M NOT A LEADER AND I'M NOT GOOD AT SPEECHES...
...BUT YOU'RE MY FRIENDS. THAT MEANS I'LL GO WHERE YOU NEED ME TO GO.
"FRIENDS" IS A BIT SUDDEN. I MEAN, WE JUST MET.
THE LEGEND AIN'T WHAT SHE USED TO BE. LADY IRONHEART'S GONE A BIT LOOPY.
SHUT UP, MILES. I'M TALKING HERE.
LOOK, EVEN IF YOU DON'T REMEMBER WHO THEY ARE, THE CHAMPIONS STILL MATTER. IF STOPPING THIS ARMY IS WHAT'S RIGHT, THEN LET'S DO IT.
I SENSE GREAT STRENGTH WITHIN YOU, IRONHEART. I WOULD BE HONORED TO BATTLE BY YOUR SIDE.
SOUNDS GOOD, BUT HOW DO WE GET THERE? ESHU'S ARMY IS WAY AHEAD OF US AND THE LABYRINTH IS ON THE OTHER SIDE OF CROOKED SPINES MOUNTAIN.
WE'LL FLY, SWIFT AS AN EAGLE!
UH...THAT WORKS FOR YOU, SNOWGORE. WHAT ABOUT THE REST OF US?
I CAN TAKE CARE OF THAT...

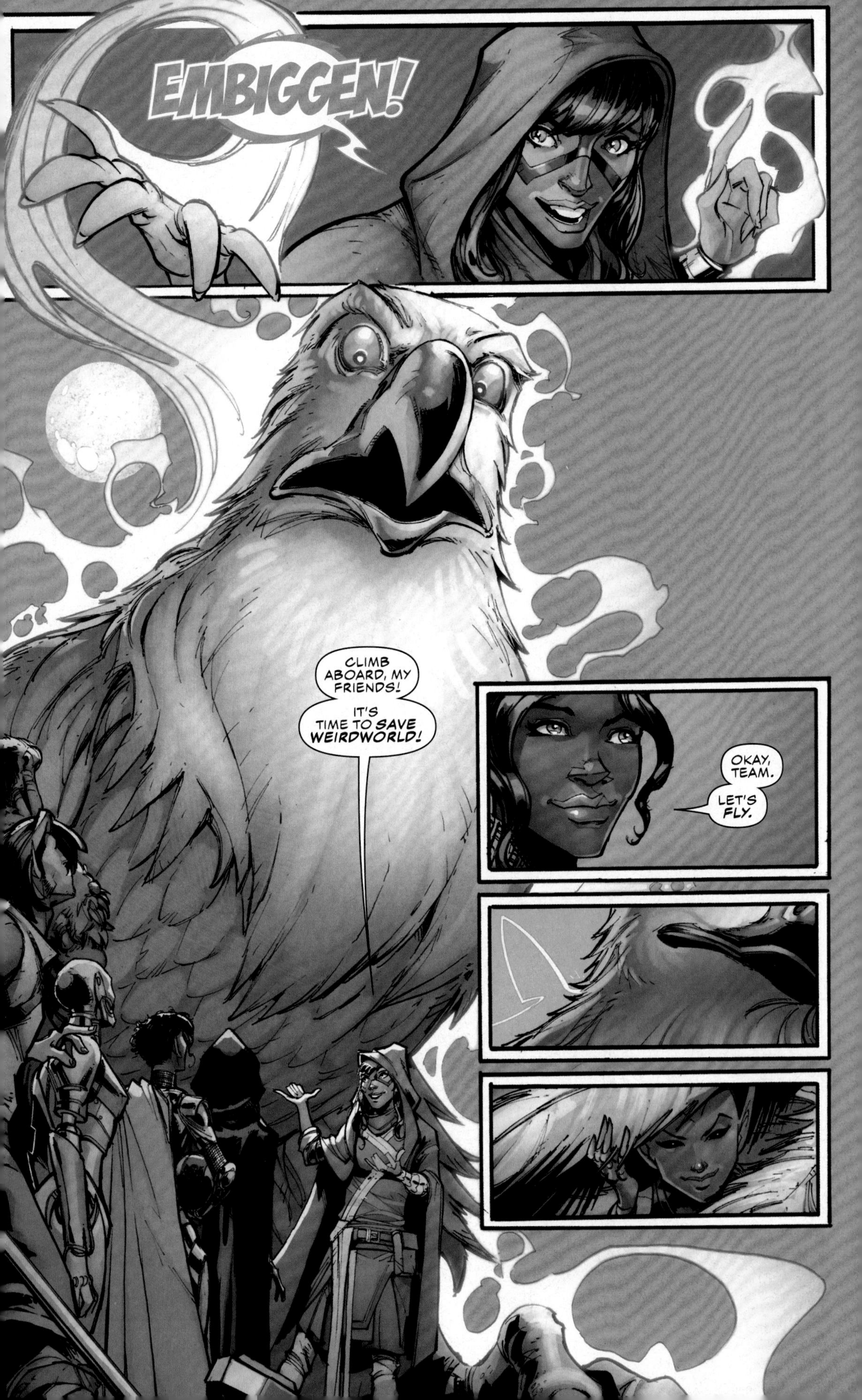

EMBIGGEN!
CLIMB ABOARD, MY FRIENDS!
IT'S TIME TO SAVE WEIRDWORLD!
OKAY, TEAM.
LET'S FLY.

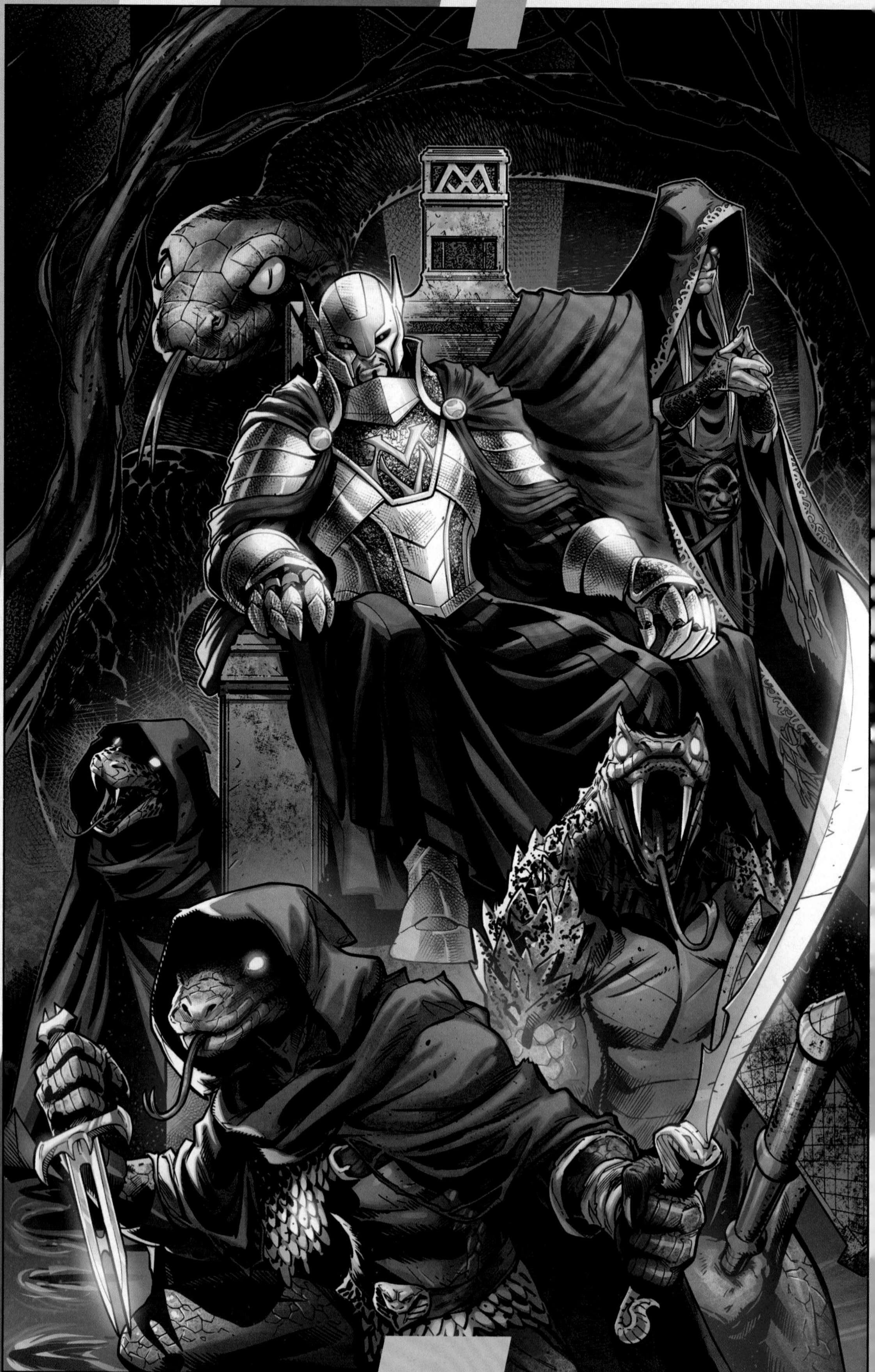

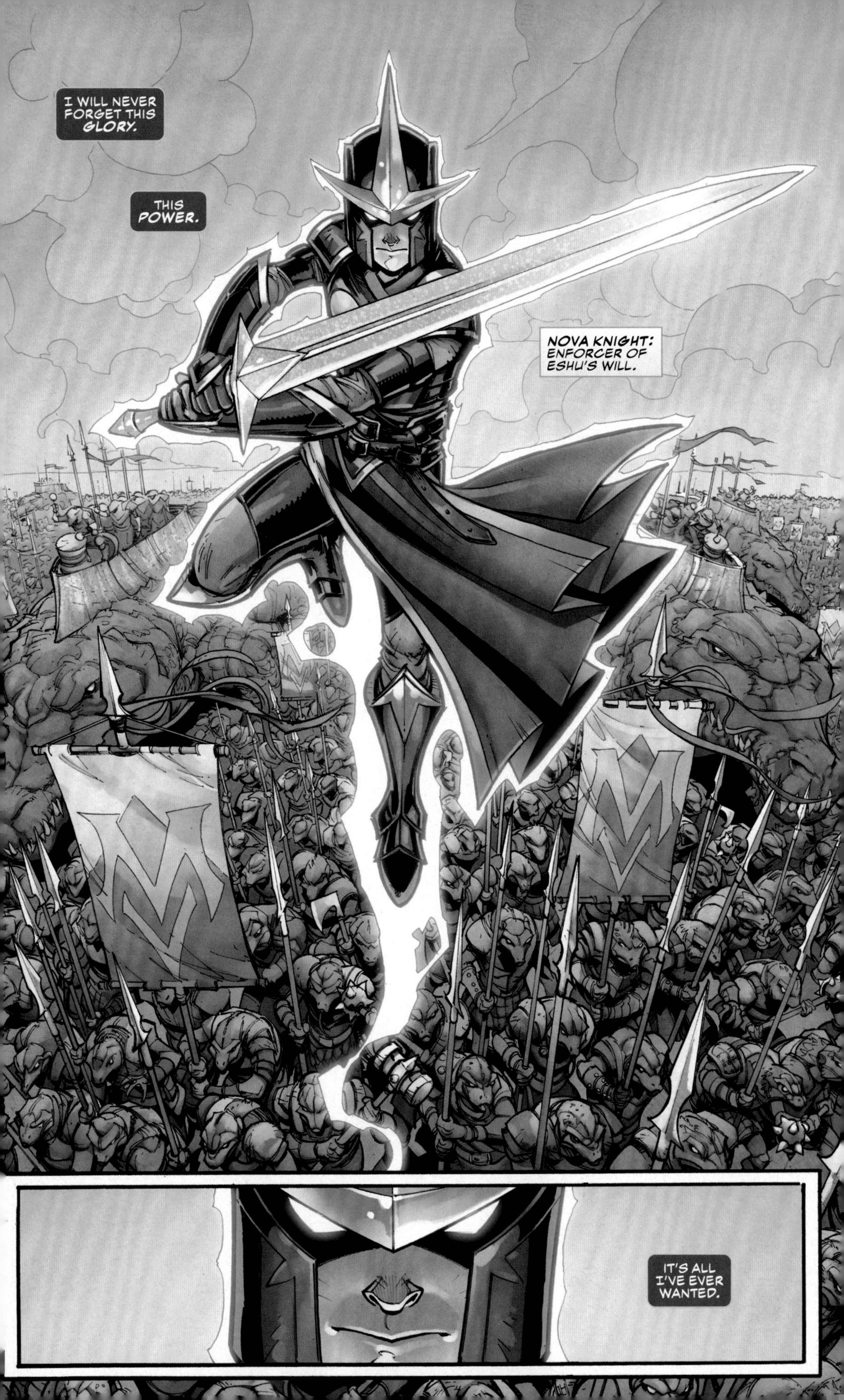
I WILL NEVER FORGET THIS GLORY.
THIS POWER.
NOVA KNIGHT: ENFORCER OF ESHU'S WILL.
IT'S ALL I'VE EVER WANTED.

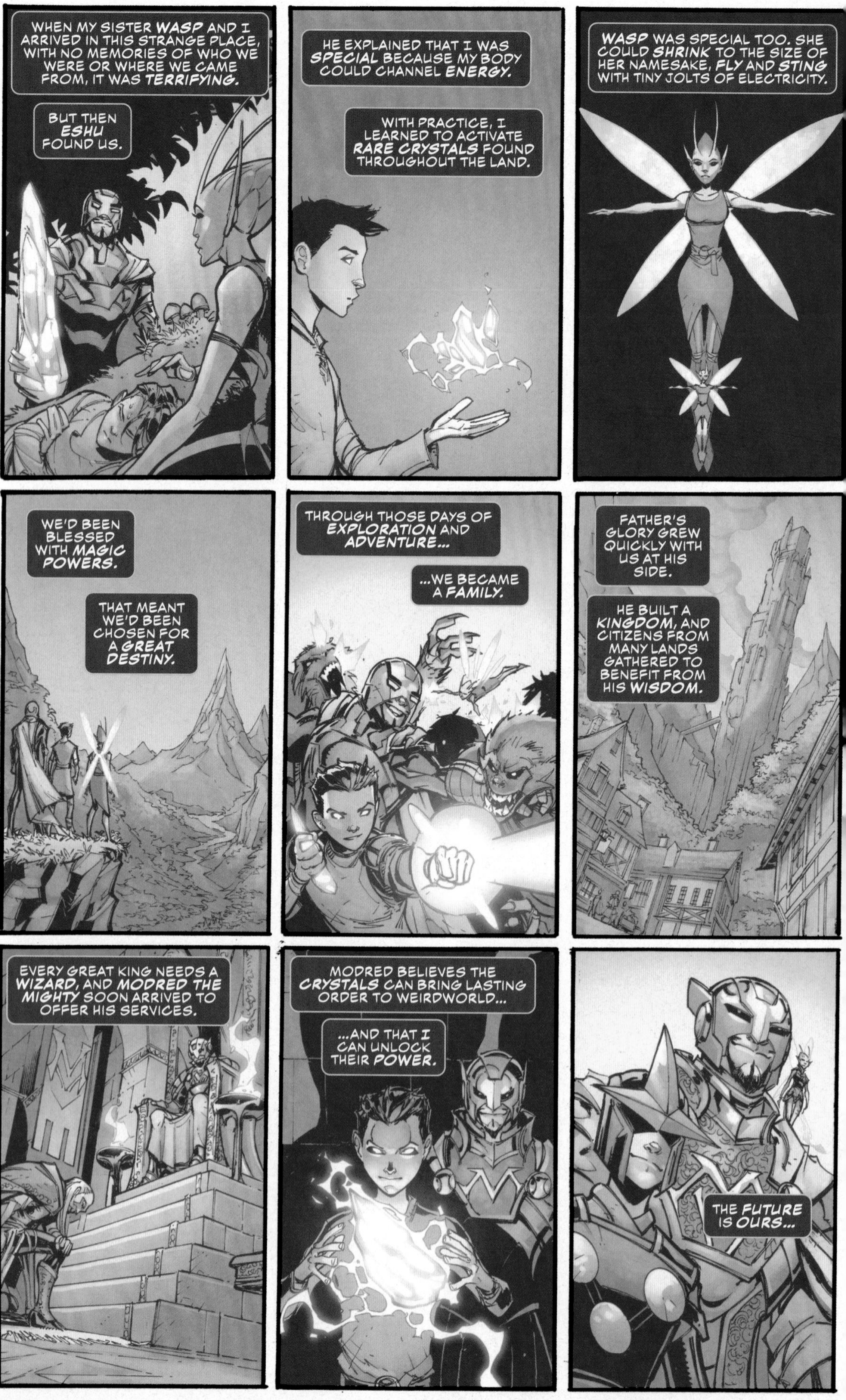
WHEN MY SISTER WASP AND I ARRIVED IN THIS STRANGE PLACE, WITH NO MEMORIES OF WHO WE WERE OR WHERE WE CAME FROM, IT WAS TERRIFYING.
BUT THEN ESHU FOUND US.
HE EXPLAINED THAT I WAS SPECIAL BECAUSE MY BODY COULD CHANNEL ENERGY.
WITH PRACTICE, I LEARNED TO ACTIVATE RARE CRYSTALS FOUND THROUGHOUT THE LAND.
WASP WAS SPECIAL TOO. SHE COULD SHRINK TO THE SIZE OF HER NAMESAKE, FLY AND STING WITH TINY JOLTS OF ELECTRICITY.
WE'D BEEN BLESSED WITH MAGIC POWERS.
THAT MEANT WE'D BEEN CHOSEN FOR A GREAT DESTINY.
THROUGH THOSE DAYS OF EXPLORATION AND ADVENTURE...
...WE BECAME A FAMILY.
FATHER'S GLORY GREW QUICKLY WITH US AT HIS SIDE.
HE BUILT A KINGDOM, AND CITIZENS FROM MANY LANDS GATHERED TO BENEFIT FROM HIS WISDOM.
EVERY GREAT KING NEEDS A WIZARD, AND MODRED THE MIGHTY SOON ARRIVED TO OFFER HIS SERVICES.
MODRED BELIEVES THE CRYSTALS CAN BRING LASTING ORDER TO WEIRDWORLD...
...AND THAT I CAN UNLOCK THEIR POWER.
THE FUTURE IS OURS...

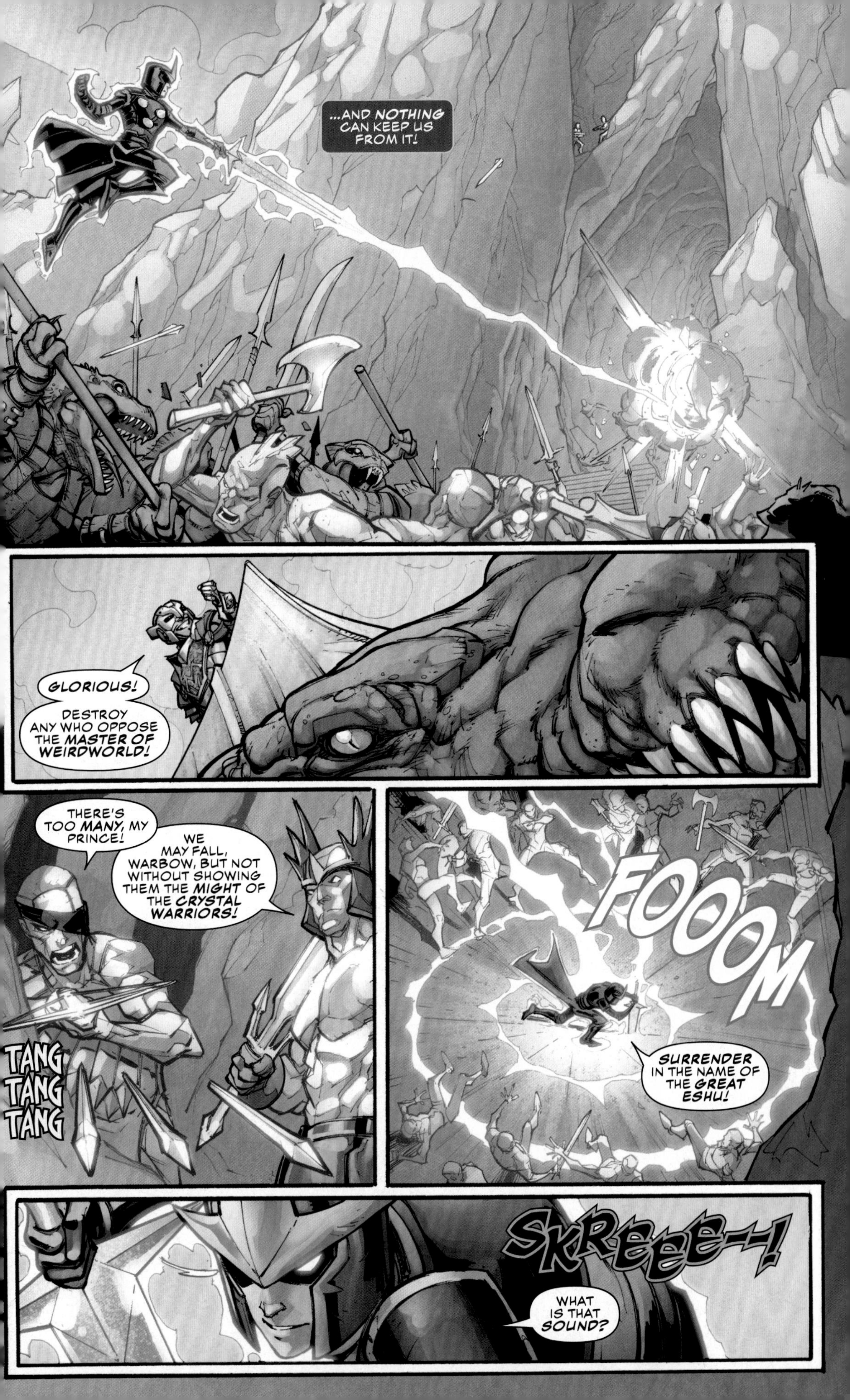
...AND NOTHING CAN KEEP US FROM IT!
GLORIOUS!
DESTROY ANY WHO OPPOSE THE MASTER OF WEIRDWORLD!
THERE'S TOO MANY, MY PRINCE!
WE MAY FALL, WARBOW, BUT NOT WITHOUT SHOWING THEM THE MIGHT OF THE CRYSTAL WARRIORS!
TANG TANG TANG
FOOOM
SURRENDER IN THE NAME OF THE GREAT ESHU!
SKREEEE--!
WHAT IS THAT SOUND?

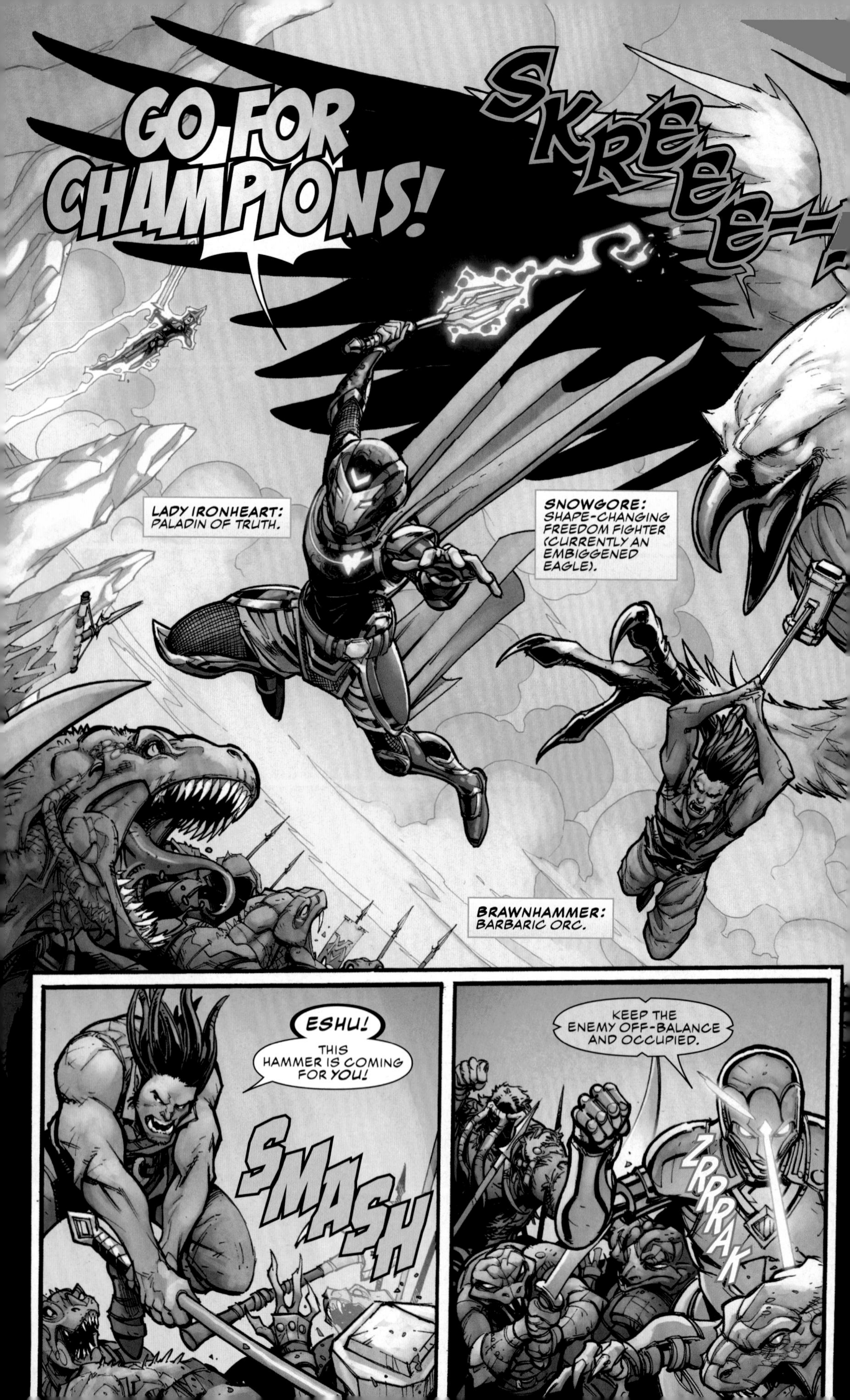
GO FOR CHAMPIONS!
SKREEE--
LADY IRONHEART: PALADIN OF TRUTH.
SNOWGORE: SHAPE-CHANGING FREEDOM FIGHTER (CURRENTLY AN EMBIGGENED EAGLE).
BRAWNHAMMER: BARBARIC ORC.
ESHU!
THIS HAMMER IS COMING FOR YOU!
SMASH
KEEP THE ENEMY OFF-BALANCE AND OCCUPIED.
ZRRRAK

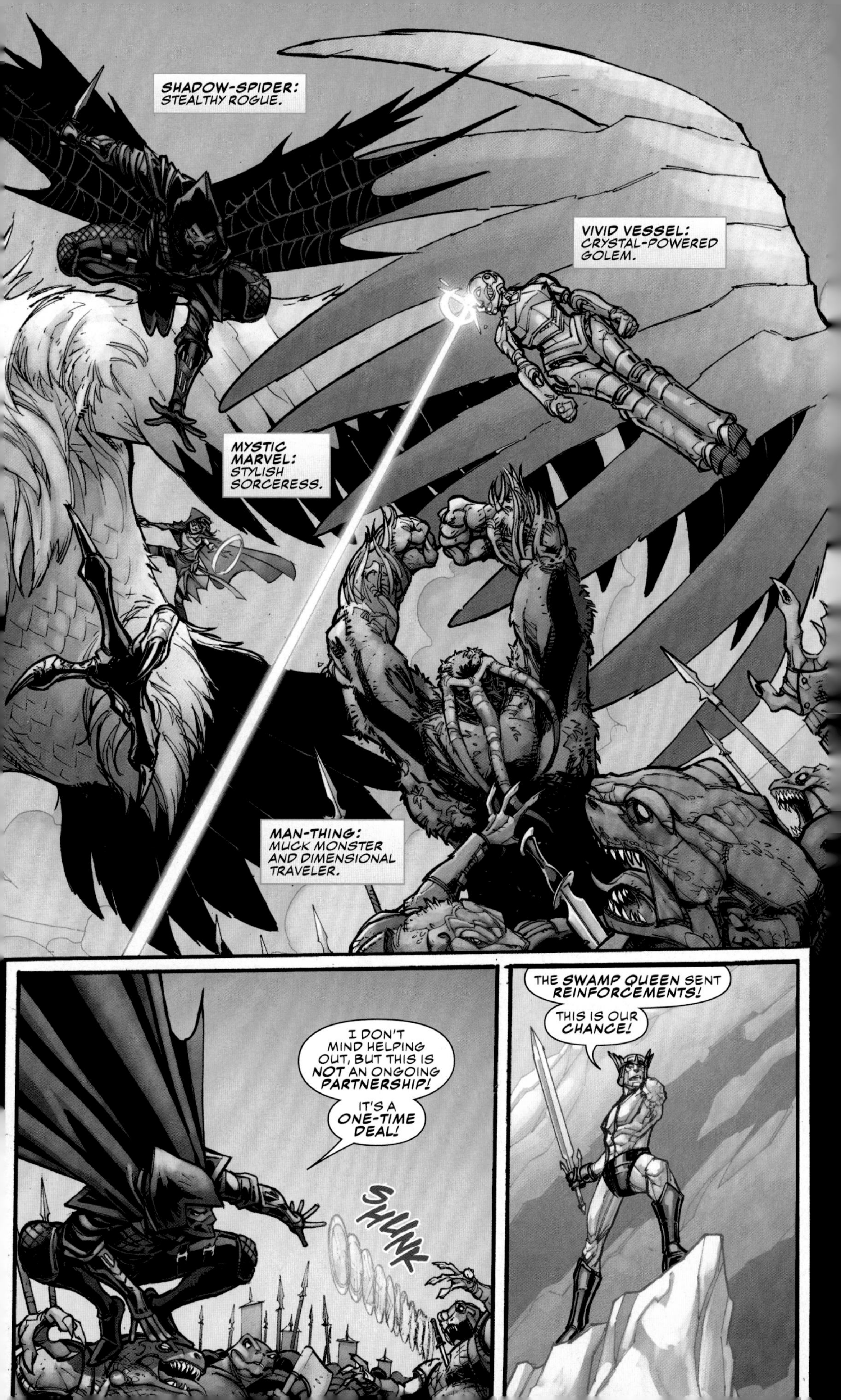
SHADOW-SPIDER: STEALTHY ROGUE.
VIVID VESSEL: CRYSTAL-POWERED GOLEM.
MYSTIC MARVEL: STYLISH SORCERESS.
MAN-THING: MUCK MONSTER AND DIMENSIONAL TRAVELER.
I DON'T MIND HELPING OUT, BUT THIS IS NOT AN ONGOING PARTNERSHIP!
IT'S A ONE-TIME DEAL!
SHUNK
THE SWAMP QUEEN SENT REINFORCEMENTS!
THIS IS OUR CHANCE!

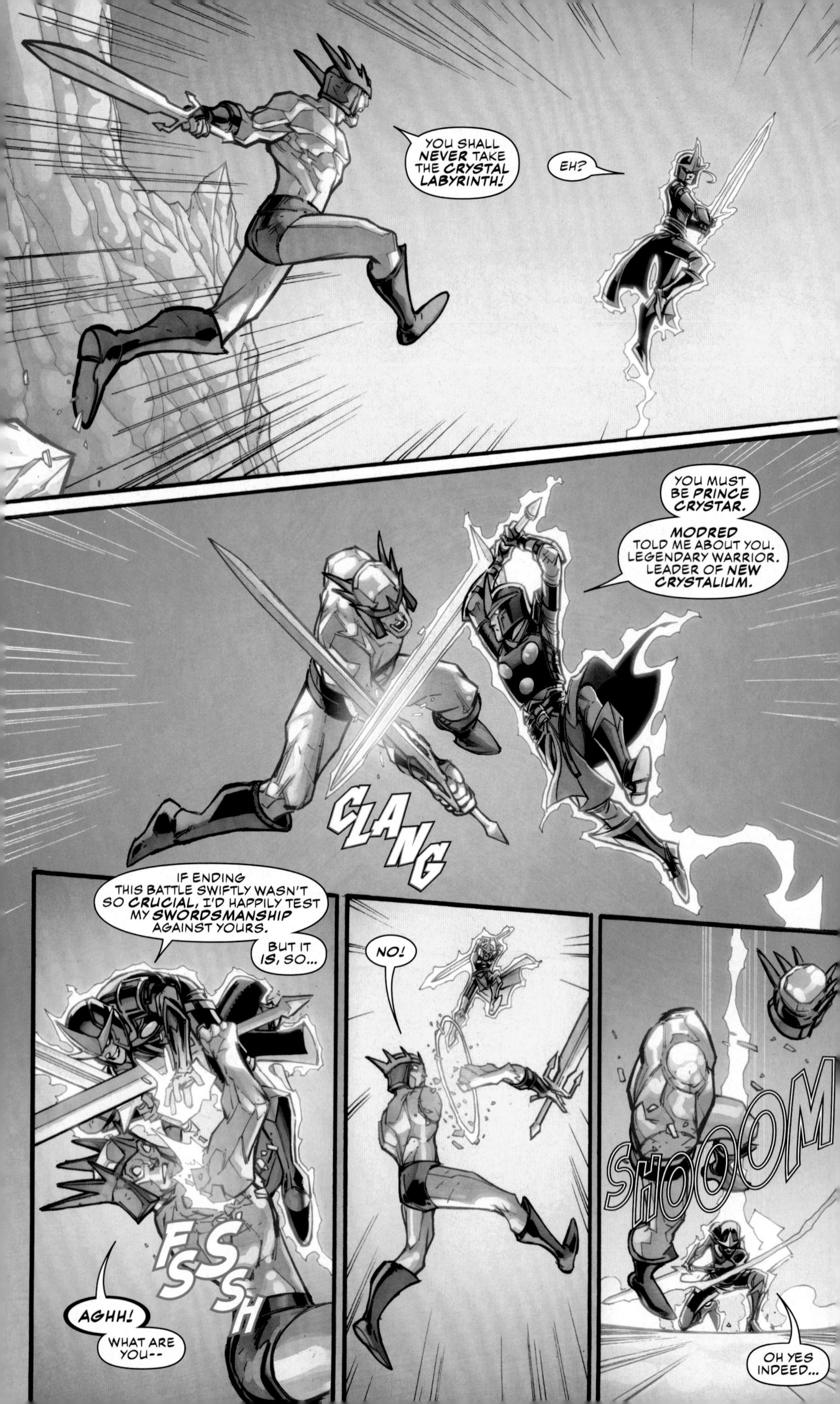
YOU SHALL NEVER TAKE THE CRYSTAL LABYRINTH!
EH?
YOU MUST BE PRINCE CRYSTAR.
MODRED TOLD ME ABOUT YOU. LEGENDARY WARRIOR. LEADER OF NEW CRYSTALIUM.
CLANG
IF ENDING THIS BATTLE SWIFTLY WASN'T SO CRUCIAL, I'D HAPPILY TEST MY SWORDSMANSHIP AGAINST YOURS.
BUT IT IS, SO...
FSSSH
AGHH!
WHAT ARE YOU--
NO!
SHOOOOM
OH YES INDEED...

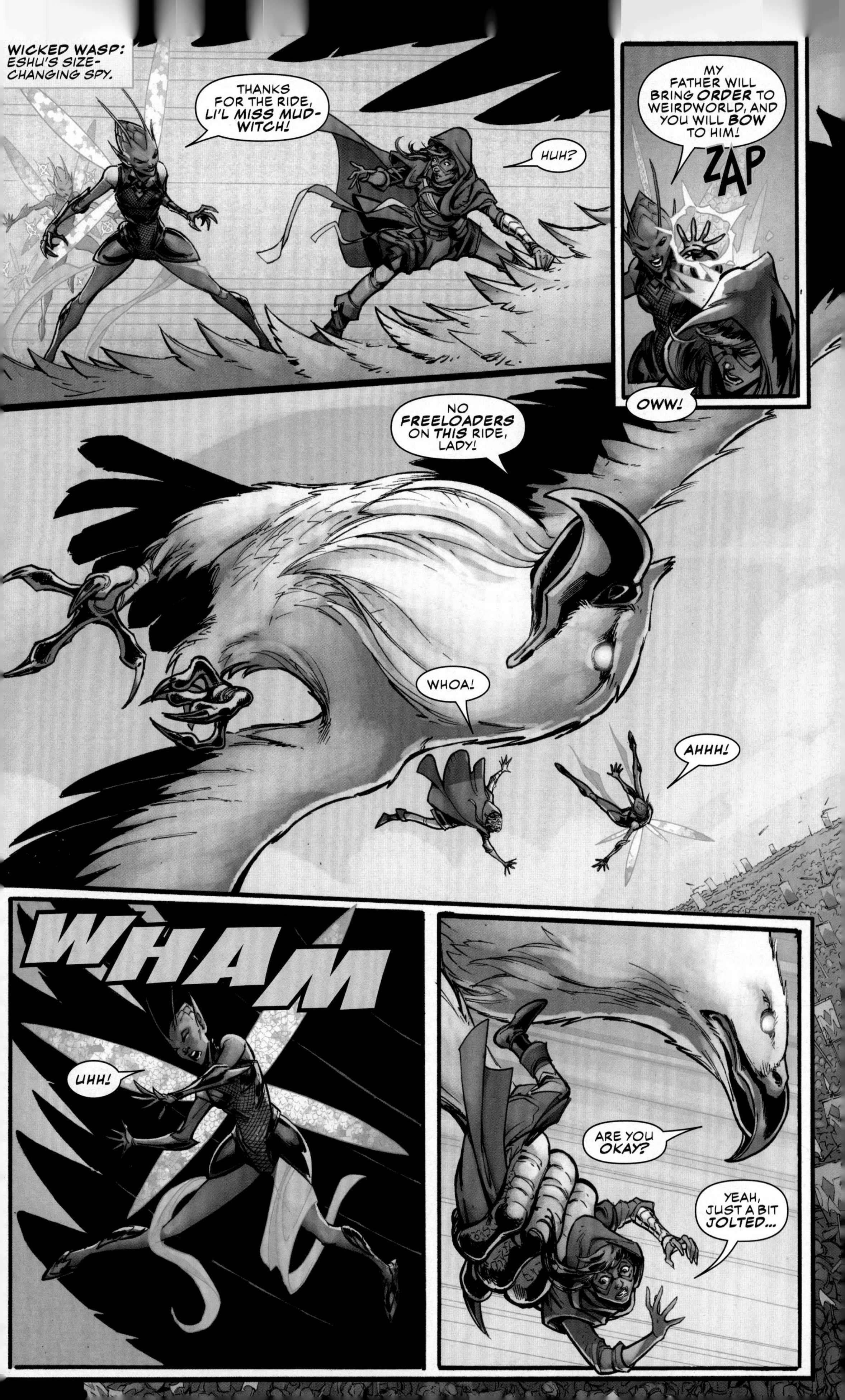
WICKED WASP: ESHU'S SIZE-CHANGING SPY.
THANKS FOR THE RIDE, LI'L MISS MUD-WITCH!
HUH?
MY FATHER WILL BRING ORDER TO WEIRDWORLD, AND YOU WILL BOW TO HIM!
ZAP
OWW!
NO FREELOADERS ON THIS RIDE, LADY!
WHOA!
AHHH!
WHAM
UHH!
ARE YOU OKAY?
YEAH, JUST A BIT JOLTED...

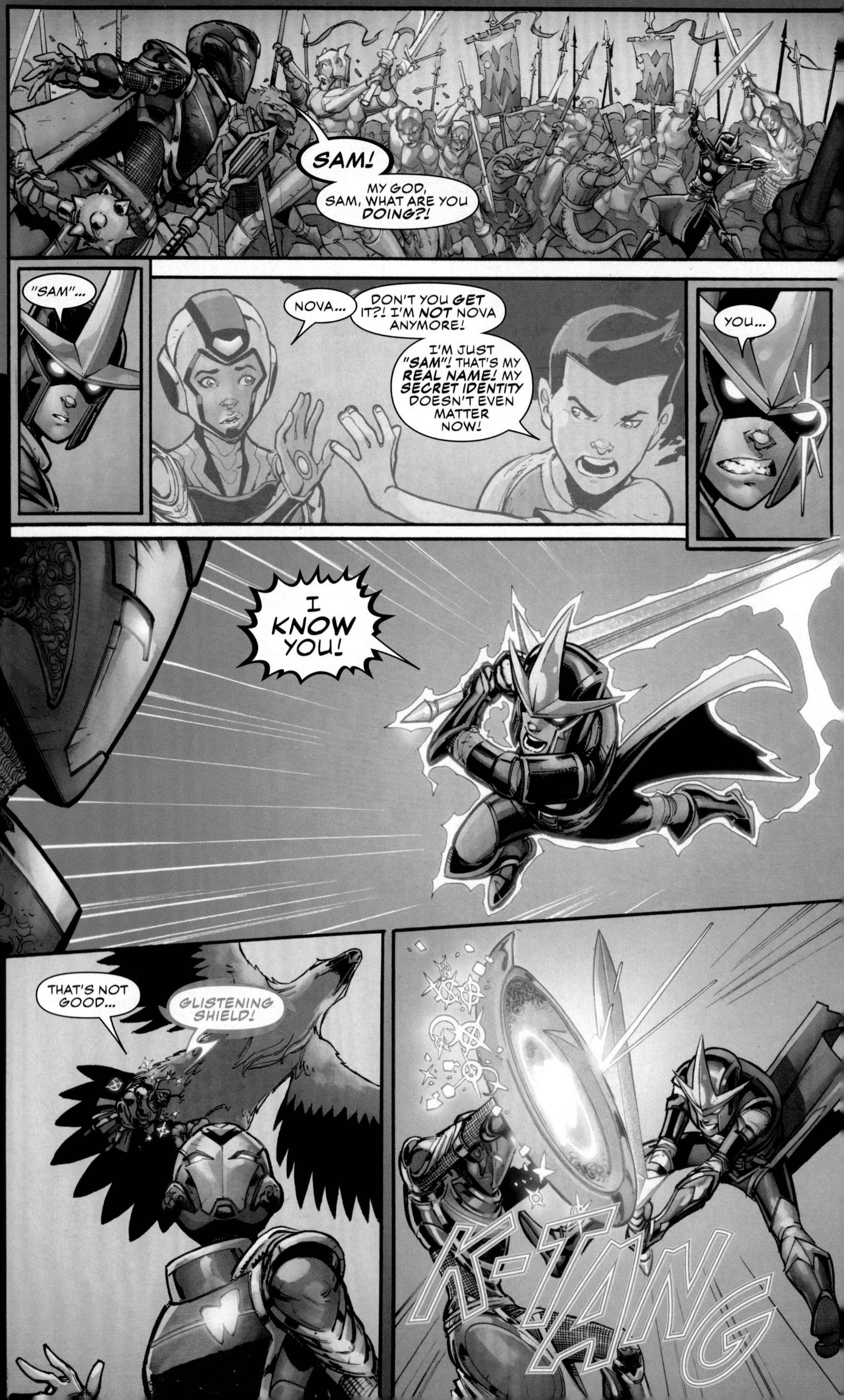
SAM!
MY GOD, SAM, WHAT ARE YOU DOING?!
"SAM"...
NOVA...
DON'T YOU GET IT?! I'M NOT NOVA ANYMORE!
I'M JUST "SAM"! THAT'S MY REAL NAME! MY SECRET IDENTITY DOESN'T EVEN MATTER NOW!
YOU...
I KNOW YOU!
THAT'S NOT GOOD...
GLISTENING SHIELD!
K-TANG

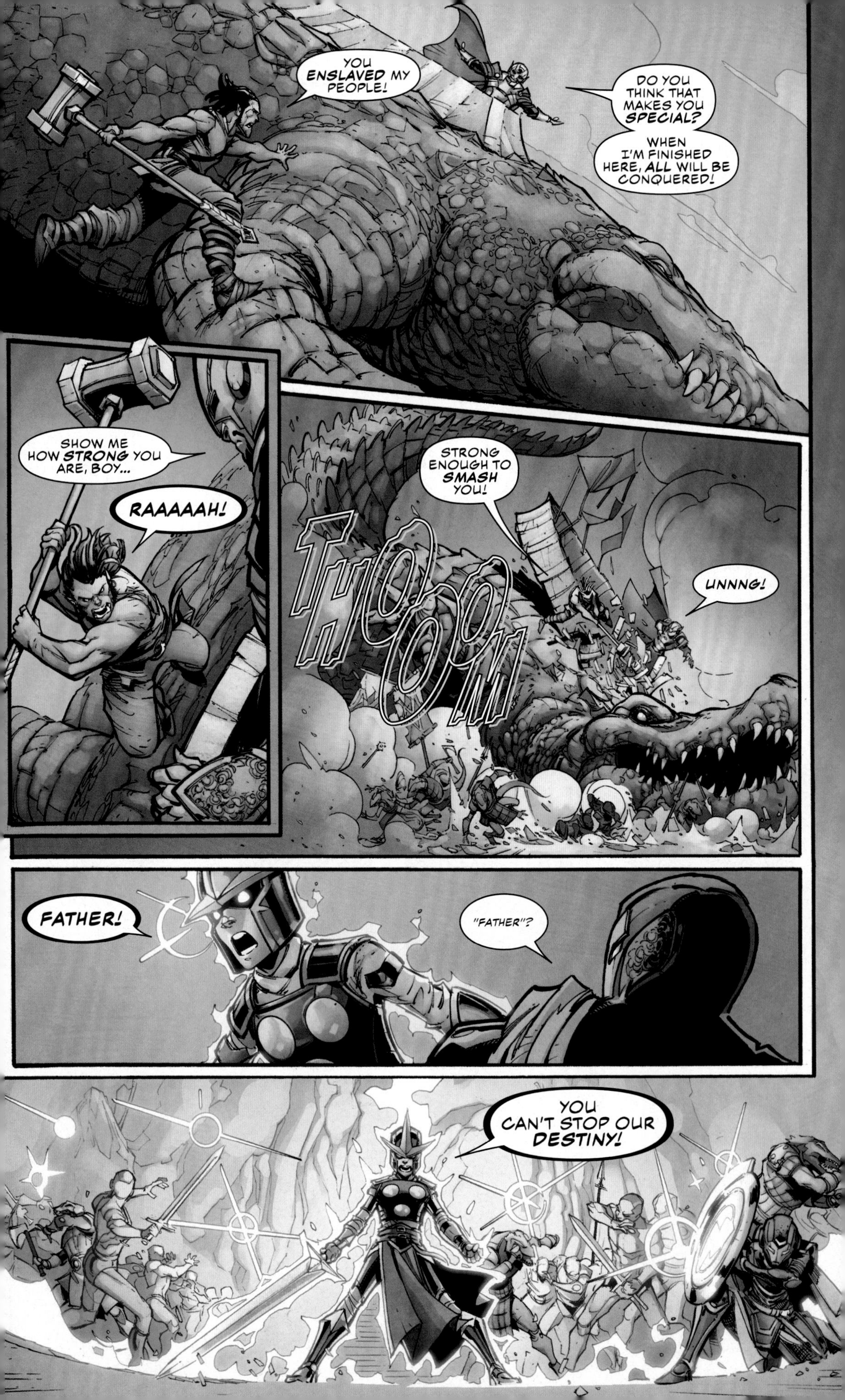
YOU ENSLAVED MY PEOPLE!
DO YOU THINK THAT MAKES YOU SPECIAL?
WHEN I'M FINISHED HERE, ALL WILL BE CONQUERED!
SHOW ME HOW STRONG YOU ARE, BOY...
RAAAAAH!
STRONG ENOUGH TO SMASH YOU!
THOOOM
UNNNG!
FATHER!
"FATHER"?
YOU CAN'T STOP OUR DESTINY!

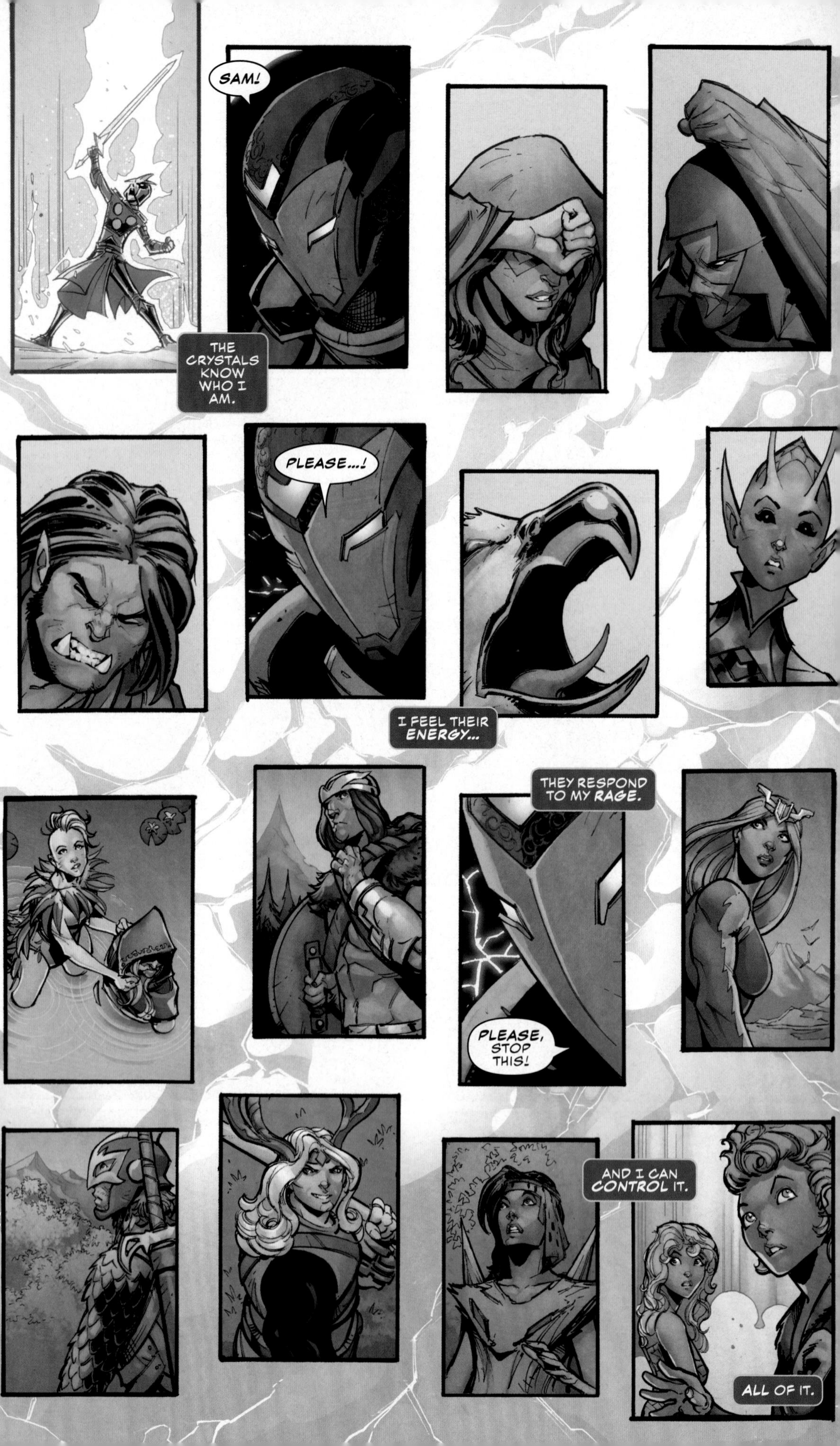
SAM!
THE CRYSTALS KNOW WHO I AM.
PLEASE...!
I FEEL THEIR ENERGY...
THEY RESPOND TO MY RAGE.
PLEASE, STOP THIS!
AND I CAN CONTROL IT.
ALL OF IT.

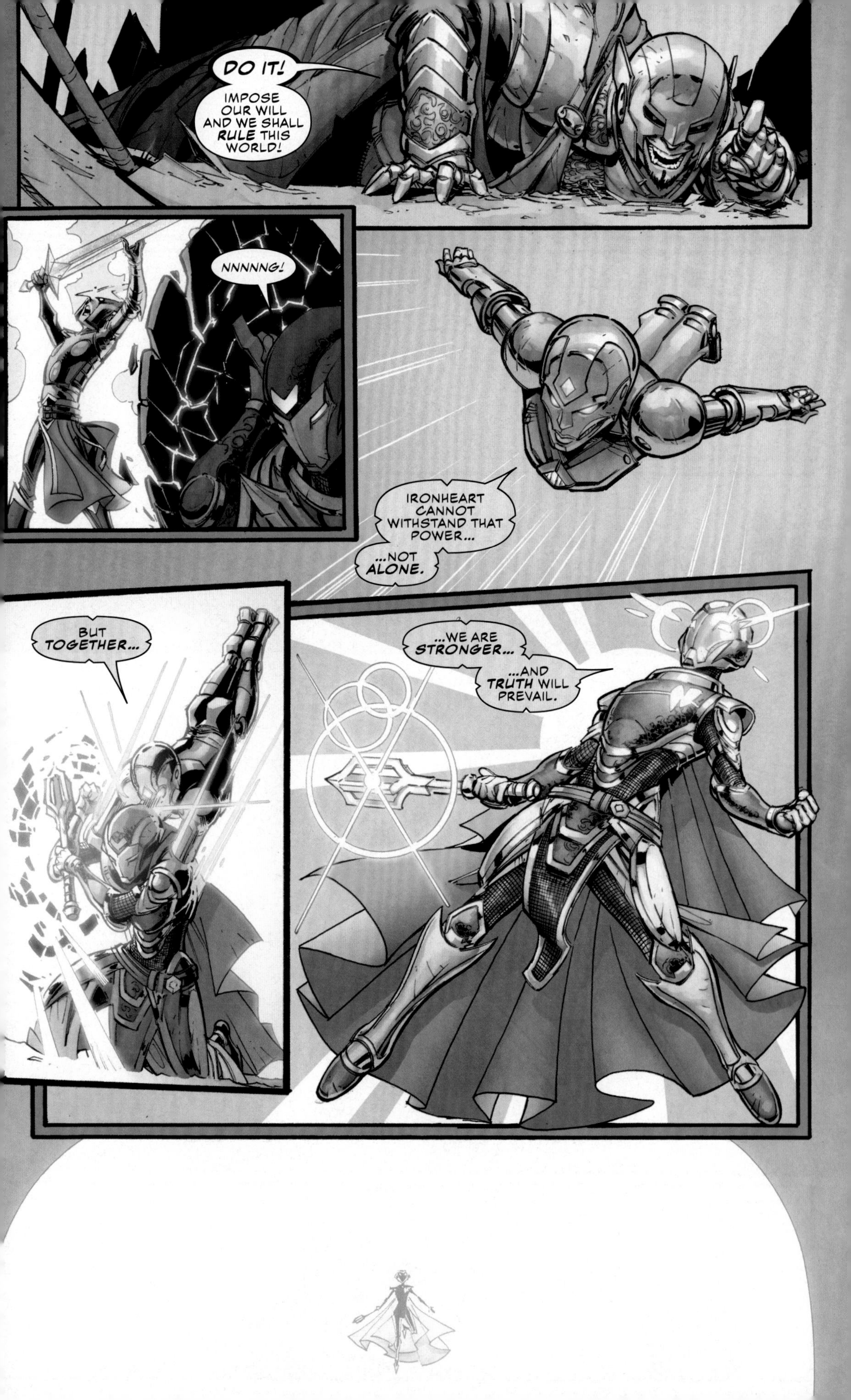
DO IT!
IMPOSE OUR WILL AND WE SHALL RULE THIS WORLD!
NNNNNG!
IRONHEART CANNOT WITHSTAND THAT POWER...
...NOT ALONE.
BUT TOGETHER...
...WE ARE STRONGER...
...AND TRUTH WILL PREVAIL.

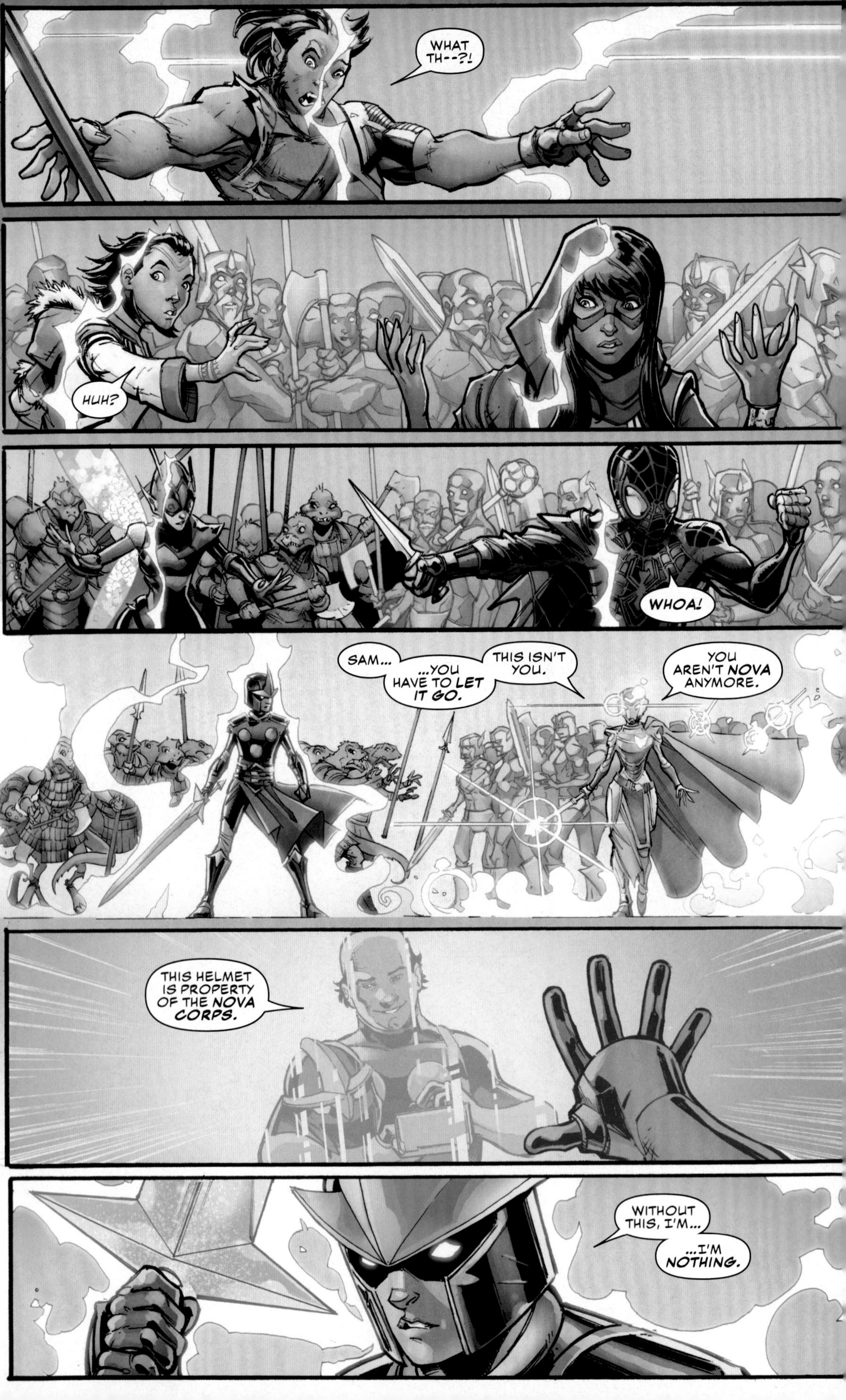
WHAT TH--?!
HUH?
WHOA!
SAM...
...YOU HAVE TO LET IT GO.
THIS ISN'T YOU.
YOU AREN'T NOVA ANYMORE.
THIS HELMET IS PROPERTY OF THE NOVA CORPS.
WITHOUT THIS, I'M...
...I'M NOTHING.

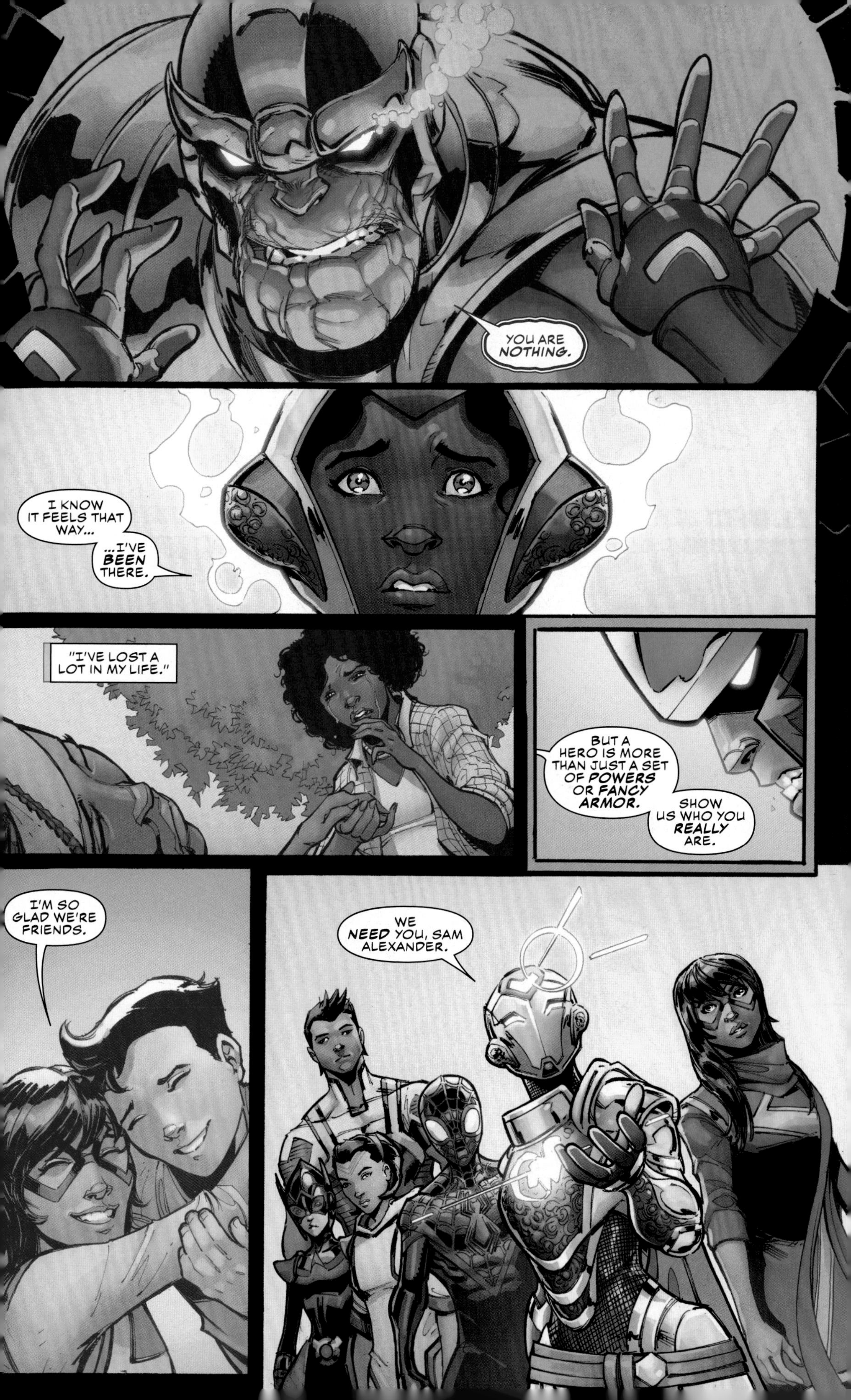
YOU ARE NOTHING.
I KNOW IT FEELS THAT WAY...
...I'VE BEEN THERE.
"I'VE LOST A LOT IN MY LIFE."
BUT A HERO IS MORE THAN JUST A SET OF POWERS OR FANCY ARMOR.
SHOW US WHO YOU REALLY ARE.
I'M SO GLAD WE'RE FRIENDS.
WE NEED YOU, SAM ALEXANDER.

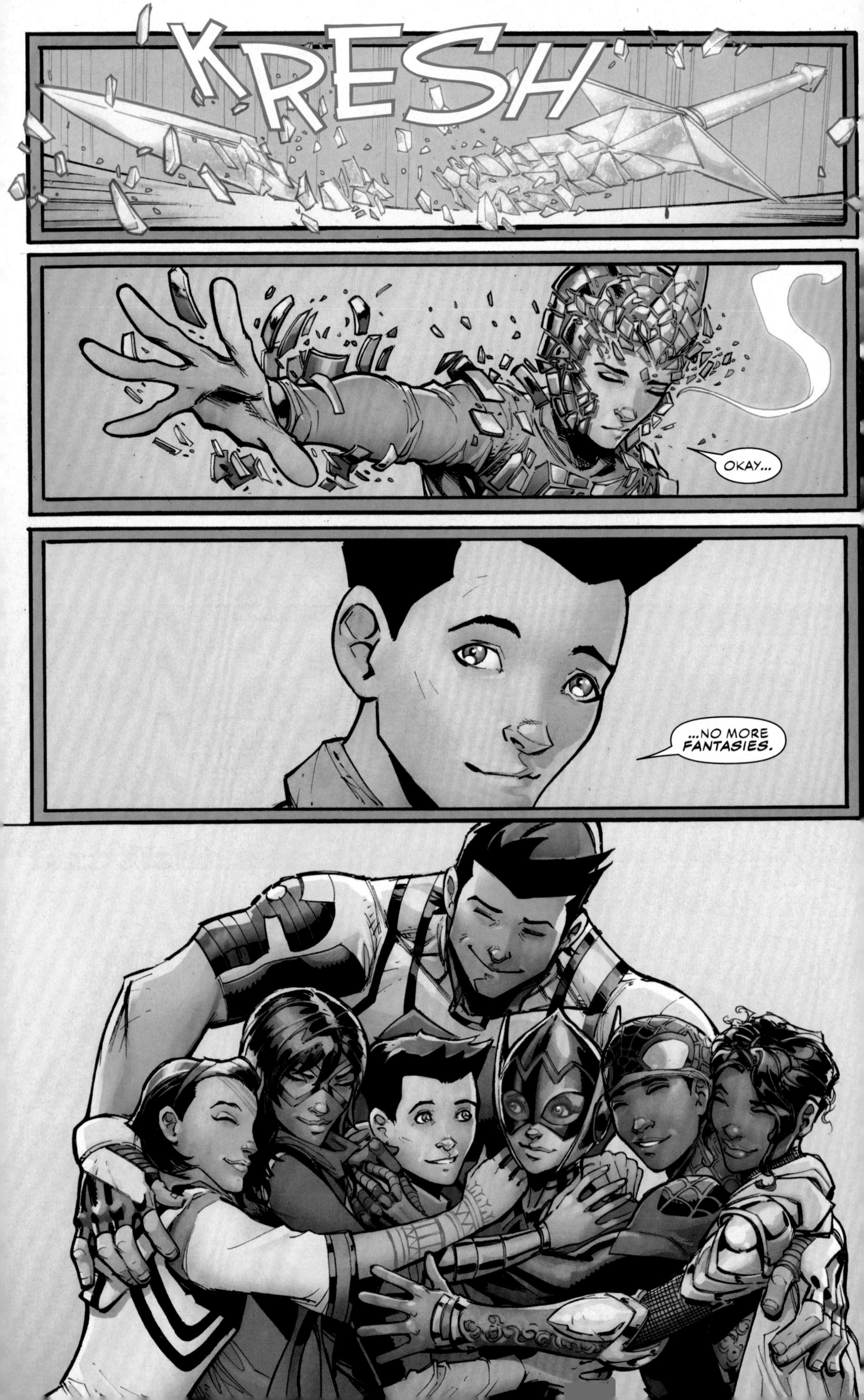
KRESH
OKAY...
...NO MORE FANTASIES.

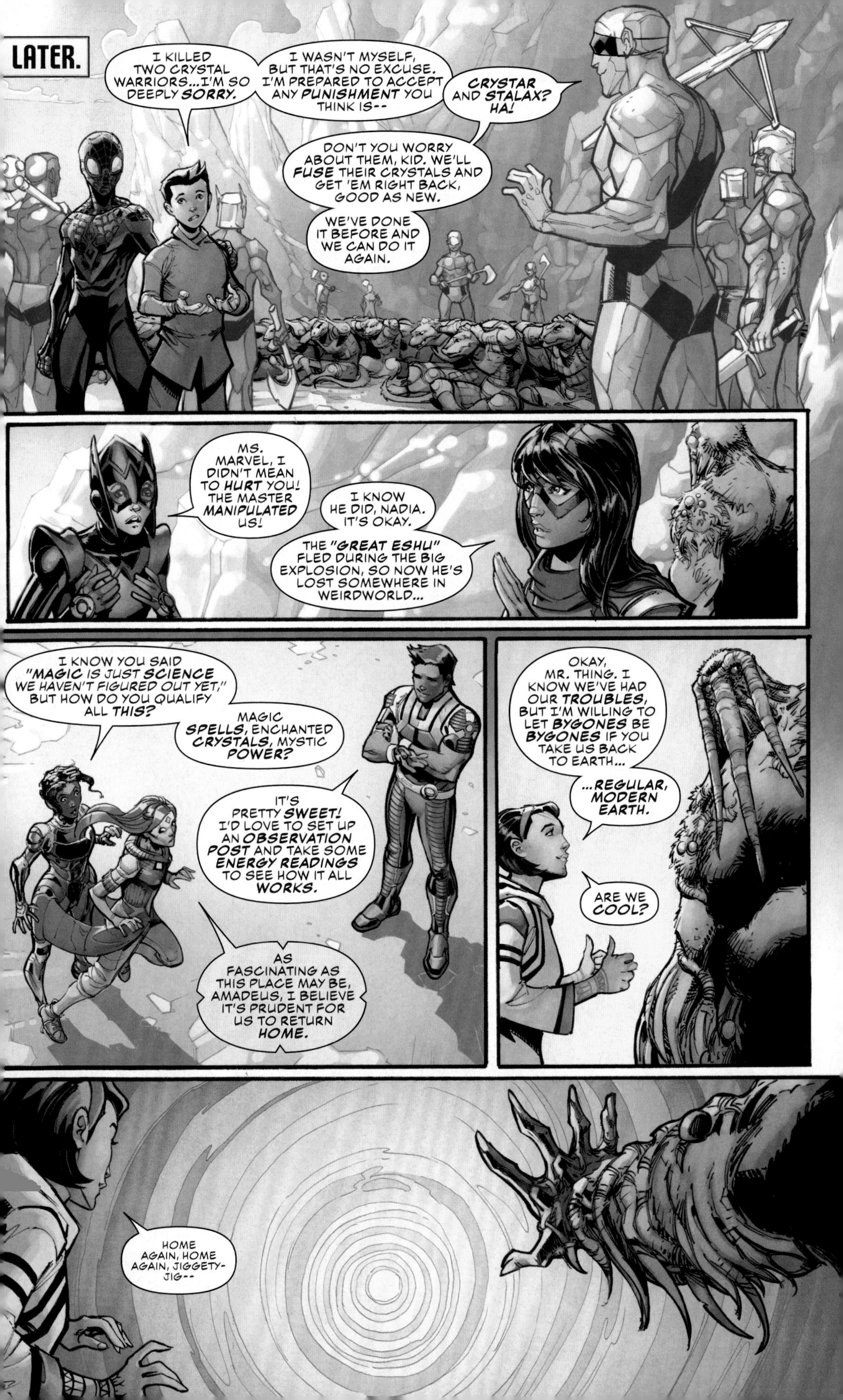
LATER.
I KILLED TWO CRYSTAL WARRIORS...I'M SO DEEPLY SORRY.
I WASN'T MYSELF, BUT THAT'S NO EXCUSE. I'M PREPARED TO ACCEPT ANY PUNISHMENT YOU THINK IS--
CRYSTAR AND STALAX? HA!
DON'T YOU WORRY ABOUT THEM, KID. WE'LL FUSE THEIR CRYSTALS AND GET 'EM RIGHT BACK, GOOD AS NEW.
WE'VE DONE IT BEFORE AND WE CAN DO IT AGAIN.
MS. MARVEL, I DIDN'T MEAN TO HURT YOU! THE MASTER MANIPULATED US!
I KNOW HE DID, NADIA. IT'S OKAY.
THE "GREAT ESHU" FLED DURING THE BIG EXPLOSION, SO NOW HE'S LOST SOMEWHERE IN WEIRDWORLD...
I KNOW YOU SAID "MAGIC IS JUST SCIENCE WE HAVEN'T FIGURED OUT YET," BUT HOW DO YOU QUALIFY ALL THIS?
MAGIC SPELLS, ENCHANTED CRYSTALS, MYSTIC POWER?
IT'S PRETTY SWEET! I'D LOVE TO SET UP AN OBSERVATION POST AND TAKE SOME ENERGY READINGS TO SEE HOW IT ALL WORKS.
AS FASCINATING AS THIS PLACE MAY BE, AMADEUS, I BELIEVE IT'S PRUDENT FOR US TO RETURN HOME.
OKAY, MR. THING. I KNOW WE'VE HAD OUR TROUBLES, BUT I'M WILLING TO LET BYGONES BE BYGONES IF YOU TAKE US BACK TO EARTH...
...REGULAR, MODERN EARTH.
ARE WE COOL?
HOME AGAIN, HOME AGAIN, JIGGETY-JIG--

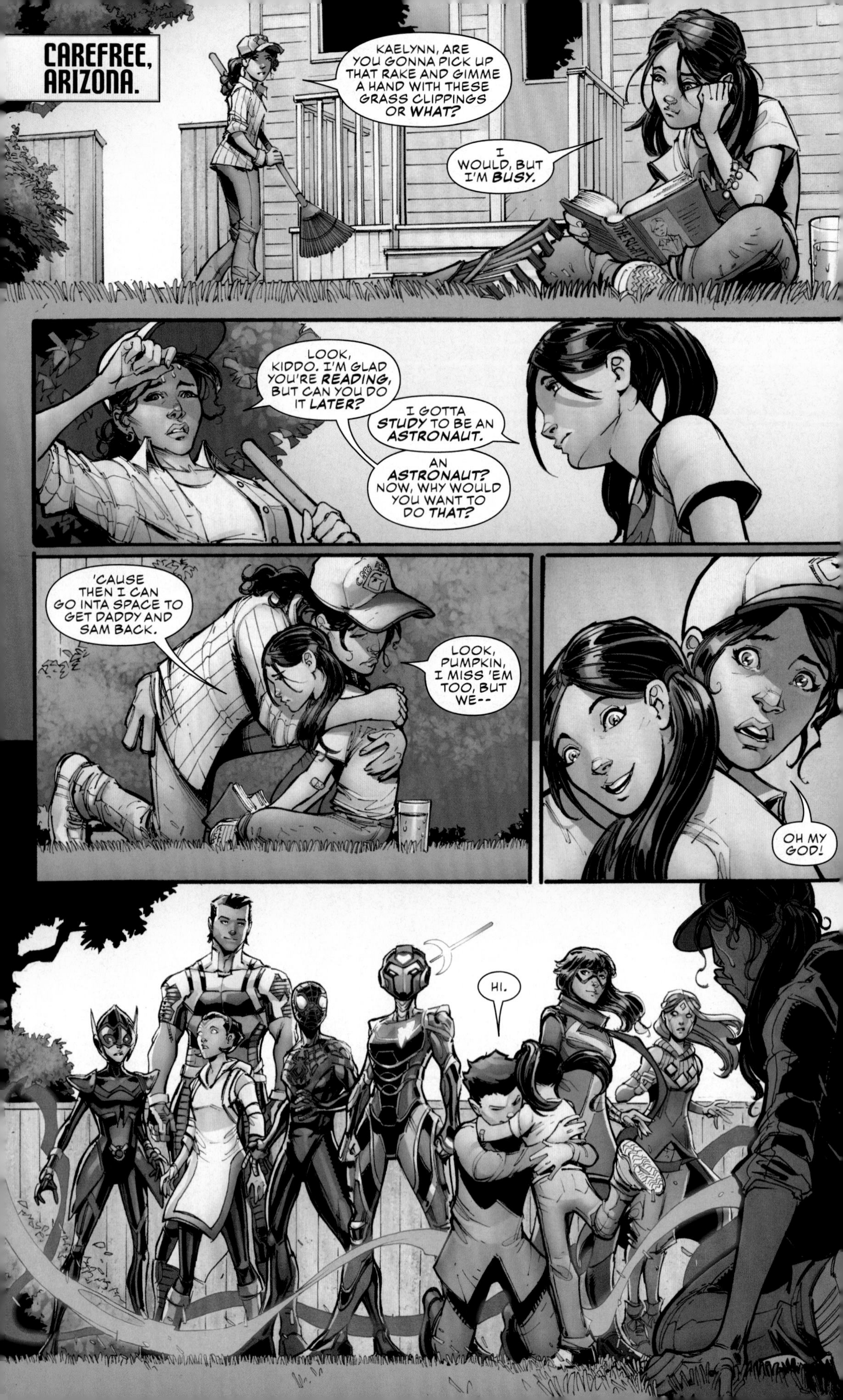
CAREFREE, ARIZONA.
KAELYNN, ARE YOU GONNA PICK UP THAT RAKE AND GIMME A HAND WITH THESE GRASS CLIPPINGS OR WHAT?
I WOULD, BUT I'M BUSY.
LOOK, KIDDO. I'M GLAD YOU'RE READING, BUT CAN YOU DO IT LATER?
I GOTTA STUDY TO BE AN ASTRONAUT.
AN ASTRONAUT? NOW, WHY WOULD YOU WANT TO DO THAT?
'CAUSE THEN I CAN GO INTA SPACE TO GET DADDY AND SAM BACK.
LOOK, PUMPKIN, I MISS 'EM TOO, BUT WE--
OH MY GOD!
HI.

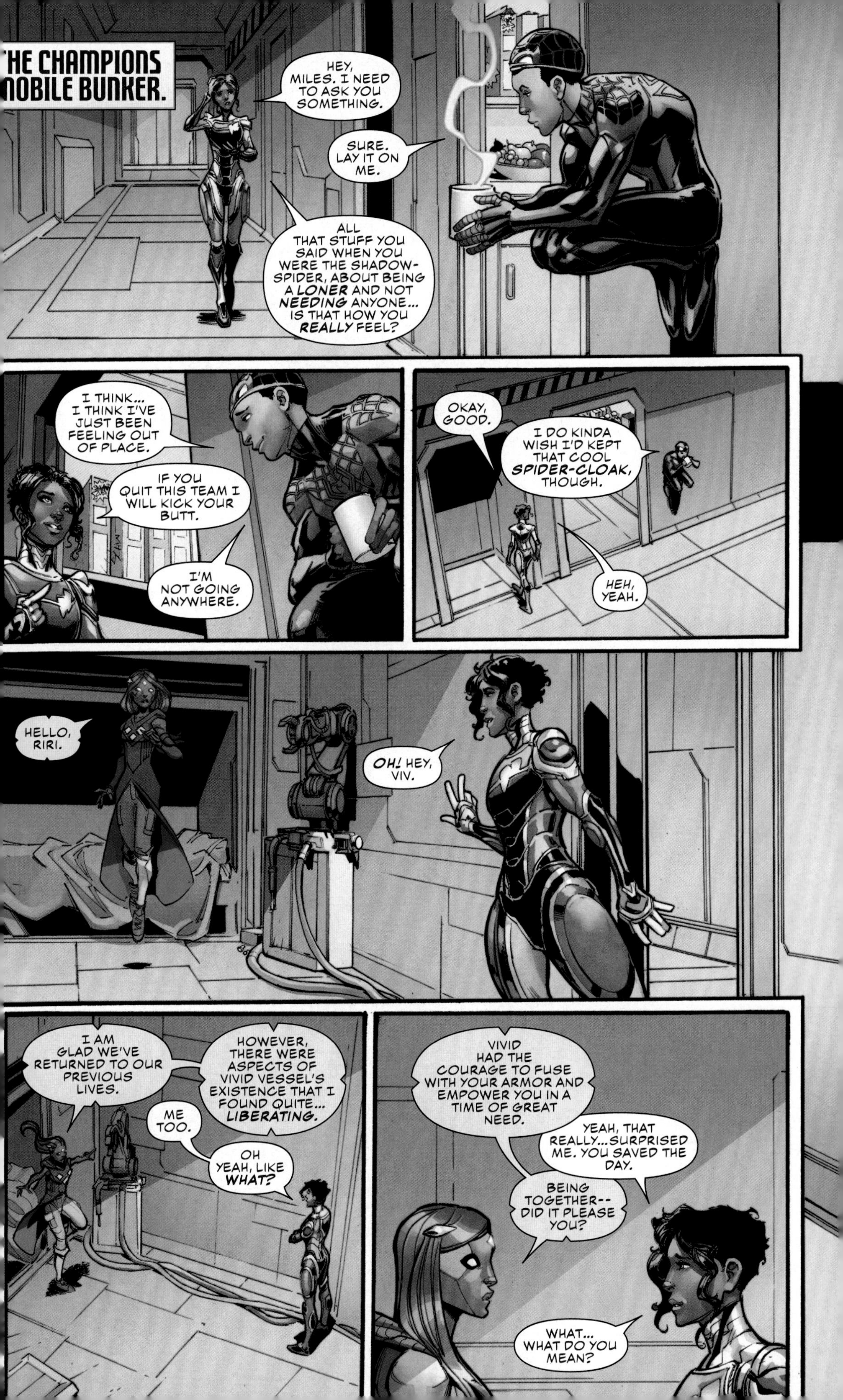
THE CHAMPIONS MOBILE BUNKER.
HEY, MILES. I NEED TO ASK YOU SOMETHING.
SURE. LAY IT ON ME.
ALL THAT STUFF YOU SAID WHEN YOU WERE THE SHADOW-SPIDER, ABOUT BEING A LONER AND NOT NEEDING ANYONE... IS THAT HOW YOU REALLY FEEL?
I THINK... I THINK I'VE JUST BEEN FEELING OUT OF PLACE.
IF YOU QUIT THIS TEAM I WILL KICK YOUR BUTT.
I'M NOT GOING ANYWHERE.
OKAY, GOOD.
I DO KINDA WISH I'D KEPT THAT COOL SPIDER-CLOAK, THOUGH.
HEH, YEAH.
HELLO, RIRI.
OH! HEY, VIV.
I AM GLAD WE'VE RETURNED TO OUR PREVIOUS LIVES.
HOWEVER, THERE WERE ASPECTS OF VIVID VESSEL'S EXISTENCE THAT I FOUND QUITE... LIBERATING.
ME TOO.
OH YEAH, LIKE WHAT?
VIVID HAD THE COURAGE TO FUSE WITH YOUR ARMOR AND EMPOWER YOU IN A TIME OF GREAT NEED.
YEAH, THAT REALLY... SURPRISED ME. YOU SAVED THE DAY.
BEING TOGETHER--DID IT PLEASE YOU?
WHAT... WHAT DO YOU MEAN?

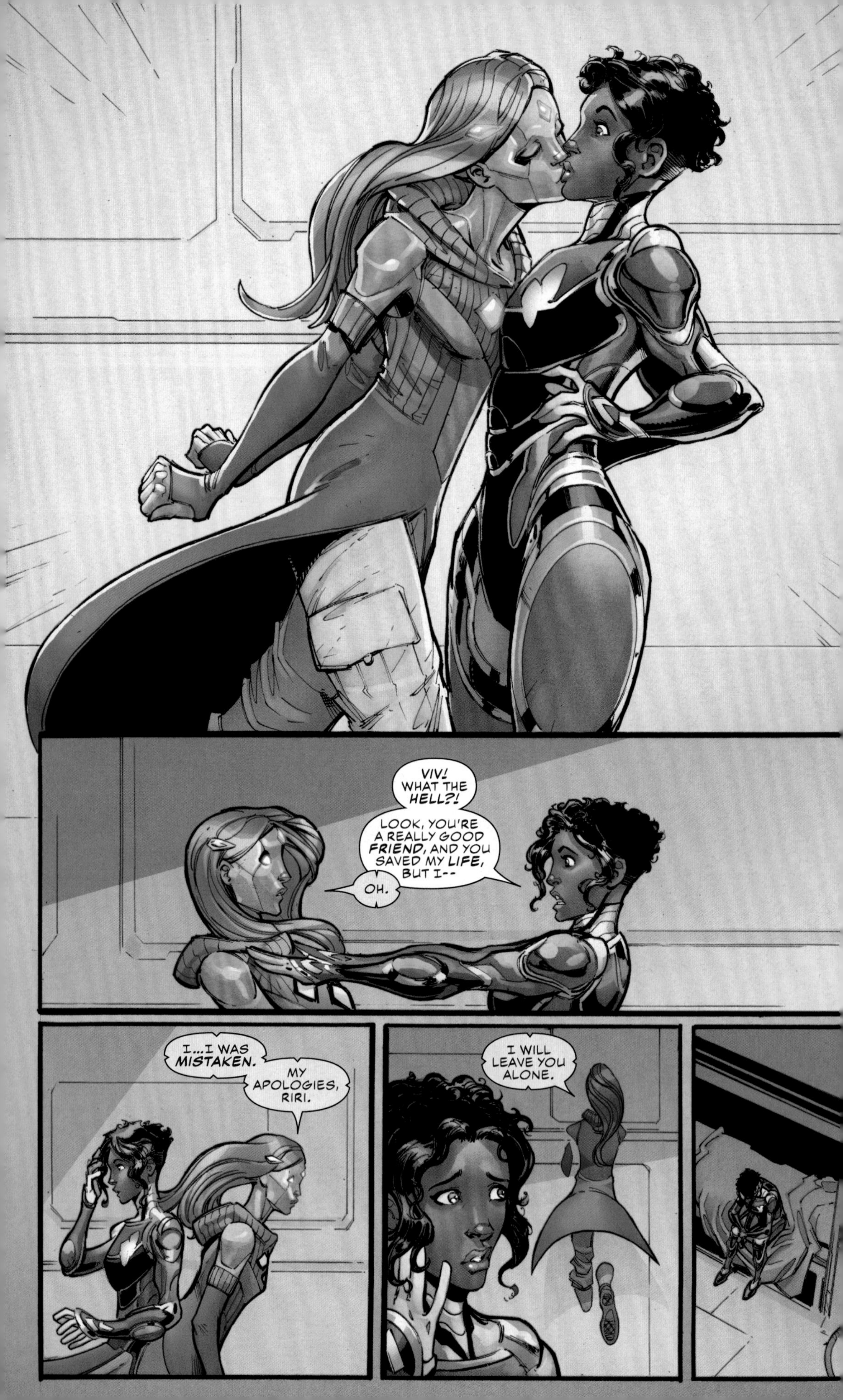
VIV! WHAT THE HELL?!
LOOK, YOU'RE A REALLY GOOD FRIEND, AND YOU SAVED MY LIFE, BUT I--
OH.
I...I WAS MISTAKEN.
MY APOLOGIES, RIRI.
I WILL LEAVE YOU ALONE.

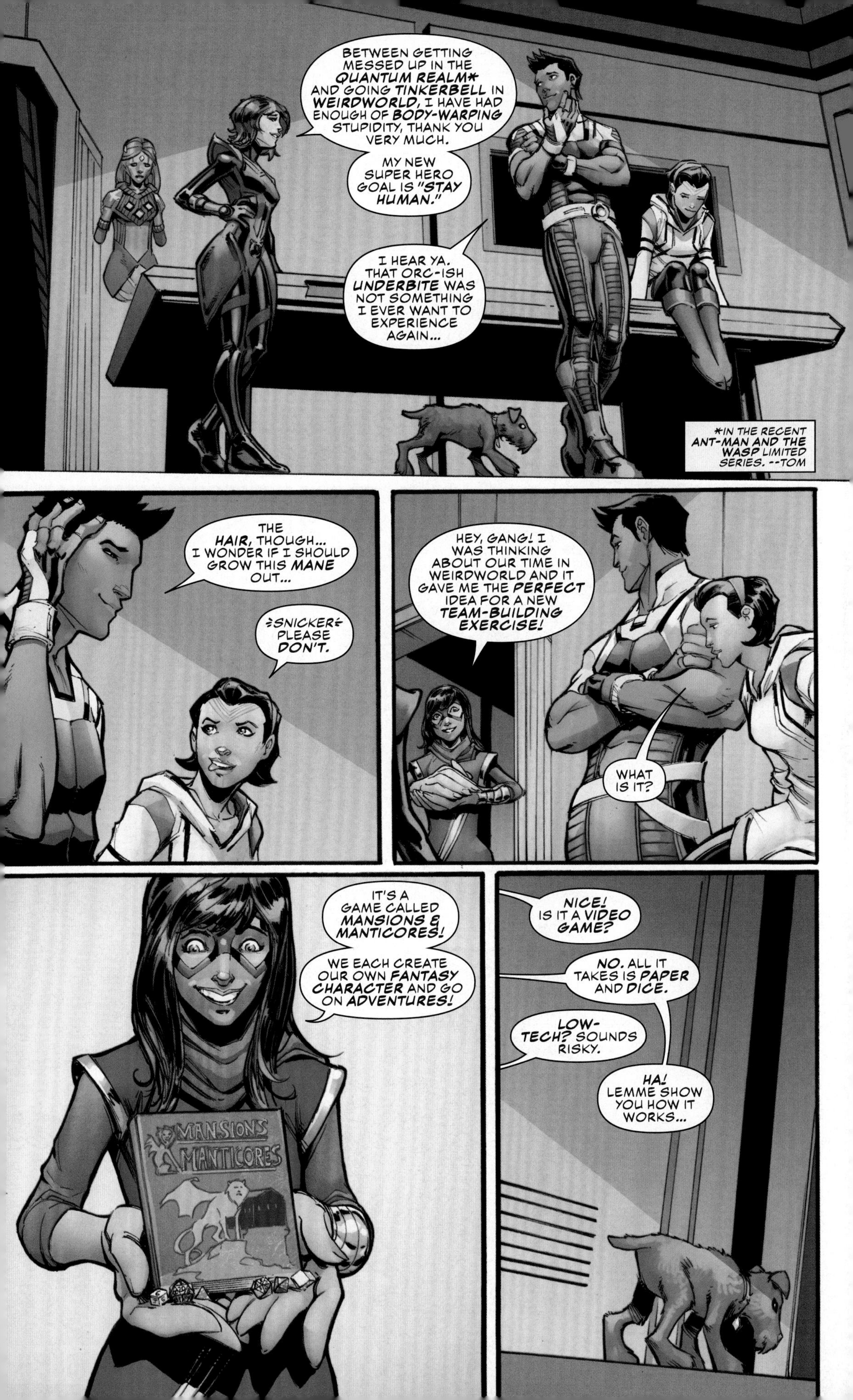
BETWEEN GETTING MESSED UP IN THE QUANTUM REALM* AND GOING TINKERBELL IN WEIRDWORLD, I HAVE HAD ENOUGH OF BODY-WARPING STUPIDITY, THANK YOU VERY MUCH.
MY NEW SUPER HERO GOAL IS "STAY HUMAN."
I HEAR YA. THAT ORC-ISH UNDERBITE WAS NOT SOMETHING I EVER WANT TO EXPERIENCE AGAIN...
*IN THE RECENT ANT-MAN AND THE WASP LIMITED SERIES. --TOM
THE HAIR, THOUGH... I WONDER IF I SHOULD GROW THIS MANE OUT...
≈SNICKER≈ PLEASE DON'T.
HEY, GANG! I WAS THINKING ABOUT OUR TIME IN WEIRDWORLD AND IT GAVE ME THE PERFECT IDEA FOR A NEW TEAM-BUILDING EXERCISE!
WHAT IS IT?
IT'S A GAME CALLED MANSIONS & MANTICORES!
WE EACH CREATE OUR OWN FANTASY CHARACTER AND GO ON ADVENTURES!
MANSIONS MANTICORES
NICE! IS IT A VIDEO GAME?
NO. ALL IT TAKES IS PAPER AND DICE.
LOW-TECH? SOUNDS RISKY.
HA! LEMME SHOW YOU HOW IT WORKS...

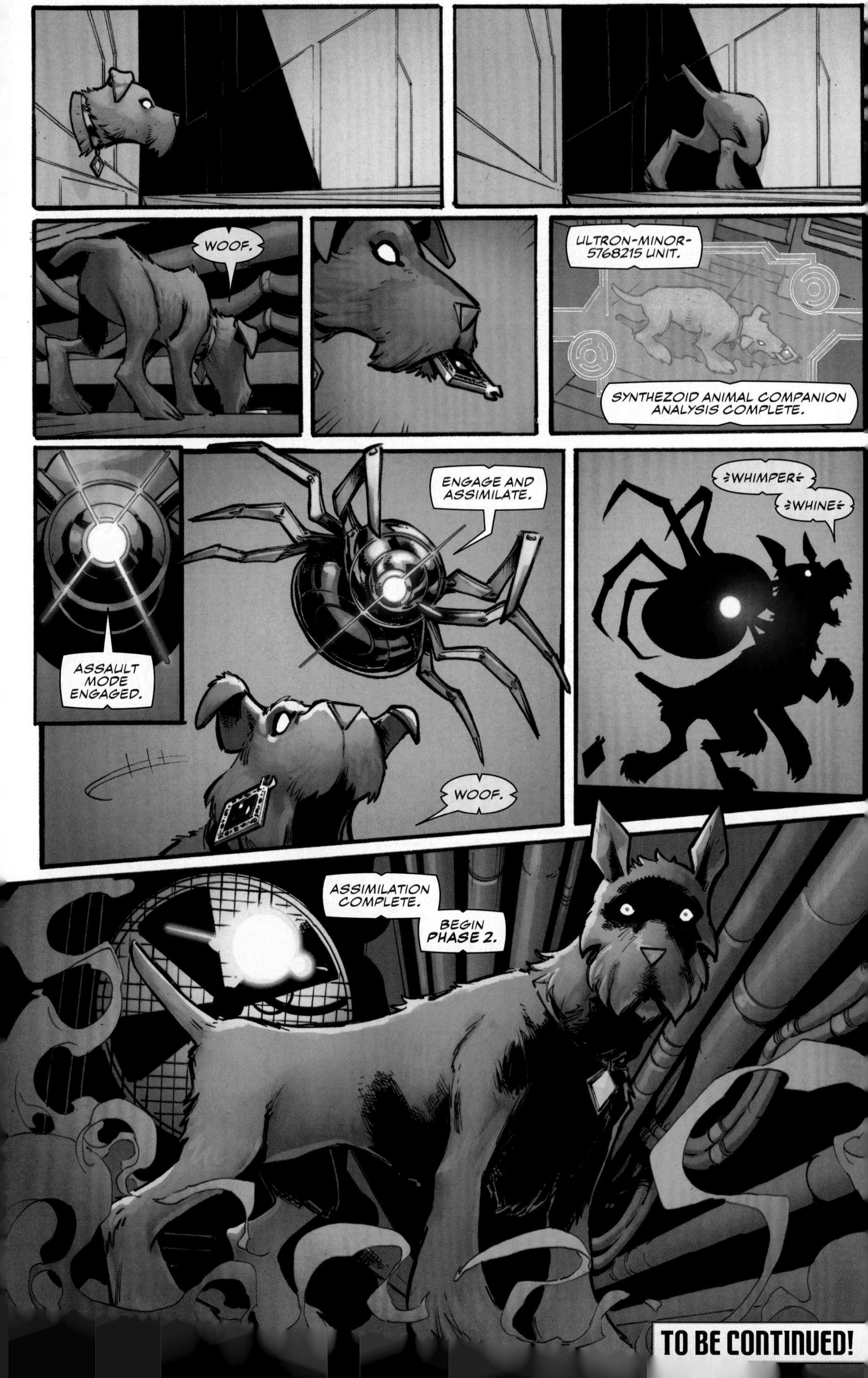
WOOF.
ULTRON-MINOR-5768215 UNIT.
SYNTHEZOID ANIMAL COMPANION ANALYSIS COMPLETE.
ASSAULT MODE ENGAGED.
ENGAGE AND ASSIMILATE.
WOOF.
WHIMPER
WHINE
ASSIMILATION COMPLETE.
BEGIN PHASE 2.
TO BE CONTINUED!

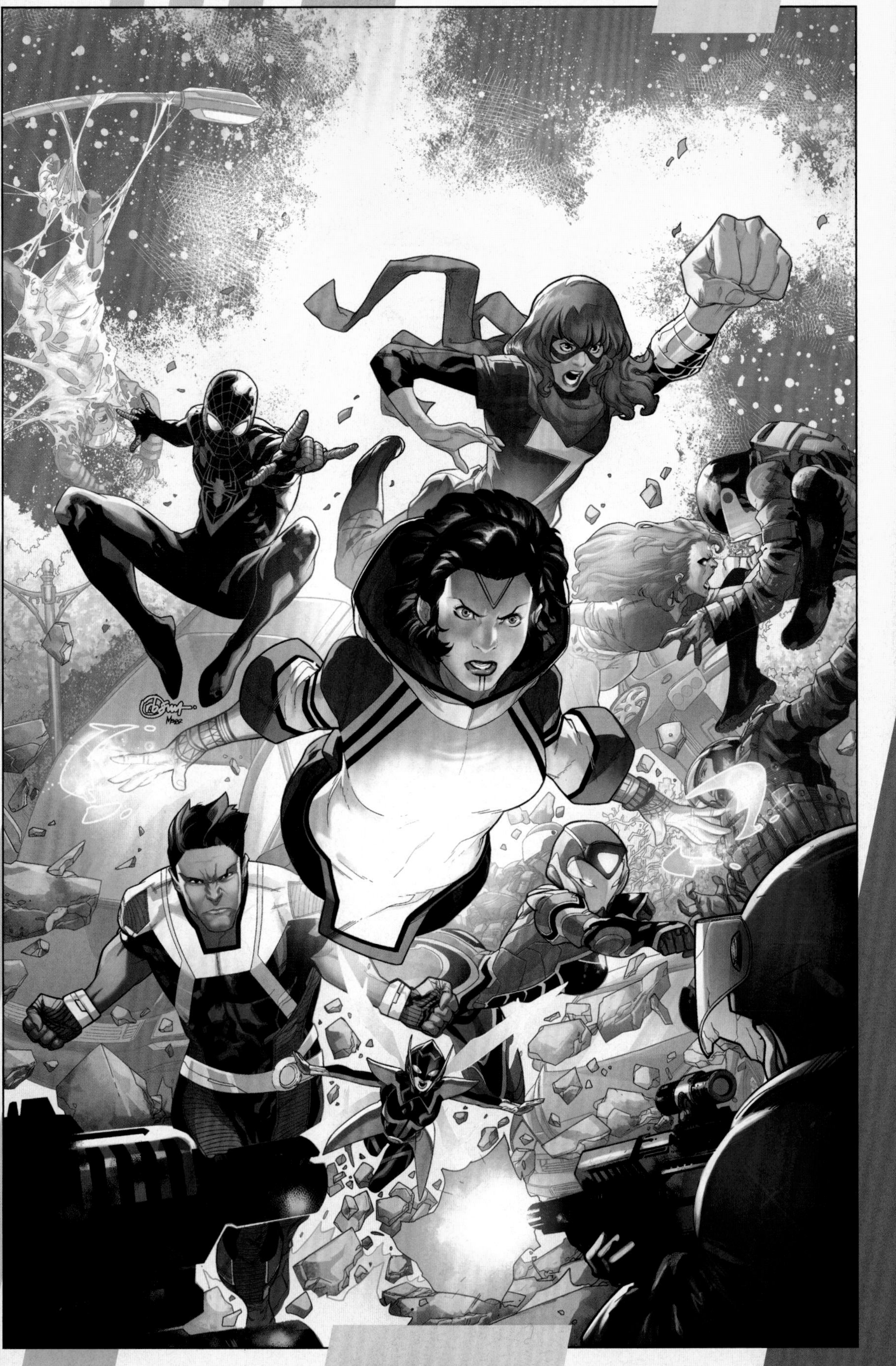

ANNUAL 1

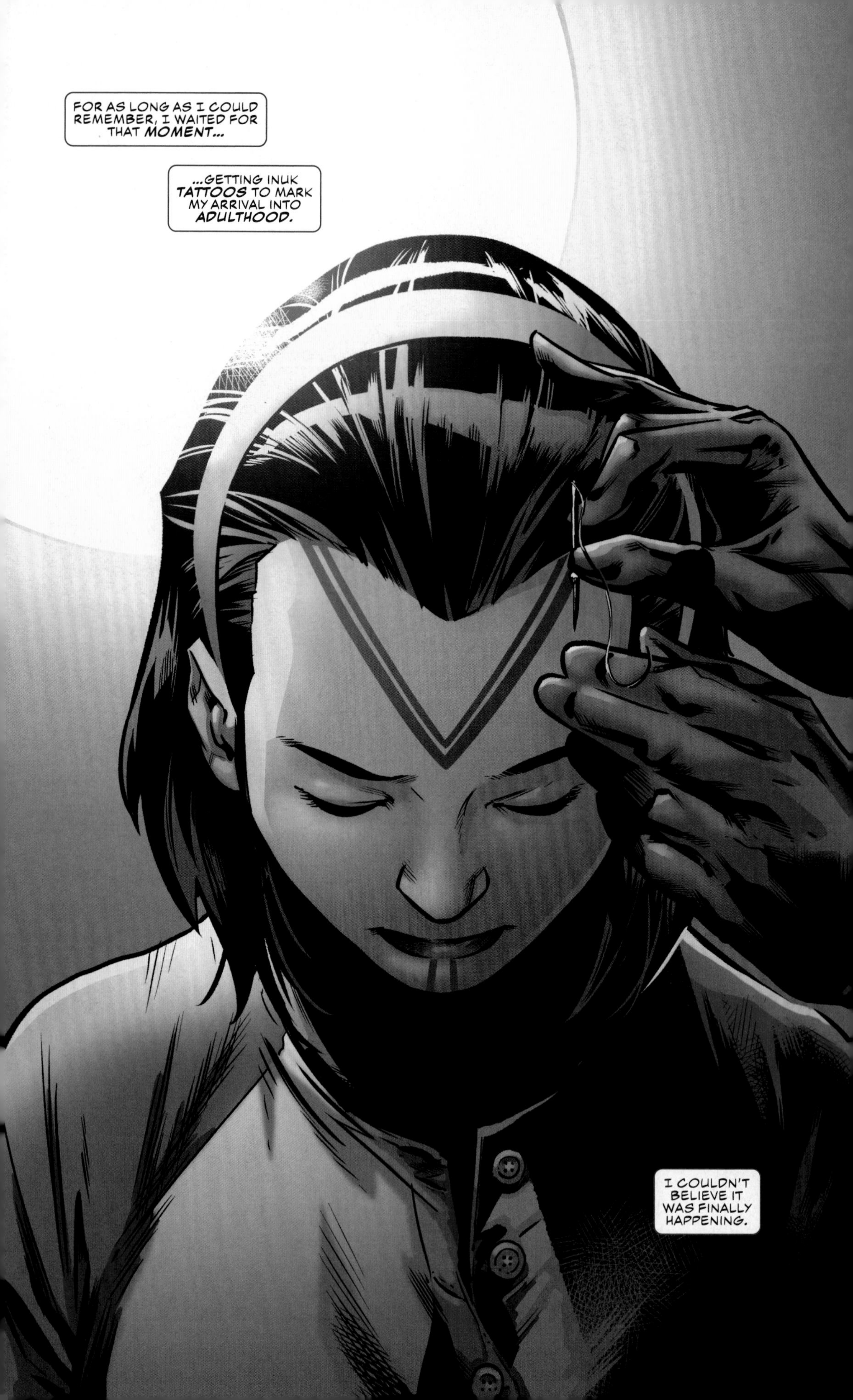

FOR AS LONG AS I COULD REMEMBER, I WAITED FOR THAT MOMENT...
...GETTING INUK TATTOOS TO MARK MY ARRIVAL INTO ADULTHOOD.
I COULDN'T BELIEVE IT WAS FINALLY HAPPENING.

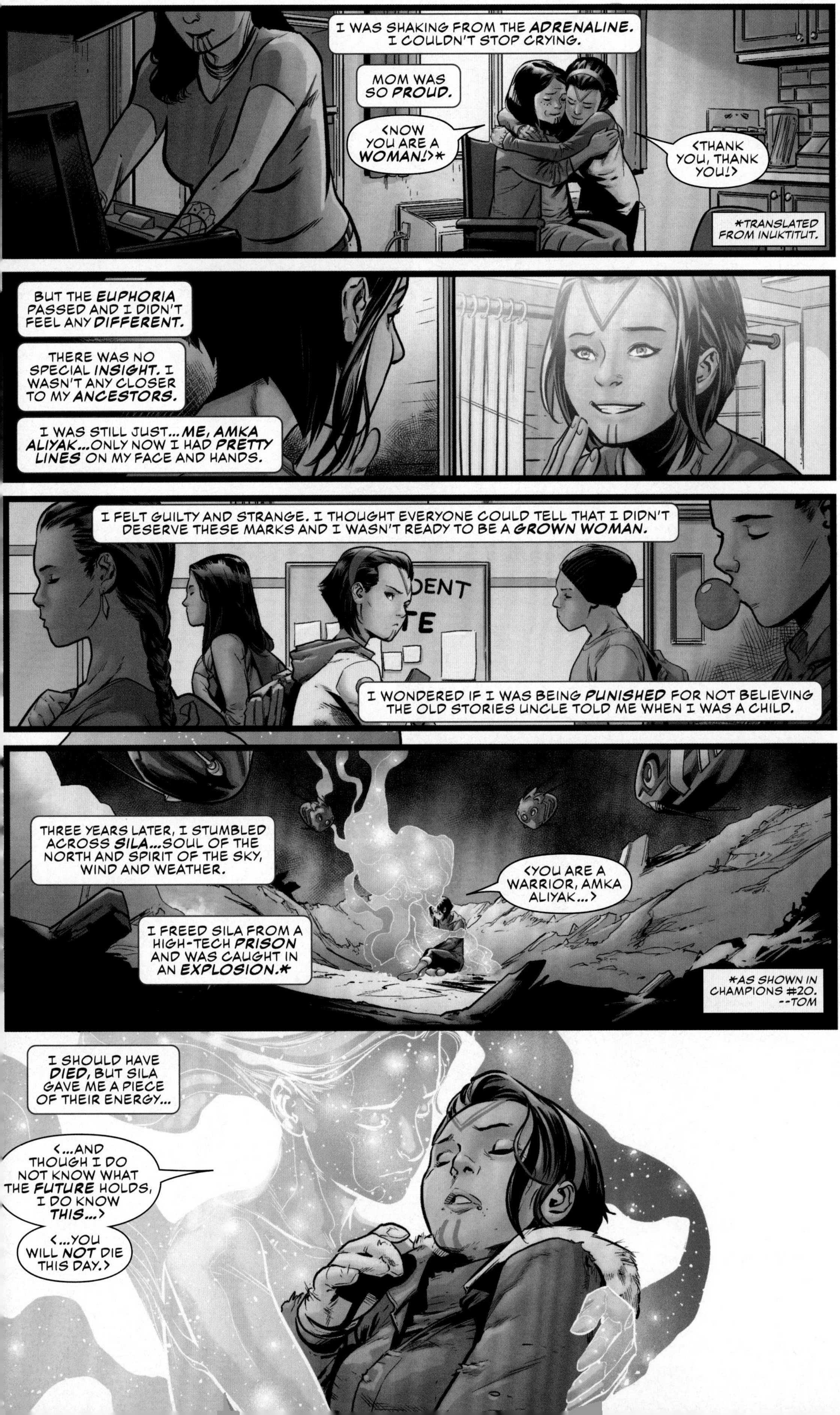

I WAS SHAKING FROM THE ADRENALINE. I COULDN'T STOP CRYING.
MOM WAS SO PROUD.
<NOW YOU ARE A WOMAN!>*
<THANK YOU, THANK YOU!>
*TRANSLATED FROM INUKTITUT.
BUT THE EUPHORIA PASSED AND I DIDN'T FEEL ANY DIFFERENT.
THERE WAS NO SPECIAL INSIGHT. I WASN'T ANY CLOSER TO MY ANCESTORS.
I WAS STILL JUST... ME, AMKA ALIYAK... ONLY NOW I HAD PRETTY LINES ON MY FACE AND HANDS.
I FELT GUILTY AND STRANGE. I THOUGHT EVERYONE COULD TELL THAT I DIDN'T DESERVE THESE MARKS AND I WASN'T READY TO BE A GROWN WOMAN.
I WONDERED IF I WAS BEING PUNISHED FOR NOT BELIEVING THE OLD STORIES UNCLE TOLD ME WHEN I WAS A CHILD.
THREE YEARS LATER, I STUMBLED ACROSS SILA... SOUL OF THE NORTH AND SPIRIT OF THE SKY, WIND AND WEATHER.
<YOU ARE A WARRIOR, AMKA ALIYAK...>
I FREED SILA FROM A HIGH-TECH PRISON AND WAS CAUGHT IN AN EXPLOSION.*
*AS SHOWN IN CHAMPIONS #20. --TOM
I SHOULD HAVE DIED, BUT SILA GAVE ME A PIECE OF THEIR ENERGY...
<...AND THOUGH I DO NOT KNOW WHAT THE FUTURE HOLDS, I DO KNOW THIS...>
<...YOU WILL NOT DIE THIS DAY.>

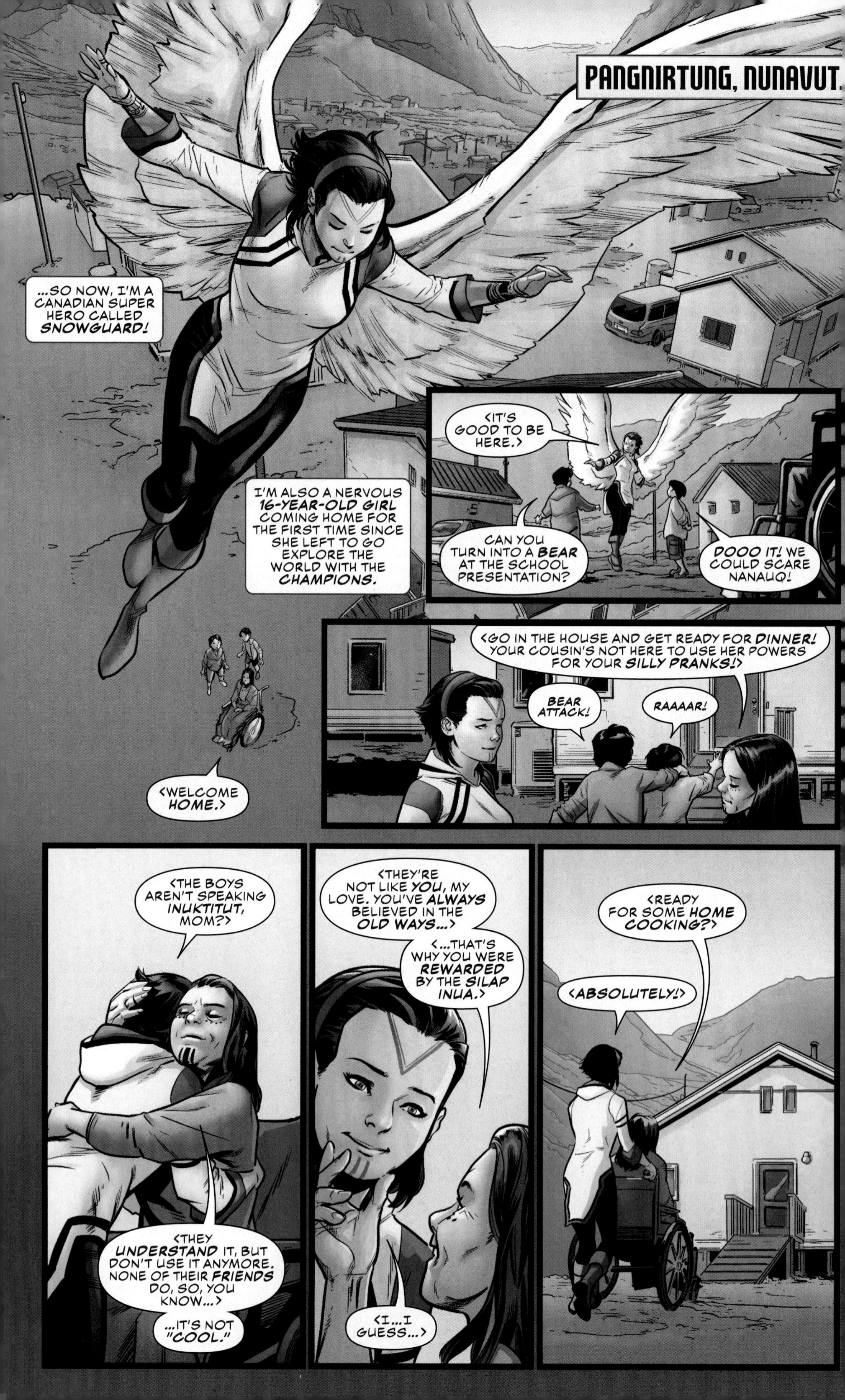
PANGNIRTUNG, NUNAVUT.
...SO NOW, I'M A CANADIAN SUPER HERO CALLED SNOWGUARD!
I'M ALSO A NERVOUS 16-YEAR-OLD GIRL COMING HOME FOR THE FIRST TIME SINCE SHE LEFT TO GO EXPLORE THE WORLD WITH THE CHAMPIONS.
<WELCOME HOME.>
<IT'S GOOD TO BE HERE.>
CAN YOU TURN INTO A BEAR AT THE SCHOOL PRESENTATION?
DOOO IT! WE COULD SCARE NANAUQ!
<GO IN THE HOUSE AND GET READY FOR DINNER! YOUR COUSIN'S NOT HERE TO USE HER POWERS FOR YOUR SILLY PRANKS!>
BEAR ATTACK!
RAAAAR!
<THE BOYS AREN'T SPEAKING INUKTITUT, MOM?>
<THEY UNDERSTAND IT, BUT DON'T USE IT ANYMORE. NONE OF THEIR FRIENDS DO, SO, YOU KNOW...>
...IT'S NOT "COOL."
<THEY'RE NOT LIKE YOU, MY LOVE. YOU'VE ALWAYS BELIEVED IN THE OLD WAYS...>
<...THAT'S WHY YOU WERE REWARDED BY THE SILAP INUA.>
<I...I GUESS...>
<READY FOR SOME HOME COOKING?>
<ABSOLUTELY!>

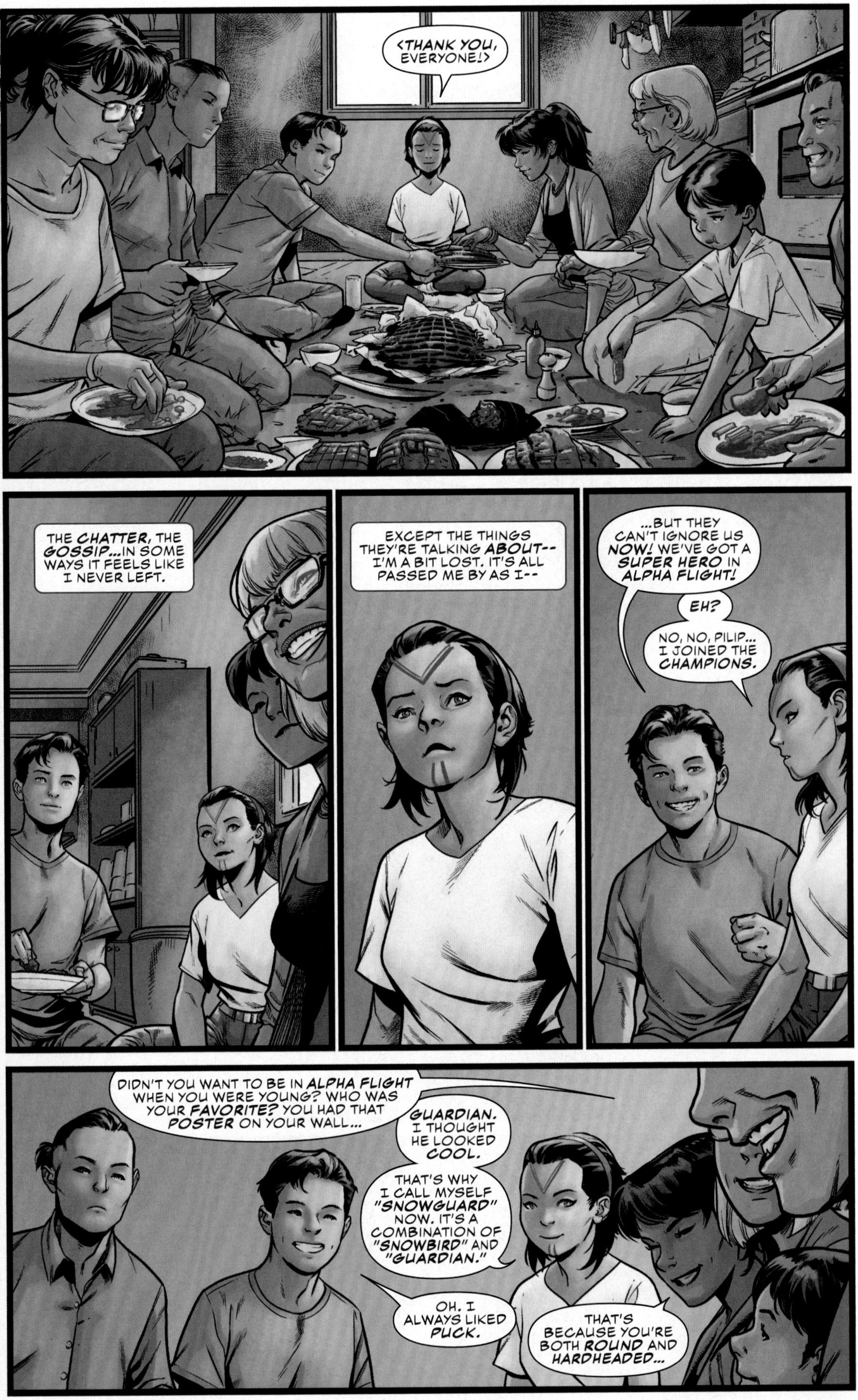

<THANK YOU, EVERYONE!>
THE CHATTER, THE GOSSIP...IN SOME WAYS IT FEELS LIKE I NEVER LEFT.
EXCEPT THE THINGS THEY'RE TALKING ABOUT-- I'M A BIT LOST. IT'S ALL PASSED ME BY AS I--
...BUT THEY CAN'T IGNORE US NOW! WE'VE GOT A SUPER HERO IN ALPHA FLIGHT!
EH?
NO, NO, PILIP... I JOINED THE CHAMPIONS.
DIDN'T YOU WANT TO BE IN ALPHA FLIGHT WHEN YOU WERE YOUNG? WHO WAS YOUR FAVORITE? YOU HAD THAT POSTER ON YOUR WALL...
GUARDIAN. I THOUGHT HE LOOKED COOL.
THAT'S WHY I CALL MYSELF "SNOWGUARD" NOW. IT'S A COMBINATION OF "SNOWBIRD" AND "GUARDIAN."
OH. I ALWAYS LIKED PUCK.
THAT'S BECAUSE YOU'RE BOTH ROUND AND HARDHEADED...

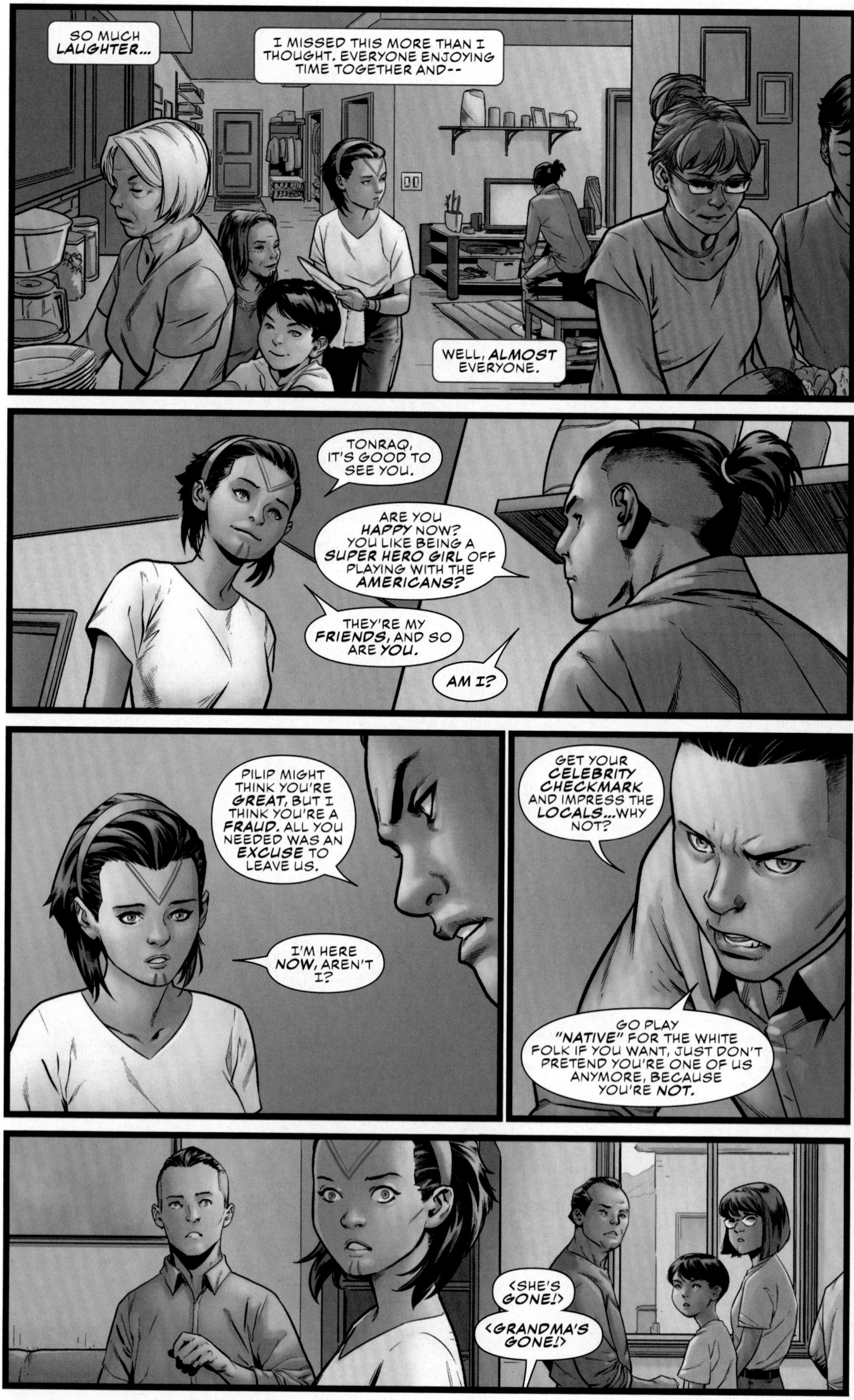
SO MUCH LAUGHTER...
I MISSED THIS MORE THAN I THOUGHT. EVERYONE ENJOYING TIME TOGETHER AND--
WELL, ALMOST EVERYONE.
TONRAQ, IT'S GOOD TO SEE YOU.
ARE YOU HAPPY NOW? YOU LIKE BEING A SUPER HERO GIRL OFF PLAYING WITH THE AMERICANS?
THEY'RE MY FRIENDS, AND SO ARE YOU.
AM I?
PILIP MIGHT THINK YOU'RE GREAT, BUT I THINK YOU'RE A FRAUD. ALL YOU NEEDED WAS AN EXCUSE TO LEAVE US.
I'M HERE NOW, AREN'T I?
GET YOUR CELEBRITY CHECKMARK AND IMPRESS THE LOCALS...WHY NOT?
GO PLAY "NATIVE" FOR THE WHITE FOLK IF YOU WANT, JUST DON'T PRETEND YOU'RE ONE OF US ANYMORE, BECAUSE YOU'RE NOT.
<SHE'S GONE!>
<GRANDMA'S GONE!>

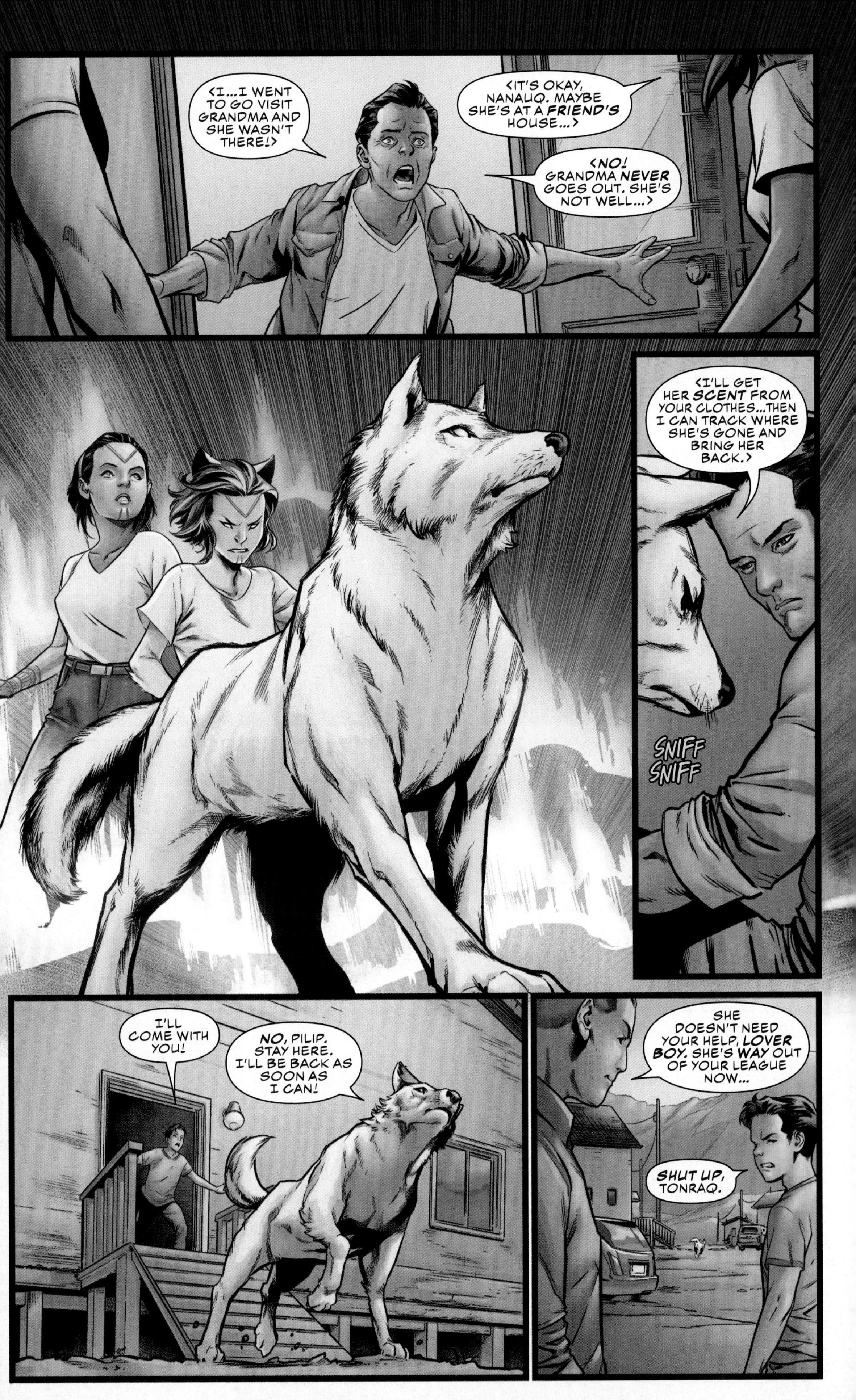
<I...I WENT TO GO VISIT GRANDMA AND SHE WASN'T THERE!>
<IT'S OKAY, NANAUQ. MAYBE SHE'S AT A FRIEND'S HOUSE...>
<NO! GRANDMA NEVER GOES OUT. SHE'S NOT WELL...>
<I'LL GET HER SCENT FROM YOUR CLOTHES...THEN I CAN TRACK WHERE SHE'S GONE AND BRING HER BACK.>
SNIFF SNIFF
I'LL COME WITH YOU!
NO, PILIP. STAY HERE. I'LL BE BACK AS SOON AS I CAN!
SHE DOESN'T NEED YOUR HELP, LOVER BOY. SHE'S WAY OUT OF YOUR LEAGUE NOW...
SHUT UP, TONRAQ.

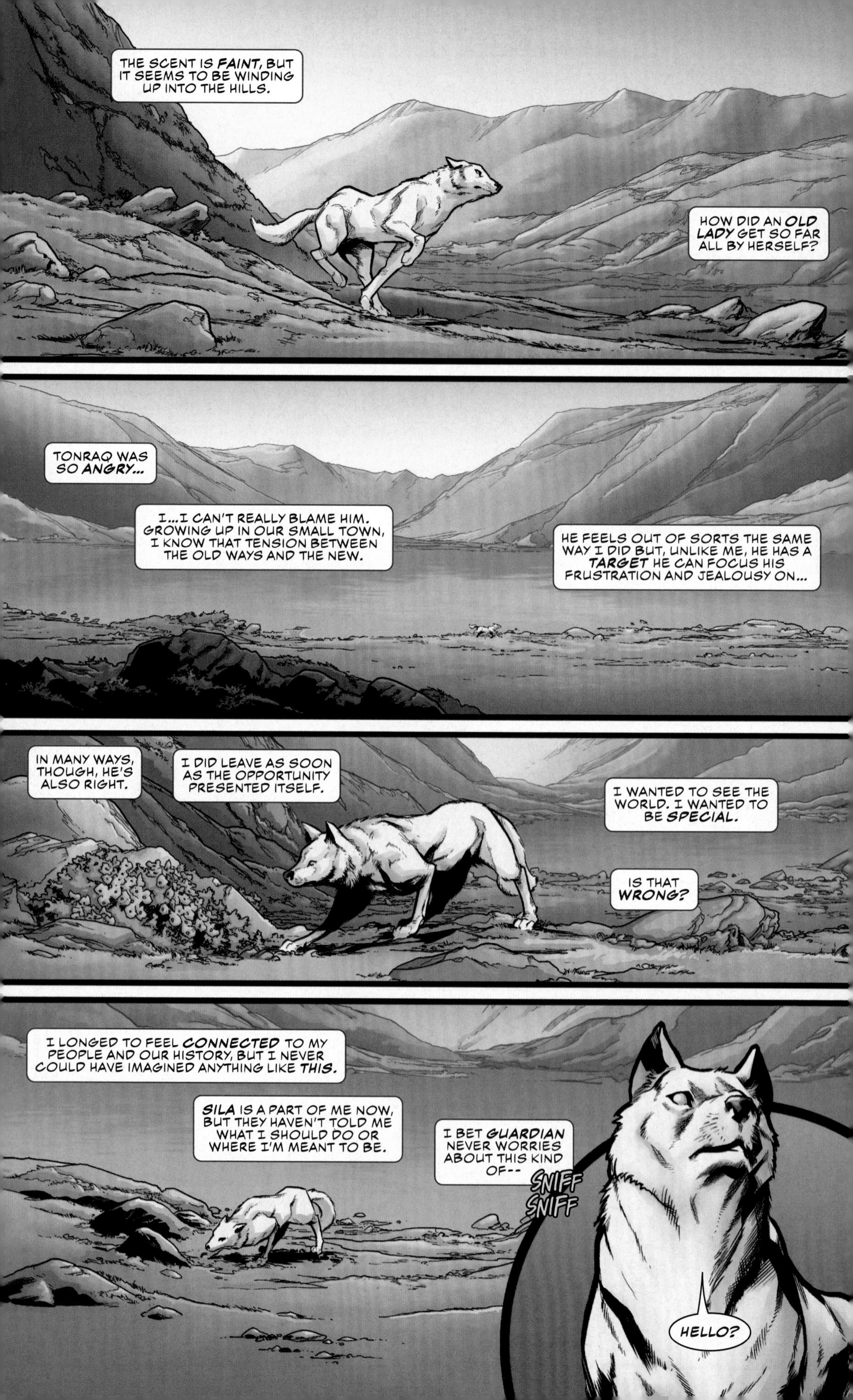
THE SCENT IS FAINT, BUT IT SEEMS TO BE WINDING UP INTO THE HILLS.
HOW DID AN OLD LADY GET SO FAR ALL BY HERSELF?
TONRAQ WAS SO ANGRY...
I...I CAN'T REALLY BLAME HIM. GROWING UP IN OUR SMALL TOWN, I KNOW THAT TENSION BETWEEN THE OLD WAYS AND THE NEW.
HE FEELS OUT OF SORTS THE SAME WAY I DID BUT, UNLIKE ME, HE HAS A TARGET HE CAN FOCUS HIS FRUSTRATION AND JEALOUSY ON...
IN MANY WAYS, THOUGH, HE'S ALSO RIGHT.
I DID LEAVE AS SOON AS THE OPPORTUNITY PRESENTED ITSELF.
I WANTED TO SEE THE WORLD. I WANTED TO BE SPECIAL.
IS THAT WRONG?
I LONGED TO FEEL CONNECTED TO MY PEOPLE AND OUR HISTORY, BUT I NEVER COULD HAVE IMAGINED ANYTHING LIKE THIS.
SILA IS A PART OF ME NOW, BUT THEY HAVEN'T TOLD ME WHAT I SHOULD DO OR WHERE I'M MEANT TO BE.
I BET GUARDIAN NEVER WORRIES ABOUT THIS KIND OF--
SNIFF SNIFF
HELLO?

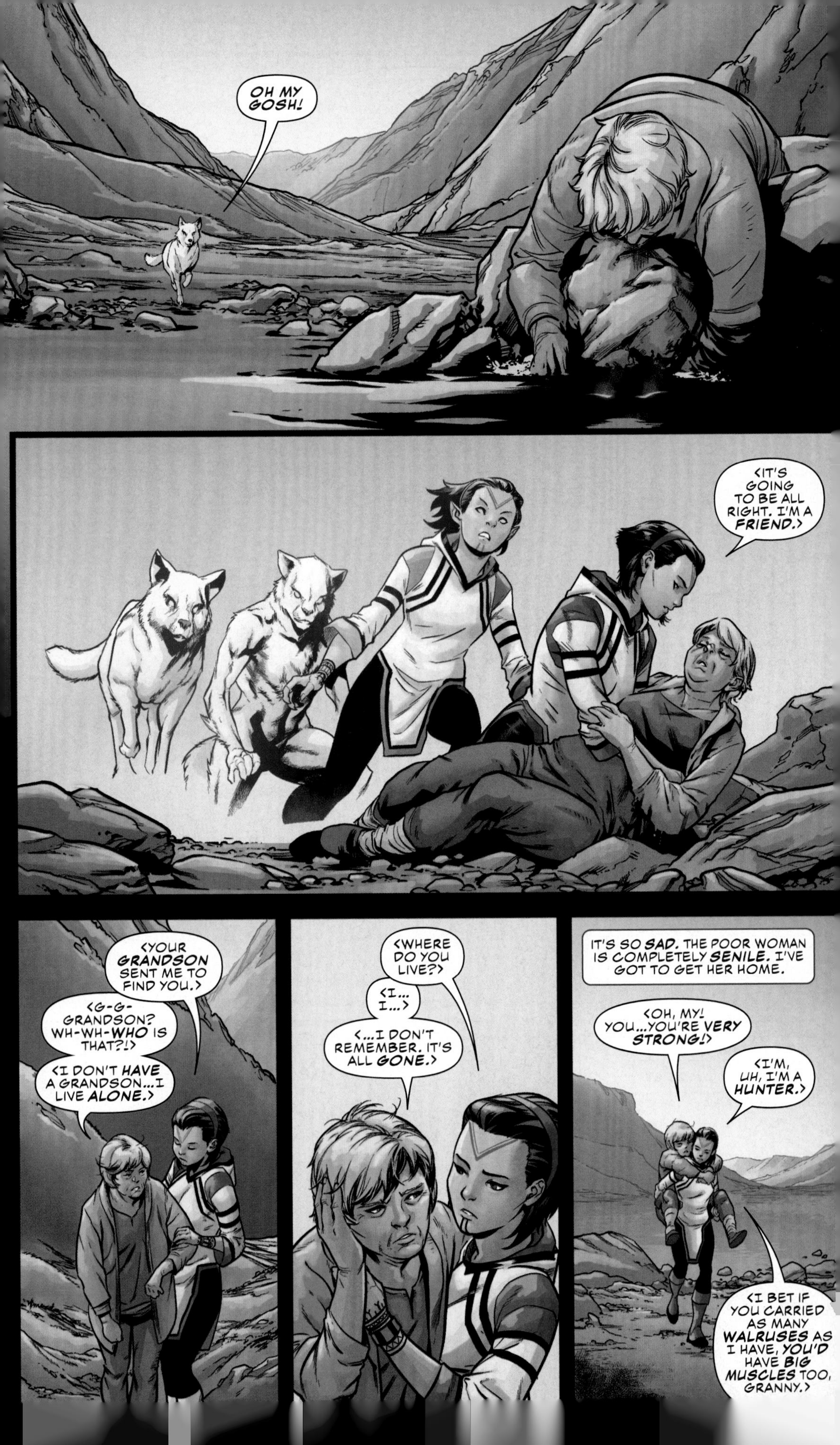
OH MY GOSH!
<IT'S GOING TO BE ALL RIGHT. I'M A FRIEND.>
<YOUR GRANDSON SENT ME TO FIND YOU.>
<G-G-GRANDSON? WH-WH-WHO IS THAT?!>
<I DON'T HAVE A GRANDSON...I LIVE ALONE.>
<WHERE DO YOU LIVE?>
<I... I...>
<...I DON'T REMEMBER. IT'S ALL GONE.>
IT'S SO SAD. THE POOR WOMAN IS COMPLETELY SENILE. I'VE GOT TO GET HER HOME.
<OH, MY! YOU...YOU'RE VERY STRONG!>
<I'M, UH, I'M A HUNTER.>
<I BET IF YOU CARRIED AS MANY WALRUSES AS I HAVE, YOU'D HAVE BIG MUSCLES TOO, GRANNY.>

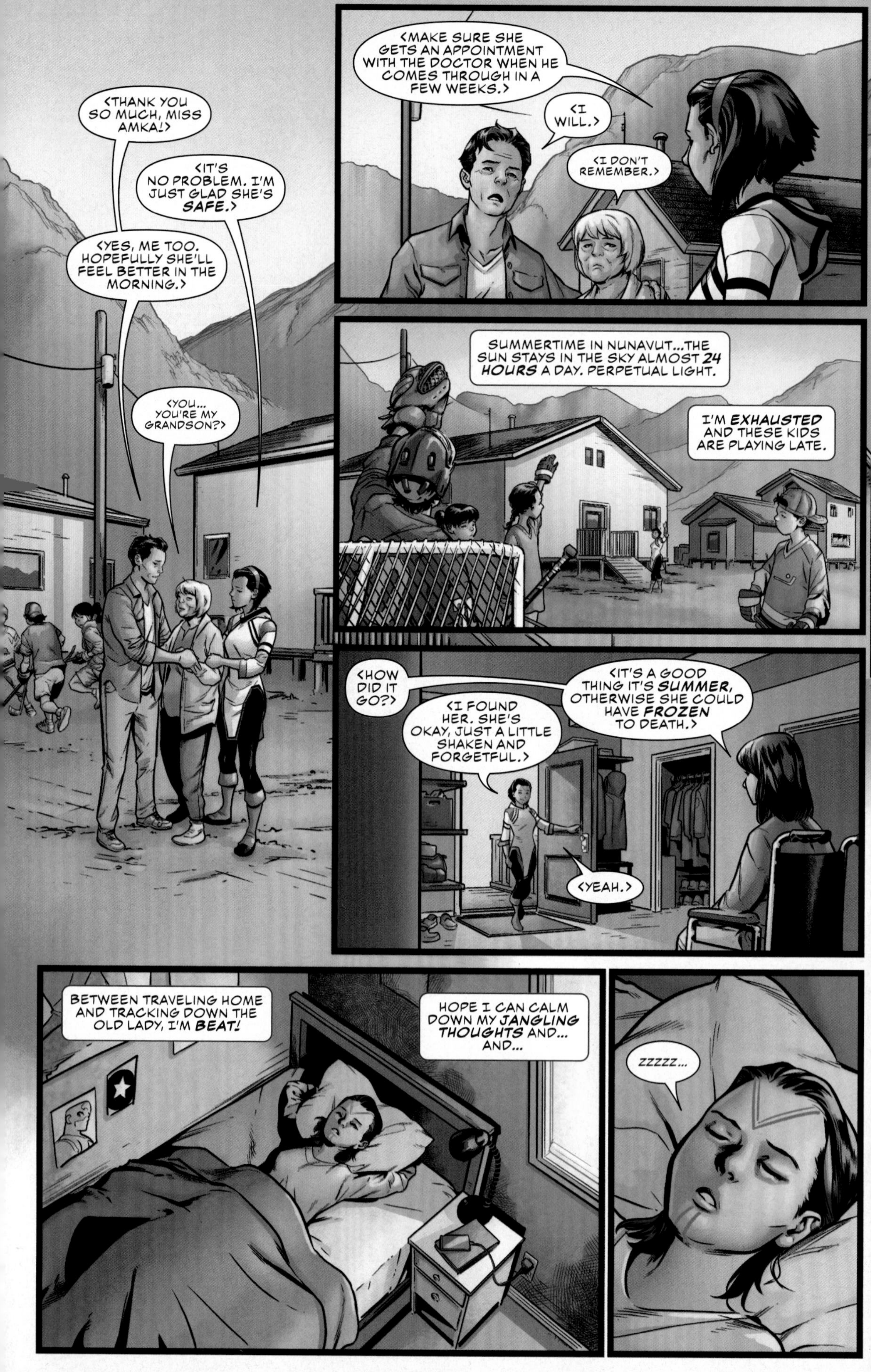
<THANK YOU SO MUCH, MISS AMKA!>
<IT'S NO PROBLEM. I'M JUST GLAD SHE'S *SAFE.*>
<YES, ME TOO. HOPEFULLY SHE'LL FEEL BETTER IN THE MORNING.>
<YOU... YOU'RE MY GRANDSON?>
<MAKE SURE SHE GETS AN APPOINTMENT WITH THE DOCTOR WHEN HE COMES THROUGH IN A FEW WEEKS.>
<I WILL.>
<I DON'T REMEMBER.>
SUMMERTIME IN NUNAVUT...THE SUN STAYS IN THE SKY ALMOST *24 HOURS* A DAY. PERPETUAL LIGHT.
I'M *EXHAUSTED* AND THESE KIDS ARE PLAYING LATE.
<HOW DID IT GO?>
<I FOUND HER. SHE'S OKAY, JUST A LITTLE SHAKEN AND FORGETFUL.>
<IT'S A GOOD THING IT'S *SUMMER*, OTHERWISE SHE COULD HAVE *FROZEN* TO DEATH.>
<YEAH.>
BETWEEN TRAVELING HOME AND TRACKING DOWN THE OLD LADY, I'M *BEAT!*
HOPE I CAN CALM DOWN MY *JANGLING THOUGHTS* AND... AND...
ZZZZZ...

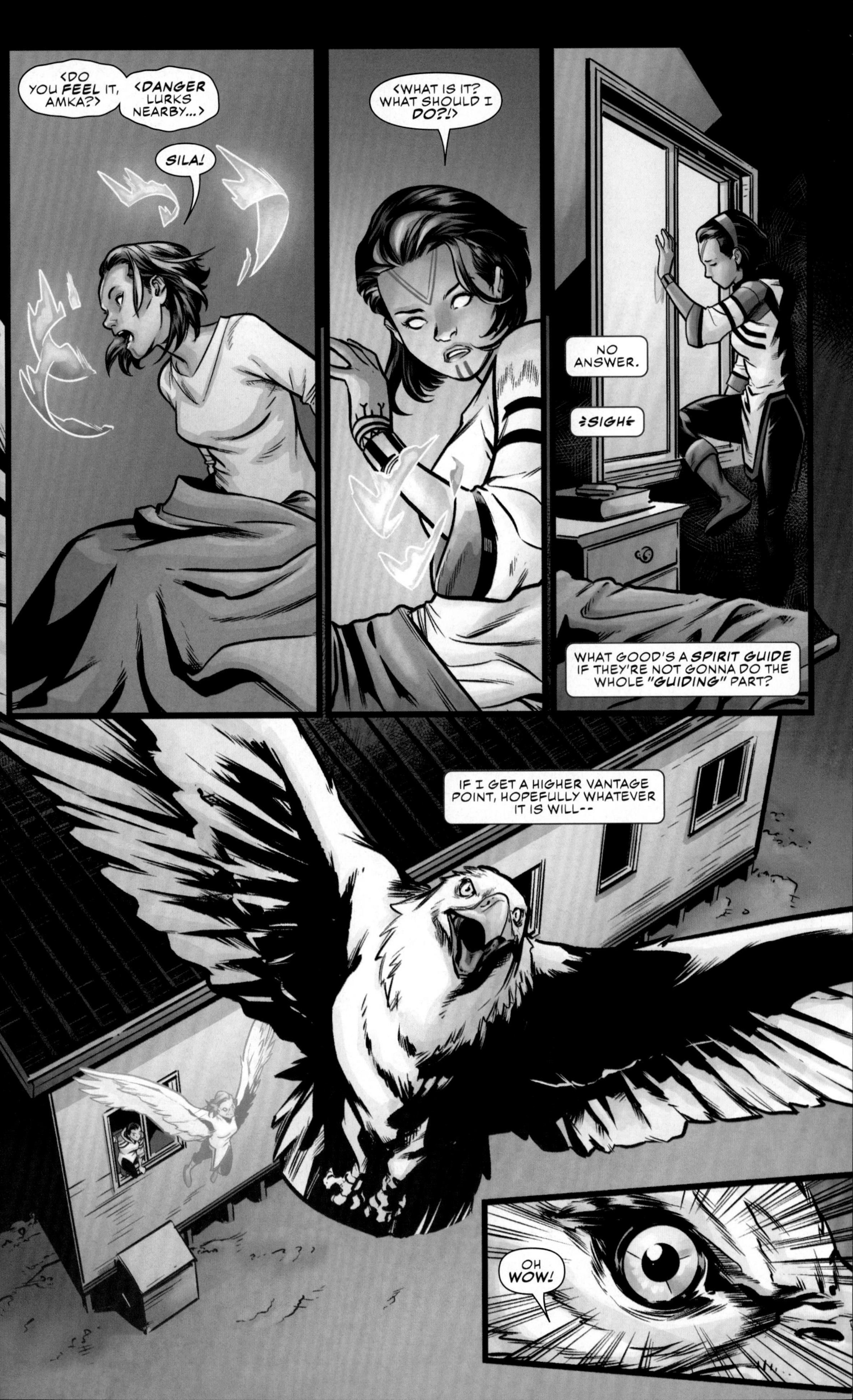

<DO YOU FEEL IT, AMKA?>
<DANGER LURKS NEARBY...>
SILA!
<WHAT IS IT? WHAT SHOULD I DO?!>
NO ANSWER.
SIGH
WHAT GOOD'S A SPIRIT GUIDE IF THEY'RE NOT GONNA DO THE WHOLE "GUIDING" PART?
IF I GET A HIGHER VANTAGE POINT, HOPEFULLY WHATEVER IT IS WILL--
OH WOW!

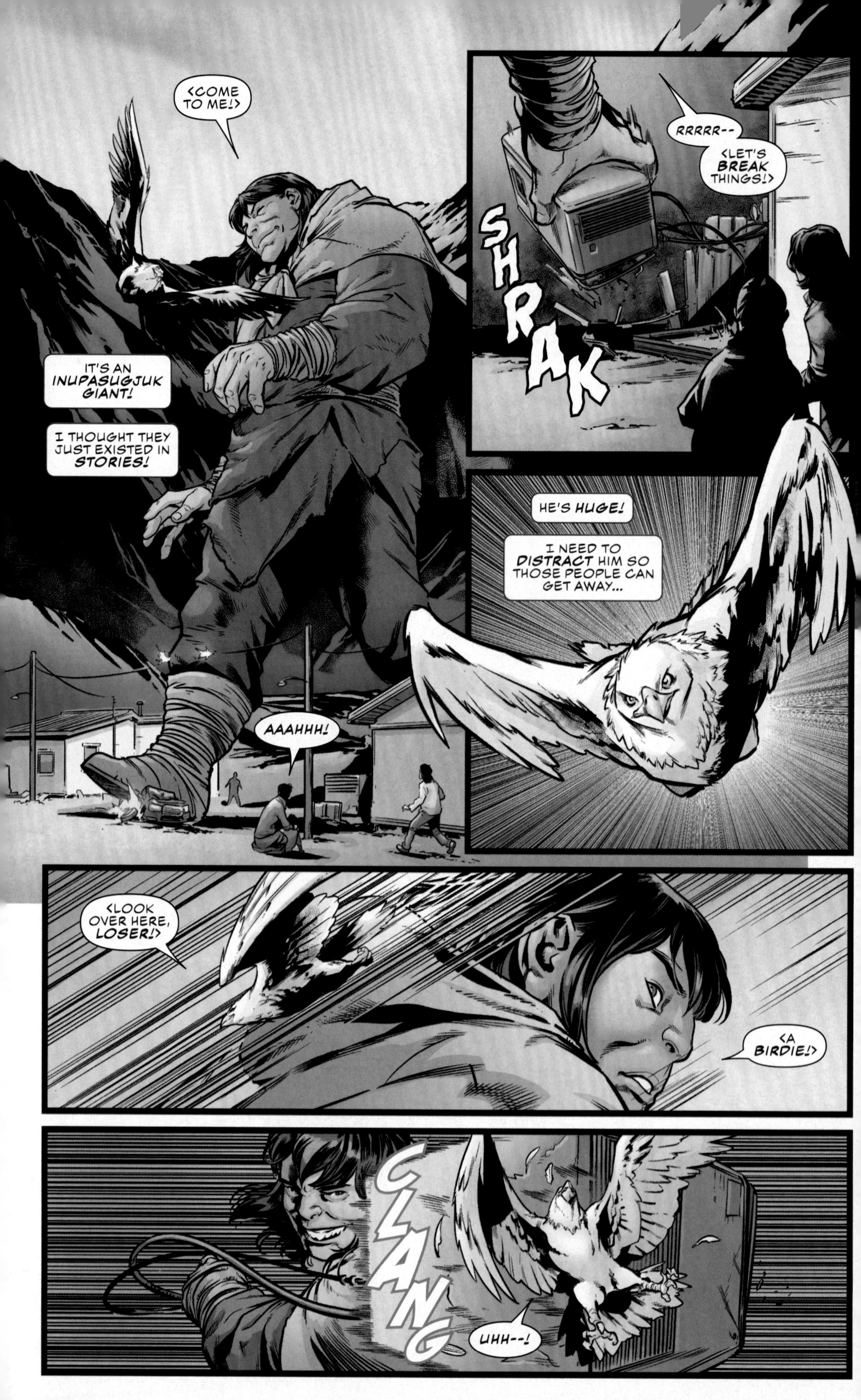

<COME TO ME!>
IT'S AN INUPASUGJUK GIANT!
I THOUGHT THEY JUST EXISTED IN STORIES!
AAAHHH!
RRRRR--
<LET'S BREAK THINGS!>
SHRAK
HE'S HUGE!
I NEED TO DISTRACT HIM SO THOSE PEOPLE CAN GET AWAY...
<LOOK OVER HERE, LOSER!>
<A BIRDIE!>
CLANG
UHH--!

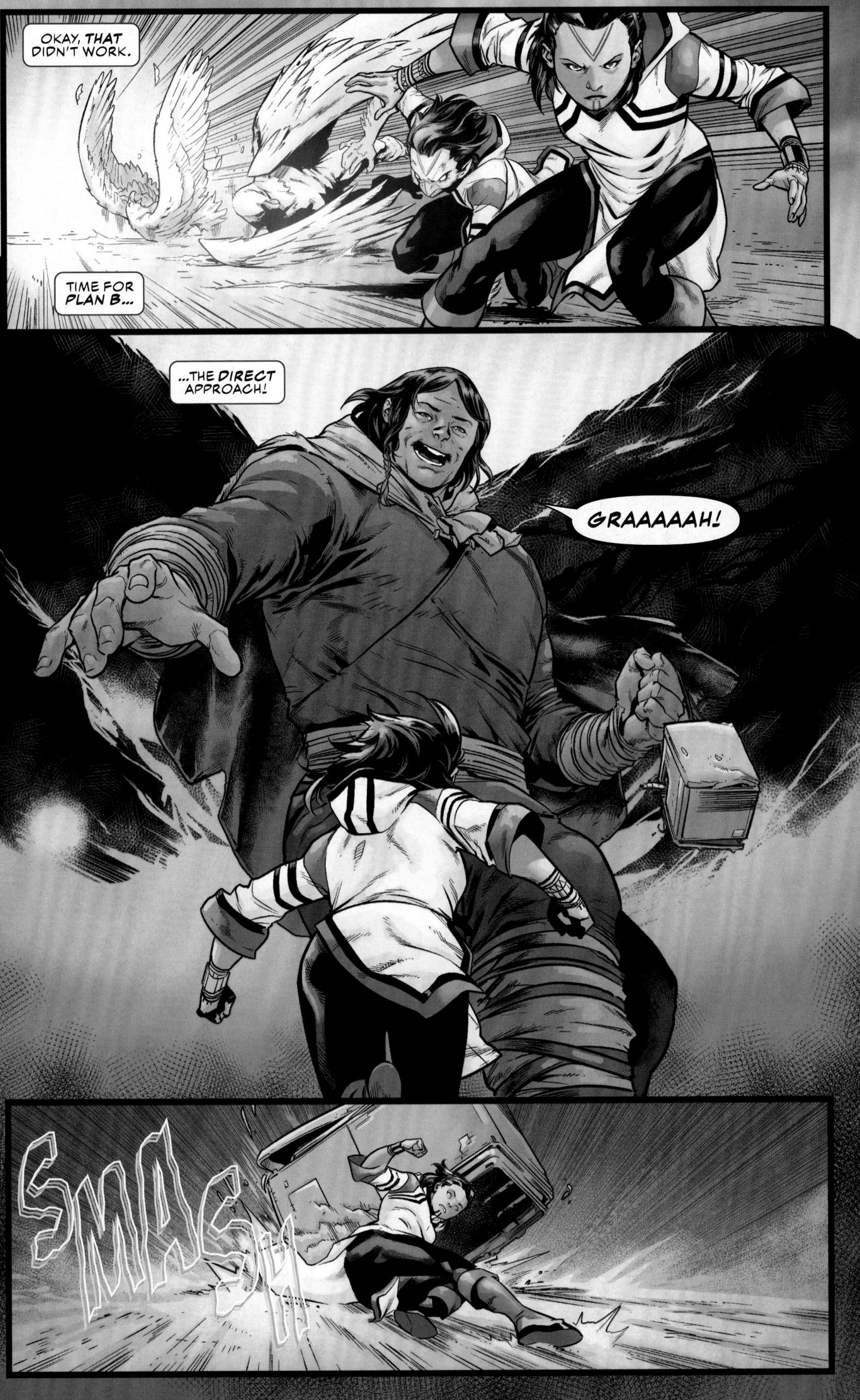

OKAY, THAT DIDN'T WORK.
TIME FOR PLAN B...
...THE DIRECT APPROACH!
GRAAAAAH!
SMASH

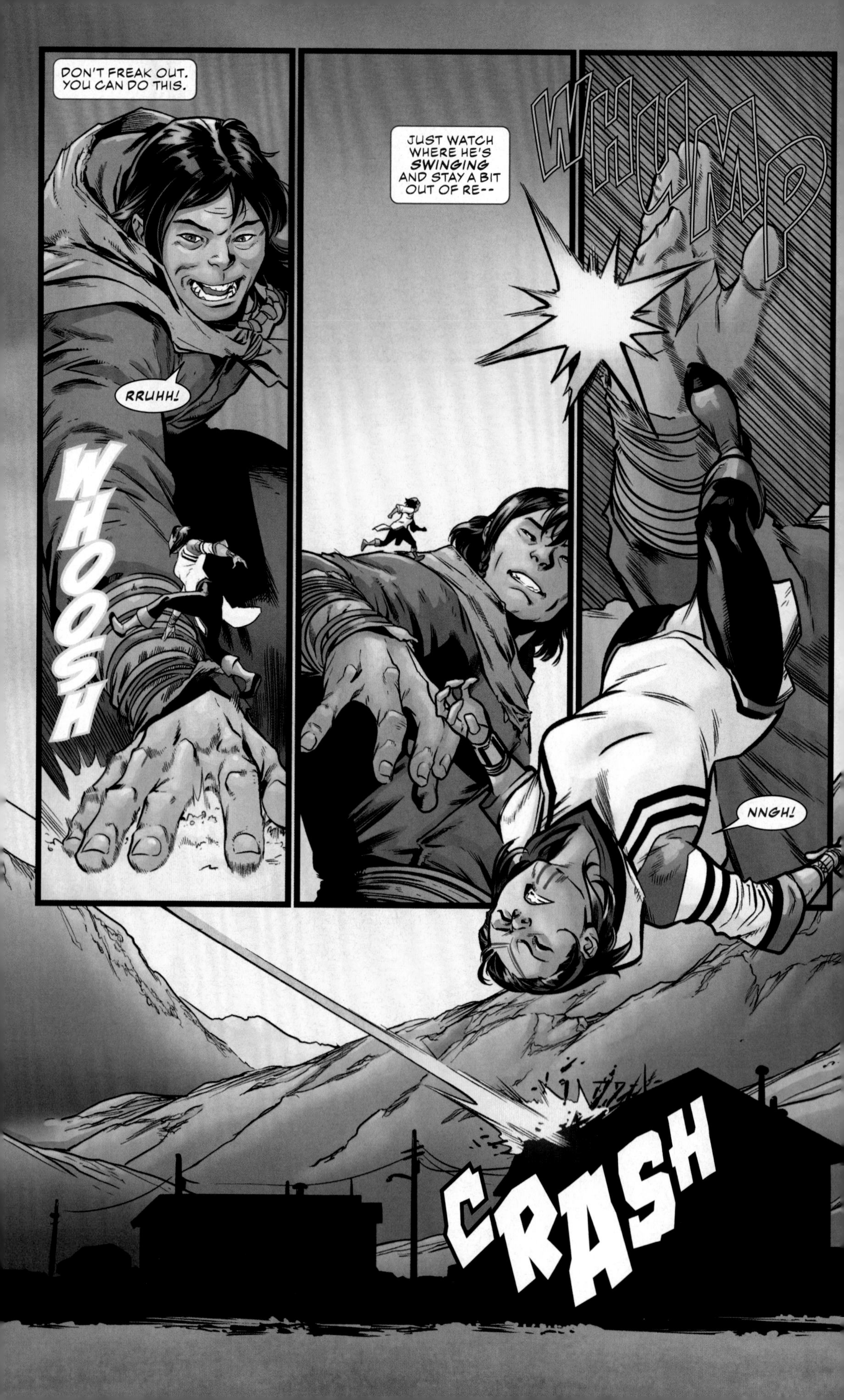
DON'T FREAK OUT. YOU CAN DO THIS.
RRUHH!
WHOOOSH
JUST WATCH WHERE HE'S SWINGING AND STAY A BIT OUT OF RE--
WHUMP
NNGH!
CRASH

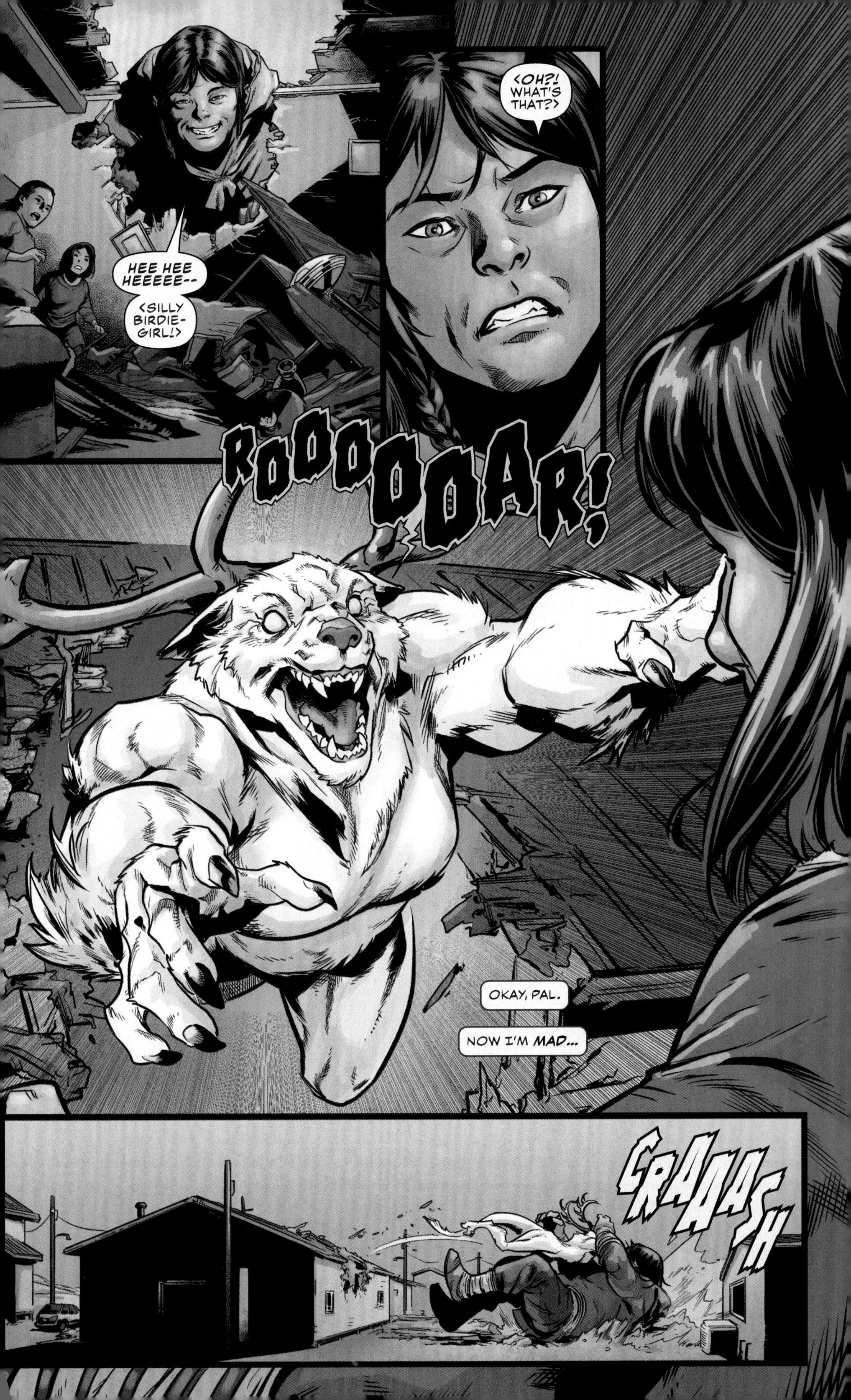
HEE HEE HEEEEE--
<SILLY BIRDIE-GIRL!>
<OH?! WHAT'S THAT?>
ROOOOOAR!
OKAY, PAL.
NOW I'M MAD...
CRAAASH

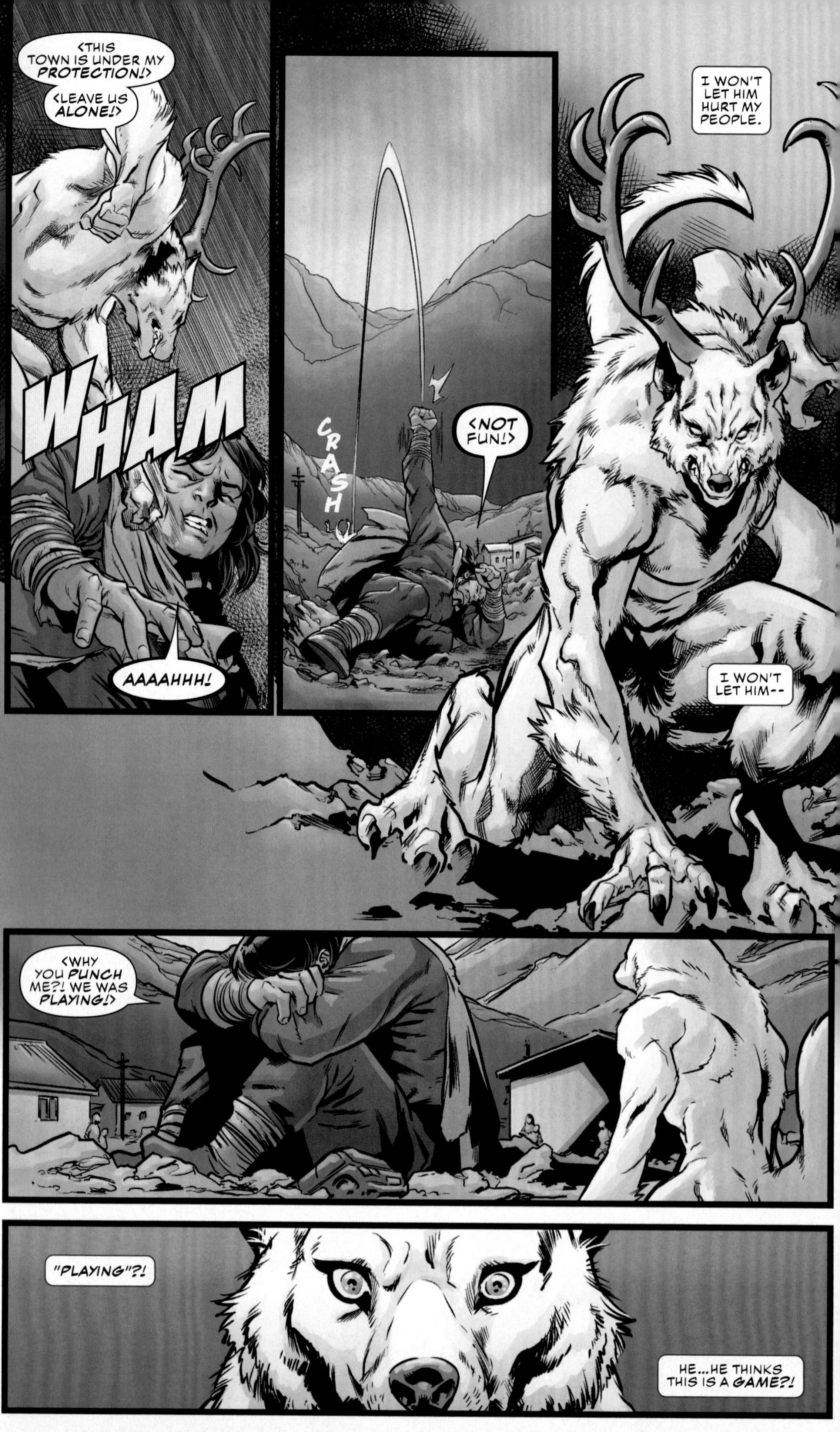
<THIS TOWN IS UNDER MY PROTECTION!>
<LEAVE US ALONE!>
WHAM
AAAAHHH!
CRASH
<NOT FUN!>
I WON'T LET HIM HURT MY PEOPLE.
I WON'T LET HIM--
<WHY YOU PUNCH ME?! WE WAS PLAYING!>
"PLAYING"?!
HE...HE THINKS THIS IS A GAME?!

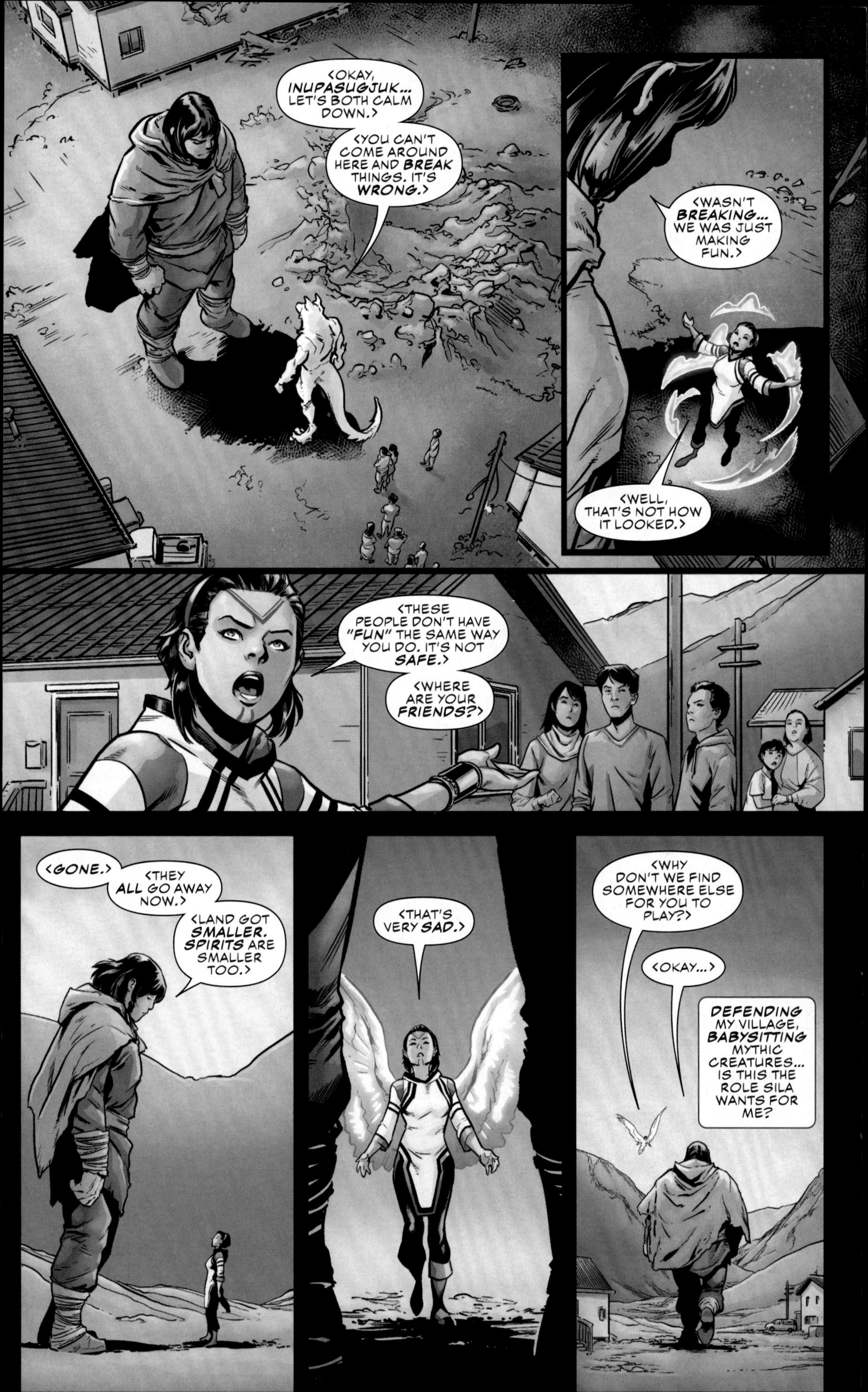
<OKAY, INUPASUGJUK... LET'S BOTH CALM DOWN.>
<YOU CAN'T COME AROUND HERE AND BREAK THINGS. IT'S WRONG.>
<WASN'T BREAKING... WE WAS JUST MAKING FUN.>
<WELL, THAT'S NOT HOW IT LOOKED.>
<THESE PEOPLE DON'T HAVE "FUN" THE SAME WAY YOU DO. IT'S NOT SAFE.>
<WHERE ARE YOUR FRIENDS?>
<GONE.>
<THEY ALL GO AWAY NOW.>
<LAND GOT SMALLER. SPIRITS ARE SMALLER TOO.>
<THAT'S VERY SAD.>
<WHY DON'T WE FIND SOMEWHERE ELSE FOR YOU TO PLAY?>
<OKAY...>
DEFENDING MY VILLAGE, BABYSITTING MYTHIC CREATURES... IS THIS THE ROLE SILA WANTS FOR ME?

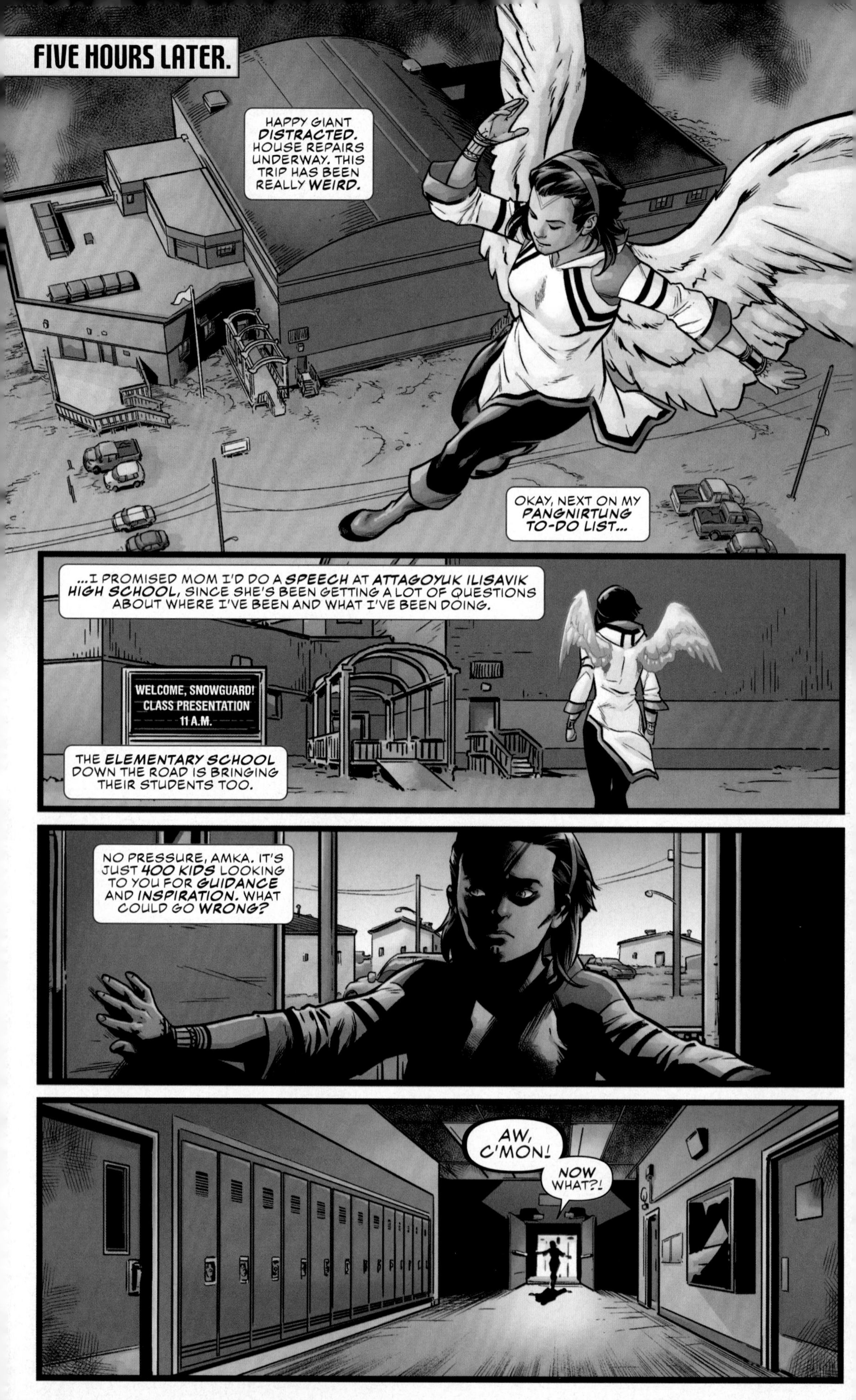
FIVE HOURS LATER.
HAPPY GIANT DISTRACTED. HOUSE REPAIRS UNDERWAY. THIS TRIP HAS BEEN REALLY WEIRD.
OKAY, NEXT ON MY PANGNIRTUNG TO-DO LIST...
...I PROMISED MOM I'D DO A SPEECH AT ATTAGOYUK ILISAVIK HIGH SCHOOL, SINCE SHE'S BEEN GETTING A LOT OF QUESTIONS ABOUT WHERE I'VE BEEN AND WHAT I'VE BEEN DOING.
WELCOME, SNOWGUARD! CLASS PRESENTATION 11 A.M.
THE ELEMENTARY SCHOOL DOWN THE ROAD IS BRINGING THEIR STUDENTS TOO.
NO PRESSURE, AMKA. IT'S JUST 400 KIDS LOOKING TO YOU FOR GUIDANCE AND INSPIRATION. WHAT COULD GO WRONG?
AW, C'MON!
NOW WHAT?!

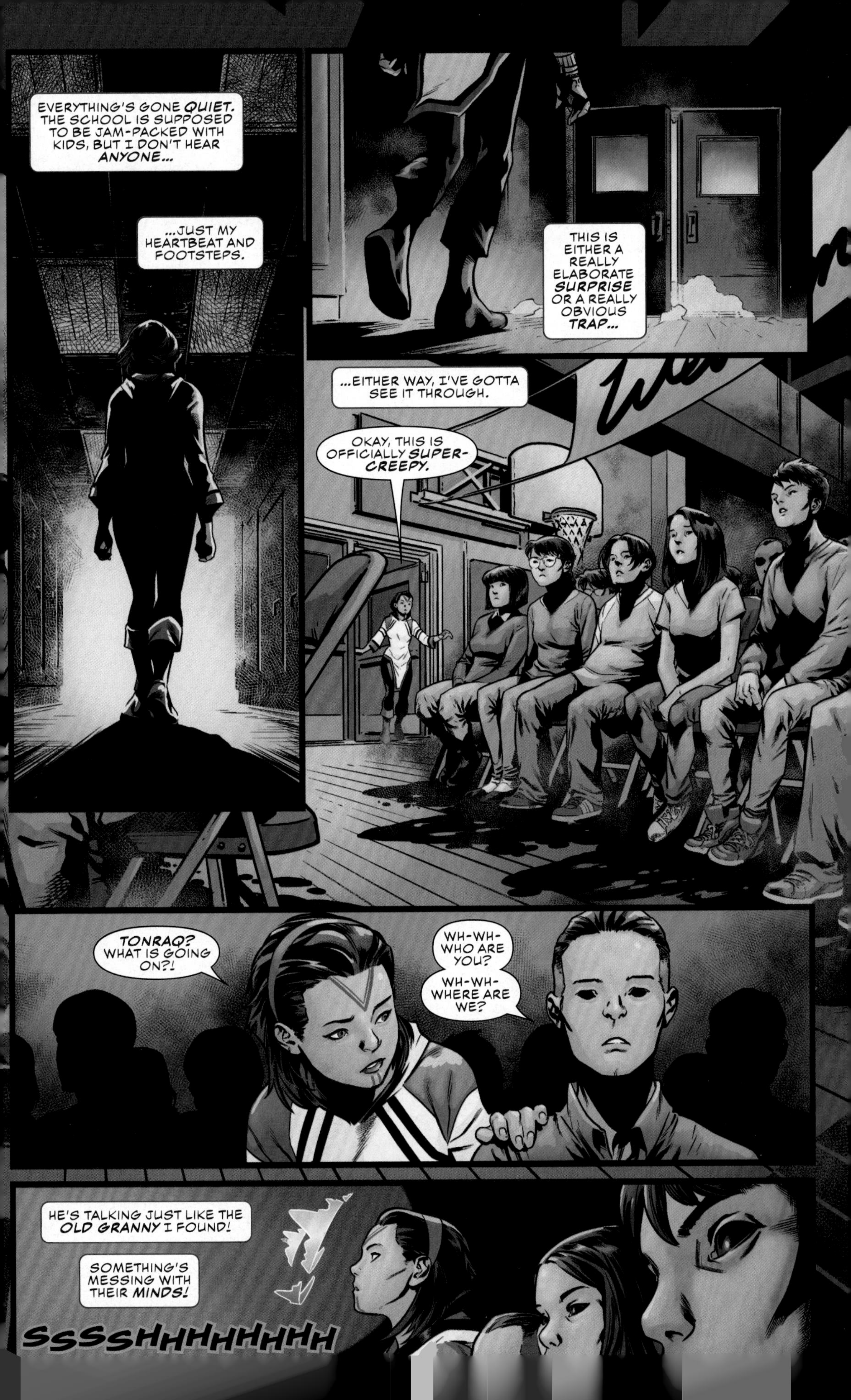
EVERYTHING'S GONE QUIET. THE SCHOOL IS SUPPOSED TO BE JAM-PACKED WITH KIDS, BUT I DON'T HEAR ANYONE...
...JUST MY HEARTBEAT AND FOOTSTEPS.
THIS IS EITHER A REALLY ELABORATE SURPRISE OR A REALLY OBVIOUS TRAP...
...EITHER WAY, I'VE GOTTA SEE IT THROUGH.
OKAY, THIS IS OFFICIALLY SUPER-CREEPY.
TONRAQ? WHAT IS GOING ON?!
WH-WH-WHO ARE YOU?
WH-WH-WHERE ARE WE?
HE'S TALKING JUST LIKE THE OLD GRANNY I FOUND!
SOMETHING'S MESSING WITH THEIR MINDS!
SSSSHHHHHHHHH

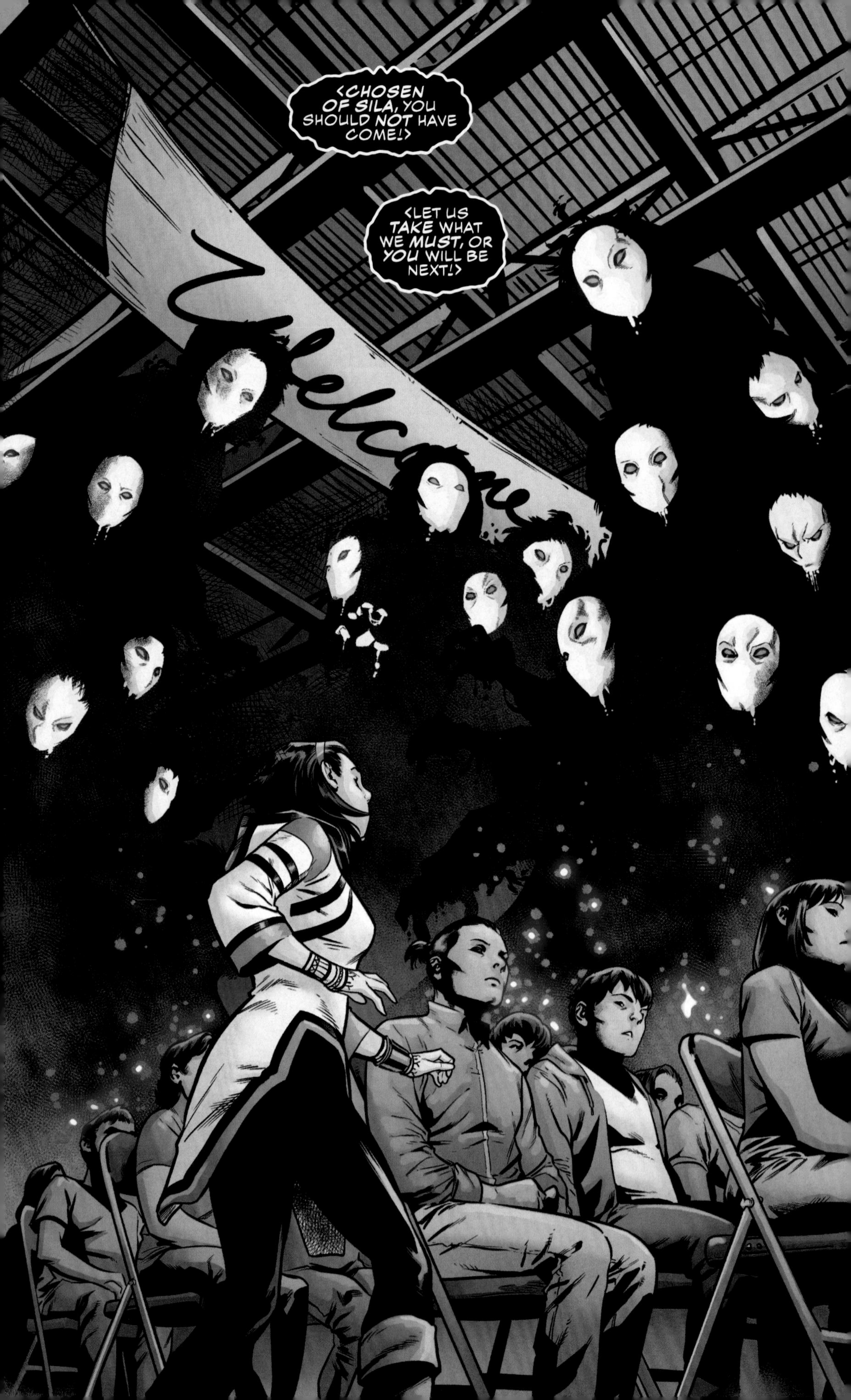
<CHOSEN OF SILA, YOU SHOULD NOT HAVE COME!>
<LET US TAKE WHAT WE MUST, OR YOU WILL BE NEXT!>
Welcome

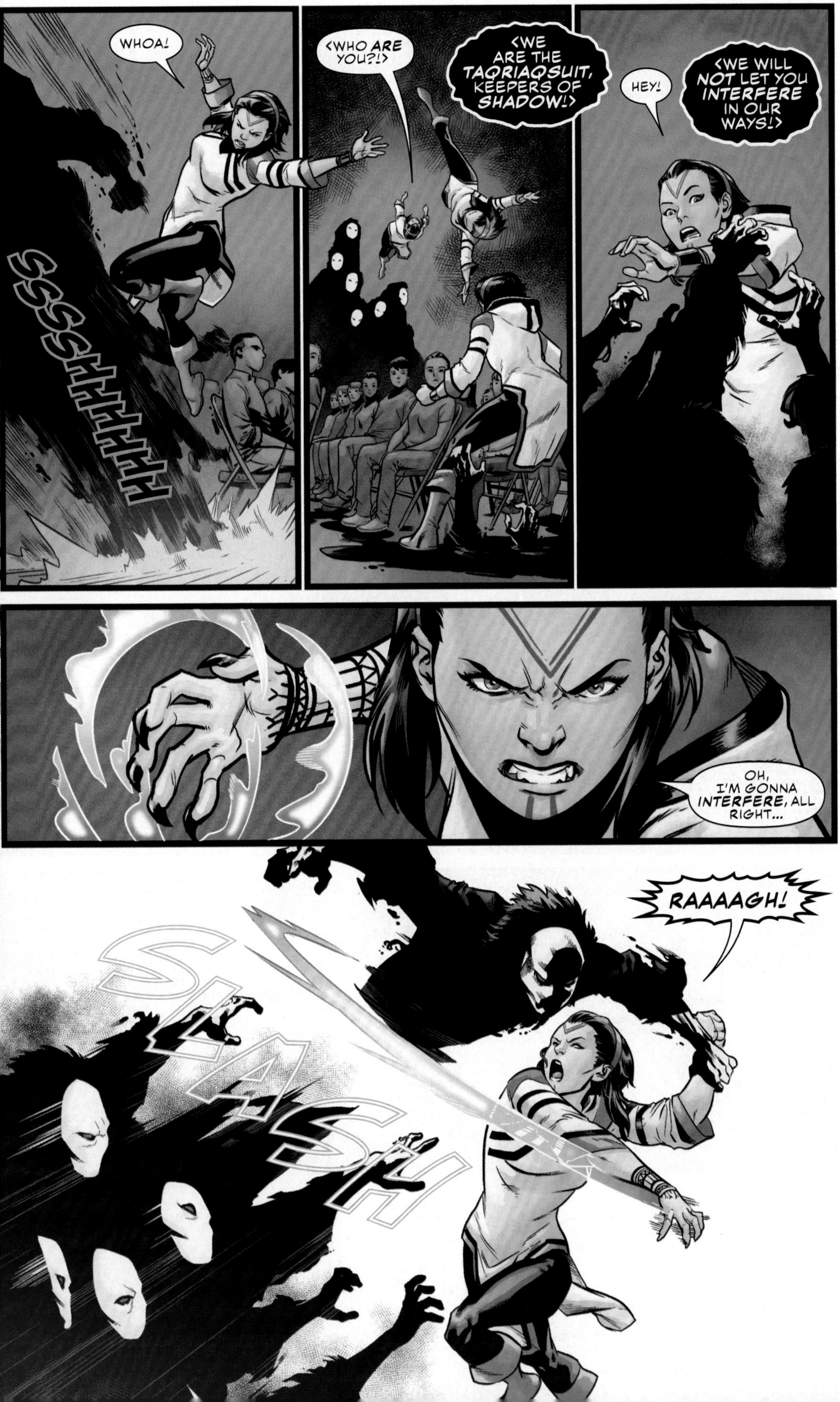
WHOA!
SSSSHHHHHHH
<WHO ARE YOU?!>
<WE ARE THE TAQRIAQSUIT, KEEPERS OF SHADOW!>
HEY!
<WE WILL NOT LET YOU INTERFERE IN OUR WAYS!>
OH, I'M GONNA INTERFERE, ALL RIGHT...
RAAAAGH!
SLASH

THE TAQRIAQSUIT.

SILENT SHADOWS, WHISPERS IN THE DARKNESS... NORMALLY THEY STAY *HIDDEN*, BUT SOMETHING HAS MADE THEM *BOLD*.

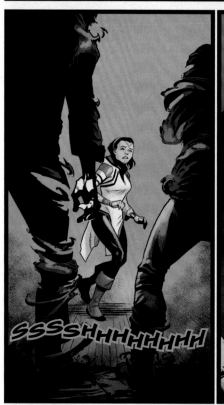
SSSSHHHHHHHH

Oh crap...

TIME FOR SOME *EVASIVE ACTION!*

WH-WH-WHO--?

PILIP, ARE YOU THERE?! CAN YOU *SPEAK?*

SSSSHHHHHHHH

WHY DIDN'T I PAY MORE ATTENTION TO *UNCLE'S STORIES* BEFORE HE PASSED?

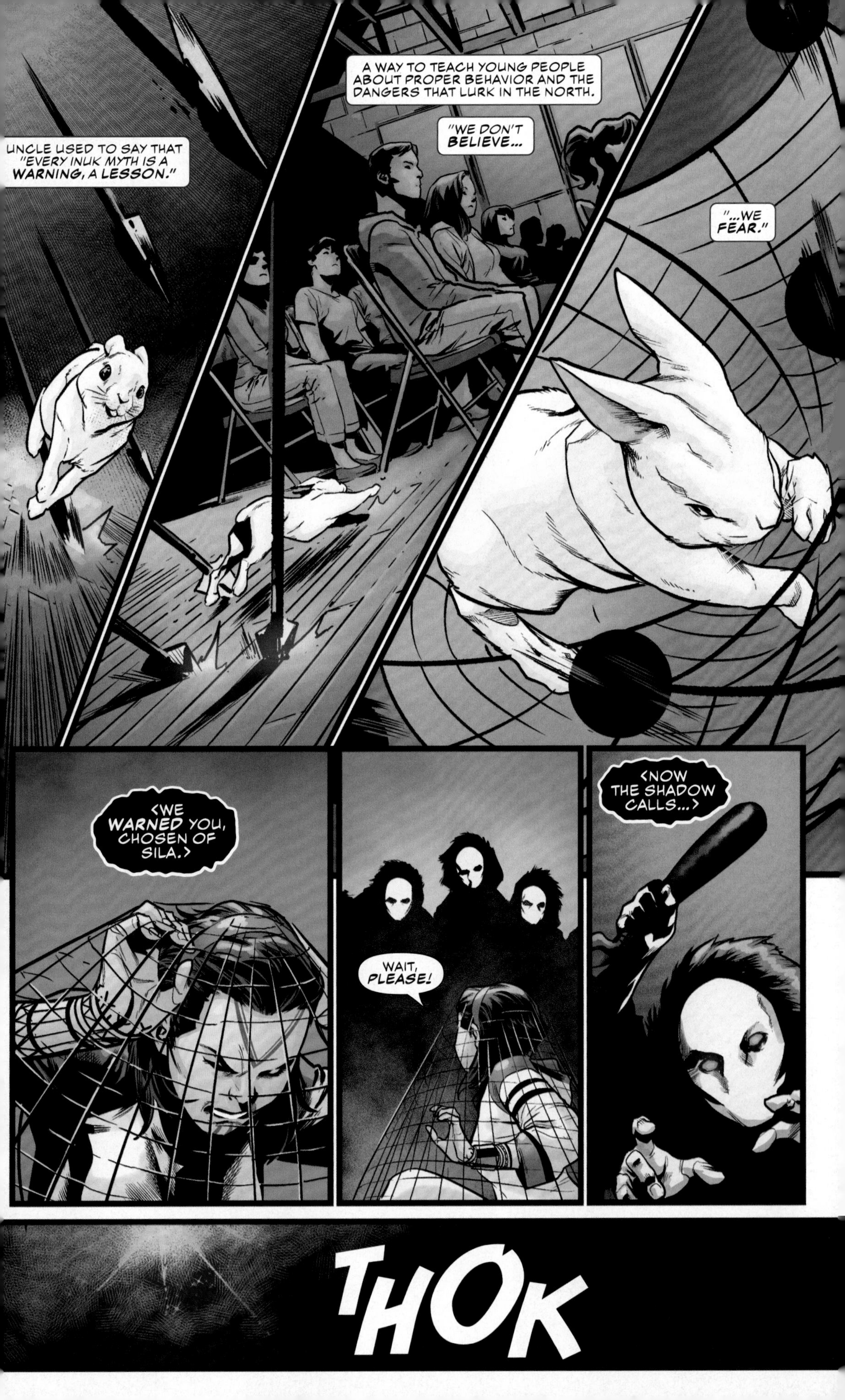
UNCLE USED TO SAY THAT "EVERY INUK MYTH IS A WARNING, A LESSON."
A WAY TO TEACH YOUNG PEOPLE ABOUT PROPER BEHAVIOR AND THE DANGERS THAT LURK IN THE NORTH.
"WE DON'T BELIEVE...
"...WE FEAR."
<WE WARNED YOU, CHOSEN OF SILA.>
WAIT, PLEASE!
<NOW THE SHADOW CALLS...>
THOK

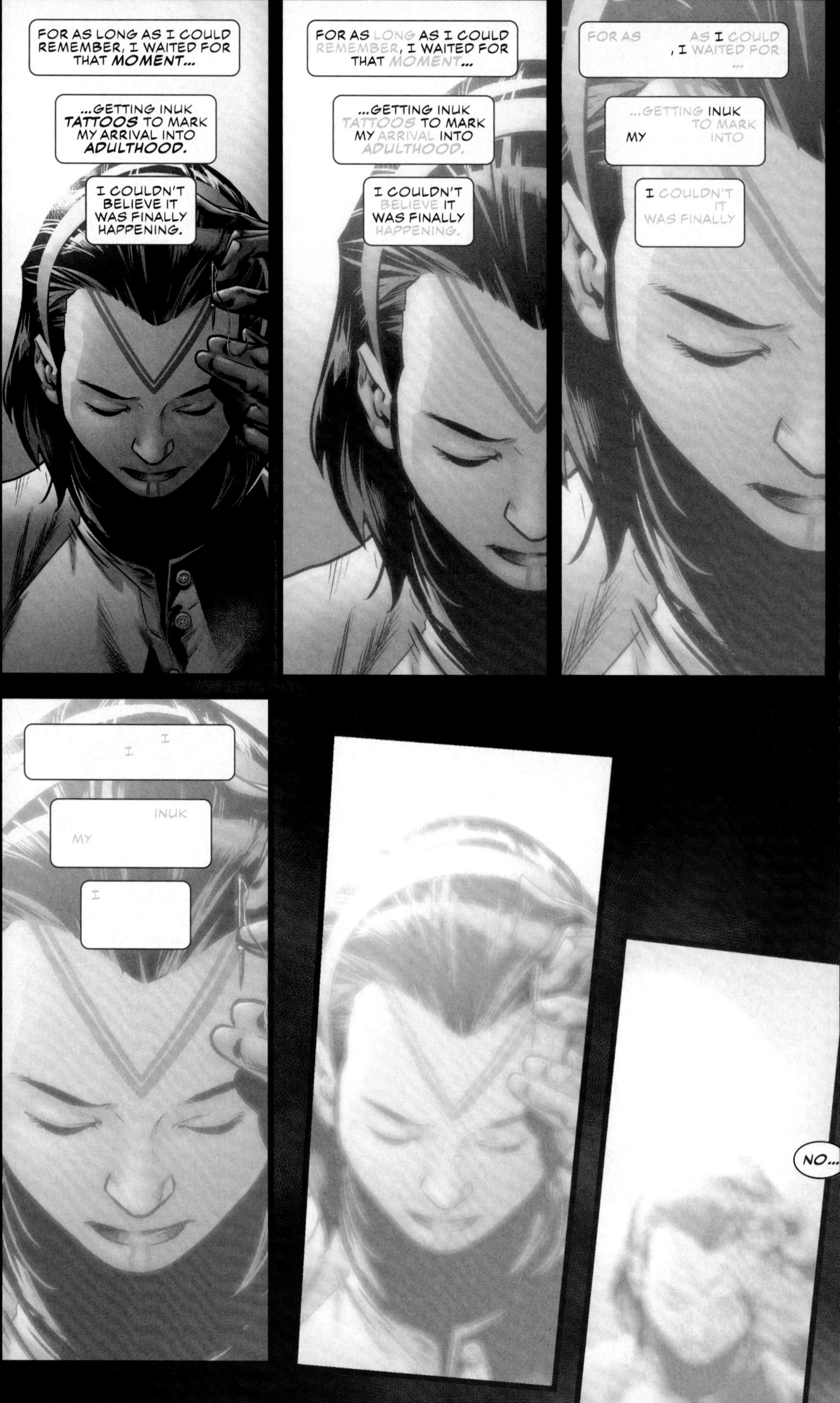
FOR AS LONG AS I COULD REMEMBER, I WAITED FOR THAT MOMENT...
...GETTING INUK TATTOOS TO MARK MY ARRIVAL INTO ADULTHOOD.
I COULDN'T BELIEVE IT WAS FINALLY HAPPENING.
FOR AS LONG AS I COULD REMEMBER, I WAITED FOR THAT MOMENT...
...GETTING INUK TATTOOS TO MARK MY ARRIVAL INTO ADULTHOOD.
I COULDN'T BELIEVE IT WAS FINALLY HAPPENING.
FOR AS AS I COULD , I WAITED FOR ...
...GETTING INUK TO MARK MY INTO
I COULDN'T IT WAS FINALLY
I I
INUK MY
I
NO...

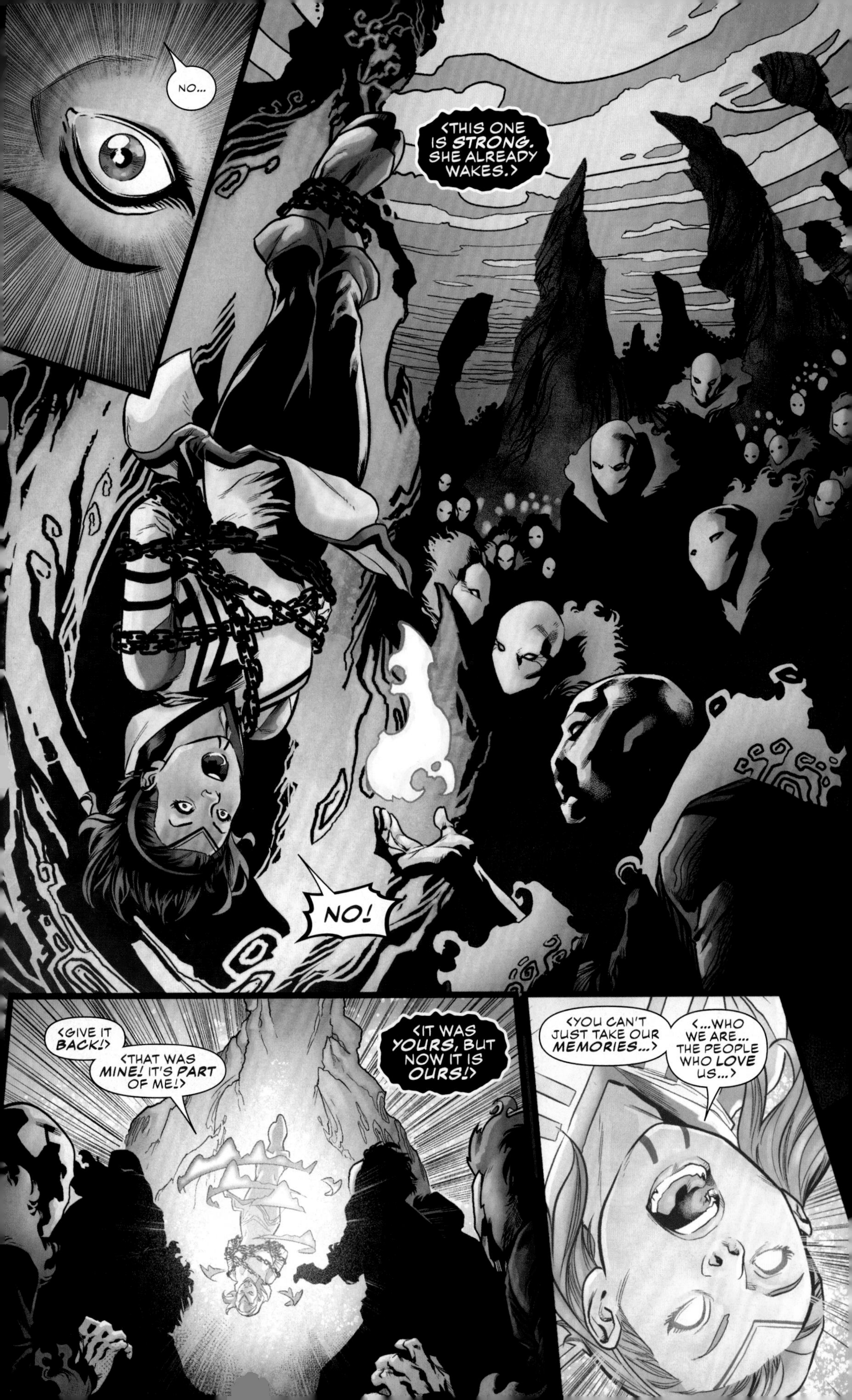
NO...
<THIS ONE IS STRONG. SHE ALREADY WAKES.>
NO!
<GIVE IT BACK!>
<THAT WAS MINE! IT'S PART OF ME!>
<IT WAS YOURS, BUT NOW IT IS OURS!>
<YOU CAN'T JUST TAKE OUR MEMORIES...>
<...WHO WE ARE... THE PEOPLE WHO LOVE US...>

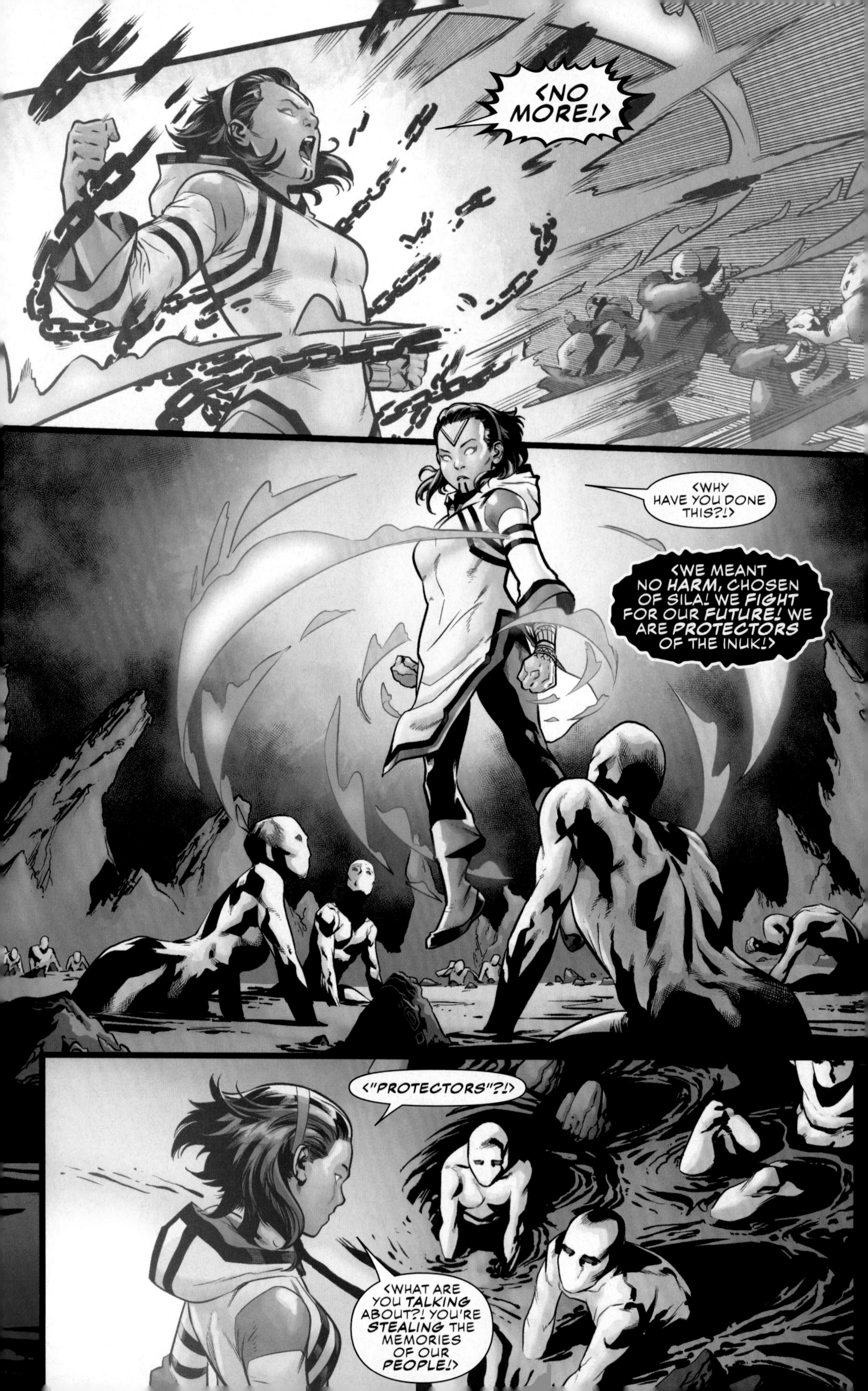
<NO MORE!>
<WHY HAVE YOU DONE THIS?!>
<WE MEANT NO HARM, CHOSEN OF SILA! WE FIGHT FOR OUR FUTURE! WE ARE PROTECTORS OF THE INUK!>
<"PROTECTORS"?!>
<WHAT ARE YOU TALKING ABOUT?! YOU'RE STEALING THE MEMORIES OF OUR PEOPLE!>

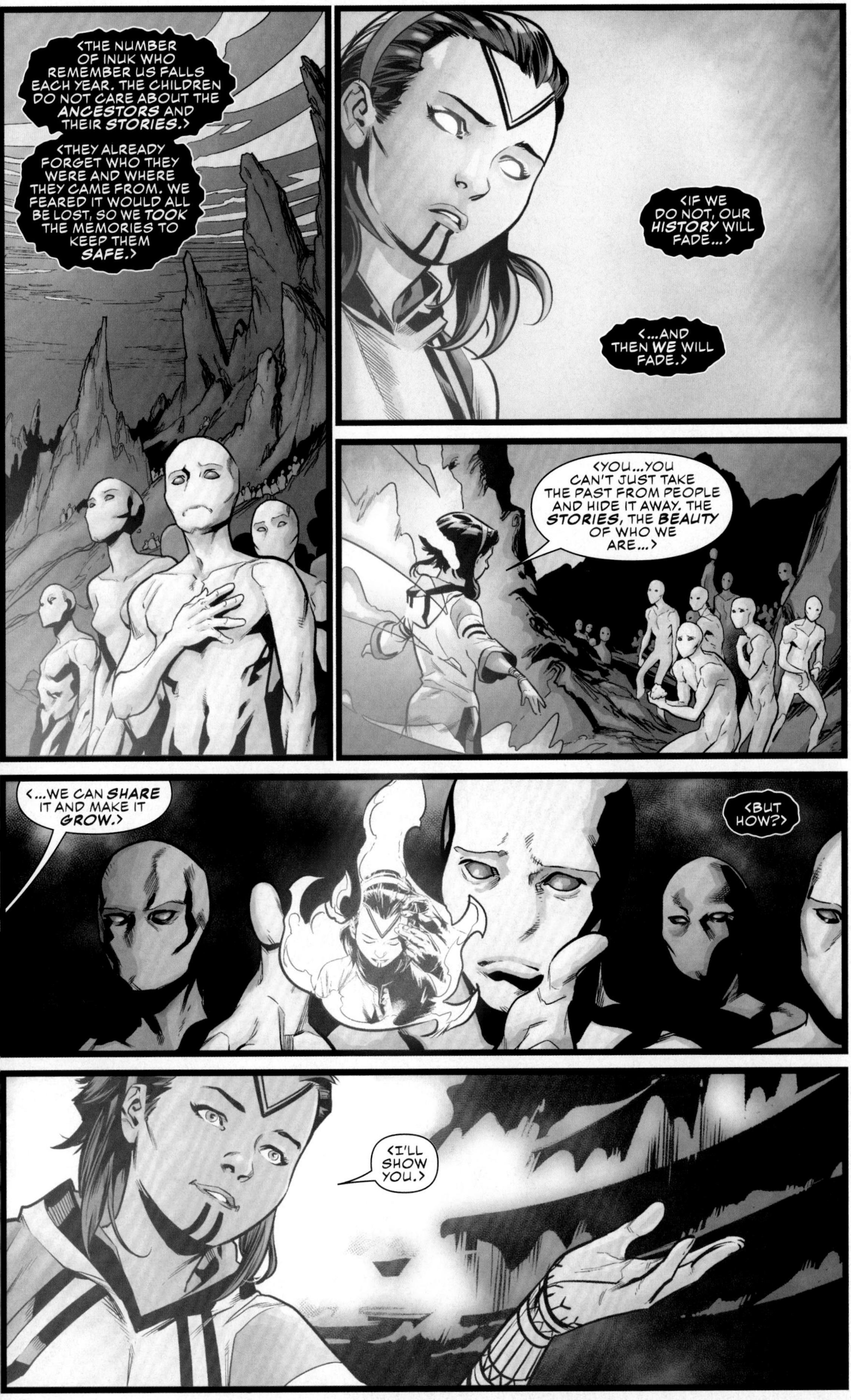
<THE NUMBER OF INUK WHO REMEMBER US FALLS EACH YEAR. THE CHILDREN DO NOT CARE ABOUT THE ANCESTORS AND THEIR STORIES.>
<THEY ALREADY FORGET WHO THEY WERE AND WHERE THEY CAME FROM. WE FEARED IT WOULD ALL BE LOST, SO WE TOOK THE MEMORIES TO KEEP THEM SAFE.>
<IF WE DO NOT, OUR HISTORY WILL FADE...>
<...AND THEN WE WILL FADE.>
<YOU...YOU CAN'T JUST TAKE THE PAST FROM PEOPLE AND HIDE IT AWAY. THE STORIES, THE BEAUTY OF WHO WE ARE...>
<...WE CAN SHARE IT AND MAKE IT GROW.>
<BUT HOW?>
<I'LL SHOW YOU.>

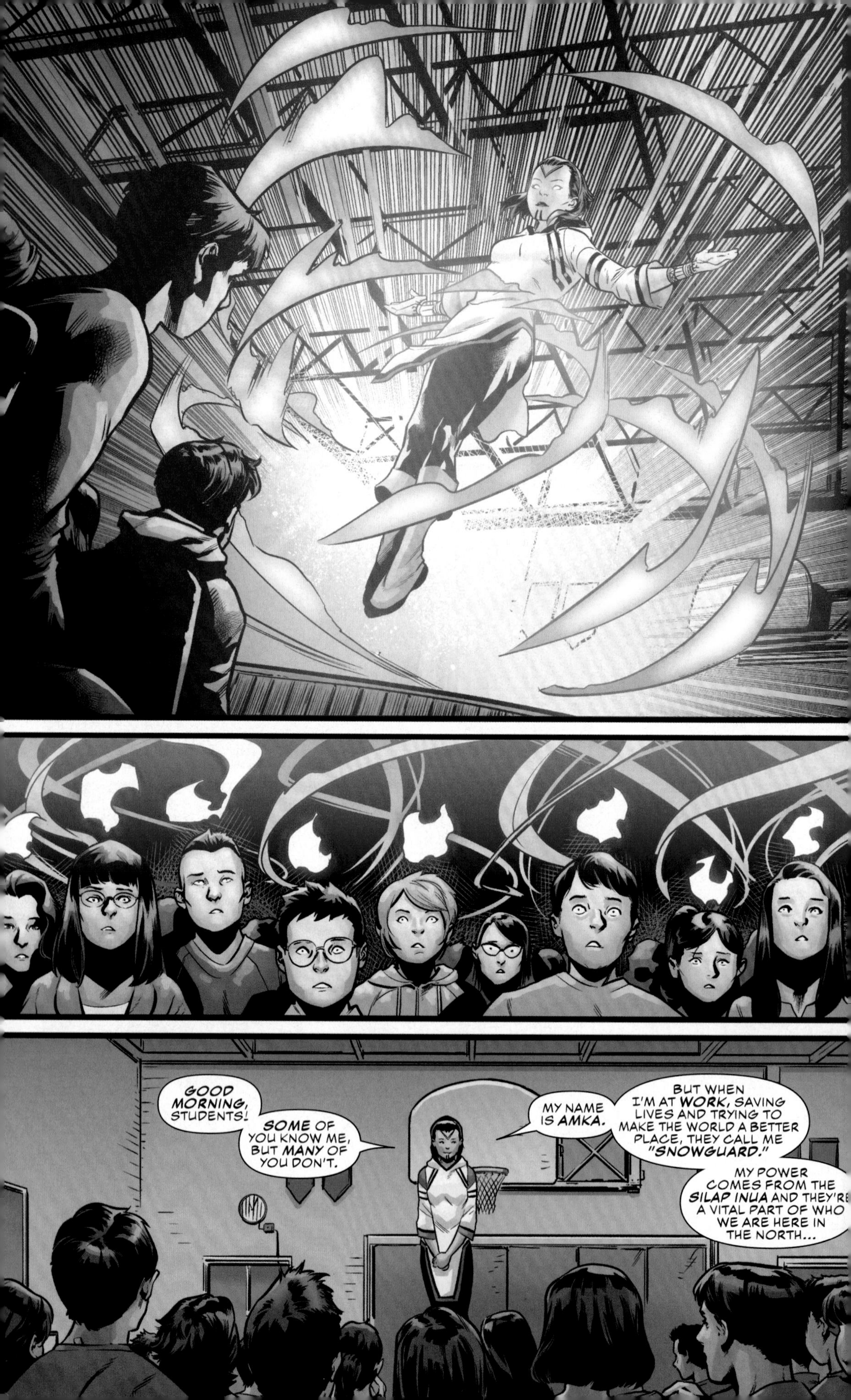
GOOD MORNING, STUDENTS!
SOME OF YOU KNOW ME, BUT MANY OF YOU DON'T.
MY NAME IS AMKA.
BUT WHEN I'M AT WORK, SAVING LIVES AND TRYING TO MAKE THE WORLD A BETTER PLACE, THEY CALL ME "SNOWGUARD."
MY POWER COMES FROM THE SILAP INUA AND THEY'RE A VITAL PART OF WHO WE ARE HERE IN THE NORTH...

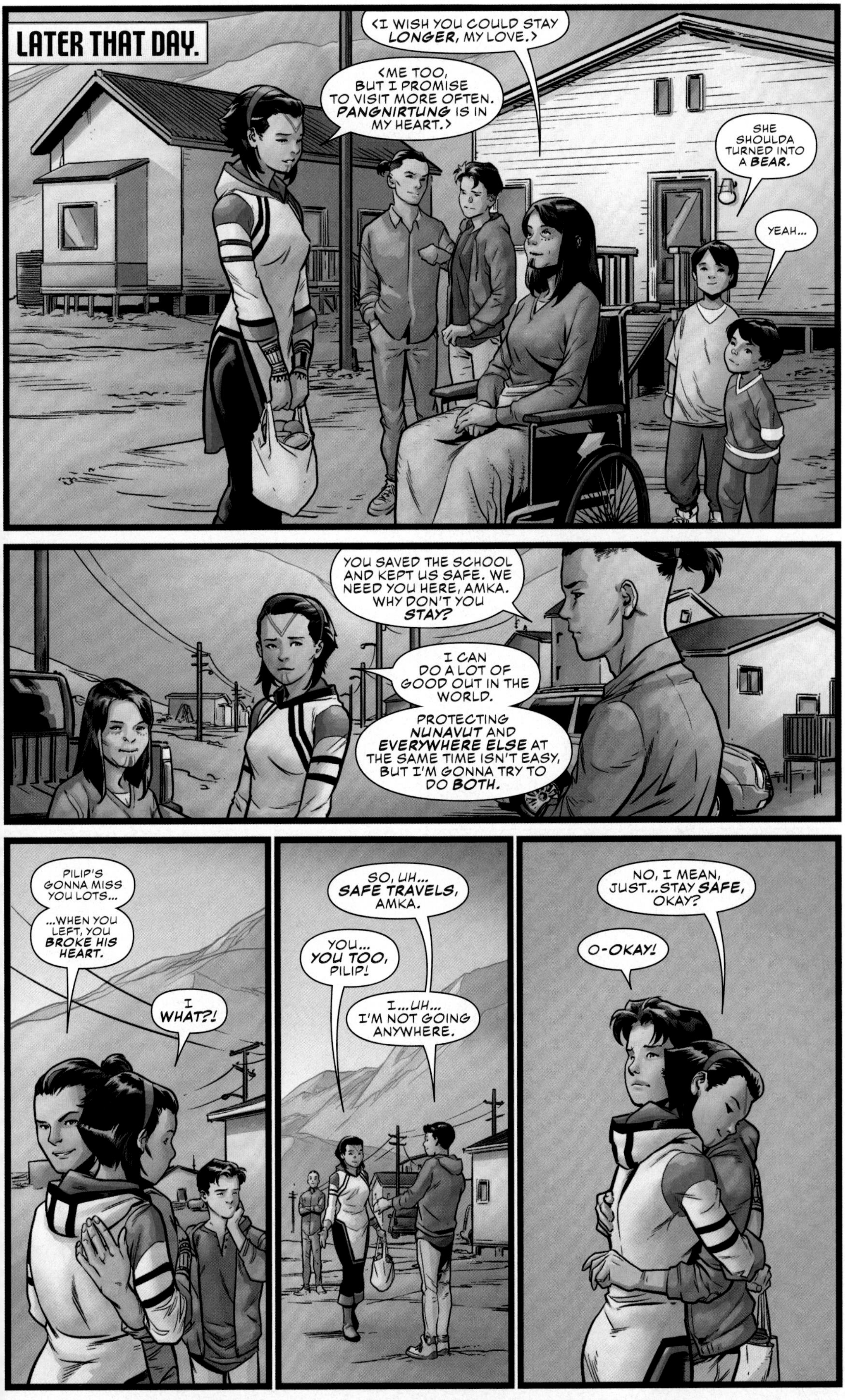
LATER THAT DAY.
<I WISH YOU COULD STAY LONGER, MY LOVE.>
<ME TOO, BUT I PROMISE TO VISIT MORE OFTEN. PANGNIRTUNG IS IN MY HEART.>
SHE SHOULDA TURNED INTO A BEAR.
YEAH...
YOU SAVED THE SCHOOL AND KEPT US SAFE. WE NEED YOU HERE, AMKA. WHY DON'T YOU STAY?
I CAN DO A LOT OF GOOD OUT IN THE WORLD.
PROTECTING NUNAVUT AND EVERYWHERE ELSE AT THE SAME TIME ISN'T EASY, BUT I'M GONNA TRY TO DO BOTH.
PILIP'S GONNA MISS YOU LOTS...
...WHEN YOU LEFT, YOU BROKE HIS HEART.
I WHAT?!
SO, UH... SAFE TRAVELS, AMKA.
YOU... YOU TOO, PILIP!
I...UH... I'M NOT GOING ANYWHERE.
NO, I MEAN, JUST...STAY SAFE, OKAY?
O-OKAY!

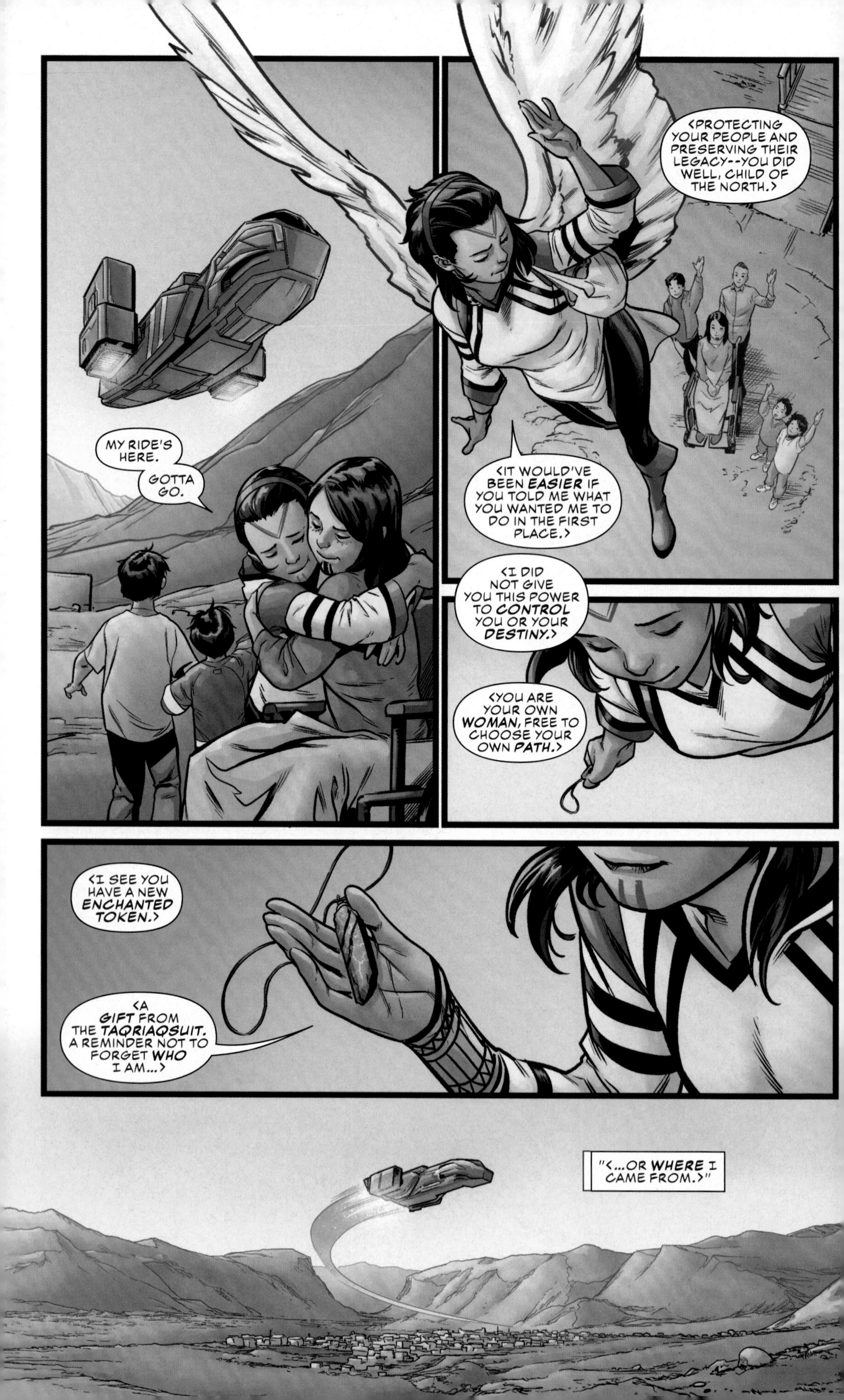
MY RIDE'S HERE.
GOTTA GO.
<PROTECTING YOUR PEOPLE AND PRESERVING THEIR LEGACY--YOU DID WELL, CHILD OF THE NORTH.>
<IT WOULD'VE BEEN EASIER IF YOU TOLD ME WHAT YOU WANTED ME TO DO IN THE FIRST PLACE.>
<I DID NOT GIVE YOU THIS POWER TO CONTROL YOU OR YOUR DESTINY.>
<YOU ARE YOUR OWN WOMAN, FREE TO CHOOSE YOUR OWN PATH.>
<I SEE YOU HAVE A NEW ENCHANTED TOKEN.>
<A GIFT FROM THE TAQRIAQSUIT. A REMINDER NOT TO FORGET WHO I AM...>
"<...OR WHERE I CAME FROM.>"

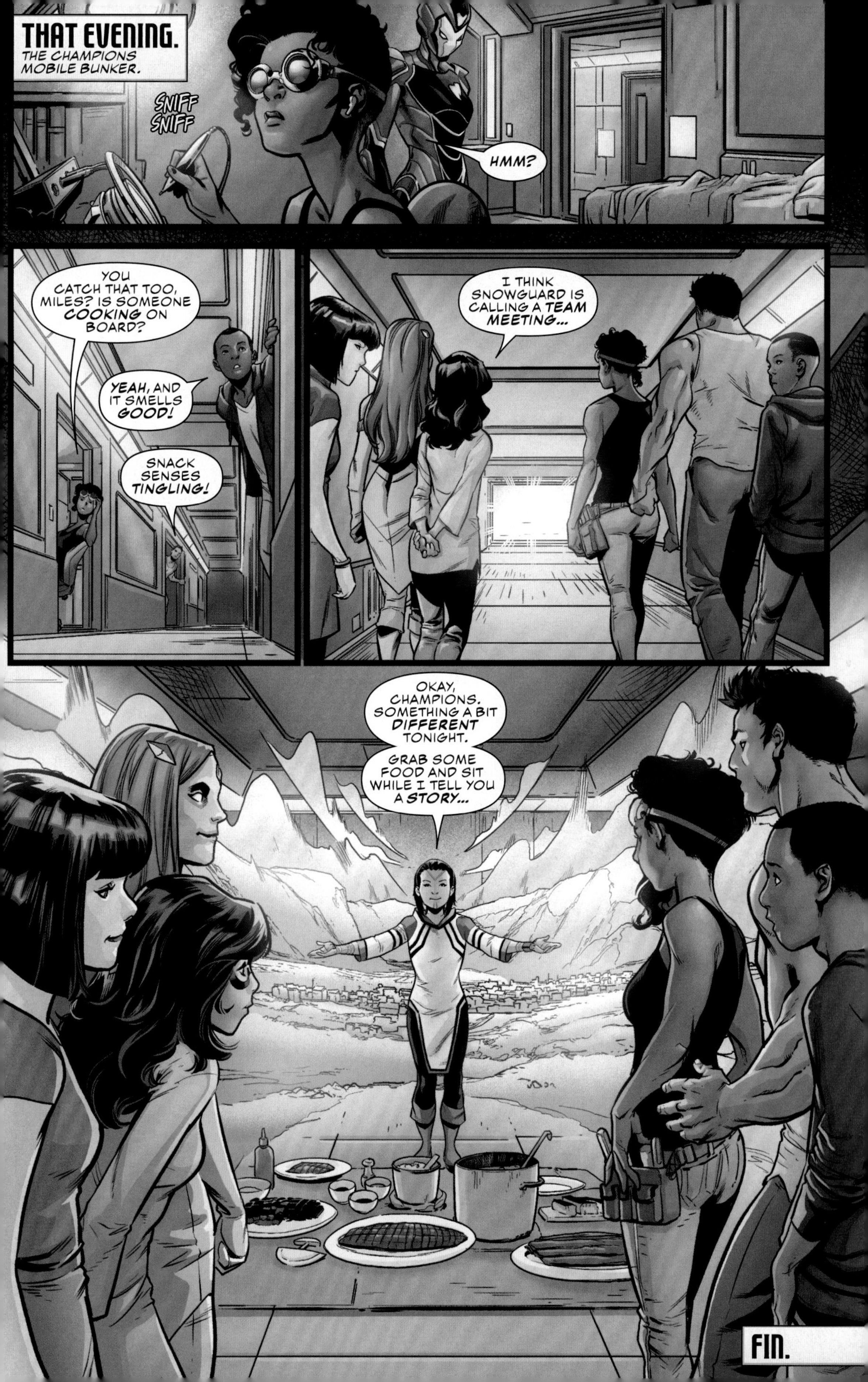

THAT EVENING.
THE CHAMPIONS MOBILE BUNKER.
SNIFF SNIFF
HMM?
YOU CATCH THAT TOO, MILES? IS SOMEONE COOKING ON BOARD?
YEAH, AND IT SMELLS GOOD!
SNACK SENSES TINGLING!
I THINK SNOWGUARD IS CALLING A TEAM MEETING...
OKAY, CHAMPIONS. SOMETHING A BIT DIFFERENT TONIGHT.
GRAB SOME FOOD AND SIT WHILE I TELL YOU A STORY...
FIN.

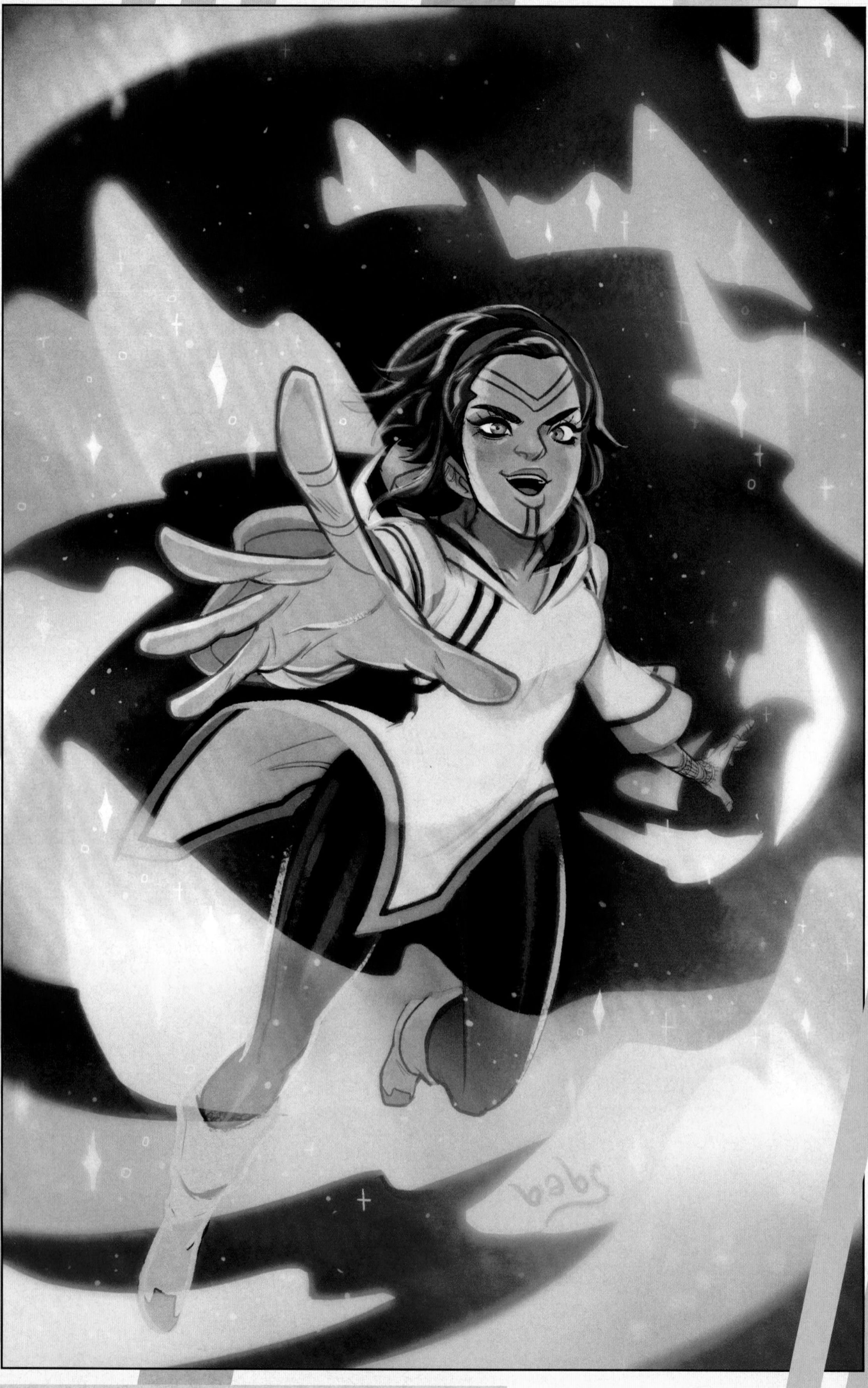
babs

CHAMPIONS ANNUAL #1 VARIANT BY **BABS TARR**

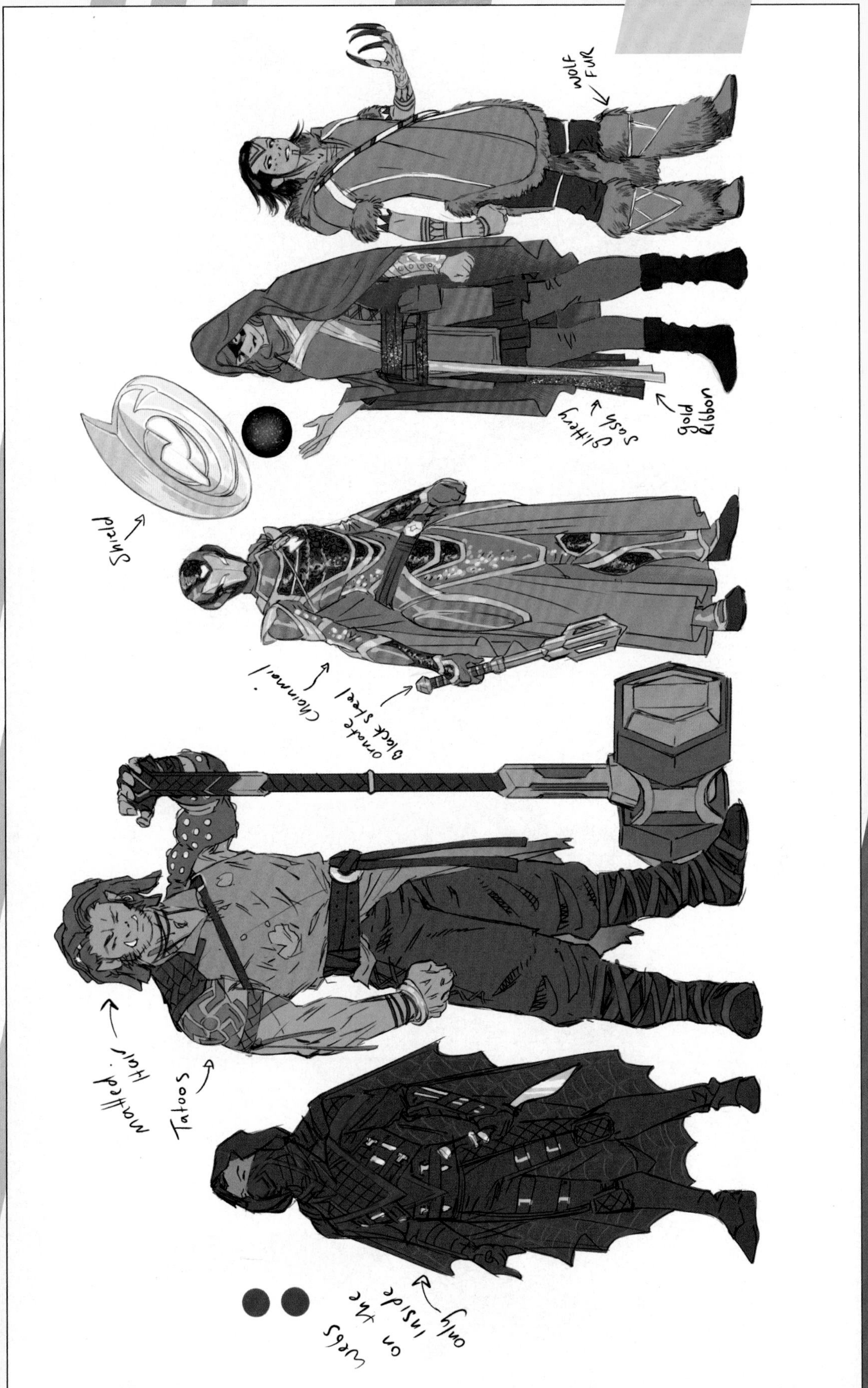
wolf FUR
glittery sash
gold Ribbon
Shield
ornate Chainmail
black steel
matted Hair
Tatoos
webs on the inside only

CHARACTER DESIGNS BY **SEAN IZAAKSE**

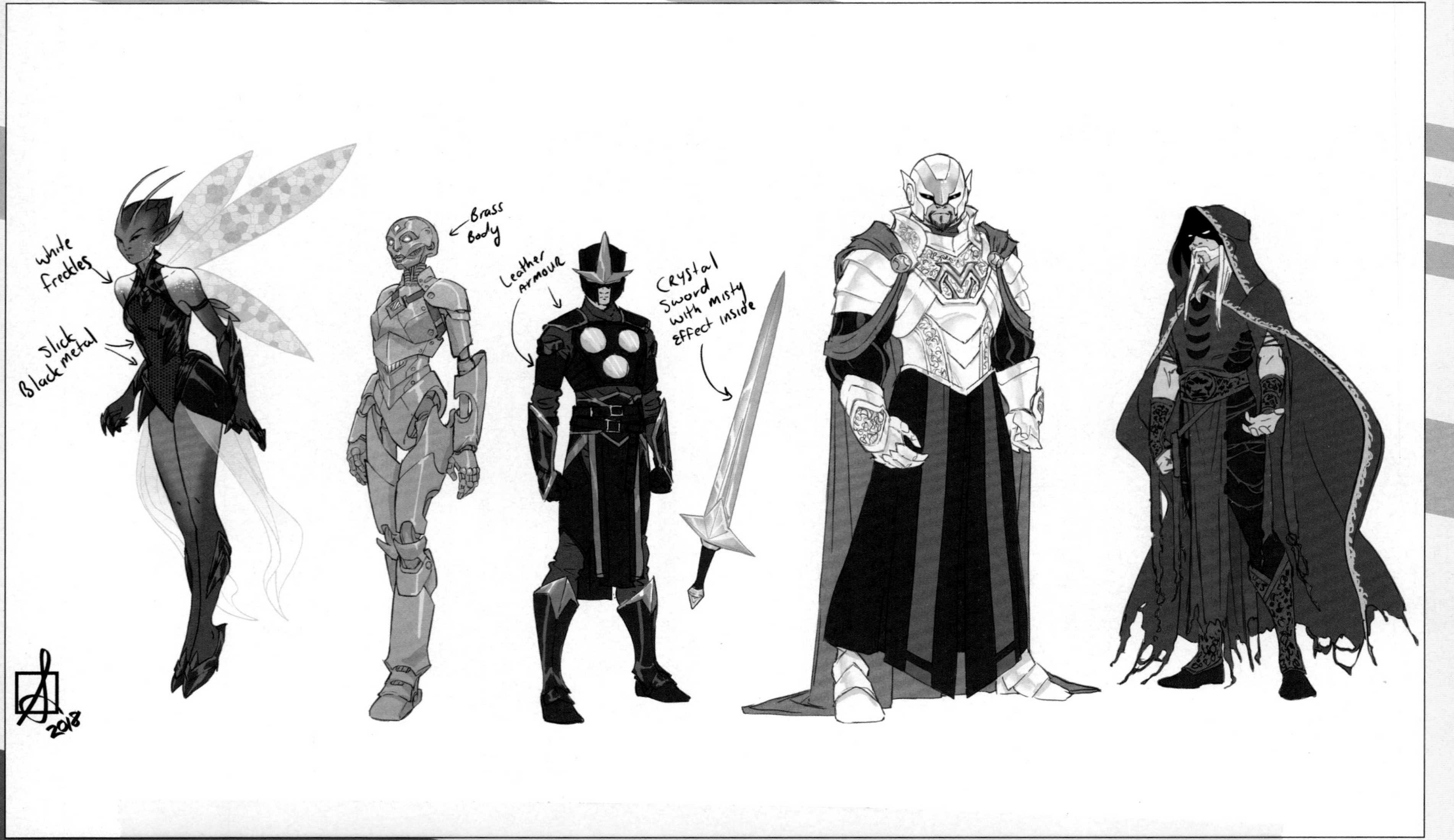
white freckles
slick Black metal
Brass Body
Leather Armour
Crystal Sword with Misty Effect inside
2018